SOMETHING ABOUT THE AUTHOR

ISSN 0276-816X

SOMETHING ABOUT THE AUTHOR

Facts and Pictures about Authors
and Illustrators of Books for Young People

EDITED BY
ANNE COMMIRE

VOLUME 58

Please see note on new index policy, page x.

 Gale Research Inc.

DETROIT • NEW YORK • FORT LAUDERDALE • LONDON

Editor: Anne Commire

Associate Editors: Agnes Garrett, Helga P. McCue

Assistant Editors: Dianne H. Anderson, Elisa Ann Ferraro, Eunice L. Petrini, Linda Shedd

Sketchwriters: Catherine Coray, Cathy Courtney, Marguerite Feitlowitz,
Mimi H. Hutson, Deborah Klezmer, Dieter Miller, Beatrice Smedley

Researcher: Catherine Ruello

Editorial Assistants: Joanne J. Ferraro, Marja T. Hiltunen, June Lee, Susan Pfanner

Production Manager: Mary Beth Trimper

Assistant Production Manager: Evi Seoud

Production Supervisor: Laura Bryant

Internal Production Associate: Louise Gagné

Internal Production Assistants: Kelly Krust, Sharana Wier

Art Director: Arthur Chartow

Keyliner: C. J. Jonik

Special acknowledgment is due to the members of the *Something about the Author Autobiography Series* staff
who assisted in the preparation of this volume.

Library of Congress Catalog Card Number 72-27107

ISBN 0-8103-2268-4
ISSN 0276-816X

Printed in the United States

Contents

Z

Introduction

As the only annually published ongoing reference series that deals with the lives and works of authors and illustrators of children's books, *Something about the Author (SATA)* is a unique source of information. The *SATA* series includes not only well-known authors and illustrators whose books are most widely read, but also those less prominent people whose works are just coming to be recognized. *SATA* is often the only readily available information source for less well-known writers or artists. You'll find *SATA* informative and entertaining whether you are:

> —a student in junior high school (or perhaps one to two grades higher or lower) who needs information for a book report or some other assignment for an English class;

> —a children's librarian who is searching for the answer to yet another question from a young reader or collecting background material to use for a story hour;

> —an English teacher who is drawing up an assignment for your students or gathering information for a book talk;

> —a student in a college of education or library science who is studying children's literature and reference sources in the field;

> —a parent who is looking for a new way to interest your child in reading something more than the school curriculum prescribes;

> —an adult who enjoys children's literature for its own sake, knowing that a good children's book has no age limits.

Scope

In *SATA* you will find detailed information about authors and illustrators who span the full time range of children's literature, from early figures like John Newbery and L. Frank Baum to contemporary figures like Judy Blume and Richard Peck. Authors in the series represent primarily English-speaking countries, particularly the United States, Canada, and the United Kingdom. Also included, however, are authors from around the world whose works are available in English translation, for example: from France, Jean and Laurent De Brunhoff; from Italy, Emanuele Luzzati; from the Netherlands, Jaap ter Haar; from Germany, James Krüss; from Norway, Babbis Friis-Baastad; from Japan, Toshiko Kanzawa; from the Soviet Union, Kornei Chukovsky; from Switzerland, Alois Carigiet, to name only a few. Also appearing in *SATA* are Newbery medalists from Hendrik Van Loon (1922) to Paul Fleischman (1989). The writings represented in *SATA* include those created intentionally for children and young adults as well as those written for a general audience and known to interest younger readers. These writings cover the spectrum from picture books, humor, folk and fairy tales, animal stories, mystery and adventure, science fiction and fantasy, historical fiction, poetry and nonsense verse, to drama, biography, and nonfiction.

Information Features

In *SATA* you will find full-length entries that are being presented in the series for the first time. This volume, for example, marks the first full-length appearance of Joy Berry, John Carpenter, Frank Frazetta, Garrison Keillor, and Hans Wilhelm.

Obituaries have been included in *SATA* since Volume 20. An Obituary is intended not only as a death notice but also as a concise view of a person's life and work. Obituaries may appear for persons who have entries in earlier *SATA* volumes, as well as for people who have not yet appeared in the series. In this volume Obituaries mark the recent deaths of Miriam Gurko, Marilyn Hirsh, Kenneth Hopkins, and Patricia C. Lord.

Revised Entries

Since Volume 25, each *SATA* volume also includes newly revised and updated entries for a selection of *SATA* listees (usually four to six) who remain of interest to today's readers and who have been active enough to require extensive revision of their earlier biographies. For example, when Beverly Cleary first appeared in *SATA* Volume 2, she was the author of twenty-one books for children and young adults and the recipient of numerous awards. By the time her updated sketch appeared in Volume 43 (a span of fifteen years), this creator of the indefatigable Ramona Quimby and other memorable characters had produced a dozen new titles and garnered nearly fifty additional awards, including the 1984 Newbery Medal.

The entry for a given biographee may be revised as often as there is substantial new information to provide. In this volume, look for revised entries on Michael Bond, Peter Firmin, Jan Pienkowski, Barbara Wersba, and Paul Zindel.

Illustrations

While the textual information in *SATA* is its primary reason for existing, photographs and illustrations not only enliven the text but are an integral part of the information that *SATA* provides. Illustrations and text are wedded in such a special way in children's literature that artists and their works naturally occupy a prominent place among *SATA*'s listees. The illustrators that you'll find in the series include such past masters of children's book illustration as Randolph Caldecott, Walter Crane, Arthur Rackham, and Ernest H. Shepard, as well as such noted contemporary artists as Maurice Sendak, Edward Gorey, Tomie de Paola, and Margot Zemach. There are Caldecott medalists from Dorothy Lathrop (the first recipient in 1938) to Stephen Gammell (the latest winner in 1989); cartoonists like Charles Schulz ("Peanuts"), Walt Kelly ("Pogo"), Hank Ketcham ("Dennis the Menace"), and Georges Rémi ("Tintin"); photographers like Jill Krementz, Tana Hoban, Bruce McMillan, and Bruce Curtis; and filmmakers like Walt Disney, Alfred Hitchcock, and Steven Spielberg.

In more than a dozen years of recording the metamorphosis of children's literature from the printed page to other media, *SATA* has become something of a repository of photographs that are unique in themselves and exist nowhere else as a group, particularly many of the classics of motion picture and stage history and photographs that have been specially loaned to us from private collections.

New Index Policy

In response to suggestions from librarians, *SATA* indexes will no longer appear in each volume but will be included in each alternate (odd-numbered) volume of the series, beginning with Volume 58.

SATA will continue to include two indexes that will cumulate with each volume: the **Illustrations Index,** arranged by the name of the illustrator, gives the number of the volume and page where the illustrator's work appears in the current volume as well as all preceding volumes in the series; the **Author Index** gives the number of the volume in which a person's Biographical Sketch, Brief Entry, or Obituary appears in the current volume as well as all preceding volumes in the series.

These indexes also include references to authors and illustrators who appear in *Yesterday's Authors of Books for Children* (described in detail below). Beginning with Volume 36, the *SATA* Author Index provides cross-references to authors who are included in Gale's *Children's Literature Review.* Starting with Volume 42, you will also find cross-references to authors who are included in the *Something about the Author Autobiography Series* (described in detail below).

What a *SATA* Entry Provides

Whether you're already familiar with the *SATA* series or just getting acquainted, you will want to be aware of the kind of information that an entry provides. In every *SATA* entry the editors attempt to give as complete a picture of the person's life and work as possible. In some cases that full range of information may simply be unavailable, or a biographee may choose not to reveal complete personal details. The information that the editors attempt to provide in every entry is arranged in the following categories:

1. The "head" of the entry gives

 —the most complete form of the name,
 —any part of the name not commonly used, included in parentheses,
 —birth and death dates, if known; a (?) indicates a discrepancy in published sources,
 —pseudonyms or name variants under which the person has had books published or is publicly known, in parentheses in the second line.

2. "Personal" section gives

 —date and place of birth and death,
 —parents' names and occupations,
 —name of spouse, date of marriage, and names of children,
 —educational institutions attended, degrees received, and dates,
 —religious and political affiliations,
 —agent's name and address,
 —home and/or office address.

3. "Career" section gives

 —name of employer, position, and dates for each career post,
 —military service,
 —memberships,
 —awards and honors.

4. "Writings" section gives

 —title, first publisher and date of publication, and illustration information for each book written; revised editions and other significant editions for books with particularly long publishing histories; genre, when known.

5. "Adaptations" section gives

 —title, major performers, producer, and date of all known reworkings of an author's material in another medium, like movies, filmstrips, television, recordings, plays, etc.

6. "Sidelights" section gives

 —commentary on the life or work of the biographee either directly from the person (and often written specifically for the *SATA* entry), or gathered from biographies, diaries, letters, interviews, or other published sources.

7. "For More Information See" section gives

 —books, feature articles, films, plays, and reviews in which the biographee's life or work has been treated.

How a *SATA* Entry Is Compiled

A *SATA* entry progresses through a series of steps. If the biographee is living, the *SATA* editors try to secure information directly from him or her through a questionnaire. From the information that the biographee supplies, the editors prepare an entry, filling in any essential missing details with research. The author or illustrator is then sent a copy of the entry to check for accuracy and completeness.

If the biographee is deceased or cannot be reached by questionnaire, the *SATA* editors examine a wide variety of published sources to gather information for an entry. Biographical sources are searched with the aid of Gale's *Biography and Genealogy Master Index*. Bibliographic sources like the *National Union Catalog*, the *Cumulative Book Index*, *American Book Publishing Record*, and the *British Museum Catalogue* are consulted, as are book reviews, feature articles, published interviews, and material sometimes obtained from the biographee's family, publishers, agent, or other associates.

For each entry presented in *SATA*, the editors also attempt to locate a photograph of the biographee as well as representative illustrations from his or her books. After surveying the available books which the biographee has written and/or illustrated, and then making a selection of appropriate photographs and illustrations, the editors request permission of the current copyright holders to reprint the material. In the case of older books for which the copyright may have passed through several hands, even locating the current copyright holder is often a long and involved process.

We invite you to examine the entire *SATA* series, starting with this volume. Described below are some of the people in Volume 58 that you may find particularly interesting.

Highlights of This Volume

MICHAEL BOND......got the idea for his first book, *A Bear Called Paddington,* while shopping for a Christmas gift for his wife. "I wandered into a London store...and found myself in the toy department. On one of the shelves I came across a small bear, looking, I thought, very sorry for himself as he was the only one who hadn't been sold....He sat on a shelf of our one-roomed apartment for a while, and then one day when I was sitting in front of my typewriter staring at a blank sheet of paper wondering what to write, I idly tapped out the words 'Mr. and Mrs. Brown first met Paddington on a railway platform....' It was a simple act, and in terms of deathless prose, not exactly earth shattering, but it was to change my life considerably." In addition to his more than seventy Paddington books, Bond has delighted children with stories of extraordinary animals like Thursday, the mouse, and Olga da Polga, the guinea pig. "I get depressed about a third of the way through a book, when I can't really see the end, but by the time I'm three-quarters of the way through and know how it will finish I start to think about the next one."

PETER FIRMIN......was fortunate to have a mother who encouraged his creativity. "She would sit us at a table with pencils and paper to draw and make models....We made our first animated film by painstakingly sticking a strip of paper down the middle of a piece of film and drawing pictures....We couldn't actually project it but we were able to look through the front hole, turn the handle and see the little moving picture happen." At fifteen Firmin was accepted into an art school in Colchester. From there, he went to Central School of Art in London, where he met Oliver Postgate, with whom he collaborated on a variety of films and books including the "Bagpuss" and "Noggin" series for children. Firmin's most recent project marks a departure from his work for children. "My wife suggested that I illustrate an edition of Vita Sackville-West's *The Land,* a long philosophical poem about England and its countryside....I'm not a very literary person, but I get the same sort of pleasure from these poems as I do from some of Shakespeare's sonnets."

S. E. HINTON......found her inspiration for writing by reading "everything, including Comet cans and coffee labels." At age fifteen she began her first novel about a teenage gang because she felt that "...there was no realistic fiction being written for teenagers. It was all Mary Jane goes to the prom,...I'd been to a few proms and they weren't anything like that. There weren't any books that dealt realistically with teenage life so I wrote *The Outsiders* to fill that gap...." The majority of Hinton's novels have been adapted for film, though she was at first reluctant to move from the page to the screen. "I guess I thought I'd collect some really funny, cynical Hollywood stories. And that's where I got disillusioned. The movies are damn near as good as my books."

JAN PIENKOWSKI......lived in Poland when World War II began. "We were only allowed to kill a pig once a year. More than one was a crime punishable by death....Making butter was punishable by death, too...." Following the war, the Pienkowski family moved to England where he studied classics at King's College, Cambridge. He began designing posters and sets for university drama groups. After graduation he met Helen Nicoll, the director of a children's educational program for the BBC, with whom he developed the "Meg and Mog" books. Even after years of steady writing for children, he has not come to take his skills for granted. "All creative people need reassurance. When you show what you've done, every single thing you've got is there. And if you've had a little success it gets worse because there's more at stake."

BARBARA WERSBA......spent her younger years determined to become an actress. After her parents divorced, she moved with her mother to New York. "By age fifteen, I was taking acting classes at the Neighborhood Playhouse. By sixteen, I was studying dance with Martha Graham....I look back on these days with a kind of sadness, for I, on my way to becoming an actress, did not like to act. What I really liked was being alone, reading and writing, and collecting books." With plans to put a show on Broadway, she came down with hepatitis. "Lying there in bed day after day, staring at the ocean, free of responsibility for the first time in years, I knew that I would never return to the theatre....After fifteen years of struggle I was free." Within a few weeks she had completed *The Boy Who Loved the Sea.* "For every manuscript that succeeds there are five that fail, but I can never bring myself to throw the failures away, and they are all kept in a trunk labeled *In Progress.* I have had my share of rejections and disappointments, and a certain number of calamities...but the impulse to write persists. What keeps it alive is simple curiosity."

PAUL ZINDEL......came from a broken home and was raised by his mother. "I felt worthless as a kid, and dared to speak and act my true feelings only in fantasy and secret. That's probably what made me a writer....When I write, I hear the voices of my mother and sister." Those perceptions became the basis of his Pulitzer Prize-winning play, *The Effect of Gamma Rays on the Man-in-the-Moon Marigolds.* "*Marigolds* is the kind of story that just sort of pops right out of you, because you've lived it. One morning I awoke and discovered the manuscript next to my typewriter." Zindel's writing career took a turn when an editor for Harper saw a production of *Marigolds.* "Charlotte Zolotow...tracked me down and got me to write my first novel, *The Pigman.* She brought me into an area that I never explored before." With the success of his first novel, Zindel quit his job as a high school chemistry teacher and dedicated himself full time to writing. He felt he could better serve young students outside of the classroom by writing "for the people who don't like to read."

These are only a few of the authors and illustrators that you'll find in this volume. We hope you find all the entries in *SATA* both interesting and useful.

Yesterday's Authors of Books for Children

In a two-volume companion set to *SATA, Yesterday's Authors of Books for Children (YABC)* focuses on early authors and illustrators, from the beginnings of children's literature through 1960, whose books are still being read by children today. Here you will find "old favorites" like Hans Christian Andersen, J. M. Barrie, Kenneth Grahame, Betty MacDonald, A. A. Milne, Beatrix Potter, Samuel Clemens, Kate Greenaway, Rudyard Kipling, Robert Louis Stevenson, and many more.

Similar in format to *SATA, YABC* features bio-bibliographical entries that are divided into information categories such as Personal, Career, Writings, and Sidelights. The entries are further enhanced by book illustrations, author photos, movie stills, and many rare old photographs.

In Volume 2 you will find cumulative indexes to the authors and to the illustrations that appear in *YABC.* These listings can also be located in the *SATA* cumulative indexes.

By exploring both volumes of *YABC,* you will discover a special group of more than seventy authors and illustrators who represent some of the best in children's literature—individuals whose timeless works continue to delight children and adults of all ages. Other authors and illustrators from early children's literature are listed in *SATA,* starting with Volume 15.

Something about the Author Autobiography Series

You can complement the information in *SATA* with the *Something about the Author Autobiography Series (SAAS),* which provides autobiographical essays written by important current authors and illustrators of books for children and young adults. In every volume of *SAAS* you will find about twenty specially commissioned autobiographies, each accompanied by a selection of personal photographs supplied by the authors. The wide range of contemporary writers and artists who describe their lives and interests in the *Autobiography Series* includes Joan Aiken, Betsy Byars, Leonard Everett Fisher, Milton Meltzer, Maia Wojciechowska, and Jane Yolen, among others. Though the information presented in the autobiographies is as varied and unique as the authors, you can learn about the people and events that influenced these writers' early lives, how they began their careers, what problems they faced in becoming established in their professions, what prompted them to write or illustrate particular books, what they now find most challenging or rewarding in their lives, and what advice they may have for young people interested in following in their footsteps, among many other subjects.

Autobiographies included in the *SATA Autobiography Series* can be located through both the *SATA* cumulative index and the *SAAS* cumulative index, which lists not only the authors' names but also the subjects mentioned in their essays, such as titles of works and geographical and personal names.

The *SATA Autobiography Series* gives you the opportunity to view "close up" some of the fascinating people who are included in the *SATA* parent series. The combined *SATA* series makes available to you an unequaled range of comprehensive and in-depth information about the authors and illustrators of young people's literature.

Please write and tell us if we can make *SATA* even more helpful to you.

Acknowledgments

Grateful acknowledgment is made to the following publishers, authors, and artists for their kind permission to reproduce copyrighted material.

ATHENEUM PUBLISHERS. Jacket illustration by Jerry Pinkney from *The Country of the Heart* by Barbara Wersba. Copyright © 1975 by Barbara Wersba./ Sidelight excerpt from "Introduction" of *Happy to Be Here* by Garrison Keillor. Copyright © 1982 by Garrison Keillor./ Jacket illustration by Viqui Maggio from *View from the Pighouse Roof* by Violet Olsen. Illustrations © 1987 by Viqui Maggio. All reprinted by permission of Atheneum Publishers, an imprint of Macmillan Publishing Co.

ATLANTIS KINDERBUCHER VERLAG. Illustration by Peter Bailey from *Das Kanguruh Viktoria* by Carolyn Sloan. Copyright © 1973 by Atlantis Kinderbucher bei Pro Juventute Zurich. Illustrations © 1973 by Peter Bailey. Reprinted by permission of Atlantis Kinderbucher Verlag.

BANTAM BOOKS. Cover illustration by John Thompson from *My Darling, My Hamburger* by Paul Zindel. Cover art © 1984 by John Thompson. Reprinted by permission of Bantam Books, a division of Bantam Doubleday Dell Publishing Group, Inc.

A & C BLACK (PUBLISHERS) LTD. Illustration by Peter Firmin from *Nina's Machines* by Peter Firmin. Reprinted by permission of A & C Black (Publishers) Ltd.

JONATHAN CAPE LTD. Illustration by Jan Pienkowski from *The Kingdom Under the Sea and Other Stories* by Joan Aiken. Text © 1971 by Joan Aiken. Illustrations © 1971 by Jan Pienkowski./ Illustration by Jan Pienkowski from *Past Eight O'Clock* by Joan Aiken. Illustrations © 1986 by Jan Pienkowski. Both reprinted by permission of Jonathan Cape Ltd.

THOMAS Y. CROWELL. Illustration by George Ford from *Ray Charles* by Sharon Bell Mathis. Illustrations © 1973 by George Ford. Reprinted by permission of Thomas Y. Crowell, a division of Harper & Row, Publishers, Inc.

CROWN PUBLISHERS. Jacket illustration by Hans Wilhelm from *I'll Always Love You* by Hans Wilhelm. Copyright © 1985 by Hans Wilhelm, Inc./ Illustration by Hans Wilhelm from *Oh, What a Mess* by Hans Wilhelm. Copyright © 1988 by Hans Wilhelm, Inc. Both reprinted by permission of Crown Publishers, a Division of Random House, Inc.

DELACORTE PRESS. Illustration by Hans Helweg from *The Complete Adventures of Olga da Polga* by Michael Bond. Illustrations © 1976 by Hans Helweg./ Jacket illustration by David Weisner from *So You Want to Be a Wizard* by Diane Duane. Jacket illustration © 1983 by David Weisner. Both reprinted by permission of Delacorte Press, a division of Bantam Doubleday Dell Publishing Group, Inc.

DELL PUBLISHING. Cover illustration from *The Outsiders* by S.E. Hinton. Copyright © 1967 by S.E. Hinton./ Cover illustration from *Tex* by S.E. Hinton. Copyright © 1979 by S.E. Hinton. Both reprinted by permission of Dell Publishing, a division of Bantam Doubleday Dell Publishing Group, Inc.

DODD, MEAD & CO. Photograph from *A Pup Grows Up* by Sally Foster. Text and photographs © 1984 by Sally Foster./ Photograph from *Where Time Stands Still* by Sally Foster. Text and photograph © 1987 by Sally Foster. Both reprinted by permission of Dodd, Mead & Co., a division of G.P. Putnam's Sons.

DOUBLEDAY. Illustration by Cecile Gagnon from *O Canada!* by Isabel Barclay. Copyright © 1964 by Isabel Barclay Dobell. Illustrations © 1964 by Cecile Gagnon./ Jacket illustration by Jon Lomberg from *The Cosmic Connection: An Extraterrestrial Perspective* by Carl Sagan. Copyright © 1973 by Carl Sagan and Jerome Agel. Both reprinted by permission of Doubleday, a division of Bantam Doubleday Dell Publishing Group, Inc.

Maryann Kovalski from *The Wheels on the Bus* by Maryann Kovalski. Copyright © 1987 by Maryann Kovalski. Both reprinted by permission of Little, Brown & Co.

LOTHROP, LEE & SHEPARD BOOKS. Illustration by Virginia Wright-Frierson from *When the Tide Is Low* by Sheila Cole. Illustrations © 1985 by Virginia Wright-Frierson. Reprinted by permission of Lothrop, Lee & Shepard Books, a division of William Morrow and Company, Inc.

MacDONALD & CO. (PUBLISHERS) LTD. Illustration by Peter Firmin from *The Last of the Dragons* by Edith Nesbit. Reprinted by permission of MacDonald & Co. (Publishers) Ltd.

MARGARET K. McELDERRY BOOKS. Illustration by Ian Wallace from *The Very Last Time* by Jan Andrews. Illustrations © 1985 by Ian Wallace. Reprinted by permission of Margaret K. McElderry Books, an imprint of Macmillan Publishing Company.

PRICE STERN SLOAN INC. Illustration by Jan Pienkowski from *Small Talk* by Jan Pienkowski. Copyright © 1981, 1982, 1983 by Jan Pienkowski. Reprinted by permission of Price Stern Sloan Inc.

RADIANT BOOKS. Illustration from *Mystery at Pier 14* by Betty Swinford. Radiant Books, copyrighted by Gospel Publishing House, Springfield, MO, USA. Used by permission.

RANDOM HOUSE, INC. Illustration by Fred Banbery from *Paddington's Garden* by Michael Bond. Illustrations © 1972 by Fred Banbery. Reprinted by permission of Random House, Inc.

EDITIONS PIERRE TISSEYRE. Illustration by Darcia Labrosse from *Histoire d'Adele Viau et de Fabien Petit* by Cecil Gagnon. Copyright © 1982 Ottawa, Canada. Reprinted by permission of Editions Pierre Tisseyre.

VIKING PENGUIN. Illustration by Leo Carty from *Sidewalk Story* by Sharon Bell Mathis. Copyright © 1971 by Sharon Bell Mathis./ Jacket illustration by Leo and Diane Dillon from *Listen for the Fig Tree* by Sharon Bell Mathis. Copyright © 1974 by The Viking Press, Inc./ Illustration by Leo and Diane Dillon from *The Hundred Penny Box* by Sharon Bell Mathis. Illustrations © 1975 by Leo and Diane Dillon./ Cover illustration by Daryl Zudeck from *Sidewalk Story* by Sharon Bell Mathis. Cover illustration © 1986 by Viking Penguin Inc./ Jacket illustration by Wendell Minor from *We Are Still Married* by Garrison Keillor. Copyright © 1989 by Viking Penguin Inc./ Sidelight excerpts from "A Letter from Copenhagen," in *Leaving Home* by Garrison Keillor. Copyright © 1987 by Garrison Keillor. These excerpts reprinted by permission of Penguin Books Canada. All reprinted by permission of Viking Penguin, a division of Penguin Books USA Inc.

FRANKLIN WATTS, INC. Illustration by Jacqui Morgan from *Children of Infinity: Original Science Fiction Stories for Young Readers*, edited by Roger Elwood. Copyright © 1973 by Franklin Watts, Inc. Reprinted by permission of Franklin Watts, Inc.

WEIDENFELD & NICOLSON LTD. Sidelight excerpts from *Return to Go: My Autobiography* by Jim Slater. Reprinted by permission of George Weidenfeld & Nicolson Ltd.

Sidelight excerpts from "Frank Frazetta at Bat," by Nick Miglin, May, 1976, in *American Artist*. Copyright © 1976 by Billboard Publications, Inc./ Sidelight excerpts from "Carpenter Builds Directing Dynasty on Past Successes," by Scott Cain, July 13, 1986, in *Atlanta Journal & Constitution*. Reprinted by permission of *Atlanta Journal & Constitution*./ Sidelight excerpts from *Frank Frazetta: Book Two* and *Frank Frazetta: Book Five*, edited by Betty Ballantine. Bantam./ Illustration by John Costanza from *Let's Talk about Teasing* by Joy Berry. Copyright © 1982 by Joy Berry. Courtesy of Joy Berry./ Illustration by John Costanza from *Let's Talk about Gossiping* by Joy Berry. Copyright © 1984 by Joy Berry. Courtesy of Joy Berry./ Sidelight excerpts from "Christmas," by Jan Pienkowski, Winter 1984, in *Bookcase*./ Sidelight excerpts from *Books for Keeps*, November, 1981. Copyright © 1981 School Bookshop Association./ Sidelight excerpts from "Director Carpenter Mixes His Genres," June 25, 1986, in *The Boston Globe*. Copyright © 1986 Globe Newspaper Co.

Sidelight excerpts from "A Love Story from the Director of 'Halloween'?" by Tom Hinckly, January 1986, in *Cable Guide*. Reprinted by permission of *Cable Guide*./ Sidelight excerpts from "In a Lake Wobegon Daze," by Les Lindeman, amended by G. Keillor, September 13, 1985, in *The Chicago Sun-Times*./ Sidelight excerpts from " 'Little China' Kicks Out Gloom," by Lloyd Sachs, July 6, 1986, in *The Chicago Sun-Times*. Reprinted by permission of *The Chicago Sun-Times*./ Sidelight excerpts from "Writer of 'Tex' Is Comfortable Dealing with

Sidelight excerpts from a National Press Club Speech by Garrison Keillor, Washington, D.C., 1987./ Sidelight excerpts from "China Doll," by Betty Bao Lord, May 12, 1986, in *New York* Magazine. Copyright © 1986 by News America Publishing, Inc. Reprinted by permission of *New York* Magazine./ Sidelight excerpts from "Hearts and Marigolds," by Jerry Tallmer, May 8, 1971, in *New York Post*. Copyright © 1971 by *New York Post*. Reprinted by permission of *New York Post*./ Sidelight excerpts from "Paul Zindel," by Jerry Tallmer, November 20, 1976, in *New York Post*. Copyright © 1976 by *New York Post*. Reprinted by permission of *New York Post*./ Sidelight excerpts from "And Gamma Rays Did It!" by Guy Flatley, April 19, 1970, in *The New York Times*. Copyright © 1970 by The New York Times Company. Reprinted by permission of The New York Times Company./ Sidelight excerpts from "The Theatre Is Born within Us," by Paul Zindel, July 26, 1970, in *The New York Times*. Copyright © 1970 by The New York Times Company. Reprinted by permission of The New York Times Company./ Sidelight excerpts from an article by Anna Quindlen, February 24, 1980, (section 2, page 1) in *The New York Times*. Copyright © 1980 by The New York Times Company./ Sidelight excerpts from "Small-Town America," by Edward Fishe, October 31, 1982, in *The New York Times*. Copyright © 1982 by The New York Times Company./ Sidelight excerpts from "Directors Join the S.E. Hinton Fan Club," by Stephen Farber, March 20, 1983, in *The New York Times*. Copyright © 1982 by The New York Times Company. Reprinted by permission of The New York Times Company./ Sidelight excerpts from "Making 'The Outsiders,' a Librarian's Dream," by Aljean Harmetz, March 23, 1983, in *The New York Times*. Copyright © 1983 by The New York Times Company.

Sidelight excerpts from "Prairie Humor Comes to the Big City," by Jon Pareles, May 13, 1983, in *The New York Times*. Copyright © 1983 by The New York Times Company./ Sidelight excerpts from "John Carpenter after 'Big Trouble,'" by Lawrence Van Gelder, June 27, 1986, in *The New York Times*. Copyright © 1986 by The New York Times Company. Reprinted by permission of The New York Times Company./ Sidelight excerpts from " 'Prairie Home Companion' Exits," by Steve Schneider, March 1, 1987, in *The New York Times*. Copyright © 1987 by The New York Times Company./ Sidelight excerpts from "With Singing, Satire and Sentiment, Lake Wobegon Fades," by Dirk Johnson, June 14, 1987, in *The New York Times*. Copyright © 1987 by The New York Times Company./ Sidelight excerpts from "Teen Agers Are for Real," by Susan Hinton, August 27, 1967, in *The New York Times Book Review*. Copyright © 1967 by The New York Times Company. Reprinted by permission of The New York Times Company./ Sidelight excerpts from "Teacup Full of Roses," by Janet Harris, September 10, 1972, in *The New York Times Book Review*. Copyright © 1972 by The New York Times Company./ Sidelight excerpts from "Profiles of John Carpenter: People Start Running," by James Stevenson, January 28, 1980, in *The New Yorker*. Copyright © 1980 by The New Yorker Magazine, Inc. Reprinted by special permission./ Sidelight excerpts from "Wobegon and the Burden of Celebrity," by Peg Meier, April 20, 1987, in *Newsday*. Copyright © 1987 by Newsday, Inc./ Sidelight excerpts from "Rumble Fish," Production Notes, No Weather Films, 1983./ Sidelight excerpts from *The Complete Guide to Greeting Card Design and Illustration* by Eva Szela, amended by Peggy Ackley, North Light Books, 1987.

Sidelight excerpts from "Phoebe Gilman: *The Balloon Tree*," amended by Phoebe Gilman. *Our Choice/Your Choice*, 1985-86. Reprinted by permission of *Our Choice/Your Choice*./ Sidelight excerpts from "Margaret Cusack: Fabric Illustrator Extraordinaire," by Chris Hunter, amended by Margaret Cusack, December, 1986, in *Palm Beach Life*. Reprinted by permission of *Palm Beach Life*./ Sidelight excerpts from "Lake Wobegon's Garrison Keillor Finds a Love That Time Forgot and the Decades Can't Improve," November 25, 1985, in *People Weekly*. Copyright © 1985 by Time, Inc./ Sidelight excerpts from an article by Ellen Glassman, amended by Margaret Cusack, volume 2, number 2, 1984, in *Prattfolio*. Reprinted by permission of *Prattfolio*./ Sidelight excerpts from "PW Interviews: Garrison Keillor," by Diane Roback, amended by Garrison Keillor, September 13, 1985, in *Publishers Weekly*. Copyright © 1985 by Xerox Corporation. Reprinted from *Publishers Weekly*, published by R.R. Bowker Company, a Xerox Company, by permission./ Sidelight excerpts from "Leaving the Shores of Lake Wobegon," by Diane Roback, August 21, 1987, in *Publishers Weekly*./ Sidelight excerpts from "How Girls with Nimble Fingers in Columbia Have Helped in a Publishing Success," by Tony Bradman, October 16, 1981, in *Publishing News*. Reprinted by permission of *Publishing News*./ Sidelight excerpts from " 'That One's Me!'—New Books for Black Children That Mirror Their World," by Liz Gant, August, 1972, in *Redbook Magazine*./ Front illustration from the boxed set of four Garrison Keillor audio cassettes. Reprinted by permission of Rivertown Trading./ Sidelight excerpts from "The Cosmos," by Jonathan Cott, December 25, 1980, in *Rolling Stone*. Copyright © 1980 by Straight Arrow Publishers, Inc.

Sidelight excerpts from "All the News from Lake Wobegon," by John Bordsen, amended by Garrison Keiller, May-June 1983, in *Saturday Review*. Copyright © 1983 by *Saturday Review* Magazine./ Sidelight excerpts from "Face to Face with a Teen-Age Novelist," October 1967, in

Seventeen Magazine. Copyright © 1967 by Triangle Communications Inc. Reprinted by permission of Triangle Communications Inc./ Sidelight excerpts from "Advice from a Penwoman," by Lisa Ehrichs, November 1981, in *Seventeen* Magazine. Copyright © 1981 by Triangle Communications Inc. Reprinted by permission of Triangle Communications Inc./ Sidelight excerpts from "High Adventure in the Future," by Steve Swires, December, 1980, in *Starlog*. Copyright © 1980 by O'Quinn Studios, Inc. Reprinted by permission of *Starlog*./ Sidelight excerpts from "On the Set with 'Escape from New York,' " by Samuel J. Maronie, April 1981, in *Starlog*. Copyright © 1981 by O'Quinn Studios, Inc./ Sidelight excerpts from "John Carpenter: Directing 'The Thing,' " by Steve Swires, July, 1982, in *Starlog*. Copyright © 1982 by O'Quinn Studios, Inc. Reprinted by permission of *Starlog*./ Sidelight excerpts from "Nina Bohlen on Her Life and Art as Told to Karin Stephen," by Karin Stephen, Boston Public Library, 1987. Copyright © 1987 by Karin Stephen. Reprinted by permission of Karin Stephen.

Sidelight excerpts from "Tex and Other Teen Tales," July 1982, in *Teen*./ Jacket illustration by Peter Thorpe from *Leaving Home* by Garrison Keillor. Reprinted by permission of Peter Thorpe./ Sidelight excerpts from "Season's Bleedings in Tinseltown," by Richard Corliss, December 19, 1983, in *Time*, New York./ Sidelight excerpts from "Lonesome Whistling Blowing," by John Skow, amended by Garrison Keillor, November 4, 1985, in *Time*, New York. Copyright © 1985 by Time Inc. Reprinted by permission of *Time*./ Sidelight excerpts from "Education: Lake Wobegon Chronicler Garrison Keillor at Gettysburg College, Gettysburg, Pa.," June 22, 1987, in *Time*, New York./ Sidelight excerpts from "People," June 5, 1989, in *Time*, New York./ Sidelight excerpts from "For Garrison Keillor Fantasy Is a Lot More Fun than Reality," by Ira Letofsky, July 29, 1976, in *Tribune* (Minneapolis). Reprinted by permission of Star Tribune, Minneapolis-St. Paul./ Sidelight excerpts from "Beyond Viking: Where Missions to Mars Could Lead," August 30, 1976, in *U.S. News & World Report*. Copyright © 1976 by *U.S. News & World Report*./ Sidelight excerpts from "A Dream Career," by Hollie I. West, March 21, 1971, in *The Washington Post*. Copyright © 1971 by The Washington Post Company./ Sidelight excerpts from "Double Visions: A Special Tool for Young Adult Writers," by Cheryl Zach, November 1988, in *The Writer*. Copyright © 1988 by The Writer, Inc. Reprinted by permission of Cheryl Zach./ Sidelight excerpts from "Sharing the Laughter with Garrison Keillor," by Michael Schumacher, amended by Garrison Keillor, January 1986, in *Writer's Digest*. Copyright © 1986 by Michael Schumacher. Reprinted by permission of Michael Shumacher.

PHOTOGRAPH CREDITS

Michael Bond (Paddington toy shop): Cathy Courtney; Shirlee Evans: copyright © 1989 by Dave's Studio; Barbara Jane Feinberg: Carole Freedman; Peter Firmin: Cathy Courtney; Sally Foster: Ruth Zook; Sally Foster (standing by wagon): courtesy of Sally Foster; Cecile Gagnon: Diane Hardy; S. E. Hinton: David Inhofe; Maryann Kovalski: Steven Jack; Bette Bao Lord: copyright © by Jim Kalett; Sharon Bell Mathis: Dexter Oliver; Roxie Munro: Bo Zaunders; Uri Orlev: copyright © by Aliza Auerbach; Jan Pienkowski: Jane Brown; Carolyn Polese: Peter Lehman; Jane Rosenberg: Robert F. Porter; Carolyn Sloan: Peter Hollis; Barbara Wersba: Charles Caron; Paul Zindel: Deforest.

SOMETHING ABOUT THE AUTHOR

ABRAMS, Lawrence F. 1944-

PERSONAL: Born March 1, 1944, in Detroit, Mich.; son of Carl (a teacher) and Dorothy (a secretary; maiden name, Mires) Abrams; married Kathleen S. (a writer and teacher), 1969; children: Nathaniel. *Education:* Received B.S., 1966, and M.S.T. *Politics:* Republican. *Religion:* Lutheran. *Home:* Wausau, Wis. *Agent:* Peekner Literary Agency, 3418 Shelton Ave., Bethlehem, Pa. 18017.

CAREER: D. C. Everest High School, Schofield, Wis., English teacher, 1969—; author and photographer, 1972—; University of Wisconsin—Marathon, photography teacher, 1979-88; University of Wisconsin—Madison, photography teacher, 1988—. Member of board of directors of College for Kids. *Member:* Council for Wisconsin Writers (board member). *Awards, honors:* Council for Wisconsin Writers Third Place, 1984, for *Throw It Out of Sight!*, and Second Place in outdoor writing, 1985, for *Biking the Great Lakes Islands*.

WRITINGS:

Mysterious Powers of the Mind (juvenile), Messner, 1982.
Throw It Out of Sight! Building and Flying a Hand-Launched Glider (juvenile; self-illustrated with photographs), Dillon, 1984.
Photography for Writers, Entwood, 1986.

WITH WIFE, KATHLEEN S. ABRAMS

Logging and Lumbering (juvenile; self-illustrated with photographs), Messner, 1980.
Successful Landlording (adult), Structures, 1980, revised edition, Entwood, 1985.
One Hundred Years from Now (juvenile), Messner, 1983.
Exploring Wisconsin (adult), Rand McNally, 1983.
Salvaging Old Barns and Houses: Tear It Down and Save the Pieces (adult), Sterling, 1983.

Biking the Great Lakes Islands: A Guide to Biking Seven Islands in the Great Lakes, Entwood, 1985.

ILLUSTRATOR

Kathleen S. Abrams, *The Big Rigs: Trucks, Truckers, and Trucking* (juvenile; illustrated with photographs), Messner, 1981.
Beverly Butler Olson, *Maggie by My Side* (Junior Literary Guild selection), Dodd, 1987.
K. S. Abrams, *Alternative Careers*, F. Watts, 1988.

Contributor of about one hundred and fifty articles to magazines, including *Trailer Boats, Better Camping, Wisconsin Trails, Fins and Feathers,* and *Fur/Fish/Game*.

SIDELIGHTS: "I have an interest in nearly every subject, so my books and illustrations span a variety of topics. I enjoy providing useful information in a readable and entertaining form.

"By the time I was in second grade I had developed a love for books, reading and writing. I started writing a novel in parts that I shared with second grade friends, who seemed to enjoy reading it. In the ninth grade I won my first essay contest and won two more before I left high school. Always, though, I have spent much of my time in the outdoors, often far from civilization. My experiences helped me in writing articles on hunting, fishing, canoeing, and kayaking for magazines where I first published my work. I added photography to my activities as I continued writing. This allowed me to illustrate my articles and books. Before long I was teaching photography classes on a regular basis.

"I like to do research for articles and books on location. This forces me to travel, often to places I would not have visited without the need for research."

LAWRENCE F. ABRAMS

HOBBIES AND OTHER INTERESTS: Rowing and paddling small boats, playing guitar and folksinging, collecting knives, mountain biking, flying model gliders, hunting and fishing, photography.

FOR MORE INFORMATION SEE:

Appraisal, fall, 1984.

ACKLEY, Peggy Jo   1955-

PERSONAL: Born October 18, 1955, in Sacramento, Calif.; daughter of Harry Albright (a superior court judge) and Lois Irene (an opera house manager; maiden name, Johnson) Ackley; married Fredrick Harold Mosher (a caterer), October 8, 1983. *Education:* Attended New York University, 1975-76; University of California, Davis, B.A., 1977. *Home and office:* 3343 Folsom St., San Francisco, Calif. 94110. *Agent:* Joan Brandt, Literistic, One Madison Ave., New York, N.Y. 10010.

CAREER: Shapiro, Wisan & Krassner (law firm), New York City, receptionist, 1977-1979; Jerome Lemelson (private inventor), New York City, patent illustrator, 1979-80; Family Line, Inc., Westmont, Ill., greeting card and giftwrap illustrator, 1979-85; Renaissance Greeting Cards, Sanford, Me., greeting card illustrator, 1985—; free-lance illustrator and designer, 1987—.

ILLUSTRATOR:

Ronnie Sellers, *If Christmas Were a Poem,* Caedmon, 1983.
R. Sellers, *When Springtime Comes,* Caedmon, 1984.
Our Baby's First Seven Years, Gibson, 1989.

WORK IN PROGRESS: A monthly calendar column entitled "Month of Menus" for *Woman's Day,* 1989.

SIDELIGHTS: "I was born October 18, 1955, and I grew up in a small, agriculturally-oriented town in the Sacramento Valley of Northern California and attended public schools there. I have *always* drawn! My mother used to buy rolls of plain white shelf paper, give me a box of crayons, and I would fill the whole roll with pictures. I also loved coloring books and all kinds of crafty-stuff as a child. I won my first art award (Best in Show under ten years) at the county fair at age five. And I won again at age seventeen in the under-eighteen category. So artwork has been a part of my life for a long time.

"I focused on fine arts in high school and had some wonderfully encouraging teachers who spurred me on. After high school I attended the University of California, Davis, and studied there under some very well-respected artists and teachers: Wayne Thiebaud, William Wiley, and Roland Peterson. In my junior year I took a break from studio art and spent a year at New York University studying primarily art history and literature. I also discovered life in the big city!

"After graduating from U. C., Davis I returned to New York. I worked at different jobs (law office receptionist, patent illustrator) until a good friend encouraged me to make up a portfolio of greeting cards and take it to the New York Stationery Show. I sold two designs on the spot and that was all the encouragement I needed! After about two years of drawing cards in my spare time and cutting back on my regular job hours, I was offered a full-time, art-oriented job if I would move to the Chicago area. Eager to do this and ready for a change, I moved to the midwest in July, 1980.

PEGGY JO ACKLEY

"I lived and worked there for almost two years. During this time I also did trade show duty and one of my locations was San Francisco (about eighty miles from where I had grown up). On one of these business trips I met my future husband, and after an eight-month long-distance romance I decided I'd had enough of the harsh Chicago winters and moved to San Francisco.

"I was very lucky to be able to take my job with me. I began doing illustrations solely, sending them back to Chicago and discussing projects and changes over the phone. I still work out of my home as I have for over five years now.

"Through my greeting card connections, I was asked to illustrate a seasonal (Christmas) book for Caedmon in 1983, and due to its positive reception they decided to follow it with a spring sequel. Stylistically, the two books reflect the same look as my greeting cards, although I found the continuity of character necessary in a book format to be quite a challenge. The baby record book that I have illustrated for C. R. Gibson is much more design-orientated, although the illustrations themselves still have a story-book quality. I'm proud of the results and think it has a much more professional look than the previous two efforts.

"I approach children's books the way I approach greeting cards. I try to make each greeting card *inviting;* it should hold something so the reader will give it closer scrutiny. This makes the art special to me as the illustrator, and consequently it's more fun to work on. . . .I've developed a style and feeling that people relate to. Again, it's the detail, plus a sense of color and a sense of what can be *charming* and *sweet* without crossing the border of being sickeningly saccharine. . . .I do use source material—old children's books (my current passion), art books, museum shows, magazines: trade, home, fashions, food, and so on. Inspiration comes from *many* sources and have very varied results.

"One of the things that attracts me to greeting cards is their *size*. They are to me (at least the very best ones) like little jewels. Small pieces of wonderment that invite you to step inside the world they've created. And being small, *and* relatively affordable, you can buy this piece of art and *keep* it to treasure.

"Even when I'm doing art, I enjoy the smallness of it and I do almost all my work to size. I enjoy details (perhaps compulsively so) and patterns. You'll find them in a lot of my work. I like the fact that most of it is upbeat subject matter. I like the fact that it's printed because: (1) You get to see the results fairly fast. . .and (2) you can send your art to all your friends and relatives!"[1]

FOOTNOTE SOURCES

[1]Eva Szela, *The Complete Guide to Greeting Card Design and Illustration,* Northlight Books, 1987. Amended by Peggy Ackley.

FOR MORE INFORMATION SEE:

Artist's, May, 1988.
Leisure Arts, December, 1988.

ANDREWS, Jan   1942-

PERSONAL: Born June 6, 1942, in Shoreham-by-Sea, Sussex, England; came to Canada, 1963; became Canadian citizen, 1971; daughter of Sydney Frederick (an accountant) and Geor-

JAN ANDREWS

gina (a dog breeder; maiden name, Welsman) Ellins; married Christopher Andrews (a research scientist), August 10, 1963; children: Miriam, Kieran; (foster children) Elaine, Annette, Nicola. *Education:* University of Reading, B.A. (with honors), 1963; University of Saskatoon, M.A., 1969; attended Carson Grove Language Centre, 1975. *Home and office:* 444 Athlone Ave., Ottawa, Ontario, Canada K1Z 5M7.

CAREER: CFQC-Radio, Saskatoon, Saskatchewan, copywriter, 1963; University of Saskatoon, Saskatchewan, instructor in English, summer, 1965; Murray Memorial Library, Saskatoon, library clerk, 1965; Office of the Secretary of State, Ottawa, Ontario, grants officer in citizenship branch, 1972, program officer with Native Citizens Program, 1973, literary projects officer in Multiculturalism Directorate, 1976, 1978, writing and publications officer and acting head of academic and cultural resources in Multiculturalism Directorate, 1984, developer of oral history program "Out of Everywhere" for Expo '86, 1985-86; free-lance writer, editor, and organizer of children's literature workshops, readings, exhibitions, and panel discussions, 1977—; Ottawa Board of Education, presenter of workshops at public schools, 1979-85, teacher of evening classes for adults, 1983; Counterpoint School (parent-run cooperative), Ottawa, coordinator, 1981, 1984-85; Andrews-Cayley Enterprises, Ottawa, founder and partner, 1987—. Organizer of "Come Hear a Writer," series of readings for children at Glebe Community Theatre, 1982-83; writer and coordinator for children's record "A Band of Storytellers," Marc Productions, Ottawa, 1985; researcher for "The Chance to Give," an exhibition at National Library of Canada, 1986-87; organizer of school events in the multicultural "The Chance to Give" series, 1986-88; organizer of "Uncharted Territory" a multicultural reading series, 1987-88; programmer of summer performances at the National Gallery of Canada, 1988; programmer for the Cultures Canada Festival, Ottawa, 1988; researcher of children's literature exhibition "The Secret Self," for the National Library of Canada, 1988.

MEMBER: Writers Union of Canada, Canadian Society of Children's Authors, Illustrators, and Performers. *Awards, honors:* Canada Council Grant, 1983, and 1987; *Very Last First Time* was exhibited at the Bologna International Children's Book Fair, 1985, nominated for the Ruth Schwartz Award from the Ontario Arts Council, Children's Literature Prize from the Canada Council, and selected one of *School Library Journal*'s Best Books for Young Adults, all 1986, selected one of Child Study Association of America's Children's Books of the Year, 1987, and shortlisted for the Washington State Children's Choice Picturebook Award, 1989.

WRITINGS:

JUVENILE

Fresh Fish. . .and Chips (illustrated by Linda Donnelly), Canadian Women's Educational Press, 1973.
Ella, an Elephant: Ella, un elephant (illustrated by Pat Bonn), Tundra Books, 1976.
A Good Place to Be, Gage, 1980.
(Editor) *The Dancing Sun: Stories and Poems Celebrating Canadian Children* (anthology; illustrated by Renee Mansfield), Press Porcepic, 1981.
Very Last First Time (Junior Literary Guild selection; illustrated by Ian Wallace), Douglas & McIntyre, 1985, Atheneum, 1986 (published in England as *Eva's Ice Adventure*, Methuen, 1986).

SCRIPTWRITER

"Coming of Age" (dramatic montage), first produced at the National Library of Canada, 1985.

OTHER

(Contributor) *The Canadian Family Tree*, Don Mills, 1979.

Contributor to periodicals, including *Canadian Children's Annual, Cricket, Ahoy,* and language arts publications in Canada and the United States.

WORK IN PROGRESS: Picture books: the story of a boy's visit to the family farm the night before the farm is to be sold, working title *Farm Auction,* for Groundwood Books; a story about three children whose mother has stayed up late working and turned into a pumpkin; a short fantasy piece about the bringing of joy and light and color when all the world is cold and dark; a story about a boy in Cape Breton who flies in his imagination through the night-time with the gulls.

SIDELIGHTS: "Most of my writing seems to be very firmly rooted in some place or other. I often wonder whether, if I had not come to North America, I would ever have started writing at all. There is something about the way of the land—its vastness and strength, the space of it—that speaks to me very deeply. I go out into it whenever possible in canoes and kayaks and on my own two feet.

"I write for children because I can't seem to help it. I have a passionate interest in adult life, but still the children's stories are the ones that grow in my head. Not only because of my writing, but also because of all sorts of other things I can't explain too well, children are important to me. I think about young people a great deal and about how, when it comes to raising them, we really ought to be doing a better job.

The lap, lap of the waves sounded louder and nearer. ■ (From *Very Last First Time* by Jan Andrews. Illustrated by Ian Wallace.)

"Recently my life seems to have taken sundry new directions, and I have been providing material for exhibits and planning a variety of special events. To me, all of this seems to come out of the same place, however—out of a concern with making and shaping, with dreaming and seeking, with hoping and being alive.

"I like. . .to give readings and workshops in schools, and enjoy quite simply being where children are around."

HOBBIES AND OTHER INTERESTS: Canoeing, kayaking, cross-country skiing, gardening, investigating the world of storytelling.

ARNOLD, Susan (Riser) 1951-

PERSONAL: Born October 11, 1951, in Salt Lake City, Utah; daughter of Frederick F. (a retired engineer and president of wholesale company) and Denise (a volunteer; maiden name, Bintz) Riser; married Robert L. Arnold (an architect), October 13, 1973; children: Benjamin R., Christopher Karrick. *Education:* University of Pau, France, language degree, 1973; University of Utah, B.F.A., 1974; attended Colorado Mountain College. *Home and office:* P.O. Box 3262, Vail, Colo. 81658.

CAREER: Free-lance author and artist. Teacher of aerobics, creative dancing, and art to children. Member of the board of directors of Vail Junior Hockey League, 1985-88; organizes art appreciation for Red Sandstone Elementary School.

WRITINGS:

SELF-ILLUSTRATED

(With Barbara Williams) *Pins, Picks, and Popsicle Sticks: A Straight Line Crafts Book,* Holt, 1977.
Eggshells to Objects: A New Approach to Eggcraft, Holt, 1979.

WORK IN PROGRESS: Illustrations for *Simon,* a French conversational/storybook for one- to three-year-olds; *Charlotte's Long Blonde Beautiful Hair,* a storybook.

SIDELIGHTS: "I enjoy working on children's books because I like to see the world and experience it once again from their eyes. Also, it is my hope that my illustrations will be so beautiful as to inspire a child to experience art as well. The craft books that I wrote and illustrated will hopefully give pleasure to all of those who create the projects as well as show the potential of taking a common object and creating something special from it. Beauty is of utmost importance to me. I like to create it and hope that others will appreciate it as well. I think that one's state of mind is actually influenced by one's surroundings. I hope to give pleasure and ideas to any audience I might have. Children are very special and deserve the very best.

"I wrote a book in third grade and used plants and details from nature. In fifth grade I used to finish my work early and then write and illustrate books in the back of the room.

"I grew up in a neighborhood that had lots of woods where I spent a great deal of time. Nature has always been my refuge. The ability to even slightly express the beauty of natural botanical plants especially, has been a constant goal.

"Fantasy has always been present in our family. My mother encouraged it, and we read tons of books while growing up. Reading, fantasy, writing, painting, and observing are my past

and present. I always treasure Arthur Rackham books and have always wanted to be able to draw and illustrate as beautifully as he does. Art is a way of life. Beauty is a way of life, too. Children are special in that they are so open to new things and seem to experience things more thoroughly than adults. I gravitate to the children, and children gravitate to me. We must have something in common.

"I went to the University of Utah and took a lot of drawing classes. Life drawing, botanical drawing, advanced problem solving, painting in all mediums, lithography and more art history than needed for the degree.

"Every advertising agency I interviewed with said I should be illustrating children's books. Then, I met Barbara Williams and we collaborated on my first book.

"I have started a specialized painting business. It entails painting on furniture and walls. Also, stenciling and wall glazes using different materials and glazes to add depth to walls. Examples of this are marbelizing, ragging, and sponging.

"Our family spends a lot of time in southern Utah hiking and camping. The light, air, color, and structure in that part of the country is magical."

BERRY, Joy (Wilt) 1944-

PERSONAL: Born April 15, 1944, in Southgate, Calif.; daughter of Richard Jackson and Doris Opal (owners and operators of a small manufacturing company) Berry; married James S. Gough (a psychiatrist), February 14, 1987; children: Christopher Todd, Lisa Renee. *Education:* Laverne College, B.A., 1966; Pacific Oaks College, M.A., 1971. *Home:* Sebastopol, Calif. *Office:* Living Skills Press, P.O. Box 83, Sebastopol, Calif. 95473.

JOY BERRY

CAREER: Ontario School District, Calif., teacher, 1966-67; El Monte School District, Calif., teacher, 1967-70; Arcadia Preschool and Family Education Center, Calif., administrator, 1970-75; Tri-City Recreation Program, Calif., director, 1973-79; Pasadena Probation Department, Calif., consultant, 1973-79; Pasadena Child Welfare Agency, Calif., counselor, 1973-79; Arcadia Child Development Center, Calif., administrator, 1975-79; Institute of Living Skills, Sebastopol, Calif., founder, lecturer, director of seminars, 1975—; Living Skills Press, Sebastopal, Calif, founder and author, 1980—; creator and director of Children's Ministries, Pasadena, Calif.; founder of the Human Race Club. *Member:* National Association for the Education of Young Children. *Awards, honors:* Finalist for Children's Instructional Video from the American Film Institute, 1988, for "The Unforgettable Pen Pal."

WRITINGS:

An Uncomplicated Guide to Becoming a Superparent, Word Books, 1983.

"READY-SET-GROW" SERIES; ALL ILLUSTRATED BY ERNIE HERGENROEDER

Mine and Yours, Weekly Reader, 1978.
Needing Each Other, Weekly Reader, 1978.
Keeping Your Body Alive and Well, Weekly Reader, 1978.
Saying What You Mean, Weekly Reader, 1978.
Surviving Fights with Your Brothers and Sisters, Weekly Reader, 1978.
The Nitty-Gritty of Family Life, Weekly Reader, 1978.
A Kid's Guide to Making Friends, Weekly Reader, 1978.
Making Up Your Own Mind, Weekly Reader, 1978.
Handling Your Ups and Downs, Weekly Reader, 1979.
Using Your Head, Weekly Reader, 1979.
May I? Please? Thank You!, Weekly Reader, 1979.
Danger, Weekly Reader, 1979.
You're All Right, Weekly Reader, 1979.
You're One of a Kind, Weekly Reader, 1979.
A Kid's TV Guide, Weekly Reader, 1979.
A Kid's Guide to Managing Time, Weekly Reader, 1979.
A Kid's Guide to Managing Money, Weekly Reader, 1979.
A Consumer's Guide for Kids, Weekly Reader, 1979.
You Can Do It, Weekly Reader, 1980.
You're Either One or the Other, Weekly Reader, 1980.
Handling Your Disagreements, Weekly Reader, 1980.
A Kid's Guide to Understanding Parents, Weekly Reader, 1980.
Checking 'Em Out and Sizing 'Em Up, Weekly Reader, 1980.
Tuff Stuff, Weekly Reader, 1980.

"SURVIVAL" SERIES; ALL ILLUSTRATED BY BARTHOLOMEW

What to Do When Your Mom or Dad Says. . .Clean Your Room!, Living Skills Press, 1981.
. . .Get Good Grades!, Living Skills Press, 1981.
. . .Be Prepared!, Living Skills Press, 1981.
. . .Earn Your Allowance!, Living Skills Press, 1981.
. . .Clean Yourself Up!, Living Skills Press, 1982.
. . .Be Kind to Your Guest!, Living Skills Press, 1982.
. . .Take Care of Your Clothes!, Living Skills Press, 1982.
. . .Be Good While You're There!, Living Skills Press, 1982.
. . .Don't Hang around with the Wrong Crowd!, Living Skills Press, 1982.
. . .Help!, Living Skills Press, 1982.
. . .Do Something besides Watch TV!, Living Skills Press, 1982.
. . .Do Your Homework and Schoolwork!, Living Skills Press, 1982.
. . .Don't Overdo with Video Games!, Living Skills Press, 1982.
. . .Be Careful!, Living Skills Press, 1983.
. . .We Can't Afford It!, Living Skills Press, 1983.
. . .Get the Phone!, Living Skills Press, 1983.

. . .Be Good!, Living Skills Press, 1983.
. . .Go to Bed!, Living Skills Press, 1983.
. . .What Should You Say Dear?, Living Skills Press, 1983.
. . .Stand Up Straight!, Living Skills Press, 1983.
. . .Don't Slurp Your Soup!, Living Skills Press, 1984.
. . .Write to Grandma!, Living Skills Press, 1984.
. . .Make Your Breakfast and Lunch!, Living Skills Press, 1984.
. . .Turn Off the Water and Lights!, Living Skills Press, 1984.
. . .Get Dressed!, Living Skills Press, 1986.
. . .Baby-Sit!, Living Skills Press, 1986.
. . .Do the Yardwork!, Living Skills Press, 1986.
. . .You Want a Pet?, Living Skills Press, 1986.
. . .Behave in Public!, Living Skills Press, l986.

"LET'S TALK ABOUT" SERIES; ALL ILLUSTRATED BY JOHN COSTANZA; NEW EDITIONS PUBLISHED AS "HELP ME BE GOOD" SERIES; INCLUDES CASSETTE; ALL ILLUSTRATED BY BARTHOLOMEW; ALL PUBLISHED BY LIVING SKILLS PRESS, 1988; ALL TITLED A CHILDREN'S BOOK ABOUT. . .

Let's Talk about Being Selfish, Grolier, 1982.
. . .Being Lazy, Grolier, 1982.
. . .Overdoing It, Grolier, 1982.
. . .Breaking Promises, Grolier, 1982.
. . .Disobeying, Grolier, 1982.
. . .Showing Off, Grolier, 1982.
. . .Whining, Grolier, 1982.
. . .Throwing Tantrums, Grolier, 1982.
. . .Complaining, Grolier, 1982.
. . .Tattling, Grolier, 1982.
. . .Teasing, Grolier, 1982.
. . .Being Rude, Grolier, 1982.
. . .Snooping, Grolier, 1982.
. . .Lying, Grolier, 1982.
. . .Cheating, Grolier, 1982.
. . .Stealing, Grolier, 1982.
. . .Being Destructive, Grolier, 1982.
. . .Fighting, Grolier, 1982.
. . .Being Messy, Grolier, 1984.
. . .Being Greedy, Grolier, 1984.
. . .Interrupting, Grolier, 1984.
. . .Gossiping, Grolier, 1984.
. . .Being Bullied, Grolier, 1984.
. . .Being Bossy, Grolier, 1984.
. . .Being Wasteful, Grolier, 1984.
. . .Being Careless, Grolier, 1984.
. . .Being Forgetful, Grolier, 1984.
. . .Being a Bad Sport, Grolier, 1984.
. . .Being Mean, Living Skills Press, 1988.

"NO MORE" SERIES; RECORDS

No More Feeling Weird, Peter Pan, 1982.
. . .Feeling Cheated, Peter Pan, 1982.
. . .Feeling Yucky, Peter Pan, 1982.
. . .Boredom, Peter Pan, 1982.
. . .Fighting, Peter Pan, 1982.
. . .Losing, Peter Pan, 1982.

"DANGER ZONES" SERIES

Abuse and Neglect (illustrated by Bartholomew), Living Skills Press, 1984.
Kidnapping (illustrated by Bartholomew), Living Skills Press, 1984.
Sexual Abuse (illustrated by Bartholomew), Living Skills Press, 1984.
(With Kathy McBride) *A Parent's Guide to the Danger Zones,* Word Books, 1985.

Anger might cause you to be destructive. ■ (From *Let's Talk about Being Destructive* by Joy Wilt Berry. Illustrated by John Costanza.)

"TEACH ME ABOUT" SERIES; INCLUDES CASSETTE; ALL ILLUS-TRATED BY BARTHOLOMEW

Teach Me about Mealtime, Living Skills Press, 1984.
. . .*Getting Dressed*, Living Skills Press, 1984.
. . .*Potty Training*, Living Skills Press, 1984.
. . .*Bathtime*, Living Skills Press, 1984.
. . .*Bedtime*, Living Skills Press, 1984.
. . .*Boredom*, Living Skills Press, 1984.
. . .*Crying*, Living Skills Press, 1984.
. . .*Danger*, Living Skills Press, 1984.
. . .*Illness*, Living Skills Press, 1984.
. . .*Security Objects*, Living Skills Press, 1984.
. . .*Separation*, Living Skills Press, 1984.
. . .*Travel*, Living Skills Press, 1984.
. . .*Pets*, Living Skills Press, 1986.
. . .*Brothers and Sisters*, Living Skills Press, 1986.
. . .*Pretending*, Living Skills Press, 1986.
. . .*Relatives*, Living Skills Press, 1986.

. . .*Friends*, Living Skills Press, 1986.
. . .*the Dentist*, Living Skills Press, 1986.
. . .*Listening*, Living Skills Press, 1986.
. . .*Looking*, Living Skills Press, 1986.
. . .*the Baby-Sitter*, Living Skills Press, 1986.
. . .*Mommies and Daddies*, Living Skills Press, 1986.
. . .*the Doctor*, Living Skills Press, 1986.
. . .*My Body*, Living Skills Press, 1986.
. . .*School*, Living Skills Press, 1986.
. . .*Smelling*, Living Skills Press, 1986.
. . .*Tasting*, Living Skills Press, 1986.
. . .*Touching*, Living Skills Press, 1986.

"LIVING SKILLS" SERIES; ALL ILLUSTRATED BY BARTHOLOMEW

Every Kid's Guide to Decision Making and Problem Solving, Living Skills Press, 1987.
. . .*Handling Fights with Brothers or Sisters*, Living Skills Press, 1987.

(From *Let's Talk About Gossiping* by Joy Berry. Illustrated by John Costanza.)

. . .*Laws that Relate to Parents and Children*, Living Skills Press, 1987.
. . .*Laws that Relate to School and Work*, Living Skills Press, 1987.
. . .*Overcoming Prejudice and Discrimination*, Living Skills Press, 1987.
. . .*Nutrition and Health Care*, Living Skills Press, 1987.
. . .*Understanding Human Rights*, Living Skills Press, 1987.
. . .*Understanding Parents*, Living Skills Press, 1987.
. . .*Watching TV Intelligently*, Living Skills Press, 1987.
. . .*Being a Communicator*, Living Skills Press, 1987.
. . .*Family Rules and Responsibilities*, Living Skills Press, 1987.
. . .*Good Manners*, Living Skills Press, 1987.
. . .*Handling Disagreements*, Living Skills Press, 1987.
. . .*Laws that Relate to Kids in the Community*, Living Skills Press, 1987.
. . .*the Juvenile Justice System*, Living Skills Press, 1987.
. . .*Thinking and Learning*, Living Skills Press, 1987.
. . .*Using Time Wisely*, Living Skills Press, 1987.
. . .*Being Special*, Living Skills Press, 1988.
. . .*Handling Family Arguments*, Living Skills Press, 1988.
. . .*Handling Feelings*, Living Skills Press, 1988.
. . .*Making and Managing Money*, Living Skills Press, 1988.
. . .*Making Friends*, Living Skills Press, 1988.
. . .*Responding to Danger*, Living Skills Press, 1988.

. . .*Understanding Nightmares*, Living Skills Press, 1988.
. . .*Coping with Childhood Traumas*, Living Skills Press, 1988.
. . .*Handling Illness*, Living Skills Press, 1988.
. . .*Intelligent Spending*, Living Skills Press, 1988.

*"HUMAN RACE CLUB" SERIES; BOOK AND CASSETTE; ALL-ILLUS-
TRATED BY BARTHOLOMEW*

The Lean Mean Machine, Living Skills Press, 1987.
The Letter on Light Blue Stationery, Living Skills Press, 1987.
The Battle at the McGoverns', Living Skills Press, 1987.
The Fair Weather Friend, Living Skills Press, 1987.
What Happened to A. J.?, Living Skills Press, 1987.
A High Price to Pay, Living Skills Press, 1987.
Casey's Revenge, Living Skills Press, 1987.
The Saturday Night Stalker, Living Skills Press, 1987.

ADAPTATIONS

CASSETTES

"Handling Your Disagreements," Word Books.
"Handling Your Ups and Downs," Word Books.
"Keeping Your Body Alive and Well," Word Books.
"A Kid's Guide to Understanding Parents," Word Books.
"Mine and Yours," Peter Pan.

(From *Let's Talk About Teasing* by Joy Berry. Illustrated by John Costanza.)

"Saying What You Mean," Peter Pan.
"Surviving Fights with Your Brothers and Sisters," Peter Pan.
"Using Your Head," Peter Pan.
"You Can Do It," Peter Pan.
"You're All Right," Peter Pan.
"You're Either One or the Other," Peter Pan.
"You're One of a Kind," Peter Pan.

VIDEOCASSETTES

"The Lean Mean Machine," Children's Media Group, 1987.
"The Letter on Light Blue Stationery," Children's Media Group, 1987.
"A High Price to Pay," Children's Media Group, 1987.
"The Fair Weather Friend," Children's Media Group, 1988.
"Casey's Revenge," Children's Media Group, 1988.
"The Unforgettable Pen Pal" (based on *Every Kid's Guide to*

Overcoming Prejudice and Discrimination), Children's Media Group, 1988.

WORK IN PROGRESS: "Good Answers to Tough Questions," a series of twenty-four books; "Winning Skills," a series of eighteen books.

SIDELIGHTS: "I can't for the life of me remember ever reading a book when I was a kid. Somehow I had acquired the idea that reading was work, and I was determined not to do it unless I absolutely had to. Considering my lack of fondness for books, was it any wonder that I never considered the possibility of becoming an author when I grew up?

"What I *did* want to become was a school teacher, a goal my first-grade teacher had inspired in me. Once I started in that direction, I never once looked back, even though obtaining an education and teaching credentials wasn't easy for me. Having been too busy being a cheerleader, class president, and homecoming queen to concentrate on getting very good grades in high school, I had to buckle down in college to catch up academically. And, with two older brothers and a younger sister, money was scarce in my family, so I worked as a dishwasher, house-cleaner, camp counselor, and child-care worker to pay for my education.

"I recall the night before my first day as a third-grade teacher. I was so excited after laboring all summer to have my classroom ready for the first day of school that I brought my sleeping bag and spent the night in my classroom.

"In the beginning, I was sure that the five years it had taken me to earn my teaching credentials was time well spent. I loved being a teacher! However, as I taught for the next four years, something about the curriculum and my role as a teacher began to bother me. No matter how hard I tried, I couldn't quite shake the feeling that something was missing.

"In one sense, it all began in the fifth grade, when I had talked my classmates into staging a 'walk-out' to protest the fact that we kids had nothing to say about what happened to us at school and that what happened at school seemed to have nothing to do with our lives and what *we* felt was important.

"When all of my peers broke down and re-entered the classroom, I chose to stay outside, a decision that cost me the only field trip our class took that entire year. Sitting all alone in the principal's office while my classmates were having fun at the dairy, I vowed then and there that if I couldn't change the way school was while I was a kid, I would surely do it when I became a grown-up.

"I found that things didn't change much during the eleven years it took me to return to the elementary school classroom as a teacher. Deep down inside I knew that the situation wasn't right, but it took a ten-year-old boy named Guy to get me to act on the promise I had made to myself that day in the fifth grade.

"Guy, one of the kids in my after-school program, was having serious problems in school when his parents called on me for help. During a visit with Guy in his home, I discovered that he had masterminded the construction of an elaborate, three-story tree house in his backyard. The impressive structure had become the meeting place for a group of neighborhood children who called themselves 'The Tree House Club.' Under Guy's capable leadership, the Tree House Club members undertook a variety of creative enterprises that earned the group a substantial amount of money.

"In spite of Guy's failing in school, it was obvious to me that he was both intelligent and talented. However, this was *not* obvious to Guy or to his parents. Guy's sense of failure and his parents' disappointment with their son's academic performance led me to re-evaluate the school curriculum and also my role as a teacher. As a result, I developed an entirely new educational approach designed to teach children living skills.

"I realized that I would need appropriate printed materials. To be effective, these materials had to be illustrated in a way that children would find appealing and entertaining. Using the Tree House Club as a model, I developed a group of cartoon characters—The Human Race Club—and used them as the basis for illustrating my self-help books and other materials for teaching living skills.

"Along the way, I also earned a master's degree in human development from Pacific Oaks College in Southern California. However, it wasn't in school that I gained the practical experience I needed to write self-help books for kids. Instead, it was by working directly with children and by raising two children of my own.

"I've always said that kids have a way of getting your head out of the clouds and putting your feet on the ground. That's what Christopher Todd (my son) and Lisa Renee (my daughter) have done for me. Their influence and the influence of the other children I've worked with have helped me write and produce books and other materials that are realistic as well as practical.

"When I was a kid, I had no idea that I would write more than 200 self-help books for children. I don't think anyone else did, either. Life is full of many wonderful surprises!"

FOR MORE INFORMATION SEE:

Belinda Busteed, "Aren't Children People Too?," *Star-News* (Pasadena, Calif.), October 2, 1977.
"Wilt Offers Seminar on Child Care," *Danville Register* (Va.), September 23, 1978.
Press Democrat (Santa Rosa, Calif.), June 19, 1979, January 2, 1989.
Argus-Courier, September 25, 1979.
Janet Pierson, "Kids Need Skills for Living: Author," *News World* (New York, N.Y.), April 5, 1982.
"Children's Books Are Growing Up," *Fort Lauderdale News*, November 18, 1982.
Lynn Rumley, "Children's Authors Use Various Methods," *Seattle Times*, December 9, 1982.
Margaret Carlin, "Joy Berry: An Adult in a Child's World," *Rocky Mountain News* (Denver, Colo.), February 6, 1983.
Us, February 14, 1983 (p. 10).
Betsy Kline, "Childhood Is Daring to Be, Educator Says," *Kansas City Star*, July 7, 1983.
Mary Ann Grossmann, "'Survival' Books for Kids," *Dispatch* (St. Paul, Minn.), July 18, 1983.
Paul Miller, "Peter Pan's Children's Books Address Real-Life Situations," *Toy and Hobby World*, June, 1984.
Bernice O'Connor, "Parental 'Guilt Trips' Unwarranted," *News* (Indianapolis, Ind.), June 25, 1984.
Sandra Burnett, "Responsibility Ought to Be Taught to Kids," *Times* (San Mateo, Calif.), November 1, 1986.
Instructor, January, 1988.
Sonoma Business, April, 1988.
Dallas Morning News, September 21, 1988.
USA Today, September 27, 1988.
Copley News Service, October 5, 1988.
Chicago Tribune, November 4, 1988.

BIRD, E(lzy) J(ay)   1911-

PERSONAL: Born April 3, 1911, in Salt Lake City, Utah; son of Joseph M. (a farmer and carpenter) and Fanny (a homemaker; maiden name, Beutler) Bird; married Nan Fugate (a homemaker), November 3, 1932; children: Robyn Lamm. *Education:* Attended University of Utah, 1929-31, and Chinauard School of Art, 1933. *Home:* 6980 Essex Circle, #2, Midvale, Utah 84047.

CAREER: Works Project Administration Federal Art Project, Utah, state director, 1935-42; A. B. Paulson, Salt Lake City, Utah, draftsman, 1946-54; Slack Winburn, Salt Lake City, draftsman, 1954-56; John Clawson, Salt Lake City, draftsman

E. J. BIRD

and designer, 1956-64; FFK&R, Salt Lake City, draftsman and designer, 1964-77. Past-member of board of directors, Utah State Institute of Fine Arts, 1930s, and Art Barn, Salt Lake City, 1950s. *Exhibitions*—Group shows: Artists West of the Mississippi, Colorado Springs, 1938; New York World's Fair, 1939; exhibited in many Utah shows prior to World War II. One-man shows: Denver Art Museum, Colo., 1939; Santa Barbara Museum, Calif., 1946; University of Utah, 1946. Permanent collections: Utah State Institute of Fine Arts, Utah State Fair, works are also included in many private collections and in Utah schools and public buildings. *Military service:* U.S. Army Engineers, first sergeant, 1942-46. *Awards, honors:* Purchase Award for paintings from Utah State Institute of Fine Arts, and the Utah State Fair, both in the 1930s; *Ten Tall Tales* was exhibited at the Bologna International Children's Book Fair, 1985.

WRITINGS:

SELF-ILLUSTRATED

Ten Tall Tales, Carolrhoda, 1984, 2nd edition, 1986.
Chuck Wagon Stew, Carolrhoda, 1988.

WORK IN PROGRESS: How Do Bears Sleep?; The Blizzard of Eighteen and Ninety Six; a children's picture book about an old mare that I used to ride to school; a book illustrated with pictographs and petroglyphs about a young Anasazi Indian boy (800 years ago) and his pet bear.

SIDELIGHTS: "In my retirement my wife and I have traveled, three times to Hawaii and once to Mexico down as far as the Yucatan. All this for pleasure and to experience far places. Four trips to Europe brought us into contact with all the great museums we had only read about. Then there is our own wide country, north, south, east and west, where we've seen the great museums and scattered works of art.

"I was born in the West when it was young and vital, and what I think was the most interesting time in the history of this country. I have watched it grow from the days of the horse and wagon to the day of the computer and the jet. I have watched the old things and the old ways disappear like smoke from the old campfires.

"I thought, in my retirement, I would like to leave something to my grandkids that I had seen and experienced—something of the West I knew that is now long gone.

"Drawing and painting I could handle, and my friends convinced me that I had a way with words. So I started with the things I knew and put them down honestly and without any frosting. I have been pleased that so many people have enjoyed the results of the things I have put together. I've enjoyed it myself—every minute of it."

BOHLEN, Nina 1931-

PERSONAL: Born March 5, 1931, in Boston, Mass.; daughter of Henry Morgan (in real estate) and Margaret (Curtis) Bohlen. *Education:* Radcliffe College, B.A., 1953; studied drawing and painting under Hyman Bloom, 1952-57; studied sculpture under Frank Tock and Harold Tovish and painting with Morton Sacks. *Home and office:* 55 Hagen Rd., Newton, Mass. 02159.

NINA BOHLEN

CAREER: Artist. Private drawing teacher, 1970—; Newton Arts Center, Newton, Mass., teacher, 1984-88; Pine Manor College, Chestnut Hill, Mass., visiting faculty, 1985-88.

EXHIBITIONS—Group shows: Swetzoff Gallery, Boston, Mass., 1957; Boston Arts Festival, 1962; Boston Museum School, 1963; Brockton Museum, Mass., 1969; Westmoreland Museum, Pa., 1973; Far Gallery, New York City, 1974; Library of Boston Athenaeum, 1976, 1978; Impressions Gallery, Boston, 1977, 1978, 1979; American Academy of Arts and Letters, 1977, 1978, 1982; Harvard Museum of Comparative Zoology, 1982; DeCordova Museum, Lincoln, Mass., 1987; Bumpus Gallery, Duxbury, Mass., 1987; Boston Public Library, 1987. One-woman shows: Carl Siembab Gallery, Boston, 1959; Shore Gallery, Boston, 1965; Tragos Gallery, Boston, 1968; Library of Boston Athenaeum, 1971, 1975; Duxbury Free Library, Mass., 1973; Far Gallery, New York City, 1979; Radcliffe College, 1983; (two-woman show) Van Buren Brazelton Gallery, Cambridge, Mass., 1985; Wiggin Gallery, Boston Public Library, Mass., 1987, Pine Manor College, Chestnut Hill, Mass, 1988. *Collections:* Fogg Museum of Art, Brockton Museum, Boston Public Library and private collections. *Awards, honors:* Art Award from the American Academy of Arts and Letters, 1977, for drawings.

ILLUSTRATOR:

Diana Harding and Deborah Manzolillo, *Baboon Orphan*, Dutton, 1981.

WORK IN PROGRESS: Oil paintings.

SIDELIGHTS: "Two events in my early childhood saved me from the rigid conventions of a Brahmin upbringing. When I was three, my mother and father were separated, and my older brother and I went to live with my aunt and uncle on a farm in Dover, Massachusetts. I became fascinated with the animals and the countryside. While I grew to love the beauty of all the animals on the farm, and was always extremely sad when they were killed, I developed the eye of a biologist. I learned to study these animals after death in a way I might not have otherwise.

"Then when I was five, my mother married a man from Eastern Maine. Although we lived in Boston in the winter, we spent our summers in Maine. My stepfather's relatives were botanists, ornithologists, farmers, fishermen and hunters, so once again I was in close contact with nature. During the shooting season there was always an ample supply of dead birds to draw. These two situations gave me a special approach to nature which has influenced me all my life. Recently, I came across a quote about the writer Rachel Carson which seemed to sum up that approach. It said: 'Her attitude toward nature combined a spiritual feel with scientific observation.'

"As a child, I read books about animals, books that had beautiful illustrations. I made many copies of these illustrations. My aunt, an amateur artist, encouraged me. During these younger years, two pictures inspired me particularly. One was a small painting of a dog done by my aunt. The fact that the dog's eyes followed me wherever I went amazed me. The other was Gainsborough's 'Blue Boy.' Oh, to paint satin like that!

"My real life as an artist, however, began when I was a junior at Radcliffe. That was when I met Hyman Bloom and became his student. He was teaching drawing at the Fogg Museum, a method of composing a picture from the imagination taught to him by Harold Zimmerman. We used an H.B. pencil and a kneaded eraser on smooth Bristol paper. I took the course for

credit for two years. During my senior year I also studied painting with Hyman two nights a week at his studio on Huntington Avenue. Also studying with him then was the painter Ellen Sinclair. At the time he was doing large cadaver drawings in conte crayon, and I had glimpses of these phenomenal pictures when I came into his studio. Hyman taught us to paint with a limited palette, based on the Denman Ross palette system. After the class, we would have tea in tall glasses and would look at books on art and talk about the old masters. Hyman would also encourage us to study the old masters, but it was *his* skill as an artist which inspired me most of all, and I admired the religious dedication he brought to his work. These were wonderful evenings.

"After graduating from Radcliffe, I continued studying with Hyman, doing large charcoal drawings, learning to compose from my imagination in light and shade. Hyman also introduced me to the world of Newbury Street and its art galleries, in particular, the Swetzoff Gallery, run by Hyman Swetzoff. There you could drop in and meet friends, see avant-garde art in the main gallery and old master drawings in the back room.

"The first piece of work I ever exhibited was a large charcoal drawing of the interior of a stable. It was in a group show at the Swetzoff Gallery. The drawing was bought by Jerry Goldberg, an avid collector of Boston artists. My first solo exhibition on Newbury Street was at the Siembab Gallery in 1959.

"During the fifties, I studied sculpture with both Frank Tock and Harold Tovish. Frank had a fascinating way of building his small sculptures out of many cone-shaped pieces of plasteline. He had a small foundry in his basement, and we cast several pieces in lead. My works from this period are very much in the style of Frank Tock. With Tovish, I worked in clay, modeling a series of falling horses, casting them in plaster and ultimately in bronze. I also studied painting for a brief period of time with Morton Sacks. In 1965 I had a drawing show at the Shore Gallery, a show of paintings at the Tragos Gallery in 1968, and in 1971, the first of several exhibitions at the Boston Anthenaeum organized by Donald Kelley.

"In 1968, the sculptress Susan Smyly moved to Boston. At the time, she was doing large sculptures of fat women. The boldness of her imagery was very liberating to me. She also taught me a method of drawing from life, a method taught her by Sandy Kincannon at the Memphis Academy of Art. Until this time I had worked only from my imagination. These small drawings on gesso required close observation of the object being drawn. I think the most important thing I retained from this method, aside from the ability to draw what was in front of me with accuracy, was a way of using the eraser up against the edge of a card, producing a very crisp edge.

"My drawings from the imagination at this time were sometimes a mixture of a tone of etching ink, rolled onto the paper and then worked on with one color of prismacolor pencil, or colored pencil on a commercially toned paper, or directly onto white paper. Among other things which I did at that time was a series of freaks, both animal and human. The first freak of nature I had ever seen was a two-headed calf, when I was a child. I suppose I see freaks as something very much part of nature, but a part which has gone wrong. These drawings were done with a spruce green pencil made by Colorama which looks like blue on paper. From there it was a natural progression to more than one color. My first multicolored pencil drawings were of feathers and large exotic birds. I had a number of friends who kept tropical birds, and they would give me their feathers as the birds molted. These made wonderfully colored bouquets.

Quanette and Gargantua begin to groom each other. ■ (From *Baboon Orphan* by Diana Harding and Deborah Manzolillo. Illustrated by Nina Bohlen.)

"In the summer of 1969, Hyman, Susan, and I were in Lubec, Maine. The painter Frank Parker had lent me a small nineteenth-century French etching press, so we began doing monotypes. Until then lithography was the only printing method I had experimented with, but Susan had done monotypes before. My first monotypes were of fishheads. Later, Hyman, seeing me try to carry my etching press through the woods in a basket, decided to design one which could be attached to a back pack. It was built by Peter Lindenmuth, of Nexus Design, and weighs only thirty pounds, truly a wonderful invention. In the autumn of 1972, I stayed in Lubec through the shooting season, and that's when I did the monotypes of dead birds.

"Most of my monotypes are from life, and I like to use them as a way of making studies. Because one is forced to work fairly rapidly, they are liberating. The beauty of a monotype is in its spontaneity. The less you alter the finished print, the better. Many of my monotypes were in group shows in the early seventies in both Boston and New York. In 1979, I had

a one-woman show of drawings and monotypes at the Far Gallery in New York. It was at this time that Sinclair Hitchings bought three that are now in the collection of the Boston Public Library. In 1984, I gave a ten-day monotype workshop in Lubec, and many of the works we did were shown. . .at the Helen Bumpus Gallery in Duxbury.

"I began working with puppets in 1977 when my younger brother, who lives in Thailand, gave me an antique Burmese puppet for Christmas. I had never seen anything like this extraordinary female with wooden breasts and a brightly painted crotch. My first puppet drawings were of this single female. One of them now is in the permanent drawing collection at the Fogg Art Museum. Several years later, my brother brought me another puppet, this time a male puppet from India. Using both the male and female puppet as a metaphor for human couples, I began a series of colored-pencil and watercolor pencil drawings. Since then my brother has returned home with more puppets, Chinese, Indonesian, and Burmese, and they continue to fascinate me.

"In 1979, my sister invited me to go to Kenya in East Africa. She had written a true children's story about a troop of Olive baboons who lived on the Kekopey Ranch, and she wanted me to illustrate the book. It was a fantastic experience. We lived in a little house atop a cliff, and every morning very early we would walk down into the valley and look for baboons. Sometimes they were hard to see because they looked like large rocks when they were sleeping. The baboons were used to people so we would walk with them all day long and watch them eating, scratching, arguing, and playing, leading a regular baboon life. The original drawings for the book were exhibited in 1982 at the Harvard Museum of Comparative Zoology. The book itself, entitled *Baboon Orphan*, was published by E. P. Dutton in 1981.

"When I won an art award from the Academy of Arts and Letters in New York, in 1977, Hyman Bloom wrote the citation: 'To Nina Bohlen, born in Boston in 1931. An individualist, she has created a mythology of which animals play a mythic role. Her work is sensitive and poetic and runs counter to the cynicism of current art fashion.'

"Anthony Burgess once said something which I found important. He said: 'Art begins with craft, and there is no art until craft has been mastered.' A work of art should be a pleasure to look at. What makes it a pleasure, apart from its content, is a sense of dexterity and skill, like that which is involved in making a beautiful watch or a fine violin. To some degree, I feel that my work as an artist is an effort to pay homage to skill in art as an enduring value. The influence of Hyman Bloom, whose works I feel combine this love of craft with a contemporary psychological point of view, has been a lasting one in that regard. To me, Hyman is not only a great artist, but a great teacher as well. Once he said that learning to compose from the imagination was the greatest contribution that Zimmerman had made to his education. I feel that learning to compose from the imagination was the greatest contribution Hyman has made to *my* education."[1]

FOOTNOTE SOURCES

[1]Karin Stephan, "Nina Bohlen on Her Life and Art as Told to Karin Stephan," Boston Public Library, 1987.

BOND, (Thomas) Michael 1926-

PERSONAL: Born January 13, 1926, in Newbury, Berkshire, England; son of Norman Robert (a civil servant) and Frances Mary (Offer) Bond; married Brenda Mary Johnson, June 29, 1950 (divorced, 1981); married Susan Marfrey Rogers, 1982; children: Karen Mary Jankel, Anthony Thomas. *Home:* "Fairacre," Farnham Lane, Haslemere, Surrey, England. *Agent:* Harvey Unna & Stephen Durbridge Ltd., 24 Pottery Lane, Holland Park, London W11 4LZ, England. *Office:* c/o 94B Tachbrook St., London SWN 2NB, England.

CAREER: British Broadcasting Corp., Reading, England, engineer's assistant, 1941-43, Faversham, England, with monitoring service, 1947-50, London, England, television cameraman, 1950-65; full-time writer, 1965—; Paddington Productions, Ltd., London, director. *Military service:* Royal Air Force, 1943-44, air crew; British Army, Middlesex Regiment, 1944-47. *Awards, honors: The Tales of Olga da Polga* was selected one of Child Study Association of America's Children's Books of the Year, 1973, *The Complete Adventures of Olga Da Polga*, 1983.

MICHAEL BOND

WRITINGS:

JUVENILE, EXCEPT AS NOTED

(Editor) *Michael Bond's Book of Bears*, Purnell, 1971.
The Day the Animals Went on Strike (picture book; illustrated by Jim Hodgson), American Heritage, 1972.
(Editor) *Michael Bond's Book of Mice*, Purnell, 1972.
(Translator with Barbara von Johnson) *The Motormalgamation*, Studio Vista, 1974.
Windmill (illustrated by Tony Cattaneo), Studio Vista, 1975.
How to Make Flying Things (nonfiction; illustrated with photographs by Peter Kibble), Studio Vista, 1975.
Mr. Cram's Magic Bubbles (illustrated by Gioia Fiammenghi), Penguin, 1975.
Picnic on the River, Collins, 1980.
J. D. Polson and the Liberty Head Dime (illustrated by Roger Wade Walker, hand lettering by Leslie Lee), Mayflower, 1980.
J. D. Polson and the Dillogate Affair (illustrated by R. W. Walker), Hodder & Stoughton, 1981.
The Caravan Puppets (illustrated by Vanessa Julian-Ottie), Collins, 1983.
(With Paul Parnes) *Oliver the Greedy Elephant* (illustrated by J. Hodgson), Methuen, 1985, Western Publishing, 1986.
The Pleasures of Paris: A Gastronomic Companion (adult guidebook; self-illustrated with photographs), Crown, 1987.

"PADDINGTON" SERIES

A Bear Called Paddington (illustrated by Peggy Fortnum), Collins, 1958, Houghton, 1960.

He soon grew tired of digging. ■ (From *Paddington's Garden* by Michael Bond. Illustrated by Fred Banbery.)

More about Paddington (illustrated by P. Fortnum), Collins, 1959, Houghton, 1962.

Paddington Helps Out (illustrated by P. Fortnum), Collins, 1960, Houghton, 1961.

Paddington Abroad (illustrated by P. Fortnum), Collins, 1961, Houghton, 1972.

Paddington at Large (illustrated by P. Fortnum), Collins, 1962, Houghton, 1963.

Paddington Marches On (illustrated by P. Fortnum), Collins, 1964, Houghton, 1965.

The Adventures of Paddington (contains *A Bear Called Paddington* and *More about Paddington;* illustrated by P. Fortnum), Collins, 1965.

Paddington at Work (illustrated by P. Fortnum), Collins, 1966, Houghton, 1967.

Paddington Goes to Town (illustrated by P. Fortnum), Houghton, 1968.

Paddington Takes the Air (illustrated by P. Fortnum), Collins, 1970, Houghton, 1971.

Paddington's Blue Peter Story Book (illustrated by Ivor Wood), Collins, 1973, published in America as *Paddington Takes to TV,* Houghton, 1974.

Paddington on Top (illustrated by P. Fortnum), Collins, 1974, Houghton, 1975.

Paddington Takes the Test (illustrated by P. Fortnum), Collins, 1979, Houghton, 1980.

Paddington: A Disappearing Trick and Other Stories (anthology), Collins, 1979.

Paddington for Christmas, Collins, 1979.

Paddington on Screen: The Second Blue Peter Story Book (illustrated by Barry Macey), Collins, 1981, Houghton, 1982.

The Hilarious Adventures of Paddington (contains *A Bear Called Paddington, More about Paddington, Paddington at Large, Paddington at Work,* and *Paddington Helps Out*), Dell, 1986.

(With Russell Ash) *The Life and Times of Paddington Bear,* Viking, 1989.

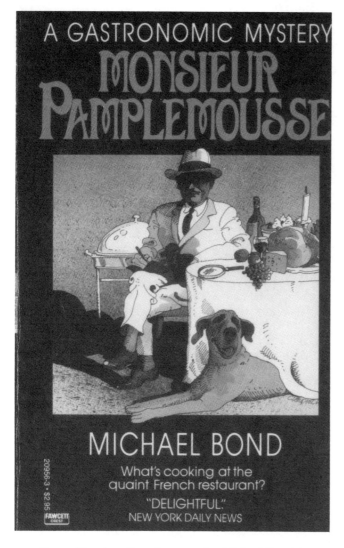

(From *Monsieur Pamplemousse* by Michael Bond.)

"PADDINGTON" PICTURE BOOKS

Paddington Bear (illustrated by Fred Banbery), Collins, 1972, Random House, 1973.

Paddington's Garden (illustrated by F. Banbery), Collins, 1972, Random House, 1973.

Paddington at the Circus (illustrated by F. Banbery), Collins, 1973, Random House, 1974.

Paddington Goes Shopping (illustrated by F. Banbery), Collins, 1973, published as *Paddington's Lucky Day*, Random House, 1974.

Paddington at the Tower (illustrated by F. Banbery), Collins, 1975, Random House, 1978.

Paddington at the Seaside (illustrated by F. Banbery), Collins, 1975, Random House, 1978.

Paddington Takes a Bath (illustrated by Barry Wilkinson), Collins, 1976.

Paddington Goes to the Sales (illustrated by B. Wilkinson), Collins, 1976.

Paddington's New Room (illustrated by B. Wilkinson), Collins, 1976.

Paddington at the Station (illustrated by B. Wilkinson), Collins, 1976.

Paddington Hits Out, Collins, 1977.

Paddington Does It Himself, Collins, 1977.

Paddington in the Kitchen, Collins, 1977.

Paddington Goes Out, Collins, 1980.

Paddington Weighs In (illustrated by B. Wilkinson), Collins, 1980.

Paddington at Home, Collins, 1980.

Paddington and Aunt Lucy (illustrated by B. Wilkinson), Collins, 1980.

Paddington in Touch (illustrated by B. Wilkinson), Collins, 1980.

Paddington Has Fun, Collins, 1982.

Paddington Works Hard, Collins, 1982.

Paddington's Storybook (illustrated by P. Fortnum), Collins, 1983, Houghton, 1984.

Paddington on the River (illustrated by B. Wilkinson), Collins, 1983.

Paddington at the Zoo (illustrated by David McKee), Collins, 1984, Putnam, 1985.

Paddington and the Knickerbocker Rainbow (illustrated by D. McKee), Collins, 1984, Putnam, 1985.

Paddington's Painting Exhibition (illustrated by D. McKee), Collins, 1985, published in America as *Paddington's Art Exhibition*, Putnam, 1986.

Paddington at the Fair (illustrated by D. McKee), Collins, 1985, Putnam, 1986.

Paddington at the Palace (illustrated by D. McKee), Putnam, 1986.

Paddington Minds the House (illustrated by D. McKee), Collins, 1986.

Paddington Spring Cleans, Collins, 1986.

Paddington Cleans Up (illustrated by D. McKee), Putnam, 1986.

Paddington's Busy Day (illustrated by D. McKee), Collins, 1987.

Paddington and the Marmalade Maze (illustrated by D. McKee), Collins, 1987.

Paddington's Magical Christmas (illustrated by D. McKee), Collins, 1988.

"PADDINGTON" LEARNING AND ACTIVITY BOOKS

The Great Big Paddington Book (illustrated by Ivor Wood), Collins, 1976, published in America as *The Great Big Paddington Bear Picture Book* Collins & World, 1977.

Paddington's Loose-End Book: An ABC of Things to Do (illustrated by I. Wood), Collins, 1976.

Paddington's Party Book (illustrated by I. Wood), Collins, 1976.

Fun and Games with Paddington (illustrated by I. Wood), Collins & World, 1977.

Paddington's Birthday Party, Collins, 1977.

Paddington Carpenter, Collins, 1977.

Paddington Conjurer, Collins, 1977.

Paddington Cook, Collins, 1977.

Paddington's First Book: An Object Recognition Book with Pictures to Colour (illustrated by B. Wilkinson), Collins, 1977.

Paddington Golfer, Collins, 1977.

Paddington's First Word Book: Words to Copy, Pictures to Colour (illustrated by B. Wilkinson), Collins, 1977.

Paddington's First Play Book: Things to Make, Games to Play, Pictures to Colour (illustrated by B. Wilkinson), Collins, 1977.

Paddington's First Counting Book: Learn the Numbers, Colour the Pictures (illustrated by B. Wilkinson), Collins, 1977.

Paddington's Picture Book, Collins, 1978.

Paddington's Cartoon Book (illustrated by I. Wood), Collins, 1979.

(With daughter, Karen Bond) *Paddington at the Airport* (illustrated by Toni Goffe), Macmillan, 1986.

(With K. Bond) *Paddington Mails a Letter* (illustrated by T. Goffe), Macmillan, 1986 (published in England as *Paddington Bear Posts a Letter*, Hutchinson, 1986).

A moment later some familiar looking whiskers, followed by an equally familiar hat, appeared in the gap. ■ (From *Paddington Takes to TV* by Michael Bond. Illustrated by Ivor Wood.)

(With K. Bond) *Paddington's Clock Book* (illustrated by T. Goffe), Hutchinson, 1986.

(With K. Bond) *Paddington's London*, Hutchinson, 1986.

Also author with K. Bond of *Paddington's Wheel Book* (illustrated by T. Goffe), published by Macmillan.

"PADDINGTON" POP-UP BOOKS

Paddington's Pop-Up Book, Collins, 1977.
Paddington and the Snowbear, Collins, 1981.
Paddington at the Launderette, Collins, 1981.
Paddington's Shopping Adventure, Collins, 1981.
Paddington's Birthday Treat, Collins, 1981.

"THURSDAY" SERIES

Here Comes Thursday! (illustrated by Daphne Rowles), Harrap, 1966, Lothrop, 1967.
Thursday Rides Again (illustrated by Beryl Sanders), Harrap, 1968, Lothrop, 1969.
Thursday Ahoy! (illustrated by Leslie Wood), Harrap, 1969, Lothrop, 1970.
Thursday in Paris (illustrated by L. Wood), Harrap, 1971, Penguin, 1974.

"OLGA DA POLGA" SERIES

The Tales of Olga da Polga (ALA Notable Book; illustrated by Hans Helweg), Penguin, 1971, Macmillan, 1973, published as *First Big Olga da Polga Book*, Longman, 1983, and *Second Big Olga da Polga Book*, Longman, 1983.
Olga Meets Her Match (illustrated by H. Helweg), Longman, 1973, Hastings House, 1975.
Olga Carries On (illustrated by H. Helweg), Kestrel, 1976, Hastings House, 1977.
Olga Takes Charge (illustrated by H. Helweg), Kestrel, 1982, Dell, 1983.
The Complete Adventures of Olga da Polga (omnibus volume; contains *The Tales of Olga da Polga, Olga Meets Her Match, Olga Carries On*, and *Olga Takes Charge;* illustrated by H. Helweg), Delacorte, 1983.

"OLGA DA POLGA" PICTURE BOOKS; BASED ON "THE TALES OF OLGA DA POLGA"

Olga Counts Her Blessings, Puffin, 1975, E.M.C., 1977.
Olga Makes a Friend, Puffin, 1975, E.M.C., 1977.
Olga Makes a Wish, Puffin, 1975, E.M.C., 1977.
Olga Makes Her Mark, Puffin, 1975, E.M.C., 1977.
Olga Takes a Bite, Puffin, 1975, E.M.C., 1977.

Entertainer Joel Grey joined Paddington on the six-part television series, "Paddington Bear."

Olga's New Home, Puffin, 1975, E.M.C., 1977.
Olga's Second House, Puffin, 1975, E.M.C., 1977.
Olga's Special Day, Puffin, 1975, E.M.C., 1977.

"PARSLEY" SERIES

Parsley's Tail (illustrated by Esor), BBC Publications, 1969.
Parsley's Good Deed (illustrated by Esor), BBC Publications, 1969.
Parsley's Last Stand, BBC Publications, 1970.
Parsley's Problem Present, BBC Publications, 1970.
Parsley's Parade (illustrated by I. Wood), Collins, 1972.
Parsley the Lion (illustrated by I. Wood), Collins, 1972.
Parsley and the Herbs, Ward, Lock, 1976.

ADULT MYSTERIES

Monsieur Pamplemousse en Fete, Hodder & Stoughton, 1981.
Monsieur Pamplemousse, Hodder & Stoughton, 1983, Beaufort, 1985.
Monsieur Pamplemousse and the Secret Mission: A Gastronomic Mystery, Hodder & Stoughton, 1985, Beaufort, 1986.
Monsieur Pamplemousse on the Spot, Hodder & Stoughton, 1986, Beaufort, 1987.
Monsieur Pamplemousse Takes the Cure, Hodder & Stoughton, 1987, Random House, 1988.

Author of radio and television plays for adults and children, including "Simon's Good Deed," "Napoleon's Day Out," "Open House," and "Paddington" (fifty-six animated film episodes and three half-hour specials for Home Box Office) which have been shown in Great Britain, the United States, France, Germany, Scandinavia, Canada, South Africa, the Netherlands, Hong Kong, Italy, Ceylon, and many other coun-

tries; of *Eight Olga Readers,* 1975. Also author for television of "The Herbs" (thirteen fifteen-minute episode puppet series) and "The Adventures of Parsley" (thirty-two five-minute episode puppet series). Contributor of stories to British periodicals, including *London Opinion.* The "Paddington Bear" series has been published in nearly twenty countries, and *Olga Meets Her Match* has been published in Spanish.

ADAPTATIONS:

(With Albert Bradley) *Paddington on Stage* (play; adapted from *The Adventures of Paddington Bear;* first produced at Nottingham Playhouse, England, 1973; illustrated by P. Fortnum), Collins, 1974, Houghton, 1977, published as *The Adventures of a Bear Called Paddington* (acting edition), Samuel French, 1976.
"Paddington Bear Series" (film series; available on videocassette), FilmFair, 1977, (animated television segments), BBC-TV, (six animated television episodes), PBS-TV, May 18, 1981.
"Paddington Bear" (cassette), Caedmon, (film), Walt Disney Productions, 1985.
"Olga Da Polga Reading Series, Sets A & B" (filmstrip with cassette), ENC Corp, 1977.
"A Bear Called Paddington" (record or cassette), Caedmon, 1978, (series; filmstrips with cassettes; with teacher's guide), Learning Tree, 1983.
"Paddington for Christmas" (record or cassette), Caedmon, 1979.
"Paddington Bear: A Visit to the Dentist and Something Nasty in the Kitchen" (record or cassette), Caedmon.
"Paddington: A Disappearing Trick and Other Stories" (record or cassette), Caedmon, 1979.
"Paddington Bear and the Christmas Shopping" (cassette), Caedmon.
"Paddington Goes to the Movies" (film).
"Please Look after This Bear" (cassette), Caedmon.
"Paddington Turns Detective" (record or cassette), Caedmon, 1979.
"Paddington Soundbook" (record or cassette).
"Paddington Bear: A Birthday Treat and Other Stories" (record or cassette), Caedmon.
"Paddington Bear—Series II" (film series), FilmFair, 1980.
"Paddington Goes to School" (cassette), Caedmon.
"Paddington Goes to Town" (cassette), Caedmon.
"Paddington Bear: Trouble at the Airport and Other Stories" (record or cassette), Caedmon.
"Paddington Bear—Volume Five" (videocassette), Walt Disney Productions.
"Paddington Soundbook" (cassette), Caedmon.
"The Complete Adventures of Olga da Polga" (record or cassette) Caedmon.
"Paddington Bear Read-Alongs" (cassette), Caedmon.
"Paddington on Top" (series; with teachers guide), Learning Tree, 1984.

WORK IN PROGRESS: "Olga da Polga" for television; *Monsieur Pamplemousse Aloft.*

SIDELIGHTS: "I was born at West Mills in Newbury, England, on January 13, 1926. The Event went unreported in the *Times* of London, who were more concerned with matters like the theft of a motor car and its contents, the adverse trade balance (nothing changes!), and something they called 'weather probabilities.'

"I weighed over eleven pounds at birth and my mother used to stand me in bowls of Tidman's Sea Salt to stop me going bandy when I started to walk. It must have done the trick because in an early photograph of me sitting on a cushion I

Paddington felt most important. ■ (From *Paddington at Large* by Michael Bond. Illustrated by Peggy Fortnum.)

look perfectly normal. When I was a little older I worried for a time about the round object lying between my legs, wondering if some vital part had become detached. If it had, then it was probably lost for ever; Mother was a great tidier-up. But I consulted my best friend and after exchanging notes we decided that all was well.

"My father was a civil servant and when I was six months old he was transferred some seventeen miles away to Reading, and that was where I spent my childhood. Life was very tranquil in those prewar days. Television hadn't been invented, so people had to devise their own entertainment. The word 'radio' still meant a crystal set to many, and if you went into a room and saw someone wearing headphones you had to be very careful how you closed the door in case the 'cat's whisker' became detached.

"Practically everything was delivered to the house; freshly baked bread arrived by horse-drawn van, vegetables came on a horse and cart, milk arrived in churns on a hand cart and it was always a high spot of the day to be allowed to take a jug into the street so that a pint could be poured from a copper and brass measure. There were no refrigerators, so in the summer it went off very quickly. For the same reason pork was only eaten when there was an *R* in the month. Strawberries arrived in time for Ascot Week and were a great treat. They stayed for Wimbledon, then disappeared again. There was no question of their being available at any other time of the year, but we enjoyed them much more because of that.

"Street games came in strict rotation. Hoops made of iron or wood came out as if by magic on a certain day; tops appeared on another. Roller skates had their place in the calendar. Mine came from Woolworth's and cost sixpence each half. They seldom lasted a season and usually ended up sagging in the middle. Conkers heralded the approach of autumn.

"Memory plays strange tricks, but the seasons also seemed more clearly defined. The winters were colder and there was always snow; ponds froze over and could be skated on. By contrast the summers were long and hot. I played endless games of cricket with my father in the local park. He did all the bowling and running for the ball, while I batted. He was a very kind and patient man and knew that the most important thing you can give a child is your time; a belief he must have been sorely tempted to forego after a hard day at the office when I stood, bat in hand, anxious to get going, watching him eat his 'high tea.' How he must have prayed for rain to stop play.

"I had a reputation for being a good little boy, largely because I kept myself to myself and didn't say very much. But I used to think a lot, and it irritated me when perfect strangers took me at face value. One morning I was standing at the front door when the baker arrived. For some reason best known to myself I was carrying a large brick. When he patted me on the head and made the inevitable remark, I let go of the brick. It landed on his foot and produced a very satisfactory cry of pain. My mother stood up for me. Knowing her, she probably said he

A toy shop on Crawford Street, London, features a famous bear.

shouldn't have had his foot there anyway and that it served him right. Shortly after that we changed our baker—or he changed us.

"My mother always saw things in black and white. In her later years, when colour television came along, she never entirely approved of it, although she was forced to admit it was very good for some things—like watching snooker, where you needed to see which ball was being played. But she still criticised it from time to time because the grass wasn't the right shade of green.

"There were never any shades of grey in her life. If she went out after dark, which she rarely did, it was always 'pitch black.' Hot drinks became 'stone cold' if they were left too long. If it rained, it rained 'cats and dogs,' and if a light was accidentally left on it was always 'full on.' Christmas presents had to be kept upright and not squeezed.

"She was also a great believer in old-fashioned remedies for aches and pains, and looking back she was probably right; at least they were all tried and tested and none of them had any side effects. Calves' Foot Jelly cured most things, a nightly spoonful of a sickly chocolate-tasting substance called Virol built me up during the week, and on Friday night a dose of California Syrup of Figs prepared me for the Sunday lunch and ensured a constipation-free weekend. The state of one's bowels was very important in those days.

"She also had a habit of coming out with statements which brooked no argument. Towards the end of her life, when she and my father were less active, I used to drive down to see

them and take them for rides in the country; my father sitting in the front of the car smoking his pipe, so that it was often difficult to see where we were going, my mother sitting in the back with a bag of boiled sweets which she sucked rather noisily in between passing comments on the passing scene, or closing her eyes when we went down a steep hill.

"'Don't like flowers much,' she announced one day as we were passing through a particularly beautiful stretch of countryside. 'The best petals fall off and make the place untidy.'

"On another occasion, thinking it would be a treat, I took them to the site of an old Roman villa. I parked the car near a group of houses and as my mother climbed out she looked around and said, 'What a funny place to build a Roman villa—right next door to a housing estate!'

"'I was lying awake last night thinking of these drives,' she said on another occasion, when we were heading down the Portsmouth road towards the sea, 'and I suddenly thought of all the murderers we must pass on the way. I hope you never give any of them lifts.'

"The latter remark probably stemmed from the fact that she was an avid reader of detective novels. Books were always part of the furniture and I was read to almost as soon as I was able to recognise sounds and never went to bed without a story. She belonged to a library and every Monday would go into Reading and return with half-a-dozen or so volumes which she devoured during the rest of the week, usually without comment, although she sometimes wrote to authors telling them she had enjoyed their latest work but that it was too short.

Books by English writers like Freeman Wills Crofts, Edgar Wallace, and John Rhode were her favourites—she didn't hold much with American crime stories—they were too violent. When I started to read to myself my choice was more catholic—Sapper's *Bulldog Drummond*, and books about a character called 'Biggles,' plus innumerable readings of *The Swiss Family Robinson*, which I enjoyed because of all the practical advice it contained about things like making a pair of Wellington boots out of old socks and rubber solution; but I read everything she read too, and it doubtless sowed the seeds of my present interest in writing detective stories.

"One day my father did me a very good deed which was to be of great benefit to me in later life; he introduced me to a weekly magazine called the *Magnet*. Until then, comics came and went; I had never been totally loyal to any one particular publication, but used to oscillate, bestowing my favours on whichever happened to have the best free gift that week. The *Magnet* was something different. Set in a fictitious English public school called Greyfriars, its hero was a character named Billy Bunter, the epitome of all one shouldn't be, always borrowing money on the expectation of postal orders which never materialised, grossly overweight, lazy, and lying his way into and out of never-ending scrapes. But he inhabited a world full of wholly believable characters, whose reactions were so totally predictable it left one with a warm feeling of security and that all was for the best in the best of all possible worlds. I used to read it from cover to cover, including the advertisements for curing spots and increasing your height, until I felt I could have written it myself. Although I didn't realise it at the time, such dedication was a wonderful grounding for someone who in later life would be writing for a living. I still have a few of the original copies, and to meet someone who was also brought up on the *Magnet* is to establish an immediate rapport.

"The *Magnet* remained my staple reading until war broke out and paper rationing brought its publication to an end. I learned that Frank Richards, the author, who in his time must have written millions of words for a pittance, was a great gambler and spent what spare time he had popping over to France to play the tables.

"Holidays were taken at a place called Sandown, on the Isle of Wight. Armed with buckets and spades, we would set off by steam train in carriages decorated with sepia photographs and maps. An added excitement was catching the ferry across to the island via Portsmouth harbour, which in those days was always packed with ocean-going liners and naval craft of every description; it was the then equivalent of 'going abroad'—a possibility which wouldn't have occurred to my parents in their wildest dreams, even if they had been able to afford it. My mother didn't really hold with such things.

"I don't remember my father ever making any concession to being on the beach other than taking his shoes and socks off and rolling up the bottoms of his flannel trousers. In all the photographs still in my possession he is wearing a jacket and tie, often a waistcoat too, and smoking the inevitable pipe. More often than not he kept his hat on as well. Being a very polite man he liked to have something to raise when he met anyone he knew and he always felt lost without it. We used to stay at a 'guest house' run by a Mrs. Gate who expected her guests to be out all day. It was situated on top of the cliffs overlooking the bay and my father would give me a piggyback up the long path home every evening. They were happy days.

"My first encounter with the opposite sex came in the traditional shape of the girl next door. Her name was Sheila and if old photographs—sadly no longer in my possession—were

"What!" exclaimed Paddington. "A fish? Inside my hat?" ■ (From *Paddington Helps Out* by Michael Bond. Illustrated by Peggy Fortnum.)

anything to go by, we seemed to spend most of our time chatting across the garden fence. I was around eight at the time and I suppose she must have been a month or two younger. One picture showed her standing on a box, her silver blonde hair glowing in the evening sun, hanging on to my every word. From the expression on her face I was obviously on to a very good thing. It was only a matter of time and playing my cards right.

"However, impatience must have got the better of me, for in the end I dealt myself a losing hand.

"One day when my parents were out I invited her round to see my train set. Without a murmur, and with an innocence I have rarely encountered since, she followed me into the cupboard under the stairs. Once inside I shut the door and obeying what must have been very primitive instincts indeed, for I had no real idea *why* I was doing it, I removed my trousers.

"Even Sheila sensed that all was not well, and to my horror she started to cry. No amount of bribing with offers of free lollipops until the end of time, or unlimited goes with my train set would make her stop.

"It was the end of a beautiful friendship, and we were never allowed to talk to each other again.

"Perhaps in an effort to teach me the facts of life without actually mentioning the dreaded word 'sex,' I was given three

One day, Olga was sitting in her outside run on the lawn, enjoying a quiet nibble in the sunshine, when she smelt a smell. ■ (From "Olga's Best Effort" in *Olga Carries On* by Michael Bond. Illustrated by Hans Helweg.)

guinea pigs. I called them Pip, Squeak, and Wilfred, after a cartoon series which was popular at the time. One of them, I was never quite sure which, let me down rather badly a few months later by producing a litter of baby guinea pigs. Perhaps whichever one it was had been as innocent as Sheila.

"After the debacle with the guinea pigs I decided to devote my attention to a dog called Binkie. At least you knew where you stood with dogs. He remained my constant companion until I went into the Forces.

"Anyway, by then I had other things to occupy my mind; school and hobbies. Hobbies consisted of photography, radio, marionettes, and cycling. For a while I was a very keen cyclist and was constantly setting forth on long trips with my best friend, Tim. A hundred miles a day was nothing, and with very little in the way of motorised traffic on the roads to impede our progress, the world was our oyster as we pedalled our way around the countryside armed with flasks of special liquid clipped to our dropped handlebars and saddlebags stuffed to capacity with camping equipment and other impedimenta.

"Photography enjoyed a brief vogue and instead of putting titles under my work I put things like '1/100 sec. at f-4.5—weather cloudy.'

"By then I had also discovered the cinema, and whenever I could afford it I used to rush off with a friend to the local cinema—Reading had no less than nine in those days; one even had an organ which rose up through the floor and made

the whole building shake when it was played. For one shilling and ninepence you entered a world of double features plus all the extras; the 'shorts' with the Ritz Brothers or the Three Stooges, a cartoon, and the inevitable newsreel. And if you felt so inclined, which I often did, you could stay where you were and see it all over again.

"Along with millions of others I fell in love many times over; Claudette Colbert one day, Deanna Durbin the next, believing that if only we could meet it would be love at first sight from them too. Hollywood was a wonderful dream factory.

"But my two great interests, apart from the cinema, were building amplifiers and radio sets, and constructing a mammoth marionette theatre complete with revolving stage and lighting equipment.

"Radio was still in its infancy. The word 'electronics' hadn't been invented, although it was just around the corner. I used to play around with ebonite and bits of wire and valves and large coils which had 'Hear What the Wild Waves Are Saying' printed on the side. I can still remember the thrill of getting them to oscillate and the distinctive smell of ebonite when it was being cut.

"The theatre occupied first the garden shed, gradually forcing my long-suffering father to remove his tools as it expanded, and later the entire inside of the loft. I never did put on any shows—the excitement was in the building. Music Hall was still popular in those days and I used to go the local Palace

Theatre at every opportunity. I had no desire to be an actor, feeling myself much too shy to stand up before an audience. But on one occasion the curtain went up to reveal a stagehand and I decided that that was what I wanted to be when I grew up—a scene shifter. My parents greeted the news with a distinct lack of enthusiasm. My school fees were costing them money they could ill afford, and it must have seemed a poor return.

"School was very much of an intrusion into all these activities and I used to long for the holidays so that I could get on with things.

"Being a day boy at a boarding school, and a Catholic one at that when I was Church of England, left me feeling a bit of an outsider and there were times when I did everything I could to avoid going. Little pills of soap covered with sugar was one method; another, much less successful because it required more skill, was to hit my knee with a stone in an effort to draw blood without inflicting too much pain—I usually ended up with badly bruised knees. To say that schooldays were among the least happy days of my life wouldn't be entirely true; there were moments of enormous fun, but on the whole I don't look back on them with any great pleasure. The statutory age for leaving was fourteen, and I couldn't wait for that day to arrive.

"In any case, it was 1939 and war on Germany was about to be declared. There had been rumblings for some while; the newsreels were coming gloomier and gloomier. One morning I arrived at school only to find my seat occupied by a large Dutch boy smoking a cigar—the first refugee I had ever encountered. Several of my form mates took advantage of the situation and produced cigarettes, for which they were speedily punished.

"The day war was declared, having listened to Neville Chamberlain on the radio, I went out into the garden with my father and we made a sandbag out of a small hessian bag filled with earth. It seemed rather futile, but it was a gesture. An air-raid warning sounded and we gazed up at the sky wondering if the heavens were about to open—I had seen H. G. Wells' *Things to Come*—but nothing happened. It was the start of what was to become known as 'the phoney war.'

"When I left school I started work in a lawyer's office, carrying enormous piles of deed boxes up from the strong room in the morning and taking them back down again at night, licking stamps, delivering letters—which I always looked forward to because it meant I could call in at the local bookshop, operating the switchboard, and generally making myself useful. During the lunch hour when I was left in charge, I used to read through the divorce files hoping I might find something juicy, but I rarely did, only a lot of sadness and bad feeling. For all of these things I was paid the princely sum of ten shillings a week and after a year I plucked up courage to ask for a raise. I was given an extra two-and-sixpence on the strict understanding that I wouldn't ask again for some time to come.

"One day we stopped work half an hour early in order to celebrate the retirement at the age of sixty-five of a Mr. Jackson. Mr. Jackson had been with the firm all his life and had never married, probably because he had never been able to afford it. We had tea and cakes and he was given a gold watch. After that he said goodbye and we never saw him again. I resolved there and then that working in an office was not for me. Somehow or other life had to have more to offer. The thought of arriving in the world and departing again, leaving scarcely a ripple behind appalled me, but I had no very clear idea of what I wanted to do.

"In desperation I replied to an advertisement in the local paper which said, quite simply, 'Wanted: Someone interested in radio.' To my great surprise it turned out to be the BBC who were opening up a small transmitter in the area and were in desperate need of staff. I answered a few simple questions on things like Ohm's law and could I use a soldering iron and found myself with a new job.

"Life with the BBC was very different to working in a lawyer's office; the BBC cast its net wider when choosing its staff, who seemed infinitely more colourful. One day I found myself working alongside someone who supplemented his income by writing short stories for one of the London evening papers. From time to time a cheque would arrive and he would take us all out for a drink. I used to look at him and wonder how he managed it? He wasn't at all my idea of how a writer should look. He made it sound as if the art of creation was very easy; a matter of tossing something off when the fancy took him, which perhaps he did, although I doubt it.

"I decided I wanted to do something creative, but not having 'lived' as he had—he'd spent some time in the Merchant Navy—it needed to be something other than writing. I decided to try my hand at drawing and after a lot of thought and lying awake at night, came up with a cartoon showing a man with two heads. He was sitting behind a desk and the caption read 'I always say, Smithers, two heads are better than one.'

The only sign that he wasn't alone in the world came from a row of milk bottle tops poking through the snow. ■ (From *Paddington Marches On* by Michael Bond. Illustrated by Peggy Fortnum.)

"The vet made it for me," explained Harris proudly, as everyone gathered round uttering cries of admiration. ■ (From *Here Comes Thursday!* by Michael Bond. Illustrated by Daphne Rowles.)

"I sent it off to *Punch*. There was nothing like starting at the top. It came back fairly promptly with the inevitable rejection slip, but whoever returned it had done a very nice thing. It had 'sorry—try again' written across it, which meant my creative enthusiasm wasn't entirely dampened.

"...On my seventeenth birthday I volunteered to become a pilot in the RAF and three months later a notice arrived telling me to report to an intake centre in Regent's Park, London."[1] Bond was able to transfer into the Army after experiencing many episodes of extreme air sickness. He was first posted in Egypt, where he began writing short stories.

"...When we arrived in Egypt we suddenly found ourselves in a land of extremes; of unbelievable poverty existing alongside untold wealth, for King Farouk was still in power and corruption was everywhere. Contact with the opposite sex if you were in the ranks was almost nonexistent. Most of the A.T.S. understandably gravitated towards the officers' clubs or Shepheard's Hotel, which was out-of-bounds to lesser mortals.

"In between futile fatigues aimed at keeping us occupied— like picking up stones in the desert 'because they made it look untidy,' saluting anything that moved and whitewashing anything that didn't, I sat down one evening and sublimated my desires of the flesh by writing a short story set in a sleazy Cairo bar. I called it 'Captain Hazel's Piece of String' and I sent it to a magazine called *London Opinion*.

"Some weeks later a cheque for seven guineas arrived out of the blue. I wish now I'd had it framed—I might just as well have done; the Army Post Office didn't want to know about it; neither did any of the local Arab traders, but apart from my first book nothing before or since has quite equalled the thrill of that first sale.

"This was it—I was a writer, fame and fortune awaited me.

"Admittedly I wasn't quite on a par with my then hero, Ernest Hemingway. *He* was getting paid something like a dollar a word for his despatches. I decided to work hard at developing a simple style which made use of lots of small words.

"I wrote home telling my parents the good news, and shortly afterwards received a letter from my mother saying they had read the story and it was very nice, but they were a bit worried about me! It taught me the perils of writing in the first person.

"More followed; short stories, articles, radio plays. Over the next ten years I spent most of my leisure time writing and learned the hard way that success doesn't come easily. It was a good year if I sold one in twelve."[1]

Married Brenda Mary Johnson on June 29, 1950. Bond's job with the BBC monitoring service ended and he was transferred to London to begin working in television. "I put the idea of getting married to Brenda very tentatively and I'm not sure that I meant to be popping the question, but I found that she had accepted. I don't think I was ready to get married, but it seemed the logical step at the time and I don't regret it. I was a romantic and I enjoyed being a suitor, remembering dates and getting little presents.

"I began to work in television, which is what I'd wanted to do, although it was quite difficult to transfer between parts of the BBC. I arrived in television at a very good time, just as commercials were starting up, so there was a great exodus of staff from the BBC to the advertising channels. I had a very rapid promotion, becoming a cameraman fairly quickly and later a senior cameraman with my own crew. I spent fifteen very happy years with them.

"It was in the days of live programmes when nothing was recorded. The adrenalin flowed not knowing whether it was going to work or end in disaster. If you were a cameraman on a big crane you needed to use all your faculties: you used your right hand for focusing and holding the panning handle, your left for signalling, both feet for moving the camera and your eyes for the viewfinder and the crib card while someone was talking in each ear. I suppose the nearest equivalent is landing an aircraft—if you land it smoothly, it was a great feeling; if it's bumpy, your day was ruined.

"I was working shifts of four thirteen- to fourteen-hour days on and three days off. On my days off I used to take the typewriter out of the cupboard and go to work. The rejection slips could have papered the room.

"Then I got myself an agent. I used to do radio plays, and he would sell them abroad to places like Radio Hong Kong who would buy several at a time and pay five guineas for a half-hour play and hold a sort of Michael Bond festival. By the time my agent had sent the plays off, and written to tell me about it, he probably lost money."[2]

"Almost at the same time as Karen was born I had my first book published: *A Bear Called Paddington*. A year before, Christmas Eve 1957 to be exact, conscious that I hadn't bought my wife anything very exciting in the way of a present, I wandered into a London store looking for ideas and found myself in the toy department. On one of the shelves I came across a small bear looking, I thought, very sorry for himself as he was the only one who hadn't been sold.

"I bought him and because we were living near Paddington station at the time, we christened him Paddington. He sat on a shelf of our one-roomed apartment for a while, and then one day when I was sitting in front of my typewriter staring at a blank sheet of paper wondering what to write, I idly tapped out the words 'Mr. and Mrs. Brown first met Paddington on a railway platform. In fact, that was how he came to have such an unusual name for a bear, for Paddington was the name of the station.'

"It was a simple act, and in terms of deathless prose, not exactly earth shattering, but it was to change my life considerably. I carried on from where I had left off and by the end of the day I had completed the first chapter; by the tenth day I found myself with a book on my hands."[1]

"The first book had Paddington come from darkest Africa, and my agent said there weren't any bears in Africa. I did a bit of research and discovered that there were some in Peru which nobody knows much about, so I made it darkest Peru, which is more mysterious. Paddington inhabits Notting Hill Gate because that's where I was living. He wore a duffle coat because they were in fashion and that's what I wore, and an old hat because I had one. The boots came later. There are

(Paddington, star of the animated television series, "Paddington Bear." Premiered on PBS-TV, May 18, 1981.)

two children, Jonathan and Judy, because I thought there ought to be one of each. I thought anyone who like Mr. and Mrs. Brown finds a bear in a station and takes it home must be a soft touch, so I needed someone in the background who could be sterner and put in the housekeeper, Mrs. Bird. Paddington is an alien and slightly different from the Brown family, so Mr. Grubber came on the scene; he keeps an antique shop and he's a foreigner too, so he and Paddington have a friendship. Then, because all these were good people, I put in Mr. Curry, the next door neighbour who is a kind of foil for Paddington. I did all that instinctively; I didn't sit down and plan it. I don't like analyzing these things too much because then you become overly conscious of them.

"The book went the rounds of seven or eight publishers before Collins bought it. They invited me out to my first lunch with an editor, a big moment for me, and asked if I had anybody in mind as an illustrator. I didn't know any illustrators. They toyed with the idea of having photographs of a bear from the zoo which, in retrospect, would not have been right. Somebody suggested Peggy Fortnum and sent her a manuscript which she liked. I told her the sort of bear I had in mind. She took details from the book about his clothes and did a lot of drawings which everybody liked. She got it right from the beginning; I think she's the one person who's really captured the spirit of Paddington with just a few lines.

"I was quite pleased with the first Paddington book because a voice inside me said I couldn't have done it any better, but I didn't expect it to be as successful as it was. When it came out, it was placed on one or two recommended reading lists and got reviews, so Collins asked for more.

Her house had been cleaned out for the night, she felt much, much better. ■ (From "Olga Carries On" in *The Complete Adventures of Olga da Polga* by Michael Bond. Illustrated by Hans Helweg.)

"I wrote one Paddington book a year for six years, followed by one every two years. The Paddington Bear toy was made by Gabrielle Designs, and I was approached by somebody who wanted to make a television series using an actor dressed up in a bearskin, a disastrous idea. I tried half hour, ten minute, and five minute scripts, but I decided it was never going to work."[2]

Bond was making enough money to leave his job at the BBC in 1966, and concentrate on writing exclusively. "I felt I could take a chance; I had my bread paid for with the books, but I didn't know if I could earn enough for the butter."[2]

He began to write about a mouse called Thursday. "Someone had given me a toy mouse as a mascot and that gave me an idea. Thursday is a mouse from a big family and is a totally different character from Paddington. In one of the books the mice went to Paris and got involved in a plot of sending high explosives through the pneumatic system used for sending messages. I don't know why I thought of that plot, but I went to Paris and was shown round the post office pneumatic system. They didn't quite know what I was planning to do!

"There are four Thursday books, I don't think the climate is right for more. The plots are probably too complicated and I don't think mice have quite the same universal appeal as a bear."[2]

Bond's popular television series, "The Herbs" was produced. The technology involved in making it showed him how Paddington could be successfully adapted for television. "One day I was looking out of the window and I happened to be thinking, for no particular reason, that Parsley would be a good name for a lion because it looked like a lion's mane. The Head of Children's Programmes at the BBC happened to phone just then to say they were revamping their programmes and did I have any ideas? I told them my idea for a series; they asked for a script.

"I dropped everything and got hold of books on herbs, like *Culpeppers Complete Herbal,* and every herb suggested a character. BBC liked my script and sent me to meet producer Graham Clutterbuck to talk about ways of doing it. We decided that stop/start animation was the best way to do it.

"Stop/start animation involves using a jointed figure in a three-dimensional set. If, for example, a character has to take his hat off, you move his arm very slightly and take a picture at every step—twenty-five frames for every second. When you run the film, it looks as if it is continuous movement. If you took the clothes and fur off the character, you would find a jointed frame underneath with working elbows and knees.

"We did 'The Herbs,' a series about Parsley himself, and then Ivor came up with an idea for doing a Paddington series using a puppet and stop/start animation. We made a pilot, which the

BBC liked, and did the first thirty-two of a series of five-minute films. It was the heyday of those kinds of films, because the BBC had a five minute spot after children's television and spots before the six o'clock news when we had an audience of children and adults.

"In the beginning it was very experimental because we had a three-dimensional puppet with two-dimensional cardboard cut-outs for the other figures and a three-dimensional set. There were lots of things we couldn't do. For instance, Paddington would have a three-dimensional suitcase and he'd have to hand it to a two-dimensional character. I was probably more involved than the average person would have been because of my television background. In the end we solved all the problems and ended up doing a half-hour special based on 'Singing in the Rain' where Paddington did the dance routine from the film.

"Finding the right voice for Paddington was difficult. I was looking for someone with a distinctive voice who could narrate the story, leaving you with an open mind about what Paddington's own voice would be like. Somebody suggested Michael Hordern and he came and read and sounded right. I find myself writing for him because I can hear in my head how he will deliver the lines.

"Although Paddington was very successful at generating a lot of gross revenue, by the time the film company had taken it's twenty-five percent, the merchandising agent had his percentage and my agent had his ten percent, the actual net money coming in was not that great. I became disenchanted with the merchandising. I'd formed a company and was working fourteen or fifteen hours a day at least. I eventually brought in a company copyright lawyer and he gradually took over and I went back to writing. Now my daughter runs Paddington and Company from an office in Pimlico.

"There have been various Paddington musicals, which mostly depressed me. Having someone dressed up in a bearskin isn't Paddington. Sometimes people do it with a whole mask, where you have a problem with the voice, and sometimes with a half-mask. One version had Paddington with a ping pong ball stuck on the end of his nose, painted black, and during one of his speeches, it fell off, bouncing all over the stage. There've been all sorts of disasters."[2]

While Paddington was becoming more and more successful, Bond was already writing his Olga da Polga books. Olga was based on a guinea pig owned by Bond's daughter. "I did four Olga books, and in a way she's more interesting and a bit more devious than Paddington who has a strong sense of right and wrong and is very solid. Olga lives in a hutch and doesn't get out like Paddington and feels she has to influence other animals by telling them fabulous stories and making things up. Olga was very vain and makes up stories about why guinea pigs have such beautiful eyes, such silky fur, or how they came to lose their tails.

"I put the idea of films about Olga to Central Television and they were keen on it. I shall do it as live action and I've scripted it like that, and Olga's fantasies will go into animation. I'm doing the filming as well as the scripts and will work from home. If I used a camera crew, Olga would go into her hay and not come out and there would be an awful lot of wasted time. As it is, I can choose my time when the weather's right and Olga's in a good mood.

"I think guinea pigs are very limited in what they can do and I don't think you can make them perform. All you can do is

For a while Paddington lay where he was. . .hardly daring to breathe. ■ (From *Paddington Takes the Test* by Michael Bond. Illustrated by Peggy Fortnum.)

see what they do and then photograph it. If I put Olga on the floor downstairs I know she will open a cupboard door by catching it in her teeth and go inside. You couldn't train her to do that but, because she does it, I can work it into the script. I'm doing a pilot just to see if I can make it work and, if it does, I shall have to do twelve more ten-minute films. It's about fifteen years since I was a cameraman, but you never forget. I'm looking forward to it, but there's a lot of work involved and I half hope the pilot won't work.''[2]

Bond's marriage to Brenda Johnson ended during the 1970s. "My marriage in Hazelmere broke up, although we're better friends now than we were at the time. I lived with someone after that and that's when Anthony was born. I'm very proud of him. When I split up from his mother, it was very traumatic, but I kept on working. I think one of the good things about writing is that when traumatic things happen you can actually lose yourself in work. There have been periods when my life has been very difficult and gloomy and my output has gone down.''[2]

Bond enjoys an amiable relationship with his son. "Anthony lives in Bath with his mother and I go down to see him and he comes up to London to stay with me. He plays the saxophone and is into computers. He's a very nice boy, and he seems to have survived all the problems.''[1]

J. D. Polson and the Liberty-Headed Dime was published in 1980. This time Bond chose an armadillo as his leading character. "It was in the days when Harrods had a small zoo in their pet department and used to sell very exotic animals. I saw an armadillo with lots of character and nearly bought him. I remembered him and developed him into a character.

"I wanted to do a picture book for young children which would have something completely different on every page because I think a lot of children are frightened of print. I set it in America because armadillos are American. The emblem of Texas is an armadillo and there are lots of armadillo clubs there.

"I did three J. D. Polson books, then the illustrator had a very bad plane accident at Biggin Hill and wasn't able to do the third. Nothing has happened about it yet. I think perhaps the stories were a bit too sophisticated for that type of book. In France there's a great tradition of picture books, but in England a picture book is considered for children only. There is some interest in doing a television version of the books, but at the moment I'm not thinking of writing any more of them.''[2]

In 1982 Bond married Susan Marfrey Rogers. The couple lives near the Regents Canal just a few miles north of Paddington Station. "Sue used to work for my agent, but I couldn't think of a way to make contact because I was shy. A musical version of Paddington was being done at a theatre in Wimbledon and I rang my agent and said, 'Its time someone from your office came to see Paddington; how about Sue?' I'd plotted to take her out to dinner after the theatre. The play started late, however, because they'd had a big party the night before and the actor playing Paddington had got drunk and fallen into the orchestra pit, so he was indisposed and the actress playing Judy was taking over his part. They began the first act and then realized that Judy should have been on stage with Paddington. At that point someone ran out saying, 'Judy can't be here, she's missed the train.' It was so awful that we came out after the interval, and Sue went back to the office, and I went home.''[2]

Monsieur Pamplemousse, the first of Bond's series of books about a French detective, written for adults, was published in 1983. "I wanted to write a book about a detective. The Mon-

sieur Pamplemousse books are tongue in cheek. I'm a great Maigret fan and I wanted to write about a detective who was all that Maigret wasn't, who solved his crimes partly by accident. I was going to set the stories in Paris, and he was to be the last detective to ride a bicycle there.

"Then I was in a restaurant south of Lyons, where they specialize in roast chicken cooked in a pig's bladder with vegetables. They bring the bladder to your table and show it to you and then the waiter pierces it. I suddenly thought, supposing there isn't a chicken inside, supposing. . . .' Then something clicked and I hit on the idea of actually making Pamplemousse a defrocked detective who has blotted his copybook and become a food inspector on travel all around France. He works for a very old established food guide, even older than the Michelin Guide, and he has a dog called Pommes Frites who does his food tasting and helps solve his cases. I rushed home and started on the book and it all gelled. Everywhere Pamplemousse goes he gets involved in some complicated crime.

"The latest book was triggered by seeing a huge balloon with advertising written on its side flying over the area where I live. I thought maybe a balloon service could start up between London and Brittany, perhaps carrying Mrs. Thatcher and the French President on its inaugural flight. Monsieur Pamplemousse is brought in to advise on the food on board. In the meantime there's a terrorist plot to hijack the balloon.

"Monsieur Pamplemousse is terribly popular in America. In New York there are lots of specialized book shops, like The Mysterious Bookshop, which just sell crime books. Also you get much more serious reviewing in American papers.

"I like doing adult books because there's more freedom in what you can say and where you can go. I buy old cookery books as background for the stories, and like exploring new restaurants. I actually enjoy the research. . .because I take in a different area of France each time. I research what the countryside is like and what flowers grow—those kinds of basic details.

"Central Television is interested in doing a television series based on the book, and there's a chance of a full-length film being done. Various American companies have shown interest, but I'd sooner it was done in Europe. One of the first questions the Americans ask is, 'Can Monsieur Pamplemousse come to the States?' I think if you've got something which works in a particular environment, you ought to work within that.''[2]

The Pleasures of Paris (1987) was published. Bond first visited France with the army during the war and he has had an apartment in Paris for the past decade. This, combined with his love of French cuisine and his skill as a photographer, led to the guidebook which he wrote and illustrated himself.

"I loved France from the first time I went there. I remembered the smell of the air and seeing people smoking Galoises and leading a totally different life from the English even though it was only the other side of the Channel. It was a life with totally different priorities and standards. I had never drunk wine until I was in France.

"I go to Paris once a month. I've got a compatible word processor there so I can go on working. France has changed from being a dreadfully inefficient country, which it was after the war, to being a terribly efficient one. When I go to Paris I feel happy and when I come back to England I actually feel unhappy until I adjust again. Probably I feel that way about France because I don't speak the language all that well and I'm not aware of the various nuances of daily life there—the grass on the other side of the fence is always greener. I've sometimes considered going to live there but, until a few years ago my parents were alive, and my daughter is married now with two children and that keeps me in England."[2]

Bond's output shows no sign of slackening. Despite his success he maintains a rigorous routine. "I work solidly, weekends included. I tend to wake up early, sometimes I start work at four in the morning. But I enjoy it. If I'm working on a book and it's going well, I'm quite happy to come down and do it when I wake up. I prefer doing books to TV scripts. I get depressed about a third of the way through a book, when I can't really see the end, but by the time I'm three-quarters of the way through and know how it will finish I start to think about the next one."[2]

FOOTNOTE SOURCES

[1]Adele Sarkissian, editor, *Something about the Author Autobiography Series*, Volume 3, Gale, 1987.
[2]Based on an interview by Cathy Courtney for *Something about the Author*.

FOR MORE INFORMATION SEE:

BOOKS

Brian Doyle, *The Who's Who of Children's Literature*, Schocken, 1968.
Doris de Montreville and Donna Hill, editors, *Third Book of Junior Authors*, H. W. Wilson, 1972.
Marcus Crouch, *The Nesbit Tradition: The Children's Novel in England, 1945-70*, Benn, 1972.
Margaret Blount, *Animal Land*, Hutchinson, 1974.
Lee Bennett Hopkins, *More Books by More People*, Citation, 1974.
Children's Literature Review, Volume 1, Gale, 1976.
Cornelia Jones and Olivia R. Way, *British Children's Authors*, American Library Association, 1976.
D. L. Kirkpatrick, editor, *Twentieth-Century Children's Writers*, St. Martin's, 1978, 2nd edition, 1983.
Martha E. Ward and Dorothy A. Marquardt, *Authors of Books for Young People*, supplement to the 2nd edition, Scarecrow, 1979.

PERIODICALS

Christian Science Monitor, November 3, 1960 (p. 5B), May 6, 1965 (p.3B), May 2, 1973 (p. 5B).
Horn Book, February, 1961 (p. 53), October, 1961 (p. 443), December, 1967 (p. 748), April, 1973, June, 1973 (p. 268), June, 1980 (p. 335).
New York Times Book Review, August 27, 1961 (p. 22), May 9, 1965 (p. 24), November 9, 1969, March 1, 1987.
Times Literary Supplement, November 24, 1966 (p. 1087), November 12, 1970, October 22, 1971 (p. 1333), November 3, 1972, December 6, 1974, October 1, 1976, September 30, 1983.
School Library Journal, March, 1968 (p. 127), December, 1973 (p. 41).
Saturday Review, November 9, 1968, April 17, 1971.
New Yorker, December 4, 1971, December 1, 1975.
Bulletin of the Center for Children's Books, November, 1973 (p. 38), February, 1974 (p. 90).
Wilson Library Bulletin, January, 1974 (p. 381).
Books and Bookmen, February, 1985.
Observer, March 10, 1985.
Los Angeles Times Book Review, June 9, 1985.
Village Voice, July 16, 1985.

BRAHM, Sumishta 1954-

PERSONAL: Born August 1, 1954, in Wiesbaden, Germany; daughter of John (a film director) and Anna (a professor of romantic languages; maiden name, Bruni) Brahm. *Education:* Attended California Arts, Immaculate Heart College, and Santa Monica College. *Politics:* Independent. *Religion:* Vedanta. *Address:* 1765 N. Highland Ave., #237, Los Angeles, Calif. 90028.

CAREER: Free-lance illustrator, 1971—.

ILLUSTRATOR:

Grant Sanders, *Solstice: Selected Poems* (cover), Pygmalion, 1974.
Elbridge Anderson, *Through the Awakening Eye*, Pygmalion, 1976.
Joyce Strauss, *How Does It Feel. . .?*, Human Science Press, 1981.
Barbara Jean Menzel, *Would You Rather?*, Human Science Press, 1982.

Contributor of illustrations to *L.A. Weekly*, *Marilyn: A Magazine of Poetry*, *Madrona*, and *Reader*.

WORK IN PROGRESS: The World Is Screaming without Fingers, a book of illustrations; writing and illustrating several children's science fiction books.

SIDELIGHTS: "Throughout the years (since 1971) I have done illustrations for various businesses and publications. The most successful illustrations were done from 1982 to 1986 for editorials in the *L.A. Weekly* and *Reader*. In 1981 I published a series of four postcards under the publishing name INSIDE-OUT, and in 1982 I published and illustrated two more greeting cards for Halloween. I also illustrated the cover and back

SUMISHTA BRAHM

of a seven-inch single record entitled 'Mouse or Rat?' by Even Worse in 1983.

"Regarding my artwork, if I was to comment on how I was influenced, I would have to include Jimi Hendrix and Janis Joplin along with Charles Dickens and Aubrey Beardsley. The thing that they all have in common is expression which has always been my interest. Another possible influence was my father who was a film director whose best works were black and white thriller films in the 1940s. My eyesight has never been very good and I have always appreciated the great detail artists like Michelangelo and Da Vinci and more recently, Parrish offered. Since I could never see that well, I have had the opportunity to focus on the basic expression of life through the single line. Occasionally I have used light watercolor washes but only to enhance and pull out certain images.

"Music has been the other half of my creative circle, and my involvement in writing and performing live has enhanced my illustrations, which are always included in the flyers I make for the shows I play."

BRUSSEL-SMITH, Bernard 1914-

PERSONAL: Born March 1, 1914, in New York, N.Y.; son of Raymond (a designer) and Belle (a housewife; maiden name, Epstein) Smith; married Mildred Cornfeld (a retired teacher), September 28, 1937; children: Peter. *Education:* Attended Pennsylvania Academy of Fine Art, 1931-36, and Atelier 17, Paris, France, 1937; studied in France under W. Stanley Hayter, 1957-58. *Home and studio:* 328 Cherry St., Bedford Hills, N.Y. 10507.

CAREER: Artist and teacher. Cooper Union, New York, N.Y., teacher, 1946; Philadelphia Museum College, Philadelphia, Pa., teacher, 1949; National Academy, teacher, 1965-72. Also taught at Brooklyn Museum, Brooklyn, N.Y., and City College, N.Y.

EXHIBITIONS: Musee Rupin, Brive, France, 1976; National Academy Annual, 1976-79, 1981, 1983; Yale University, Sterling Library, New Haven, Conn., 1977, 1988; Olthuysen Ateliers, Rotterdam, Holland, 1978; Maison de la Sirene, Collonges, France, 1979; St. Antonin, France, 1979; Deux Tetes Gallery, Toronto, Canada, 1980; Katonah Library, Katonah, N.Y., 1980; Desert Museum, Palm Spring, Calif., 1980; Bethesda Art Gallery, Md., 1980, 1981, 1982, 1983; Galerie Maas, Rotterdam, Holland, 1980; A.A.A. Gallery, New York, N.Y., 1980, 1988; Virginia Barrett Gallery, Chappaqua, N.Y., 1980, 1984; Hunterdon Art Center, N.J., 1981, 1982; A.A.A. Gallery, Philadelphia, Pa, 1981; Jane Haslem Gallery, Washington, D.C., 1981, 1984; Salon d'Ermont, France, 1981; Boston Printmakers 34th National Exhibition, 1982; Salon d'art sacre, Paris, France, 1982; Mary Ryan Gallery, New York, N.Y., 1982; Chrysler Museum, Va., 1982; Georgetown University, Washington, D.C., 1982; Tahir Gallery, New Orleans, La., 1983; Fairleigh Dickinson University, N.J., 1983; Associated American Artists, 1983, 1984, 1985, 1987; Biennale d'Ile de France, Ermont, 1984; has also participated in many exhibitions prior to 1976.

Permanent collections: Carnegie Institute, New York Library Print Collection, Philadelphia Museum of Art, University of Illinois, J. B. Speed Museum, New York City Historical Society, Brooklyn Museum, Fairleigh Dickinson University, Philadelphia Free Library, Georgetown University, Minnesota Institute of Art, Air and Space Museum, Sterling Library of Yale University.

MEMBER: National Academy of Design. *Awards, honors:* Purchase Prize from the Library of Congress, and American Artists Group Award, both 1948, both for wood engraving "Descent"; Purchase Prize from the Print Club of Phildelphia, and the Society of American Etchers; Frank Hartley Anderson Memorial Prize from the Society of American Etchers, Gravers, Lithographers and Woodcutters, 1948, for "Ecce Homo"; John Taylor Arms Award from the National Academy of Design, 1970, for lithograph "Aquarium"; Samuel Morse Award from the National Academy of Design, 1976, for wood engraving "Another World."

WRITINGS:

(With Edith Weart) *Royal Game: Chess for Young People* (self-illustrated), Vanguard, 1948.

Also author with Tom Scott and Joy Scott of *Sing of America* (self-illustrated), 1946. Contributor of articles to *America, American Artist, Graphic Arts Review, Vista, U.S.A., Today's Art,* and *La France graphique.*

FOR MORE INFORMATION SEE:

"Bernard Brussel-Smith, Wood-Engraver," *American Artist,* February, 1948.
"Wood Engraving Pays Off," *Art Direction,* September, 1949.
"Modern Portraits Resurrect Typographic Greats," *American Printer,* January, 1950.
"Drugs and Art, the Wood Engravings of Brussel-Smith," *American Artist,* May, 1952.
"Four Great Masters of Printing," *Printing Review,* winter, 1952.
Ruth Hill Viguers and others, compilers, *Illustrators of Children's Books: 1946-1956,* Horn Book, 1958.
Martha E. Ward and Dorothy A. Marquardt, *Illustrators of Books for Young People,* Scarecrow, 1975.

CANIFF, Milton (Arthur) 1907-1988

OBITUARY NOTICE: Born February 28, 1907, in Hillsboro, Ohio; died of lung cancer, April 3, 1988 (one source says April 4), in New York, N. Y. Artist, actor, and cartoonist. Caniff will be best remembered as the creator of the comic strips "Terry and the Pirates" and "Steve Canyon." He first began his career in kindergarten. "Nobody but my mother could have told me they were cartoons," he said. By the age of thirteen, he was drawing for newspapers and also landed small parts in a few films before settling on writing comic strips full time. He was grateful for the advice he received during that time: "Stick to your inkpots, kid. Actors don't eat regularly."

Caniff's first strips for the Associated Press were "Dickie Dare" and "The Gay Thirties," but he caught the public's imagination in 1934 with his adventure strip about a boy, Terry Lee, and his tutor, Pat Ryan, who traveled throughout the Orient encountering such villains as the Dragon Lady. By 1946, dissatisfied because he did not own the rights to "Terry," Caniff allowed George Wunder to take over the strip while he went on to create "Steve Canyon," an Air Force colonel who had many exciting adventures. Caniff also created a special strip, "Male Call," to boost morale in the armed forces during World War II. In addition to his cartoons, he painted oils, and some of his paintings have been exhibited in galleries in New York. Caniff received numerous awards, including awards from the armed forces, Boy Scouts, Goodwill Industries, and the Freedoms Foundation, and Ohio State University has a Milton Caniff Research Library. He was one of the original founders of the National Cartoonists Society in 1946, and was named to the National Comic Strip Hall of Fame in 1981.

FOR MORE INFORMATION SEE:

Authors in the News, Volume 1, Gale, 1976.
Contemporary Authors, Volumes 85-88, Gale, 1980.
Current Biography, H. W. Wilson, 1988.
Who's Who in American Art, 17th edition, Bowker, 1988.

OBITUARIES

Los Angeles Times, April 4, 1988.
New York Times, April 5, 1988.
Washington Post, April 5, 1988.
Chicago Tribune, April 5, 1988.

CARPENTER, John 1948-

PERSONAL: Born January 16, 1948, in Carthage, N.Y.; son of Howard Ralph (a musician) and Milton Jean (a housewife; maiden name, Carter) Carpenter; married Adrienne Barbeau (an actress), January 1, 1979 (divorced); children: John Cody. *Education:* University of Southern California, 1968-72; attended Western Kentucky University, 1966-68. *Agent:* Jim Wyatt, ICM 8899 Beverly Blvd., Los Angeles, Calif. 90048. *Office:* c/o Jim Jennings, Levy & Co., 8383 Wilshire Blvd., Suite 840, Beverly Hills, Calif. 90212.

CAREER: Director, screenwriter, composer. Began making short films in 1962; published *Fantastic Films Illustrated* (magazine), 1965; with Tommy Wallace formed the band "The Coupe

JOHN CARPENTER

de Villes," in the mid-seventies. *Member:* Directors Guild of America West, Writers Guild of America West. *Awards, honors:* Academy Award from the Academy of Motion Picture Arts and Sciences for "Best Live-Action Short," 1970, for "The Resurrection of Bronco Billy."

WRITINGS:

SCREENPLAYS

(With Dan O'Bannon; and director) "Dark Star," Jack H. Harris, 1974.
(And director) "Assault on Precinct 13," Turtle Releasing, 1976.
(And director) "Someone's Watching Me" (television movie), Warner Bros./NBC, 1978.
(With Debra Hill; and director) "Halloween," Falcon/Compass, 1978.
(With David Zelag Goodman) "The Eyes of Laura Mars," Columbia, 1978.
(With D. Hill; and director and composer) "The Fog," Avco-Embassy, 1979.
(And director) "Elvis" (television movie), ABC-TV, 1979.
(With Nick Castle; and director and co-producer) "Escape from New York," Avco-Embassy, 1981.
(And co-producer) "Halloween II," Universal, 1981.
(With Desmond Nakano and William Gray) "Black Moon Rising," New World, 1986.

CO-WRITER, EDITOR AND COMPOSER

"The Resurrection of Bronco Billy," John Longenecker, 1970.

DIRECTOR

"The Thing," Universal, 1982.
"Christine," Columbia, 1983.
"Starman," Columbia, 1984.
"Big Trouble in Little China," Twentieth Century-Fox, 1986.
"Prince of Darkness," Universal, 1987.
"They Live," Universal, 1988.

CO-PRODUCER

"Halloween III," Universal, 1983.

SIDELIGHTS: **January 16, 1948.** John Carpenter was born in Carthage, New York. "I was raised in Bowling Green, Kentucky. My father taught music history and theory at Western Kentucky University there. We lived in a log cabin on the grounds of the university museum. The cabin was rented out to faculty members for fifty dollars a month. It had a rail fence, a garden, a man-made pond; there was a creek, an open field, and woods. The university had planted samples of every kind of tree, bush, and flower that grew in Kentucky. I was an only child, somewhat lonely, and I grew up in the wilds of this extremely secluded, extremely beautiful fantasy land.

"My father is a violinist, and I heard classical music constantly—wall-to-wall string quartets. I learned violin, piano, and guitar. My mother worked in a bookstore. My parents were very encouraging about creative endeavors. We had no TV until I was twelve, and there were always a lot of books and paper and pens around—even a typewriter I could use. I remember once my father gave me a blank sheet of music paper, and I sat down and filled it in with little notes. Then he played it on the piano. It was really atonal! Their attitude was always 'Try your hand.'

"The first movie they ever took me to was 'The African Queen,' and what I remember most is Humphrey Bogart coming out of the water covered with leeches. But my monumental ex-

People magazine's November 7, 1988 issue featured ''Horror Boys'': Leatherface, Freddy, Jason and Michael Myers (right), Carpenter's maniac of the ''Halloween'' series. ■ (Photograph courtesy of Mark Sennet/*People Weekly*. Copyright © 1988 by Time, Inc.)

perience with films was in 1953, when I was five. My parents took me to 'It Came from Outer Space,' in 3-D. You had to wear special glasses. The first shot was of this meteor—it came right off the screen and exploded in my face. I couldn't believe it! It was everything I'd ever wanted! After that, I was addicted to films. I made movies in my head. The cabin and the museum grounds became my movie set, my back lot. I made up little stories.

"When I was eight, my dad gave me an 8-mm. movie camera—a Eumig, with stop motion, so you could shoot one frame at a time for 'animation.' It was a terrific camera. I still have it. . . .I got my friends from school together, and we made a movie called 'Gorgon the Space Monster.' It had a lot of special effects—toy tanks running in animation, things like that—and I put classical music (the '1812 Overture' and 'Night on Bald Mountain') on a tape, along with me doing different voices, for a soundtrack. I remember a moment during the shooting when I suddenly understood the process of editing. I was shooting two actions at once: a friend would run up, stop, and react to something; then I'd turn around and shoot what he was watching. I was editing in the camera. But suddenly I realized I could shoot the first kid all at once and then, another day, shoot what he was reacting to, and then I could splice them together. It was like a thunderbolt! I remember thinking, How clever!

"In another scene, I had a friend running down a railroad track, and I ran after him with the camera. The scene was

very jerky, and my father said, 'You should use a tripod.' But I said it looked exciting. A titling kit came with the camera: you stuck little letters on a board and shot the titles. When any of my friends came over, they'd have to sit down and watch 'Gorgon.' I kept telling my parents that I was going to go to Hollywood and be a film director. My friends quickly got tired of making movies, so I did them myself in a vacuum. I felt I was quite a bit the outsider, a little weird. I was pretty single-minded. As a matter of fact, my movies now are pretty single-minded movies. I'm a little obsessive.

"Bowling Green was very Southern—a small farm town in the Bible Belt, truly Middle America and nonsophisticated. I had an image of myself as a lonely, isolated person—not ostracized but a loner. In 1964, when the Beatles came along, I grew long hair. It was risky, and I got a lot of flak. Still, it fitted right in; maybe I was perpetuating my own isolation, even though I was always lamenting that I had no friends who were interested in movies. But by the time I was in high school I'd lost touch with making movies. I'd got interested in girls. I would borrow my father's Cutlass and take a girl driving up and down the bypass, or go to the Lost River Drive-In (they showed second-run movies) and neck, then stop at the Dairy Dip or Jerry's. The big thing in those days was drinking beer. I thought it tasted *so* bad, but I did it. Suddenly, one day, my high school class voted me president. I wondered why for days. It was an indication that I was misjudging myself, and I realized I must be reaching out to people in some way—I must have wanted their acceptance, and to be loved by them."[1]

1968. Completed undergraduate studies at Western Kentucky University. "In my senior year, I did a little acting. We did 'Queens of France,' by Thornton Wilder. My technique was totally mechanical—nothing to do with real emotion—but I began to know what actors were going through. I started getting interested in making films again, and I started researching film schools. The best seemed to be U.S.C. [University of Southern California], and I told my father I'd like to go there. He didn't say too much. He probably thought I was making a silly move, but he supported me. I wish I could describe the naive kid who got off the plane in L.A. I had two suitcases and a map. U.S.C. didn't look that far; I thought I could walk it. An hour later, I'd only moved a fraction of an inch on the map. U.S.C. was fifteen miles away."[1]

"U.S.C. was invaluable, but not in the traditional college experience where you go and train for a job and then you move into a job, because that's not how it is in film. I learned the technical aspects of film, and got to work in every area of directing—editing, camera, sound. And every day in the screening room they were showing movies. All we did was watch movies. I watched movies for four years. I saw retrospectives on every big director. I saw the directors come down. I saw a John Ford retrospective, and I'll never forget it because we started with his silent film and went all the way up to his last movie. You got to see the work of a man. I saw Howard Hawks's work, I saw Orson Welles's work. I saw Orson Welles in person. I saw John Ford in person. And these are cinematic giants. I saw Roman Polanski, and there's nothing like it. It was very exciting. It was also very unrealistic in terms of what movies were like. But that wasn't important then."[2]

"...I remember there came this big moment of truth. They encourage socially-conscious films and they wanted them to be personal, and I finally said, 'What I care about is escapist entertainment. Those are the kind of movies I grew up on and I want to do for audiences the things those movies did for me.'"[3]

1970. Carpenter assisted director Jim Rokos, co-wrote the screenplay, wrote the music and edited "The Resurrection of Bronco Bill." The film won an Academy Award for "Best Live-Action Short Subject."

1974. His first feature, "Dark Star," was released. The film is a black satire on spacemen and science-fiction films. The primary plot involves the crew of an interstellar space ship on a mission to destroy stars about to become super-novas. "...It began on the sound stage at U.S.C. and ended on a sound stage in Hollywood four years later."[1]

"I teamed up with Dan O'Bannon, who's a schoolmate of mine and we basically made 'Dark Star' ourselves. Building sets and putting it all together. It took a lot of hard work and a lot of love. We raised money as we went along, and we finally teamed up with Jack Harris, who provided the finishing money to make it into a feature. We had shot a feature on 16mm and we didn't have enough money to finish it, so he helped us out. And basically it was the will to do it, no more than that. And I think both Dan and I were young and naive enough not to realize that we were attempting the impossible."[2]

"'Dark Star'...was not successful. It was a weird little science-fiction movie, with a lot of imagination and energy but

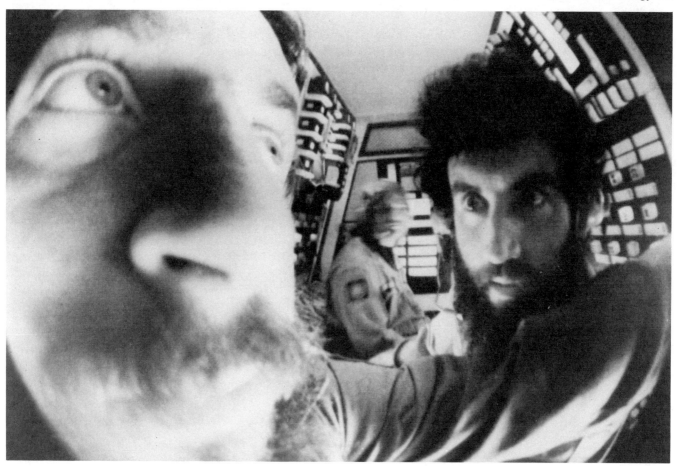

Carpenter co-authored and directed the 1974 movie "Dark Star," the story of a futuristic scoutship.

a cardboard spaceship. I wanted it to be slick and professional, with suspense and a sense of humor; it was youthful, naive, and innocent. It was exactly what I was—it reflected my cares and concerns. People said, 'What is this?' It was a tremendous disappointment, and a kind of hinge in my life: from 'Dark Star' on is a saga of getting into the film industry. I've blocked out a lot of the details, because it was so painful. I had so much faith in what I had done. Now I know the truth. I didn't listen to people; I didn't believe them.

"For a year and a half, I was so depressed. I got an agent, but nothing happened. When you're looking for work, your agent will tell you to 'take a meeting and pitch an idea.' I went to a lot of meetings, and it was like being on Mars. The fringes of Hollywood: hustlers who had a project but no money; gamblers. It was puzzling and frightening. They'd be very hostile. 'Why are you here?' they'd say. 'I'd like to make a movie with you,' but the undercurrent was 'You'll never make it, because you're not good enough or big enough.' I'd get anxiety when an agent told me to 'take a meeting.' It all comes down to selling, and I'm the worst salesman in the world. It was my first encounter with the realities. I thought, I have created this work—don't I have some credibility? I had *no* credibility. I never got a job. Most people treated me in a straight and businesslike way, but to me it was cold and brutal. I was living in an apartment off Beachwood Drive, in central Hollywood. No money. My father was sending checks; he came right through. 'Dark Star' was the end of youth for me. It didn't work. I had to find some way to cope with reality and do what I wanted to do."[1]

"I figured the only way into the business was to write my way in, so I wrote a couple of screenplays and one of them was 'Eyes.' I wanted to do it as a low budget film and through Jack Harris, who knew Jon Peters, they made me an offer to do that for Barbra Streisand—as a big budget film. It ended up as 'The Eyes of Laura Mars,' which is not one of my favorite movies."[4]

"An investor from Philadelphia approached me and basically gave me carte blanche to make a film. I'd always wanted to do an old-fashioned Howard Hawks's type of western, but that was out of the question unless you had a big star. I thought I would do a western in disguise, a modern day western. I thought I'd use youth gangs as Indians and really stylize it and go from there. It was the good versus the bad guys. I had no intention of making a political or social statement. If I ever do make a political or social statement in a film, I'll either do it unconsciously or else I'll have to be taken away, because I don't believe in that sort of thing."[2] "Assault on Precinct 13" was born.

"When I started 'Assault' I thought, well, here's another chance to direct my own films. It was the first film where I had to meet a schedule and shoot in 35mm and Panavision and Metrocolor and stuff like that. It was basically a TV schedule—I think we had twenty-five days. After we wrapped, I cut the film together myself in three months, and did the sound effects, then released it. Basically the same thing happened—it came out and no one really paid any attention to it. It was considered an exploitation picture, period. It was sold as a black violence film."[4]

Carpenter co-wrote and directed the movie "Halloween" in 1978.

(From the movie "The Thing," starring Kurt Russell. Copyright © 1982 by Universal City Studios, Inc.)

"The majors weren't interested in it; it was a strange movie, and they didn't know how to sell it. It was the second time I'd had a film make no money. I tried not to get too upset or take it too personally, but no one wanted me as a director. . . .A year later, I was in the commissary at Warner Bros., where I'd just finished directing my first TV movie, when a stranger came up and told me that 'Assault' was breaking attendance records in England. The news and reviews filtered back, and there began to be interest in me as a director. But it all came so long after I'd made the picture; I'd got used to the idea the film was going to fail. There's a disconnection between what you've put in creatively and the final response of the audience. Very strange."[1]

1979. Carpenter met his future wife, Adrienne Barbeau during the filming of "Someone's Watching Me."

Carpenter's next project was "Halloween," a horror film which opens in a small Illinois town on Halloween night, 1963. A small boy, Michael, inexplicably murders his sister and is sent to an institution for the mentally insane. Exactly fifteen years later he escapes and returns to his home town where he terrorizes three teenage girls played by Jamie Lee Curtis, P. J. Soles, and Nancy Loomis. Donald Pleasance plays the psychiatrist who has treated Michael for fifteen years without results. With total costs of approximately $300,000, "Halloween" grossed over $80,000,000, making it proportionally the most profitable film ever.

". . .Around the time 'Assault' was shown at the London Film Festival, one of [producer Irwin Yablan's] contacts was around

and I went to meet him. Through that he put up $300,000 to do a movie. Irwin had an idea to do 'the babysitter murders,' and I went along because I wanted to make movies. At one point Irwin called up and said, how about calling it Halloween and having it take place on Halloween night? At that point, this thing really took shape. What a great premise! Not making a movie about a babysitter killer, but make a movie about Halloween night."[4]

"When I was a kid, I'd go to the Southern Kentucky Fair and pay twenty-five cents to go into the Haunted House. You'd walk down a dark hallway, and when you stepped on a certain place it would make things jump out at you—it scared the hell out of me! Your expectation built up and up. I went again, and again, to learn how it worked. 'Halloween' was maybe a way of being young again and scared, and innocent in that way."[1]

"'Halloween' was the first film where I didn't storyboard everything. I just went on the set and took what I had. It was the first film I've done entirely on location, and it worked out pretty well. I storyboarded everything from the time the boy and girl make love and he goes downstairs and he's stabbed. Then, the girl upstairs gets strangled with the 'phone wire, and Jamie walks across the street, goes up the stairs, finds the bodies and runs out of the house. All that was storyboarded. What I did most of the time was figure out on paper the night before exactly what I was going to shoot. I've had a lot of editing experience at USC in addition to cutting several films, so I try now to shoot them to cut. The shooting ratio on 'Halloween' was very low."[2]

Lauren Hutton starred in the Warner Brothers' movie "Someone Is Watching Me."

Wrote and directed "Elvis," a three-hour TV movie biography of Elvis Presley starring Kurt Russell. "Elvis" was enormously successful, earning higher ratings in its head-to-head telecast with "Gone with the Wind" and "One Flew over the Cuckoo's Nest." "When I came in they were looking for a style, they didn't know what to do with it. Dick Clark was the producer and had a $3 million budget. They had Kurt Russell cast already. So off we went."[4]

"['Elvis' is a] period movie that takes place from 1945 through 1969. It's all period. We shot [it] in thirty days with 150 different locations. That means that some of the days we were moving to three and four different locations. When you have a big union crew with a lot of trucks and bullshit, you have to run very fast. You have to shoot something in the morning, shoot something in mid-afternoon, and shoot something right before you quit at night. That's what happened. We were just running. On the run.

"After it was over I was disappointed in some of my work, and I was disappointed that I didn't have more participation in the editing. The problem was; I didn't have any time. I had to run out of the country for a while, start up another film. I'm not going to do another one like that.

"Could I have [been more involved in the editing]? Again, it was a committee. It was a big network, and the producers, and I don't function very well that way. I was involved up to a point. I feel we had a pretty good film up to one point. My cut was a lot tougher than what was on television. It had a harder edge to it and it was a lot more driving; it blasted along. What they did was to bland it out, homogenize it, add some

TV music to it. One of the things that can destroy a scene or ruin a mood is inappropriate music. There was a great deal of inappropriate music in 'Elvis.' There's one scene where Elvis comes to his mother and she's living in a trailer, she's sinking, she has something wrong with her. They have a big long conversation and there's this upbeat country music in the background. They turned this sad scene into 'The Beverly Hillbillies.'"[5]

"There are basically two problems to television; one is the amount of time in which you have to do a project, and the second is censorship. You never have enough time to shoot a project. Neither in 'Highrise' [later changed to 'Someone's Watching Me'] nor 'Elvis' was there really the time required to get it perfect. I just had to storyboard as much as I could, get as prepared as I could, and do it within the time allowed. In 'Highrise' the time element wasn't too bad. But 'Elvis' is a different kind of film. We had a tremendous amount of locations, and trying to do them in a short amount of time was very difficult. The shooting schedule was eighteen days for 'Highrise' and thirty days for 'Elvis.' Secondly, there is the problem for censorship. You're constantly having to answer to Standards and Practices, which is the censoring body of the network itself—what they will and won't allow on television. There are certain things you can't get on the air. I just hate censorship in any form, especially in terms of a film. It's really aggravating. I must tell you, I've had very little problems with it. I've never shot a scene that I know of that had a censorship problem."[2]

1980. "The Fog," shot in 1979, was released. Carpenter directed, scored, and co-wrote the film with producer Debra

Janet Leigh and daughter, Jamie Lee Curtis, starring in "The Fog."

Hill. It starred Adrienne Barbeau, Hal Holbrook, Janet Leigh, Jamie Lee Curtis, and John Houseman. "['The Fog' presented] immense challenges. All the big special effects shots; the fog rolling down the street, moving in from the sea, the driftwood changing, they all had to be done a certain way to look a certain way and they were very tough. It was a boring, time consuming process. Also the story was difficult to achieve. Like the fog itself, the concept wasn't very substantial. It was light. I needed to create an evil force from something that was very light and whispy, and that applies in a dramatic sense.

"I spent a whole year working on it, and we found some dramatic problems I wrote that didn't work on the screen. I had to go back and fiddle with them. It was the first time I ever did. There are so many options in directing. There are so many ways to film things. Getting just the right one that works can be a horror story in itself. You can move the camera from ten miles away up to their nose. Which certain camera spot is going to convey what I want to convey? That's the problem. I think that's the fear that afflicts directors on the floor. I think they say, what am I going to do? My God, I can shoot this from twenty-five angles and they would all be good. So that's what they do—shoot it from twenty-five angles then hope to cut it together. You've got to make a choice. It's all about making a choice: directing, writing, editing. You've got to make a choice, have a reason for it. . .and be right."[4]

1981. Shot on a budget of $7 million, "Escape from New York" was released, starring Ken Russell, Adrienne Barbeau, Lee Van Cleef, and Ernest Borgnine. ". . .I wrote 'Escape from New York' way back in 1974; I believe I was inspired by the movie 'Death Wish' (about a vigilante killer), that was

very popular at the time. I didn't agree with the philosophy of it, taking the law into one's own hands, but the film came across with the sense of New York as a kind of jungle, and I wanted to make an SF film along those lines."[6]

"It was the first professional screenplay I ever wrote. It was always one of my favorite screenplays, and was always on a movie I wanted to make, but it was very big and I wasn't quite sure when the time would be to do it. . . .Meanwhile, a commitment with Avco came up, and I was going to do a picture for them. However, it wasn't working out, so I suggested we do 'Escape' instead.

"['Escape' is] a very tough and violent high adventure in the future. The year is 1997. The crime rate has increased enormously, resulting in a big war between the criminals and the United States Police Force, which is the size of the Army except it's all S.W.A.T. teams. The police win the war, but it is very costly and takes several cities with it. America becomes a police state, and Manhattan Island is evacuated and turned into a maximum-security prison that's walled off from the rest of the world. Every prisoner in the country is thrown in there and allowed to live the way they want, so it's basically hell on Earth. The government turns off the electricity, sterilizes the criminals and drops food into Central Park once a month, but otherwise leaves them on their own.

"The story concerns a rescue mission. A plane carrying the President is hijacked to New York, where it's crash landed inside the prison. The criminals hold him hostage, so the government has to send someone in to get him out. They send in the world's greatest criminal—Snake Plissken. The film is about what he runs into in Manhattan.

(Scene from the movie, ''The Fog.'' Directed by Carpenter, it was produced by Avco Embassy in 1979.)

''When I first wrote the script, I set it in 1982, but I've since realized I was being premature, so I moved it ahead seventeen years from today. Go back seventeen years, to 1963, and think how the world has changed. It's been subtle but significant. I know, because I grew up during that time. That's the kind of perspective I want. Things aren't too different, but they *are* different. It's enough distance so that some of the outlandishly fantastic stuff I'll have happening *could* be possible, though it won't be a fantasy like 'Star Wars.'

''In realistic terms, in today's market, $7 million is considered to be a medium budget, but this could cost $30 million if I went all the way with it. Obviously, I'm cutting some corners in certain areas, and I have some tricks in mind, so I'm going to apply the same techniques I've used in low-budget film-making as much as I can. Unfortunately, all the money won't be going on the screen, because it's a union picture and I have to play by the rules. People know who I am now, so I can't shoot non-union anymore.

''What I usually did before was to say: I think I can make 'Halloween' for $300,000, and then wrote the script to fit that. This time I wrote the script first and budgeted it afterwards. I told Avco: 'If you want this film, you're not going to get me for just a certain amount of money. You'll have to do it for what it will cost.' And I must admit, they came through. This is the first time in years that they've invested this much money in a movie, so they have a lot of faith in it.

'' 'The Fog' was the hardest movie I've ever made, and it cost a million dollars. 'Escape' will be ten times more difficult than 'The Fog,' and I have almost ten times the budget, so I figure it will be just about as hard. However, I'm not worried and I don't feel I'm under tremendous pressure. What I *do* feel is a little surprised, because I didn't know I was going to do this one next. It's just sort of a happy accident.

'The requirements of the film are such that to do all of it in New York would be ridiculous. It all takes place at night, all the lights are out except for torches, the streets are deserted, the building windows are broken out and there are wrecked planes and burning cars. It would be absurd to try to stage that in Manhattan, because it would add months to the schedule."[7]

"Halloween II" was released with a script by Carpenter. "At first I was extremely reluctant because sequels are sometimes simply money-making devices, and inferior to the originals. But then I thought about Coppola's reasons for doing 'God-father 2'—sequels are so bad so often, why not try to make a good one?

"Also there were certain things that happened in the first one that I wanted to 'clear up'; that was very attractive to me— and also kind of freeing thing. On the business aspect, it was a good move. Then there was the challenge of it—what could we do with a sequel to 'Halloween?' Could it be exciting and scary? And then the final thing; after thinking about it a long time, I thought that there really might be another story in it, and I thought it really might be a lot of fun. So I thought, let's try it.

"But my biggest problem was that I did not want to direct it—I had made that film once, and I really didn't want to do it again."[8] Rick Rosenthal was hired to direct.

Carpenter's experiences with Rosenthal were not positive, however. "The cut he delivered to me was one of the *worst*

movies I've ever seen in my life. It was an amateurish mish-mash, and was about as frightening as an episode of 'Quincy.' He didn't make the film, he didn't take responsibility for his movie, and he placed the blame on everybody else. He was a spoiled little child.

"We gave him another chance to make it work, but he didn't do it. Therefore I had to assume my contractual responsibility of sole creative control, because I wasn't going to release a piece of garbage. I came into the editing room for two weeks and cut the picture to compress his material and make it go at a decent pace. After cutting out seventeen minutes of bad, sub-television moviemaking we had a seventy-seven minute film. We needed a ninety minute movie, so I shot some connective material to fill it out."[9]

1982. Carpenter directed "The Thing," starring Kurt Russell, with a script by Bill Lancaster. It was the first Carpenter-directed feature he did not also write. "Universal wanted to do a remake of 'The Thing,' which was filmed in 1950-51, directed by Christian Nyby, co-directed by Howard Hawks, based on a short story by John Campbell called 'Who Goes There?' And it was an excellent film, one of my favorite movies, with James Arness as a giant, blood-drinking carrot from outer space.

"It was a chair-lifter, for me. Popcorn flew. But I realized that I really couldn't remake 'The Thing' from the movie; it just wouldn't work out. So we went back to the short story,

(From the futuristic adventure film "Escape from New York," starring Kurt Russell, 1981.)

(From the 1983 movie ''Christine,'' starring Keith Gordon and John Stockwell, directed by John Carpenter.)

which was an entirely different thing. It's more about a creature that can become you, rather than [about its ability to] kill you. Imitate you perfectly, cell for cell. So that these men in this arctic camp suddenly realize that their friends may not be their friends. And that if they don't stop it, it can become the population of the world in about two weeks—if it gets any further than this arctic camp. When it's threatened, the thing goes through several incantations and does some strange things to the human body; that's what the movie is about.

''I'm really fond of it; and I'm really fond of the short story. I've always thought that it never got its due. Hawks and Nyby changed it so much from what the story was—a sort of Agatha Christie mystery up in the arctic, with people walking down dark corridors. . .I thought that might be interesting to do. It's a story more about people than it is about a monster.''[10]

1983. ''Christine'' released. Directed by Carpenter, script by Bill Phillips, it is based on the novel by Stephen King. Christine is a 1958 Plymouth Fury born with a malevolent streak: her first murder is an assembly line worker who drops cigar ashes on her factory fresh upolstery. Teamed up with her eventual owner, Arnie Cunningham, a meek, repressed adolescent, she becomes an instrument of Arnie's rage against the world. Carpenter considers ''Christine'' as ''just a job.'' ''Everybody wants to get their hands on Stephen King. But they're so bad now, most of them, *so* bad. I don't think I'll do another right away. A few people are doing great horror films, like George Romero and David Cronenberg. Romero is supposed to do

'Pet Sematary,' which is the best but the most difficult of Stephen King's novels to adapt, I would think. . . .Spielberg is going to do 'The Talisman.' If he doesn't chicken out. For most of us, it's a chance to do a teenage movie, and that's not to put it down at all.''[11]

Nonetheless, ''Christine'' received generally favorable notices including one from critic Richard Corliss: ''Director John Carpenter and screenwriter Bill Phillips have compacted and customized Stephen King's screaming jalopy of a novel until it moves with sleek '50s lines and a sassy tail-fin flip at the end. Graceful tracking shots mime the killer car's gliding menace; the deserted nighttime streets are washed chrome-shiny by rain. The high-school scenes, which are neither coarse nor condescending, put every other current teen-pic to shame. Carpenter's cast mixes vigorous old pros with young comers; Keith Gordon is a hilariously intense Jekyll-and-Snide. The movie—Carpenter's best since 'Halloween'—is at heart a deadpan satire of the American male's love affair with his car. This 'Christine' is one lean mean funny machine.''[12]

1984. Carpenter's ''Starman'' won an Academy Award nomination for lead actor Jeff Bridges. ''I was offered the film in October of 1983 by the men in charge at Columbia pictures. I knew that it had been in development at the studio for quite a while. I also knew that Columbia had done market reasearch on the concepts of both 'E.T.' and 'Starman' and that 'Starman' came out ahead. And I'm aware that studios put great belief in that kind of data. With all that in mind, I went home, read the script and two days later, I knew it was going to be my next film. People seem to find this hard to believe, but it was that fast, and that simple."[13]

"Frank Prince, who was then a producer at Columbia presented 'Starman' as a love story. A friend once told me about studios, 'find out what they want and if it's not too abhorent, give it to them.' I remembered that advice, so when I heard the cue love story, I mentioned 'It Happened One Night.' It didn't seem to bother them, so I thought we were in good shape."[11]

"At one point [Columbia Pictures executives] even scrapped the project because they felt it was too much like 'E.T.' I read the script and realized immediately what the similarities were. I felt there's no way you can compete with a movie like 'E.T.' It's so unique and special; the audience has taken it to heart. It would be like trying to remake 'The Wizard of Oz.' You just can't do it. But I felt that 'E.T.' had a relationship between a boy and a rubber puppet. And I felt that 'Starman' had a relationship between two people. So I saw it as an opportunity for me, as a director, to try my hand at a large-budget love story. I rarely get the chance to do that. People don't think of me in that vein."[14]

1986. "Big Trouble in Little China" released. The film stars Kurt Russell as a truck driver named Jack Burton, Dennis Dun as Burton's Chinese friend, and a Chinese restaurateur played by Chao Li Chi. The trio sets out in search of the restaurateur's wife-to-be who has been kidnapped by the emissaries of Lo Pan, a 2,000 year-old dead (but active) Chinese ghost. "It's a mystical action-adventure-comedy-kung-fu-monster-ghost story. It's the first American film to involve all these elements. I've always wanted to make a kung fu movie and deal with Chinese mythology, the essence of Chinese tradition, by incorporating it into the melting-pot sensibility of American entertainment. It's very complicated and has a lot of twists, but also straightforward—almost like a 1940s adventure."[15]

"As a moviegoer I fell in love with kung fu movies in 1973. The first film that I saw that got me hooked was a picture called 'Five Fingers of Death.' It was pretty much the usual fare. However, it took place around the Boxer Rebellion. It was basically a costume picture, but it introduced me to the astonishing and balletic movement of kung fu. As I watched these films through the years, they had a wonderful, unsophisticated, uncynical view. They presented heroes and villains in situations without the kind of cynicism you see in American films. The heroes had an emormous macho quality to them untainted by the world, and this is true of a lot of the Chinese cinema that I researched for 'Big Trouble in Little China.'"[16]

With the birth of his son, Carpenter had re-experienced the joys of being young again "...and coming into the world without too much knowledge of nuclear weapons and human rights violations and just the horrors of life. My son is unaware of that, so to him the world is this wondrous place. Simple

(From the movie "Starman," starring Karen Allen and Jeff Bridges. Directed by John Carpenter, it was released in 1984.)

Carpenter (right) poses with actor Kurt Russell on the set of "Big Trouble in Little China," 1986.

things are wonderful. Communication is wonderful. Hugs are wonderful.

". . .It's really down to an elemental level. And I started to really change my thinking. I thought, well, before I get too old here and too set, I better kick out the jams and do something that really sort of celebrates this point of view. And so 'Big Trouble in Little China' was just the perfect vehicle. When I read the script, it was impossible for me to get too moody about it because it's so outrageous."[17]

"Big Trouble in Little China" cost $25 million and was produced by Twentieth Century-Fox. The film was not a commercial success and relations with Fox were poor. By the time "Big Trouble" was released, Carpenter was re-evaluating his relationship to the studio system. "I think the studio wanted an Indiana Jones. I don't think they realized I was going to do a high-tech Chinese farcical. I think that's what threw them. The studio didn't understand the film until they showed it to an audience.

"To me it's like 'The Wizard of Oz.' You go over the hill and there's something else. You go over another hill and there's something else. I'm very disenchanted with Hollywood. Hollywood has become a bad place for film directors. I'm exploring some options, new ways of making movies on my own terms."[18]

"One of the things I have been trying to come to grips with is that people in Hollywood are simply not the way that I always assume they are. I act like they are all from Kentucky and then, when they act differently, I feel betrayed. I have had to realize they are the way they are, not the way I wish they were. I must learn to adjust. They don't have to change. I do. I must learn to see them as they are."[19]

"I used to think when they told you how much they liked what you did, your style, your way of making a movie, that they really meant it—it was a compulsion in me to believe it. But they only like you if you make money. So I'm going to find a way to make low-budget movies, while still making films like 'Big Trouble.' I know there's a way to do it. And it should be interesting to find out exactly how.

"I've come full circle. 'Big Trouble' is much more like a (John Carpenter) film. And I'm recognizing that now. I think the next step is that I'm going to start writing my own movies again. And go right back to where I started, which is a really exciting idea. Because I've come to realize that I *like* John Carpenter movies. And they're fun to make. And they won't all be great, and they won't always make lots of money, but who cares?"[17]

". . .This is my eleventh movie as a director. I'm starting to creep toward forty and starting to leave behind certain eras, and now I realize the most important thing is how I feel about a picture. I'm always anxious that people like my work and respond to it. You always want somebody to like you, but that's not the most important thing. If I'm happy with it, then I'm going to wish it the best of luck out there. You've got to love yourself."[18]

". . .My whole philosophy of movies is that movies are not intellectual, they are not ideas, that is done in literature and all sorts of other forms. Movies are *emotional,* an audience should cry or laugh or get scared. I think the audience should project into the film, into a character, into a situation, and *react*. The great thing about some of the B movies or the *film noir,* say, is that the audience did just that. In 'The Big Sleep' they wanted to know what Humphrey Bogart was going to do. These other directors don't do that. They take the superficial

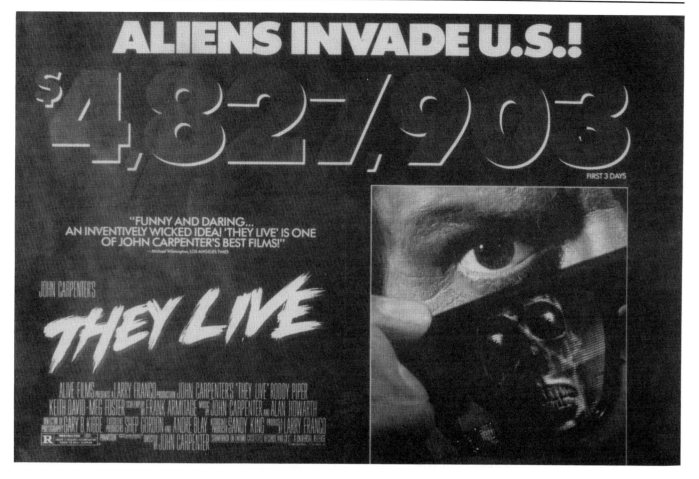

Promotional ad for Carpenter's 1988 film.

aspects of it but they don't get down to the real guts of the thing, which is that the audience has to care. I don't feel you can just sit and analyse the film intellectually, because then it has failed. So in terms of extending the genres, philosophical ideas, I'm not as interested in that as I am in getting the audience to react, really to project into the film, and come away having had an experience."[4]

FOOTNOTE SOURCES

[1]James Stevenson, "Profiles: People Start Running," *New Yorker,* January 28, 1980.
[2]Ralph Applebaum, "From Cult Homage to Creative Control," *Films and Filming* (London), June, 1979.
[3]Anna Quindlen, *New York Times,* February 24, 1980 (section 2, p. 1).
[4]Richard Meyers, "Interview: Budget-Conscious Director, John Carpenter," *Millimeter,* April, 1980.
[5]Todd McCarthy, "Trick and Treat," *Film Comment,* January/February, 1980.
[6]Samuel J. Maronie, "On the Set with 'Escape from New York,'" *Starlog,* April, 1981.
[7]Steve Swires, "High Adventure in the Future," *Starlog,* December, 1980.
[8]Bob Martin, "John Carpenter: The Multi-Talented Filmmaker Discusses His Latest Projects: 'Halloween 2' and 'The Thing!,'" *Fangoria,* number 14, August, 1981.
[9]S. Swires, "John Carpenter: Directing 'The Thing,'" *Starlog,* July, 1982.
[10]Mick Garris, "Landis, Cronenberg, Carpenter: Fear on Film Continues!," *Fangoria,* number 20, July, 1982.
[11]Karen Jaehne, "The Man Behind 'Starman,'" *Films on Screen and Video,* May, 1985.

[12]Richard Corliss, "Season's Bleedings in Tinseltown," *Time,* December 19, 1983.
[13]Susan Stark, "Carpenter's New Tack: 'Starman' Shatters His Horror Mold," *Detroit News,* December 14, 1984.
[14]Tom Hinckley, "A Love Story from the Director of 'Halloween?,'" *Cable Guide,* January, 1986.
[15]Dan Yakir, "Director Carpenter Mixes His Genres," *Boston Globe,* June 25, 1986.
[16]Lawrence Van Gelder, "John Carpenter after 'Big Trouble,'" *New York Times,* June 27, 1986.
[17]Lloyd Sachs, "'Little China' Kicks Out Gloom," *Chicago Sun-Times,* July 6, 1986.
[18]Scott Cain, "Carpenter Builds Directing Dynasty on Past Successes," *Atlanta Journal & Constitution,* July 13, 1986.
[19]Julia Cameron, "'Trouble' Director Carpenter Sees New Route to Screen," *Chicago Tribune,* July 6, 1986.

FOR MORE INFORMATION SEE:

Cinefantastique, winter, 1975 (p. 40), winter, 1979 (p. 39), summer, 1980 (p. 5).
Ecran (Paris), September, 1978.
Feature, January, 1979 (p. 12).
People Weekly, May 21, 1979 (p. 131), December 17, 1984, January 27, 1986 (p. 12), July 28, 1986.
Rolling Stone, June 28, 1979 (p. 42).
New York Post, July 13, 1979 (p. 47), January 30, 1980 (p. 24), February 28, 1980 (p. 29), October 14, 1980 (p. 21), October 15, 1981.
Soho Weekly News, July 26, 1979 (p. 46), February 27, 1980 (p. 37).
Films and Filming, September, 1979.
Fangoria, number 5, 1980 (p. 11), number 19, May, 1982.

Carpenter directs Adrienne Barbeau in a scene from "Escape from New York."

New Yorker, January 28, 1980, December 17, 1984, January 28, 1985 (p. 88).
New York, Februry 18, 1980 (p. 50), December 17, 1984.
Daily News (New York), February 24, 1980, June 20, 1982, December 23, 1984.
Filmmakers Monthly, March, 1980 (p. 17).
Christian Science Monitor, March 13, 1980 (p. 18).
Films in Review, April, 1980 (p. 218).
Tinkerbelle, "Suspense Builder John Carpenter," *Interview,* May, 1980.
Image et Son (Paris), May, 1981.
Starlog, July 1981 (p. 73).
San Francisco Chronicle, July 8, 1981 (p. 47).
Variety, July 29, 1981 (p. 28).
Contracamp (Madrid), October, 1981.
New York Times Biographical Service, November, 1981.
New York Times, November 24, 1981 (p. C-7), June 25, 1982 (p. C-10), December 7, 1984 (p. C-8), August 9, 1985 (p. C-16).
Omni, July, 1982 (p. 26).
Cahiers du Cinema, September, 1982 (p. 15).
David Quinlan, *The Illustrated Guide to Film Directors,* Barnes and Noble, 1983.
Maclean's, December 19, 1983 (p. 54), December 17, 1984 (p. 59), July 14, 1986 (p. 49).
Newsweek, December 19, 1983 (p. 66), December 17, 1984 (p. 80), July 14, 1986 (p. 69).
USA Today, March, 1984 (p. 96), March, 1985 (p. 95), September, 1986 (p. 94).
Time, December 24, 1984 (p. 65), July 14, 1986 (p. 62).
Commonweal, January 11, 1985 (p. 19).
Glenn Lovell, "'Starman' Stirs Up a Storm from Sci-Fi Fans and Experts," *Chicago Tribune,* January 18, 1985.
Andrew Kopkind, "The Cartoon Epic," *Nation,* January 26, 1985.
Saturday Review, January/February, 1985 (p. 80).

Glamour, February, 1985 (p. 134).
Mademoiselle, April, 1985 (p. 88).
Jack Sullivan, editor, *The Penguin Encyclopedia of Horror and the Supernatural,* Viking, 1986 (p. 70).
Bob Thomas, "Low-Budget Director Flies High Nowadays," *Detroit News,* July 26, 1986.

CHIEFARI, Janet D. 1942-

PERSONAL: Born October 24, 1942, in Saratoga Springs, N.Y.; daughter of Harold D. (a businessman) and Edith (a homemaker; maiden name, Dunston) Wood; married James J. Chiefari (a car dealer), August 9, 1968; children: Robert, Phillip, Amy. *Education:* Attended Albany College of Pharmacy, Hudson Valley Community College, Russell Sage, and State University at Albany. *Politics:* Conservative. *Religion:* Pentecostal. *Home:* RD1, Box 270, Cropseyville, N.Y. 12052. *Office:* G. P. Putnam's Sons, Books for Young Readers, 51 Madison Ave., 22nd floor, New York, N.Y. 10010.

CAREER: Sterling Winthrop Research Institute, Rensselaer, N.Y., laboratory technician, 1964-72; *Times Record,* Troy, N.Y., reporter, 1981-82; Tabernacle Christian School, Rensselaer, teacher, 1984—. Feingold Association, secretary, 1977-78; 4-H Leader, 1987—. *Awards, honors: Kids Are Baby Goats* was named an Outstanding Science Trade Book for Children by the National Science Teachers Association and the Children's Book Council, 1984.

WRITINGS:

JUVENILE

(With Nancy Wightman) *Better Synchronized Swimming for Girls* (illustrated with photographs by Ann Hagen Griffiths), Dodd, 1981.

Introducing the Drum and Bugle Corps (illustrated with photographs by A. H. Griffiths), Dodd, 1982.
Kids Are Baby Goats (self-illustrated with photographs), Dodd, 1984.
Logging Machines in the Forest, Dodd, 1985.

Contributor of stories and articles to periodicals, including *Highlights for Children* and *Family Life Today.*

SIDELIGHTS: "As a child I loved to read—the classics, animal stories. I had several pen pals whom I wrote to regularly—in England, New Zealand and Hawaii. Long, involved letters were my specialty. In school I studied science and worked for many years in that field.

"I began writing when my children were young—writing stories and articles for *Highlights for Children* and their 'Newsletter of Parenting.' I wrote mostly nonfiction.

"I took synchronized swimming at the swim school in Troy. My instructor, Nancy Wightman, co-authored my first book. My daughter Amy also took synchronized swimming for a year.

"I started a goat dairy in 1981. The interest in goats began because my son and I are allergic to cow's milk. This led to *Kids Are Baby Goats* featuring my daughter Amy. It was a fun book to do. I took most of the photographs myself, which was quite a challenge! I still run the dairy—we are state licensed to sell raw milk.

"I am a 'back to basics' person. My husband and I have a hundred-acre homestead on the top of a mountain, a mile from the nearest neighbors. We have pigs, chickens, a Holstein cow (milking), and 'many' goats, cats, and dogs! I am breeding sable brown, long-haired cats—perhaps to establish a new breed—and I go to the county fair every fall and enjoy showing my dairy goats. Our home is a two-hundred-year-old, one and one-half story, cedar-shingled saltbox. (Antiques, wideplank floors, rag rugs, oil lamps, and stencils abound.) I love crafts—needlepoint, embroidery, macrame, rug hooking, you name it, I've done it—my walls are full. Rocking chairs in every room. (My best form of relaxation is 'rocking' and 'reading.') My favorite book—the *Bible.*

"I teach my children at home using a Christian education program. They are now in high school courses, so this keeps me *very* busy. I have put my writing aside since September of 1984. I will resume, hopefully, when I have time again."

CHISLETT, Gail (Elaine) 1948-

PERSONAL: Born November 1, 1948, in Kingston, Ontario, Canada; daughter of Angus Macintosh (an electrician) and Doris (a secretary; maiden name, Loyst) Smith; married Wayne Chislett (a pyscho-educational consultant), June 13, 1974; children: Bram, Lachlan. *Education:* Civic Hospital School of Medical Technology, medical technologist, 1972; Trent University, Peterborough, B.Sc., 1975; Canadian Society of Laboratory Technologists, advanced registered technologist in immunohematology, 1979.

CAREER: St. Joseph's General Hospital, Peterborough, Ontario, Canada, laboratory technologist, 1973-75; The Can, Red Cross Blood Transfusion Service, Toronto, Ontario, Canada, laboratory technologist, 1975-78; Peterborough Clinic, Peterborough, part-time laboratory technologist, 1978-80; Fort Nelson General Hospital, Fort Nelson, British Columbia, Canada,

GAIL CHISLETT

registered technologist, 1982-85; free-lance writer, 1984—. Vice-chairperson, Fort Nelson Library Board, 1983-85; chairperson of Nursery Two Board, Peterborough, 1987—. *Member:* Canadian Society of Laboratory Technologists, Canadian Society of Children's Authors, Illustrators, and Performers. *Awards, honors:* Ortho Award, Immunohematology, 1980, for "Investigations of an Unclassifiable Weak Subgroup of A"; White Raven Award, West Germany, 1986, for *The Rude Visitors.*

WRITINGS:

The Rude Visitors (illustrated by Barbara Di Lella), Annick Press, 1984.
Busy Nights (illustrated by B. Di Lella), Annick Press, 1985.
Pardon Me, Mom (illustrated by Joanne Fitzgerald), Annick Press, 1986.
Whump (illustrated by Vladyana Krykorka), Annick Press, 1989.

WORK IN PROGRESS: Turn Off the Northern Lights, a youth novel about a girl adapting to life in a small town in Northern Canada after life in Vancouver; an animal adventure story; *Morgue Shift,* an adult suspense/crime novel, under the name Vanessa Smith, about serial murders in a hospital laboratory.

SIDELIGHTS: "I grew up in a small town, Napanee, Ontario, Canada, in a middle-class family. My parents were hard workers who demanded hard work from their children. Since we had no television, I read voraciously, and indiscriminately. By the time I had finished high school, I had also finished reading almost all of the fiction books in the small library in town. I have read, written, and loved poetry since childhood.

"We also had a cottage, quite private, which immersed me in nature for all the summers I lived with my parents before I left home to go to university. Perhaps it was this free, contemplative setting, after many months of rigid small town WASP life, that loosened my artistic bent. I spent many hours at the cottage drawing and painting.

"In choosing a career, I was practical: initially, a biology degree, then a medical technology registered technologist with later specialization in blood transfusion, an advanced registered technologist. It fed the rational side of my brain. But the art was not buried. It stayed active as a hobby, never one I had the time to work at to become too competent.

"Having children and staying home with them has returned me to the world of art and the magic of pretend and creation. When Bram, my first child, was of preschool age, we lived in the village of Fort Nelson in northern British Columbia. Perhaps it was a combination of a rediscovery of the joys of children's stories, the isolation and the long winters, and the vibrant creativity of the people in that community, that turned me back to artistic pursuits. I began writing children's stories, painting again, beading mukluks and trying other crafts, and then attempted novels.

"Since then I have found an increasing satisfaction from writing, even more so than from painting. Using language can be a game, and finding the one word you need to express perfectly a group of ideas or feelings to the reader is the goal. To lure him in and let him see what is in your mind and to evoke a response using written words, is to play the game of writing. Like finding the perfect colour for a painting, then adding others to create a composition. Becoming good at typing and having a word processor eases the technical strain and lets the ideas flow. A cup of tea helps too. Chocolate, music, anything to create the mood.

"The wonder of a child's perception of the world influences my writing of children's books. Five years in Fort Nelson also left me wanting to write about the uniqueness of the Canadian north. My lab experience has also found a way into my writing. Experiences and their savouring and recounting seem to me to be necessary for writers. That and hard work at writing.

"In 1972 I went to Europe and lived in Paris, France for three months, then travelled through Spain to the Canary Islands, and back to Paris again. For that brief time I was passably competent in French. I painted and sketched on the trip.

"I am an aerobics addict, and have been for a number of years now. Helps fight the aging process young kids inflict on their mothers. My second boy, Lachlan, was an aerobics baby and he's been running ever since he was delivered. After racing around after him all day, it is a treat to quietly write at night while he sleeps!"

HOBBIES AND OTHER INTERESTS: Aerobics, cooking, animals, the outdoors.

COHEN, Paul S. 1945-

PERSONAL: Born November 13, 1945, in Brooklyn, N.Y.; son of Lester and Alma (Gaster) Cohen; married Marie Padalino, July 1, 1973. *Education:* Brooklyn College of the City University of New York, B.A., 1966, M.A., 1969, Advanced Certificate in Administration, 1972. *Politics:* "Erratic." *Home:* 3303 Filmore Ave., Brooklyn, N.Y. 11234.

PAUL S. COHEN

CAREER: Edward R. Morrow High School, Brooklyn, N. Y., chemistry teacher, 1966—; writer. Athletic coach at Lafayette High School, Brooklyn. *Member:* Audubon Society, Brooklyn Botanical Gardens, Brooklyn Bird Club.

WRITINGS:

CHILDREN'S BOOKS; WITH JOANNE E. BERNSTEIN

Un-Frog-Gettable Riddles, A. Whitman, 1981.
Unidentified Flying Riddles (illustrated by Meyer Seltzer), A. Whitman, 1983.
Happy Holiday Riddles to You (illustrated by M. Seltzer), A. Whitman, 1985.
More Unidentified Flying Riddles (illustrated by M. Seltzer), A. Whitman, 1985.
What Was the Wicked Witch's Real Name? And Other Character Riddles (illustrated by Ann Iosa), A. Whitman, 1986.
Creepy, Crawly, Critter Riddles (illustrated by Rosekrans Hoffman), A. Whitman, 1986.
Riddles to Take on Vacation, A. Whitman, 1987.
Grand Slam Riddles, A. Whitman, 1987.
Out to Pasture! Jokes about Cows (illustrated by Joan Hanson), Lerner, 1987.
Grand-Slam Riddles, A. Whitman, 1988.
Touchdown Riddles (illustrated by Slug Signorino), A. Whitman, 1988.

WORK IN PROGRESS: "A sort of travel guide and comic novel, entitled *Idiots Abroad.*"

SIDELIGHTS: "I find travel and languages fascinating. My love of word play is evident in my writing. I am not fluent in

German, French, and Italian, but I can speak all three languages with an accent so bloodcurdlingly Brooklynese that the listener is immediately forced to switch to English.

"When I write riddles and jokes for children, I mix in some which they may not understand, but their parents will. Children especially enjoy evoking laughter from their parents and may gain a little knowledge from the explanation of the joke. At least I hope they do; I can't stop thinking like a teacher."

COLLINS, Michael 1930-

PERSONAL: Born October 31, 1930, in Rome, Italy; son of James L. (a U.S. Army officer) and Virginia (a housewife; maiden name, Stewart) Collins; married Patricia Mary Finnegan (a real estate broker), April 28, 1957; children: Kathleen, Ann Stewart, Michael Lawton. *Education:* U.S. Military Academy, B.S., 1952. *Agent:* Maria Downs, 1500 Massachusetts Ave., Washington, D.C. 20005. *Office:* 1025 Thomas Jefferson St. N.W., Suite 511, Washington, D.C. 20007.

CAREER: U.S. Air Force, 1952-70, became colonel; U.S. Air Force Reserve, 1970-83, retired as major general, served as experimental test officer at Edwards Air Force Base, Calif., 1960-63, and as an astronaut with the National Aeronautics and Space Administration (NASA), 1963-70, while serving as an astronaut, piloted "Gemini X," 1966, and became the third American to "walk in space," in 1969 piloted the command module of first moon landing mission, "Apollo 11"; U.S. Department of State, Washington, D.C., assistant secretary for the public affairs, 1970-71; Smithsonian Institution, Washington, D.C., director of National Air and Space Museum, 1971-78, undersecretary, 1978-80; Vought Corp., Arlington, Vir., vice-president, 1980-85; aerospace writer and consultant, 1985—. *Member:* American Institute of Aeronautics and Astronautics, Society of Experimental Test Pilots.

AWARDS, HONORS—Military: Distinguished Service Medal; Distinguished Flying Cross, 1966; General Thomas D. White Space Trophy, 1969. Civilian: Robert J. Collier Trophy from the National Aeronautic Association of the U.S.A., 1969, for the Flight of "Apollo 11" and the first landing of man on the surface of the moon; Cullum Geographical Medal from the American Geographical Society, 1969; Harmon Trophy; Presidential Medal of Freedom, 1969; Hubbard Medal from the National Geographic Society, 1970, for first to land on the moon and set up its exploration; *Flying to the Moon and Other Strange Places* was chosen one of Child Study Association of America's Children's Books of the Year, 1976; FAI Gold Space Medal from the Federation Aeronautique International (France), 1976; Frank G. Brewer Trophy from the National Aeronautic Association of the U.S.A., 1978; Spirit of St. Louis Medal from the American Society of Mechanical Engineers, 1980; D.Sc., Northeastern University, and Stonehill College; LL.D., St. Michael's College.

WRITINGS:

(With others) *First on the Moon: The Astronauts' Own Story,* Little, Brown, 1970.
Carrying the Fire: An Astronaut's Journeys, Farrar, Straus, 1974.
Flying to the Moon and Other Strange Places, Farrar, Straus, 1976.
Liftoff: The Story of America's Adventure in Space, Grove Press, 1988.

WORK IN PROGRESS: A non-fiction book about Mars for Grove Press.

HOBBIES AND OTHER INTERESTS: Long-distance running, handball.

FOR MORE INFORMATION SEE:

New York Times Book Review, August 11, 1974, February 27, 1977.
Time, August 19, 1974.
Atlantic Monthly, September, 1974.
"Meet Your Author: Michael Collins," *Cricket,* January, 1978.
Washington Post, June 19, 1988.

CUSACK, Margaret 1945-

PERSONAL: Surname sounds like Q-sack; born August 1, 1945, in Chicago, Ill.; daughter of Harold M. (a retired comptroller) and Catherine (a retired secretary; maiden name, Lynch) Weaver; married Frank Cusack (an art director), December 27, 1969; children: Katie. *Education:* Attended Queens College, 1963-64; Pratt Institute, B.F.A. (cum laude), 1968. *Politics:* Democrat. *Religion:* Unitarian. *Home and office:* 124 Hoyt St. Brooklyn, N.Y. 11217.

CAREER: Richard K. Manoff Co., Inc., New York City, art director, 1968-70; Bailey, Deardourff & Bowen, Inc., Washington, D.C., graphic designer, 1970; WETA-TV Public Television, Washington, D.C. graphic designer, 1970-71; American Broadcasting Corporation, New York City, free-lance graphic designer, 1971; C. Richard Hatch Associates, Inc., New York City, art director and graphic designer, 1971-72; free-lance graphic designer and illustrator, 1972—. Lecturer. Hoyt Street Association (president, 1974-79).

EXHIBITIONS: Scarabaeus Gallery, New York City, 1972; Automation House, New York City, 1972; Handwork Gallery, New York City, 1973, 1974; Lighting Associates Gallery, New York City, 1973-76; Art Directors Club, New York City, 1974, 1982, 1983; Society of Illustrators Show, New York City, 1974, 1975, 1981-82, 1984-86; Mari Gallery, Mamaroneck, N.Y., 1974, 1975, 1986; Fairtree Gallery, New York City, 1974, 1975; American Crafts Council Fair, Rhinebeck, N.Y., 1974, 1976; United Nations International Year of Women, New York City, 1975; Hands of Man, Bedford Hills, N.Y., 1975; Craftsman Gallery, Scarsdale, N.Y., 1975; Brooklyn College Gallery, N.Y., 1975; Philadelphia Art Alliance, Pa., 1975, 1976; Islip Gallery, N.Y., 1975, 1979; Elizabeth Fortner Gallery, Santa Barbara, Calif., 1976; Saks Fifth Avenue Gallery, White Plains, N.Y., 1976; New York Bicentennial Exhibition, New York City, 1976; Brooklyn Museum Community Gallery, N.Y., 1976, 1977, 1978, 1983; "Women's Art Symposium," Indiana State University, Terre Haute, 1977; Artspace Invitational Fibre Exhibition, Milwaukee, Wis., 1977; Intersew Exhibition, Monte Carlo, Monaco, 1978; BFM Gallery, New York City, 1978-83.

Olympic Village Exhibit, Lake Placid, N.Y., 1980; Louise Himelfarb Gallery, Southampton, N.Y., 1981; "Contemporary Graphics," Maryland Institute College of Art, Baltimore, 1981; "Art Space," Swan Gallery, Philadelphia, Pa., 1982; "Figure Exhibition," Nassau Community College, Garden City, N.Y., 1982; "Twentieth-Century Images of George Washington," Fraunces Tavern Museum, New York City, 1982; "Women," Guilford Craft Center, Conn., 1983; "1983 Fiber National," Access to the Arts, Inc., Dunkirk, N.Y., 1983; "The Christmas Carol Sampler," Skera Gallery, Hadley, Mass., 1984; "Currents '84," Middle Tennessee State University, Murfreesboro, 1984; Joske's Gallery, Dallas, Tex., 1984;

MARGARET CUSACK

McCall's Great American Needlework and Sewing Fair, San Mateo, Calif., 1984; "Texture, Form and Style," Hartwick College, Oneonta, N.Y., 1984; "New York State of Mind," Gallery at 15 Steps, Ithaca, N.Y., 1984; "American Politics and the Presidency," Renwick Gallery, Washington, D.C., 1984; "Contemporary Illustration," College D'Enseignemant General et Professionel de Sainte Foy, Quebec, Canada, 1985; National Air and Space Museum, Smithsonian Institution, Washington, D.C., 1986; "Needle Expressions" (traveling exhibition), 1986, 1988; The Chair Fair, New York City, 1986; Henry Flagler Museum, Palm Beach, Fla., 1986; Appalachian State University, Boone, N.C., 1987; "Five Contemporary Illustrators," East Tennessee State University, Johnson City, Tenn., 1989.

MEMBER: Graphic Artists Guild, American Crafts Council, Brooklyn Communication Arts Professionals, Dimensional Illustrators Group. *Awards, honors:* Emmy Award from the Academy of Television Arts and Sciences, 1971, for set design for WETA-TV's program "White House Conference on Children"; Pioneer-Moss Exhibit, Best of Show, 1974, for "Marilyn Monroe"; Award from the Society of Illustrators, 1974, for "Silver Lion," 1981, for "D.P.F. Donuts illustration," and "Perrier illustration," 1982, for Altman's catalog cover, 1984, for "Cue Still Life" and "O Christmas Tree" from *The Christmas Carol Sampler,* and 1985, for *Yankee* calendar cover illustration; Andy Award of Merit from the Advertising Club of New York, 1975, for Texaco pincushion advertisement; The One Show Award from the Art Directors Club, 1975, for epicure food illustrations and Lighthouse Album cover illustration.

Award of Merit from the Society of Publication Designers, 1976, for editoral illustration "Quilted Medicine"; Award from the Art Annual of Communication Arts, 1976, for series of editorial illustrations, and 1981, for Perrier illustration; First Prize from the Music Publishers Association, 1982, for "Songs America Sings"; Certificate of Honor from Women in Design, 1984, for fibre art; Award from *Print*'s Regional Design Annual, 1985, for 1988 *Yankee* calendar, 1986, for illustrations for *Yankee* and Avon calendar, and 1988, for "Jack and Jill" advertisement; ACE Award from the Business Professional Advertising Association, 1986, for an American Express poster; Alumni Achievement Award from Pratt Institute, 1988, for illustration.

ILLUSTRATOR:

(With others) *The Book of Christmas,* Reader's Digest, 1973.
George Orwell, *1984* [*and*] *Animal Farm,* Franklin Library, 1977.
The Christmas Carol Sampler (juvenile; musical arrangements by Kathleen Krull), Harcourt, 1983.
(With others) *The Calico Mother Goose,* Contemporary Books, 1988.
A Family Christmas, Reader's Digest, 1984.

Contributor of illustrations to periodicals, including *Woman's Day, Redbook, Cue, Encore, Parents, Emergency, New York Times, Seventeen, Creative Living, Drug Topics, Booklist, Yankee, Purchasing, Epicure, Saturday Review, Good Housekeeping, Tempo, Ladies' Home Journal,* and *Reader's Digest.*

(From ''O Christmas Tree'' in *The Christmas Carol Sampler*. Illustrated by Margaret Cusack.)

WORK IN PROGRESS: Illustrations for a book about a garden; posters, art work for advertising.

SIDELIGHTS: Cusack attended Pratt Institute. "Martha Erlebacher, who taught two-dimensional design made a big impression on me. As a teacher she gave a lot of good information that is still very valid now in making design decisions about my work.

"After graduation in 1968 I went to work for a one-person graphic design studio. It probably wasn't the greatest choice for a first job right out of school: when you make mistakes in a one-person studio they don't go unnoticed. I didn't last there very long."[1]

She married her husband, Frank, on December 27, 1969, the same year he was drafted. "We got married while he was in the army and lived in Alexandria Virginia. I got one job in a political ad agency and then did graphics for WTEA-TV Channel 26—the educational network. . . .

"We really felt that we had been snatched out of our lives by the army, so when Frank's term was up we came right back to New York—Brooklyn, in fact."[1]

Worked for Hatch Associates, a firm that produced educational kits. "I *was* the art department. I did illustration, design of teacher's manuals—anything that had to be done—it was wide open. Unfortunately the working conditions were terrible and I got very ill. I was out for a week and when I came back I was let go—lack of funding. I was psychologically blown away and physically exhausted and I decided that my first priority should be to get healthy."[1]

Cusack's appliqued collage commissioned for the cover of B. Altman's Christmas catalog.

Cusack's haunting portrait of a little girl was used to illustrate the short story "My Creek,"
in *Parents' Magazine,* June, 1980.

While recuperating from her illness, Cusack began to put to use a collection of fabrics to make fabric collages. "My work is appliqued collage—machine stitched fabric artwork. It is highly textural and makes use of my graphic design background. It also generally exhibits a subtle sense of humor in the choices of fabrics and collage materials. Although I do not sew for myself in the traditional sense of making clothes, I use the sewing machine as I would a pencil.

"My fabric work involves texture, line, form and color in both two and three dimensions. I have been working in fabric since 1972, and each project has been widely different than the next. I am a problem solver and look forward to challenges. The woodcuts are yet another direction, and an important one. I've been doing them since 1965."

"For my fabric collage work, I do thumbnail sketches. Then, I draw the final image on tracing paper. Sometimes, I use photographs, swipe material, models or Polaroids. Then I use an artograph enlarger to enlarge the images. When the drawing is finalized, I choose the fabrics and position them roughly in place. The fabric is then ironed. I trace the shapes onto the fabrics, cut out the pieces, spray glue them in position, pin them (if necessary) and sew them. The finished piece is stretched on canvas stretchers and padded if needed.

"*The Christmas Carol Sampler* has become more than a vehicle for my illustration work. I've been able to include all the faces and images that are dear to me. I suppose that this is what all artists—everyone from Michaelangelo to Norman Rockwell—have done, but it's been an engaging and important part of this whole endeavor for me. I hope that the affection and care that I've put into this work is imparted to the users of this book.

"There is a somewhat magical quality about the work that I do. I usually have *just* enough of whatever fabric or trim that's needed for the image that I'm working on. I have a good memory and a system for sorting my collection of fabrics, so that I can put my hands on even the smallest scrap of fabric. Sometimes I buy fabrics with a specific project in mind. Many pieces have been given to me by friends and relatives. I think that they get a kick out of seeing their pieces of fabric in print. Sometimes I will buy a piece of fabric and keep it for ten years before it is used. Some pieces are actually from old clothes and have memories attached to them as well.

"The cover illustration of *The Christmas Carol Sampler* will give the reader an idea of how I work. I'd bought the brocade trim about five years before because I liked it. The green trim that looks like vines, originally had pink flowers on it and had been purchased at a later date. The white moire fabric had been left over from a previous job.

"After I designed the cover roughly with those textures in mind, I went out to buy more of the brocade. I found that it was available in a larger size and a smaller size, but not in the scale that I wanted. So, I returned and re-designed the cover with the amount of trim that I had at hand. There was only an inch or so left after it was stitched in place."

Cusack's work also includes soft sculptures, samplers, woodcuts and graphic design. Her fabric collage illustrations have included the poster for the musical "Shenandoah," Altman's 1981 Christmas catalog cover, the 1986 Avon calender, a twelve-foot bus poster for Brooklyn's Fulton Street mall, a poster map for American Express, and advertisements.

"I have to give credit to my parents for giving me a sense of the importance of following through on a job that's been undertaken. I have a memory of my mother ripping out rows and rows of a knitting project because she'd discovered an error."

"I'd like my work to be taken. . .seriously. I had a piece at the Smithsonian Institution called 'Looking at Earth.' It was quite an honor to be chosen. I guess you always want more and to be thought of and to be considered. But right now, I feel pretty good and I feel very proud of my work."[2]

FOOTNOTE SOURCES

[1]*Prattfolio,* Volume 2, number 2, 1984. Amended by M. Cusack.
[2]Chris Hunter, "Margaret Cusack: Fabric Illustrator Extraordinaire," *Palm Beach Life,* December, 1986. Amended by M. Cusack.

FOR MORE INFORMATION SEE:

Art Techniques, April, 1973.
Print, December, 1973, September, 1985.
Time-Life's the Family Creative Workshop, Volume 1, Plenary, 1974.
Thelma Newman, *Quilting, Patchwork and Applique and Trapunto: Traditional Methods and Original Designs,* Crown, 1974.
Communication Arts, May, 1977.
Peggy Jo Shaw, "Illustrations in Fabric," *Decorating & Craft Ideas,* April, 1984.
How, October, 1986.

DABCOVICH, Lydia

PERSONAL: Born in Bulgaria; came to the United States; married; children: two. *Education:* Attended Boston Museum of Fine Arts School. *Home:* 29 Sargent-Beechwood, Brookline, Mass. 02146. *Office:* Art Institute of Boston, 700 Beacon St., Boston, Mass. 02159.

CAREER: Free-lance author and illustrator; teacher of illustration at Art Institute of Boston, Mass. *Awards, honors: There Once Was a Woman Who Married a Man* was selected one of *New York Times* Best Illustrated Children's Books of the Year, 1978; *Sleepy Bear* was chosen one of Library of Congress' Books of the Year, 1985; Children's Choice from the International Reading Association and the Children's Book Council, 1986, for *Mrs. Huggins and Her Hen Hannah.*

WRITINGS:

JUVENILE; SELF-ILLUSTRATED

Follow the River, Dutton, 1980.
Sleepy Bear, Dutton, 1982.
Mrs. Huggins and Her Hen Hannah ("Reading Rainbow" selection), Dutton, 1985.
Busy Beavers, Dutton, 1988.

ILLUSTRATOR

Barbara Corcoran, *A Trick of Light* (Junior Literary Guild selection), Atheneum, 1972.
Marjorie Filley Stover, *Trail Boss in Pigtails,* Atheneum, 1972.
Jack London, *White Fang,* Heritage Press, 1973.
Adrienne Richard, *The Accomplice,* Little, Brown, 1973.
Frank Emerson Andrews, *Nobody Comes to Dinner,* Little, Brown, 1977.
Norma Farber, *There Once Was a Woman Who Married a Man,* Addison-Wesley, 1978.

(With Charles Mikolaycak and Jim Arnosky) Richard Kennedy, *Delta Baby and Two Sea Songs,* Addison-Wesley, 1979.
Marjorie Lewis, *The Boy Who Would Be a Hero,* Coward, 1982.
Paul Fleischman, *The Animal Hedge,* Dutton, 1983.
Arielle North Olson, *Hurry Home, Grandma!,* Dutton, 1984.
Deborah Hartley, *Up North in Winter,* Dutton, 1986.

DETWILER, Susan Dill 1956-

PERSONAL: Born January 7, 1956, in Fort Knox, Ky.; daughter of Wade Earl (a supervisor at Baltimore Gas & Electric Company) and Barbara (a nurse; maiden name, Dallam) Dill; married Jon Detwiler (a theatrical set designer and teacher), April 22, 1978; children: Herman. *Education:* Attended Maryland Institute College of Art, 1974-77. *Politics:* Independent. *Religion:* Agnostic. *Home and office:* 2939 North Charles St., Baltimore, Md. 21218.

CAREER: Park Sign Co., Baltimore, Md., artist, 1975-78; Precision Printers, Inc., Millville, Pa., artist, 1979-80; Thompson Recruitment Advertising, Baltimore, illustrator, 1980-83; free-lance illustrator, 1984—. *Exhibitions:* Life of Maryland Gallery, 1986. *Awards, honors: The First Teddy Bear* was chosen one of Child Study Association of America's Children's Books of the Year, 1986.

ILLUSTRATOR:

Helen Kay, *The First Teddy Bear,* Stemmer House, 1985.
Susan Borges, *The Bradley Twins and the Wonderful Bicycle Parade,* Prospect Hill, 1989.

SIDELIGHTS: "I have always loved books, and when I was a child, my favorite books were the ones with the best illustrations. The pictures sparked my imagination as much as the text did, and I found that I enjoyed communicating with pictures myself. Not only did I enjoy making pictures, I enjoyed showing the pictures I had made to everyone I knew. When it occurred to me late in my teen years that I could make my living this way, I knew that nothing less would ever satisfy

SUSAN DETWILER

me. I find joy in the creation of each illustration, and I am particularly thrilled to do books because so many more people have a chance to see an illustration in a book than see a painting in a gallery, and I hope that my pictures inspire.

"I live in a sunny apartment overlooking a park and the Baltimore Museum of Art (where I took a summer art class as a third grader). With me lives my husband, Jon—also an artist— our young son, Herman, our Labrador retriever, Falstaff, and our cat, Phoebe. I have a studio overlooking the backyard.

"My favorite books as a child included anything that was illustrated by Garth Williams, particularly the 'Little House' series and *A Cricket in Times Square*. But my favorite book is *Harriet the Spy* by Louise Fitzhugh.

"I attribute the fun I have drawing pictures for children to the fact that my parents gave me a blissful childhood. . .and with each illustration I recapture a little bit of that."

HOBBIES AND OTHER INTERESTS: "I make dolls, stuffed animals, and other toys for the children I know."

DEWEY, Jennifer (Owings) 1941-

PERSONAL: Born October 2, 1941, in Chicago, Ill.; daughter of Nathaniel Alexander (an architect) and Emily Webster (a homemaker; maiden name, Otis) Owings; married Keith Monroe, 1961 (died, 1964); married Phelps Dewey (a newspaperman; divorced); children: (first marriage) Tamar. *Education:* Attended Rhode Island School of Design, 1959-60, and University of New Mexico, 1960-62. *Home and office:* 607 Old Taos Highway, Santa Fe, N.M. 87501.

CAREER: Artist and writer, 1970—. *Exhibitions:* Shorebirds Gallery (solo), Tiburon, Calif., 1966-76. *Member:* Society of Natural Science Illustrators. *Awards, honors:* Bookbinders West Award for Illustration, 1980, for *Idle Weeds;* Outstanding Science and Trade Book from the Science Teachers Association and the Children's Book Council, 1982, for *Living Fossils,* 1985, for *Snowflakes,* and 1986, for *Clem;* Award for Illustration from the National Academy of Sciences, and Children's Science Book Award from the New York Academy of Sciences, both 1984, both for *The Secret Language of Snow;* Grant for study in Antarctica from the National Science Foundation, 1985-86; *The Dinosaurs and the Dark Star* was selected one of Child Study Association of America's Children's Books of the Year, 1986.

WRITINGS:

JUVENILE; SELF-ILLUSTRATED

Clem: The Story of a Raven (Junior Literary Guild selection), Dodd, 1986.
At the Edge of the Pond, Little, Brown, 1987.
Penguin Year, Little, Brown, 1989.
The Wandering Albatross, Little, Brown, 1989.
Camouflage, Scholastic, 1989.

ILLUSTRATOR

Harriett Weaver, *Frosty: A Raccoon to Remember,* Archway, 1977.
David Rains Wallace, *Idle Weeds,* Sierra Books, 1980.
Howard E. Smith, Jr., *Living Fossils,* Dodd, 1982.
Edith Thacher Hurd, *Song of the Sea Otter,* Sierra Books/ Pantheon, 1983.
Louise B. Young, *The Blue Planet,* Little, Brown, 1983.
Richard Headstrom, *Suburban Wildlife,* Prentice-Hall, 1984.

JENNIFER DEWEY

Terry Tempest Williams and Ted Major, *The Secret Language of Snow,* Sierra Books/Pantheon, 1984.
David D. Gillette, *Walkers: Prehistoric Animals of the Southwest,* Museum of New Mexico Press, 1984.
Robin Bates and Cheryl Simon, *The Dinosaurs and the Dark Star,* Macmillan, 1985.
Lucia Anderson, *Mammals and Their Milk,* Dodd, 1985.
Joan Sugarman, *Snowflakes,* Little, Brown, 1985.
Fritz Ryser, *Birds of the Great Basin,* University of Nevada Press, 1986.
David Douglas, *Wilderness Sojourn,* Harper, 1987.
Millicent Selsam, *Strange Creatures That Lived Long Ago,* Scholastic, 1987, new edition published as *Strange Creatures That Really Lived,* 1989.
Seymour Simon, *Questions and Answers about Dinosaurs,* Morrow, 1989.
H. E. Smith, Jr., *All about Arrowheads and Spear Points,* Holt, 1989.

WORK IN PROGRESS: Writing and illustrating *Desert: Night and Day,* to be published by Little, Brown, and *Spiders Near and Far* (working title), for Dutton.

SIDELIGHTS: Born in Chicago, Dewey was raised in New Mexico from the time she was three. "As a young man, my father had explored the Southwest and had come to love it. He had always wanted to return.

"My earliest memories, and influences, all come from life on the ranch. My twin sisters and brother and I each had our own horse. Parental guidance was minimal—we roamed the hills, we hiked and rode our horses. No one ever counted how many cats, dogs, puppies or kittens we happened to have. My sisters loved white rats. I was interested in pigs. I raised two pigs for 4-H."

In high school, Dewey had some poems published at the suggestion of an English teacher. After graduation from high school,

The full-throated croaking of the male frogs
attracts the females.
Their mating goes on for several days.
When it is over, masses of frogs' eggs float
in silvery, jelly-like rafts
on the surface of the water.

(From *At the Edge of the Pond* by Jennifer Owings Dewey. Illustrated by the author.)

she attended the Rhode Island School of Design for one year, returned home and entered the University of New Mexico where she met her future husband. "The story of *Clem* begins here. I was married to Keith, we worked together on building a house, Tamar was born, and we had the owl and the raven. I went to school part time but I was primarily at home—with the house, the baby, the birds, and my drawing. The writing took second place.

"Later, after Keith died and I remarried, the writing came back into importance. I moved to California with my new husband. I lived a very middle-class life raising children (his as well as mine) and working hard on my art. In Tiburon, California I had one show a year at Shorebirds Gallery. I wrote long, detailed accounts of our life—to friends and relatives.

"I realize, now that *Clem* is written, that I took time to complete the process of incubation. Life had to go a certain distance before I was ready to put it all down. . . . I began doing illustration and writing with an eye to being published. I have been very fortunate in the way one thing has led to another. I've illustrated numbers of other people's books—mostly subjects related to the outdoors, nature, and science. I have now begun doing my own books.

"My primary interest is natural science for children, an aesthetic but still *real* approach, with the aim of making clear the connections between one part of life and another, one creature and another, one environment and another. My favorite thing to do is research in some incredible place, such as Antarctica, then writing and drawing as a result of the trip. At the present time I am proposing a book on spiders, a book on ice (life above, life at the edge, and life under the ice), and other books of a similar nature."

In 1985, Dewey, on a grant from the National Science Foundation, spent two months at Palmer Station on the Antarctic Peninsula doing field work for future books. She has now returned to New Mexico, where she lives in Santa Fe.

In addition to book illustation, she has designed and illustrated several projects for the National Park Service. "I love to travel, especially out of doors, and explore the natural world."

DUANE-SMYTH, Diane (Elizabeth) 1952-
(Diane Duane)

PERSONAL: Born May 18, 1952, in New York, N.Y.; daughter of Edward David (an aircraft engineer) and Elizabeth Kath-

DIANE DUANE

ryn (a housewife; maiden name, Burke) Duane; married Robert Peter Smyth (a writer), February 15, 1987. *Home:* c/o The Sloane Club, 52 Lower Sloane St., London SW1W 8BS, England. *Agent:* Donald Maass Literary Agency, 64 West 84th St., New York, N.Y. 10024; Meg Davis, MBA Agency, 45 Fitzroy St., London W1P 5HR, England.

CAREER: Novelist and television writer. Pilgrim State Hospital, Brentwood, N.Y., registered nurse, 1974; Payne Whitney Clinic, Cornell New York Hospital Medical Center, New York, N.Y., psychiatric nurse, 1974-76; assistant to writer, 1976-78; free-lance novelist and television writer, 1978—; Filmation Studios, Reseda, Calif., staff writer, 1983-84. *Member:* Writers Guild of America East. *Awards, honors: Deep Wizardry* was named one of *School Library Journal*'s Best Books, 1985, and was on *Voice of Youth Advocates'* list of Best Science Fiction and Fantasy Titles for Young Adults, 1986; *The Door into Shadow* was on *Voice of Youth Advocates'* list of Best Science Fiction and Fantasy Titles for Young Adults, 1986.

WRITINGS:

ALL UNDER NAME DIANE DUANE

The Door into Fire, Dell, 1979.
The Wounded Sky (based on television series "Star Trek"), Pocket Books, 1983.
So You Want to Be a Wizard, Delacorte, 1983.
My Enemy, My Ally (based on television series "Star Trek"), Pocket Books, 1984.
The Door into Shadow, Bluejay Books, 1984.
(Contributor) Donald R. Gallo, editor, *Sixteen: Short Stories by Outstanding Young Adult Writers,* Delacorte, 1984.
Deep Wizardry, Delacorte, 1985.
(Contributor) Jane Yolen and others, editors, *Dragons and Dreams: A Collection of New Fantasy and Science Fiction Stories,* Harper, 1986.
(Story editor) "Dinosaucers" (sixty-four-episode, syndicated, animated television series), DIC Enterprises, 1986-87.
(With Peter Norwood, pseudonym of husband) *Star Trek: The Romulan Way, No. 35,* Pocket Books, 1987.
Spock's World, Pocket Books, 1988.

Contributor to *Flashing Swords.*

WORK IN PROGRESS: With Peter Norwood (pseudonym of husband, Robert Peter Smyth) a fantasy, *Keeper of the City,* for Bantam; another fantasy, *High Wizardry,* for Delacorte; "Star Trek" novels, *Doctor's Orders, Swordhunt,* and *Birthright,* all for Pocket Books; science fiction with P. Norwood, *The Law of Space #1: Mindblast,* for Avon; *The Door into Sunset,* for Tor Books.

SIDELIGHTS: "My childhood was essentially quite boring and sometimes rather unhappy, but the unhappiness was tempered with a great love of books and writing in general. I have been writing for almost as long as I've been reading. This started out as an expression of discontent. . .the library simply didn't stock enough of the kinds of books that I wanted to read, so I began to write my own, occasionally illustrating them (usually in crayon). When I left high school, I went on to study astronomy (something else I had loved greatly from a young age), didn't do too well at that, and then on a friend's recommendation went on to study nursing, which I did much better at. But the writing, for my own enjoyment, went on all the time.

"I never specifically made a decision to write for young people. I always wrote what pleased me, and was rather shocked when it began to sell (though the shock was very pleasant). Occasionally I find I'm writing a story which younger readers would probably appreciate more thoroughly than older ones, or rather, it would take older readers of taste and discernment to have fun with a story that younger readers would have no problem with at all. I let my publishers label or target the markets for my books, and I myself sit home and get on with the storytelling.

(Jacket illustration by David Wiesner from *So You Want to Be a Wizard* by Diane Duane.)

"It took several years of uneven output to get used to the fact that I was going to be able to make my living as a writer. . .at least, if I got my discipline in place, for it's hard to go smoothly from a job where you 'punch the clock' to one where you are the only judge of how much work you have to do each day. I don't consider writing 'work'—at least not when it's coming easily. When I'm having to write something I don't care for (or don't care for at the moment), the situation sometimes looks different. But this rarely lasts.

"I would say that nearly half the time I spend in 'writing' a book is spent in research—especially in the sciences. Science fiction is worthless without a good solid grounding in the sciences that underlie it, though you would be surprised how many people try to write it without studying, and then fail miserably, and don't understand why. These people typically think that writing science fiction should be easy 'because you're making it all up.' Nothing could be further from the truth. I spend at least one day a week rummaging in the local library, or reading *New Scientist* or *Science News* to keep up on the latest developments. So many of these have suggested ideas for new projects that it seems unlikely I'll run out of ideas for novels before the middle of the next century or so. . .since any new discovery brings with it the question, 'How will people react to this?' And people are the heart of good science fiction.

"My fantasy work requires different sorts of research—a great deal of reading in myths and legends of all countries, comparative religion, folklore, fairy tales, and (every now and then) other people's fantasy novels. One wants to see what the colleagues are up to! But I find the oldest material the most useful for my purposes. Fraser's *Golden Bough* and the *Larousse Encyclopedia of Mythology* have been two major helps to my fantasy work: the old themes, the Jungian 'archetypes,' are what makes fantasy work best in any time and place it's set—ancient Greece or modern Manhattan.

"There are certainly themes underlying my writing, but they're subject to change without notice, and in any case I don't care to spell them out. I prefer to let the reader find them, if he or she cares to. If the themes aren't obvious, so much the better— a book made primarily for entertainment purposes is not the place for a writer to shout. People who are listening hard enough will hear even the whispers, the rest shouldn't be distracted from being entertained, which in itself is a noble thing, in this busy, crazy world. My only and daily hope is that my readers feel they're getting their money's worth."

ELWOOD, Roger   1943-

PERSONAL: Born January 13, 1943, in Atlantic City, N.J.; son of Raymond C. (an accountant) and Dorothy F. Elwood.

CAREER: Free-lance writer and editor. *Awards, honors: Children of Infinity* was selected one of Child Study Association of America's Children's Books of the Year, 1973, and *Tomorrow,* 1975.

WRITINGS:

Alien Worlds, Paperback Library, 1964.
Strange Things Are Happening: Satanism, Witchcraft, and God, David Cook, 1973.
Anita Bryant, Dale Evans Rogers: Two Stars for God, Paperback Library, 1974.
Prince of Darkness, C. R. Gibson, 1974.
Salvation behind Bars, Tower Books, 1977.
Soaring: An Odyssey of the Soul, Standard, 1978.

ROGER ELWOOD

Blessed by God: The Christian Marriage of Pat and Shirley Boone, New American Library, 1979.
People of Destiny: Outspoken Interviews about the Christian Experience, Standard, 1980.
(Compiler) *Turning Point: Christian America at the Crossroads,* Standard Publishing, 1980.
(With Myron Floren) *Believing: Myron Floren and His Friends Scrapbook,* Standard, 1981.
Angelwalk, Good News, 1988.

EDITOR

Great Spy Novels and Stories, Pyramid Books, 1965.
Invasion of the Robots, Paperback Library, 1965.
The Human Zero, Tower Books, 1967.
Little Monsters: Children of Wonder and Dread, Manor Books, 1971.
And Walk Now Gently through the Fire and Other Stories, Chilton, 1972.
Signs and Wonders, Revell, 1972.
(And author of introduction) *Demon Kind: Eleven New Stories of Children with Strange and Supernatural Powers,* Avon, 1973.
Children of Infinity: Original Science Fiction Stories for Young Readers (illustrated by Jacqui Morgan), F. Watts, 1973.
Flame Tree Planet: An Anthology of Religious Science Fantasy, Concordia, 1973.
Future City, Trident, 1973.
Monster Tales: Vampires, Werewolves, and Things, Rand McNally, 1973.
Science Fiction Tales: Invaders, Creatures, and Alien Worlds, Rand McNally, 1973.
Showcase, Harper, 1973.

*The Other Side of Tomorrow: Original Science-Fiction Stories
   about Young People of the Future*, Random House, 1973.
Children of Eden, Pyramid, 1973.
The Far Side of Time, Dodd, 1973.
Omega: A Collection of Original Science-Fiction Stories,
   Walker, 1973.
Future Quest, Avon, 1973.
The New Mind, Volume II, Macmillan/Collier, 1973.
Ten Tomorrows, Fawcett, 1973.
Tomorrow's Alternatives, Macmillan, 1973.
More Little Monsters, Manor Books, 1973.
*More Science-Fiction Tales: Crystal Creatures, Bird-Things,
   and Other Weirdies*, Rand McNally, 1974.
Continuum One, Putnam, 1974.
Continuum Two, Putnam, 1974.
Continuum Three, Putnam, 1974.
Mind Angel and Other Stories (illustrated by K. Groenjes),
   Lerner, 1974.
Adrift in Space and Other Stories (illustrated by K. Groenjes),
   Lerner, 1974.
Killer Plants and Other Stories (illustrated by K. Groenjes),
   Lerner, 1974.
The Beeseekers, Trident, 1974.
Science-Fiction Creatures, Rand McNally, 1974.
Strange Gods, Pocket Books, 1974.
You Can Win over "Innocent" Sins, Victor Books, 1974.
Vampires, Werewolves and Other Monsters, Curtis, 1974.
*Survival from Infinity: Original Science-Fiction Stories for Young
   Readers*, F. Watts, 1974.
Night of the Sphinx and Other Stories, Lerner, 1974.
The Many Worlds of Andre Norton, Chilton, 1974.
The Learning Maze and Other Science Fiction, Messner, 1974.
Horror Tales: Spirits, Spells, and the Unknown, Rand Mc-
   Nally, 1974.
Future Kin: Eight Science-Fiction Stories, Doubleday, 1974.
The Extraterrestrials, Macrae, 1974.
Crisis: Ten Original Stories of Science Fiction, T. Nelson,
   1974.
*Chronicles of a Comer and Other Religious Science-Fiction
   Stories*, John Knox, 1974.
The Berserkers, Trident, 1974.
Poul Anderson, *The Many Worlds of Poul Anderson*, Chilton,
   1974.
Long Night of Waiting and Other Stories, Aurora, 1974.
Journey to Another Star and Other Stories (illustrated by K.
   Groenjes), Lerner, 1974.
Corruption, Paperback Library, 1975.
Dystopian Visions, Prentice-Hall, 1975.
Epoch, Berkley, 1975.
Tomorrow: New Worlds of Science Fiction, M. Evans, 1975.
The Gifts of Asti and Other Stories of Science Fiction, Follett,
   1975.
Pat Boone, *My Faith*, C. R. Gibson, 1975.
Visions of Tomorrows, Pocket Books, 1976.
Six Science-Fiction Plays, Washington Square Press, 1976.
A World Named Cleopatra, Pyramid Books, 1977.
(With Howard Goldsmith) *Spine Chillers: Unforgettable Tales
   of Terror*, Doubleday, 1978.
Christian Mothers Reveal Their Joys and Sorrows, Standard,
   1979.

EDITOR WITH SAMUEL MOSKOWITZ

Strange Signposts, Holt, 1966.
The Time Curve, Tower, 1968.
Alien Earth and Other Stories, Macfadden-Bartell, 1969.
Other Worlds, Other Times, 2nd edition, Manor Books, 1974.

EDITOR WITH VIC GHIDALIA

Beware the Beasts, Manor Books, 1970.
Horror Hunters, Manor Books, 1971.

This house, which was once a fortress, has become
a prison. ■ (From *Children of Infinity: Original Science Fiction Stories for Young Readers*, edited by
Roger Elwood. Illustrated by Jacqui Morgan.)

Young Demons, Avon, 1972.
The Venus Factor, Manor Books, 1973.
*Androids, Time Machines, and Blue Giraffes: A Panorama of
   Science Fiction*, Follett, 1973.

EDITOR WITH VIRGINIA KIDD

*Saving Worlds: A Collection of Original Science-Fiction Sto-
   ries*, Doubleday, 1973.
The Wounded Planet, Bantam, 1974.

EDITOR WITH OTHERS

Missing Worlds and Other Stories, Lerner, 1974.
Graduated Robot and Other Stories (illustrated by K. Groenjes),
   Lerner, 1974.
Tunnel and Other Stories, Lerner, 1974.

Also editor of *The Extraterrestrials*, published by Macrae.

ETHERINGTON, Frank   1945-

PERSONAL: Born October 24, 1945, in Luton, England; son
of Francis George (a clerk) and Margaret (a homemaker; maiden
name, Calder) Etherington; divorced; children: Jainin (daughter), Jacob, Jeope (sons). *Education:* Regent St. Polytechnical

FRANK ETHERINGTON

Institute, London, diploma, 1966. *Home:* 140 Water St. S., Kitchener, Ontario, Canada N29 125.

CAREER: Toronto Telegram, Ontario, Canada, reporter and photographer, 1967-86; *Kitchener-Waterloo Record,*, Ontario, reporter and assignment and city editor, 1986—. Has also worked for various British newspapers. *Member:* Writers Union of Canada, Canadian Society of Children's Authors, Illustrators and Performers. *Awards, honors:* Chalmer's Award, 1987, for "The Snake Lady;" has received more than twenty journalism awards in various categories.

WRITINGS:

The Spaghetti Word Race (illustrated by Gina Calleja), Annick, 1981.
Those Words (illustrated by G. Calleja), Annick, 1982.
The General (illustrated by Jane Kirusu), Annick, 1983, revised edition, 1987.
When I Grow Up Bigger Than Five, Annick, 1984.

PLAYS

"The General," performed by Theatre Direct, Canada, 1986.
"The Snake Lady," performed by Theatre Direct, Canada, 1986.

WORK IN PROGRESS: The Snake Lady, a story about Anna Kaljas, aged seventy-five, and her work with the homeless; *Sarah,* a collection of newspaper columns that deal with conversations between an adult and a small girl.

SIDELIGHTS: "During a dreadful English education, writing was the only thing I enjoyed. This meant failing grades at everything but English. I went into journalism with the mistaken belief that it involved writing.

"I consider writing for children very important. In order to stop kids from becoming television extensions, authors have to provide them with interesting material. No matter how it is done, I believe the most essential thing is to get them to read early.

"Journalism plays a major part in my work—taking real Canadian characters and developing them into books and plays for children. I began doing books and plays for children because I did not like much of the material available in libraries and schools."

HOBBIES AND OTHER INTERESTS: Travel, home renovations, collecting junk at auctions, refinishing furniture, sleeping, "any project to avoid writing."

EVANS, Shirlee 1931-

PERSONAL: Born September 4, 1931, in Centralia, Wash.; daughter of Hershal Lee (a railway express agent) and Ivy (a homemaker; maiden name, Bonney) McDowell; married Robert D. Evans (a retired truck driver), August 19, 1950; children: Daniel, Rodney. *Politics:* Independent. *Religion:* Conservative Baptist. *Home:* 6100 199th St. N.E., Vancouver, Wash. 98686.

CAREER: Free-lance writer, 1961—; rural mail carrier, 1961-64; *Post-Record,* Camas, Wash., reporter, 1975-81; Kris' Hallmark Shop, Vancouver Mall, Wash., assistant manager, 1978—. *Member:* Oregon-California Trails Association (board of directors, Northwest Chapter, 1985—). *Awards, honors:* Washington State Sigma Delta Chi (Society of Professional Journalists) Award for investigative reporting, 1975; Award of

SHIRLEE EVANS

Merit from Religion in Media, Book of the Year by Choice Books, and one of the University of Iowa's Books for Young Adults Program Outstanding Books of the Year, all 1988, all for *A Life in Her Hands.*

WRITINGS:

Robin and the Lovable Bronc (teenage novel), Moody, 1974.
Tree Tall and the Whiteskins (junior historical fiction), Herald Press, 1985.
Tree Tall and the Horse Race (junior historical fiction; illustrated by James Ponter), Herald Press, 1986.
Tree Tall to the Rescue (junior historical fiction; illustrated by J. Ponter), Herald Press, 1987.
A Life in Her Hands (fiction), Herald Press, 1987, published in England as *Touch Choices,* Lion, 1988.
Winds of Promise (adult fiction), Herald Press, 1989.

Contributor to *Christian* and national horseman magazines. Author of column "The Listening Post," for *Community Post,* 1975-81.

WORK IN PROGRESS: Detour to Disaster, junior historical fiction; *A Life Apart,* an adult novel, sequel to *A Life in Her Hands; Wilderness Trails West: The Bonney Story,* historical nonfiction; an adult novel, *Winds of Promise,* dealing with an elderly farmer in conflict with his middle-aged son as housing developments take over the community.

SIDELIGHTS: "My father's job relocated him to Vancouver, Washington when I was six, resulting in five school changes in two years. Some bad experiences turned me into a withdrawn child, finding solace in Jesus while riding my horse Flame or roaming the woods surrounding my parent's country home.

"As a teenager I wrote stories, submitting them to the *Washington Farmer*'s youth page. The editor encouraged me to continue writing, but I married after high school, soon having two little boys who needed my time and energy.

"In 1961, with my sons in school, I went back to writing, purchasing a $25 typewriter and a book entitled, *Writing Made Simple.* My first article, 'How I Trained My Blind Horse,' was on the news stand six weeks after submitting it to *Horse Lover* magazine. With my first piece snapped up so fast I thought I had arrived as an author. Wrong! Reams of rejections later I realized how much I had to learn as my hobby became an obsession.

"I enrolled in night classes at a junior college, joined the Oregon Association of Christian Writers, and attended every writer's conference available. I continued to write and submit, with articles and short stories published in *Christian* and horseman magazines often enough to keep me at it. As our sons were on the verge of growing themselves out of the house, my first book, *Robin and the Lovable Bronc,* was published.

"Although looking forward to the time when I could write without interruption, I found the house much too quiet when my sons left home. And so, not realizing the number of trained journalists seeking newspaper positions, I walked into the office of a local weekly with a copy of my first book and asked for a job, '. . .reporting on meetings, maybe?' I suggested. Since they were planning to hire another reporter, they decided to give me a try, suggesting I find some news stories on my own.

"Before long I was reporting on local events, and writing a column, 'The Listening Post,' inviting readers to call in with whatever was on their minds. As a result I began investigating community concerns, from a man with Mafia connections, to a school superintendent accused of misusing funds. The first year with the paper I received a Sigma Delta Chi Award for investigative reporting. The editor laughingly remarked one day, 'We've turned Shirlee into a monster. She's not the same quiet lady who first walked in here.'

"Concern for others was replacing my shyness. I liked being with people. And so a few years later, with the newspaper job only part time, I took another part time job at Kris' Hallmark Shop. But I was longing to get back to my own writing which had been laid aside while with the paper. And so three years later I gave up the news job, going full time at the Hallmark Shop where I remain today, finding the work there an asset to writing.

"*A Life in Her Hands* came to be written after I was contacted by the editor of a large daily newspaper in Portland, Oregon, the *Oregon Journal.* (I had freelanced for him in the past.) He asked me to check out a junior high school said to be holding a four-day abortion seminar. I did, with my story and photo landing on the front page. Upon finding students opposed to abortion, I wrote a fictionalized account of a girl who gets pregnant. I interviewed people who worked with pregnant teens, and visited a Salvation Army Home using case histories (changed, of course) within the book which in 1988 received three awards, including the Religion in Media Merit Award, and was published in England under the title, *Tough Choices.*

"The first volume of the historical fiction series, about an Indian boy I named Tree Tall, was written while researching my mother's family who came west in 1845. A director of an outdoor camp needed an Indian story. I recalled interviewing a Siletz Indian while writing my newspaper column. He had talked about the suffering of his people when settlers arrived in Oregon. Using that background, along with the research at hand about my mother's family, I wrote the first story, expanding it to book length. With the book accepted two sequels were added. Mixed feelings churned as I wrote about Tree Tall. For while my mother's people were settlers who had a part in pushing the Indians off their land, my father's grandmother was half Cherokee.

"Currently my husband and I are involved in the Oregon-California Trails Association, working to protect what is left of our old immigrant trails. I have been researching and writing about the 1800s, as well as other topics.

"Rising at five or six every morning, I write until time for work. (A computer has replaced my typewriter.) My husband, now retired, has dinner ready when I return home. A quick read through of the paper and I am back at my computer until late.

"While I have gone about writing in an unorthodox manner, it has worked for me. Although it has taken much longer than if I had had formal training. My life is full and rewarding, with my church, writing, and work. I look forward to retiring in a few years, traveling, researching, and of course, writing."

HOBBIES AND OTHER INTERESTS: Church, horses, travel, learning more about our immigrant trails of the 1800s.

FEINBERG, Barbara Jane 1938-
(Barbara Silberdick Feinberg)

PERSONAL: Born June 1, 1938, in New York, N.Y.; daughter of Norman (an accountant) and Harriet (a homemaker; maiden

BARBARA JANE FEINBERG

name, Scheldon) Silberdick; married Gerald Feinberg (a professor of physics), August 9, 1968; children: Jeremy Russell, Douglas Loren. *Education:* Wellesley College, B.A., 1959; Yale University, M.A., 1960, Ph.D., 1963. *Home and office:* 535 East 86th St., New York, N.Y. 10028.

CAREER: City College of the City University of New York, New York City, lecturer, 1963-66, instructor in political science, 1966-67; Brooklyn College of the City University of New York, Brooklyn, N.Y., visiting lecturer in political science, 1967-68; Seton Hall University, South Orange, N.J., assistant professor of political science, 1968-70; Hunter College of the City University of New York, New York City, adjunct assistant professor of political science, 1970-73; freelance writer and editor, 1973—. *Member:* Phi Beta Kappa. *Awards, honors:* Woodrow Wilson Prize from Wellesley College, 1959, for essay on modern politics.

WRITINGS:

JUVENILE NONFICTION; UNDER NAME BARBARA SILBERDICK FEINBERG

Franklin D. Roosevelt: Gallant President, Lothrop, 1981.
Marx and Marxism, F. Watts, 1985.
The Constitution: Yesterday, Today, and Tomorrow, Scholastic, 1986.

Contributor of articles to periodicals, including *Western Political Quarterly.*

WORK IN PROGRESS: Various editorial and writing assignments.

SIDELIGHTS: "For as long as I can remember, I have always loved to read. As a child, I spent many hours reading Andrew Lang's rainbow collections of fairy tales, the 'Mary Poppins' series, Alcott's *Little Women, Little Men,* etc., and as many of the *Oz* books as I could get my hands on. At the same time, I discovered the biography section in the library and started to learn about the lives of famous people such as Anna Pavlova, Queen Elizabeth I, and Queen Victoria. At the age of twelve, I read Tolstoy's *War and Peace* for the first time. I have never ceased to admire that book for its marvelous characters, sweeping account of history, and intriguing philosophy.

As an adolescent, I was fortunate to be assigned to work in the school library so with the permission of the librarian, I was allowed to check out books even before they were processed to be put into circulation for the students and teachers. Maybe that is why I began to read at least eight books a week in addition to those required for homework!

"As an adult, I still spend many hours each day learning what I can from books. My interests still center on biography because I think it is important to learn how other people have met the challenges they faced and how they coped with adversity. In addition, I have developed an interest in history so I study various aspects of the American, European, and Asian past. I really believe that we all must know what went before in order to understand where we are now and where we may be going as a nation.

"The three nonfiction books I have written reflected my children's interests and needs as they were growing up. When my younger son was in kindergarten, he became curious about Franklin Roosevelt and could not find appropriate material that he could understand in the library. So I wrote a book for him about the crippled president who helped a crippled nation to recover from a major economic collapse. It was published several years later.

"When my older son was in eighth grade, he did some research on Marx but found most of the books about the German philosopher were ponderous and complex works directed at college students or adults. I decided to write a book about Marx's life and ideas so that young people could more readily

1887. . .Franklin dressed in a Scottish kilt. ■ (From *Franklin D. Roosevelt, Gallant President* by Barbara Silberdick Feinberg. Photograph courtesy of the Franklin D. Roosevelt Library, Hyde Park, New York.)

learn about him. So much of the world has been influenced by understandings and misunderstandings of what Marx wrote that it is most important for American teenagers to find out what Marx actually said, to whom his writings appealed and, how they have been reinterpreted to suit the needs of the contemporary world.

"I have recently written a text on the Constitution for young readers. This book came about after I looked at some of the materials my sons had read for courses in American history. I challenged myself to present complicated material to students in a form that would not underestimate their intelligence nor put them to sleep. In the constitution book, I tried to use as many examples and analogies as possible to make the ideas and background of the Constitution come alive. Unlike Professor Bork, I do see the Constitution as a living document that is adjusted and adapted to changing times, but at the same time, I recognize that the ideals of the Constitution are a timeless heritage bequeathed from one generation to the next. Today's students need to understand the document and its history so that they may preserve its beliefs and practices for their children and their children's children."

HOBBIES AND OTHER INTERESTS: Growing plants indoors under lights, needlepoint, baking chocolate desserts, knitting, raising a Yorkshire Terrier named Katie.

FIRMIN, Peter   1928-

PERSONAL: Born December 11, 1928, in Harwich, Essex, England; son of Lewis Charles (a railway telegrapher) and Lila Isobel (a homemaker; maiden name, Burnett), Firmin; married Joan Ruth Clapham (a bookbinder), July 29, 1952; children: Charlotte, Hannah, Josephine, Katharine, Lucy, Emily. *Education:* Colchester Art School, diploma, 1947; Central School of Art, diploma, 1952. *Politics:* Socialist. *Religion:* Methodist. *Home and office:* Hillside Farm, 36 Blean Hill, Blean, Canterbury, Kent CT2 9EF, England.

CAREER: Has worked as a teacher, a stained-glass artist, and as artist for a publicity studio. Free-lance book illustrator, writer, puppet maker, and cartoon film artist, 1952—. *Military service:* Royal Navy, 1947-49. *Awards, honors: Basil Brush at the Beach* was selected one of Child Study Association of America's Children's Books of the Year, 1976; PYE Award for services to children's television, 1984; honorary Master of Arts from the University of Kent, 1987.

WRITINGS:

SELF-ILLUSTRATED CHILDREN'S BOOKS

The Winter Diary of a Country Rat, Kaye & Ward, 1981.
Chicken Stew: Life with the Badd-Wolfe Family, Pelham, 1982.
Tricks and Tales, Kaye & Ward, 1982.
The Midsummer Notebook of a Country Rat, Kaye & Ward, 1983.
My Dog Sandy, Deutsch, 1988.
Making Faces, Collins, 1988.
Nina's Machines, Collins, 1989.
Hungry Mr. Fox, Delacorte, 1989.
Foolish Miss Crow, Delacorte, 1989.
Boastful Mr. Bear, Delacorte, 1989.
Happy Miss Rat, Delacorte, 1989.

SELF-ILLUSTRATED CHILDREN'S BOOKS; "BASIL BRUSH" SERIES

Basil Brush Goes Flying, Kaye & Ward, 1969, Scholastic Book Services (paperback), 1976, Prentice-Hall (hardcover), 1977.

PETER FIRMIN

. . .*Goes Boating,* Kaye & Ward, 1969, Prentice-Hall, 1976.
. . .*in the Jungle,* Kaye & Ward, 1970, Scholastic Book Services (paperback), 1976, Prentice-Hall (hardcover), 1979.
. . .*at the Seaside,* Kaye & Ward, 1970, published in America as *Basil Brush at the Beach,* Prentice-Hall, 1976.
. . .*and the Dragon,* Kaye & Ward, 1971, published in America as *Basil Brush and a Dragon,* Prentice-Hall, 1978.
. . .*Finds Treasure,* Kaye & Ward, 1971, Prentice-Hall, 1979.
. . .*Builds a House,* Kaye & Ward, 1973, Prentice-Hall, 1977.
. . .*Gets a Medal,* Kaye & Ward, 1973, Prentice-Hall, 1978.
. . .*and the Windmills,* Kaye & Ward, 1979, Prentice-Hall, 1980.
. . .*on the Trail,* Kaye & Ward, 1979, Prentice-Hall, 1981.
Three Tales of Basil Brush, Books 1-2, Kaye & Ward, 1979.
Two Tales of Basil Brush, Fontana, 1982.
Basil Brush Takes Off, Kaye & Ward, 1983.

SELF-ILLUSTRATED CHILDREN'S BOOKS; "PINNY" SERIES

Pinny Finds a House, Deutsch, 1985, Viking, 1986.
. . .*and the Bird,* Deutsch, 1985, Viking, 1986.
. . .*in the Snow,* Deutsch, 1985, Viking, 1986.
. . .*and the Floppy Frog,* Deutsch, 1987.
Pinny's Party, Deutsch, 1987.

ILLUSTRATOR; CHILDREN'S BOOKS; ALL WRITTEN BY O. POSTGATE; "STARTING TO READ" SERIES

Noggin and the Whale, Kaye & Ward, 1965.
Noggin the King, Kaye & Ward, 1965.
Noggin and the Moon Mouse, Kaye & Ward, 1967.
Noggin and the Dragon, Kaye & Ward, 1972.
Nogbad Comes Back, Kaye & Ward, 1972.
Nogbad and the Elephant, Kaye & Ward, 1972.
Noggin and the Money, Kaye & Ward, 1973.
Noggin and the Storks, Kaye & Ward, 1973.
Three Tales of Noggin, Books 1-2, Kaye & Ward, 1981.

Multi-media star, Basil Brush.

ILLUSTRATOR; CHILDREN'S BOOKS; All WRITTEN BY O. POST-GATE; "SAGA OF NOGGIN" SERIES

Ice Dragon, Kaye & Ward, 1968.
King of the Nogs, Kaye & Ward, 1968.
The Omruds, Kaye & Ward, 1968.
Flying Machine, Kaye & Ward, 1968.
The Firecake, Kaye & Ward, 1969.
The Island, Kaye & Ward, 1969, published as *Noggin and the Island*, Fontana, 1980.
The Flowers, Kaye & Ward, 1971, published as *Noggin and the Flowers*, Fontana, 1980.
The Pie, Kaye & Ward, 1971.
The Monster, Kaye & Ward, 1972.
The Game, Kaye & Ward, 1972.
The Icebergs, Kaye & Ward, 1975.
The Blackwash, Kaye & Ward, 1975.
Nogmania, Kaye & Ward, 1977.

ILLUSTRATOR; "BAGPUSS" SERIES; ALL WRITTEN BY OLIVER POSTGATE

Bagpuss in the Sun, Collins, 1974.
Bagpuss on a Rainy Day, Collins, 1974.
Mr. Rumbletum's Gumboot, Pelham Books, 1975.
Silly Old Uncle Feedle, Pelham Books, 1975.
The Song of the Pongo, Pelham Books, 1975.

ILLUSTRATOR; CHILDREN'S BOOKS; ALL WRITTEN BY O. POST-GATE; "IVOR THE ENGINE" SERIES

Ivor the Engine: The First Story, Fontana, 1977.
. . . : *The Snowdrifts*, Fontana, 1977.

(From *Nina's Machines* by Peter Firmin. Illustrated by the author.)

. . . : *The Dragon*, Collins, 1979.
. . . : *The Elephant*, Collins, 1979.
. . . : *The Foxes*, Armada, 1982.
Ivor's Birthday, Collins, 1984.

ILLUSTRATOR; CHILDREN'S BOOKS

Biddy Baxter, *The "Blue Peter" Book of Limericks*, Pan Books, 1976.
B. Baxter, *The "Blue Peter" Book of Odd Odes*, BBC Publications, 1976.
Peter Meteyard, *Stanley: The Tale of the Lizard*, Deutsch, 1979.
Edith Nesbit, *The Last of the Dragons*, McGraw, 1980.
E. Nesbit, *Melisande*, Macdonald, 1982.
Heather Amory, *Day and Night*, EDC, 1986.
H. Amory, *Summer and Winter*, EDC, 1986.
H. Amory, *Then and Now*, EDC. 1986.
Chis Powling, *Ziggy and the Ice Ogre*, Heinemann, 1988.
Dick King-Smith, *The Jenius*, Gollancz, 1988.
Pat Thomson, *Best Pest*, Gollancz, 1989.
Gillian Cross, *The Ghost from under the Ground*, Heinemann, 1989.

ILLUSTRATOR; TELEVISION FILMS

Oliver Postgate, "Alexander the Mouse" (six-episode, live animated series), Rediffusion-TV, 1958.
Robert Bolt, "The Miller and the Magic Trees" (series), Rediffusion-TV, 1958.
Rolf Harris and Wally Whyton, "Musical Box" (fifteen-minute weekly episodes), Rediffusion-TV, 1960-68.
O. Postgate, "Ivor the Engine" (series; forty, five-minute color cartoon films), Rediffusion-TV, 1960-68, BBC-TV, 1975-77, Smallfilms.
(With O. Postgate) "Noggin" (series), BBC-TV, 1960-70, 1981.
"Dogwatch" (series; with Oliver Postgate), Rediffusion-TV, 1961.
"Basil Brush" (series), Rediffusion-TV, 1962-68, BBC-TV, 1969-88.
"Olly and Fred" (series), Rediffusion-TV, 1962.
"Blue Peter" (series), BBC-TV, 1964.
(With O. Postgate) "Pogle's Wood" (series), BBC-TV, 1964.
O. Postgate, "The Clangers" (series), broadcast on "Watch with Mother" series, BBC-TV, 1969-72.
"Bagpuss" (thirteen fifteen-minute films), broadcast on "Watch with Mother" series, BBC-TV, 1972.
(With O. Postgate) "Tottie and the Dolls' House" (series; written by Rumer Godden), BBC-TV, 1983.
"Pinny's House" (based on "Pinny" series; thirteen five-minute films), BBC-TV, 1984.

ILLUSTRATOR; ADULT BOOKS

V. Sackville-West, *The Land and the Garden*, Viking, 1989.

ADAPTATIONS:

"Basil Brush in the Jungle" (record), Scholastic Book Services, 1976.
"Beebtots" (includes "Bagpuss," "Ivor," "Clangers," "Noggin"), BBC-Video, 1981.
"BBC Children's Favorites" (includes "Ivor," "Bagpuss," "Clangers"), BBC-Video, 1982.
"Ivor the Engine and the Dragons," BBC-Video, 1984.
"Ivor the Engine and the Elephants," BBC-Video, 1985.
"Ivor the Engine," BBC-Records and Tapes, 1985.

WORK IN PROGRESS: Two self-illustrated books: *Magic Mash* for A. & C. Black, and *Mask* for Belitha Press.

THE BIRMINGHAM REPERTORY THEATRE
(In Association with the Arts Council of Great Britain)

presents

The saga of
NoGGiN
the NoG

Firmin's illustration for a theater production of the Noggin tales.

SIDELIGHTS: Peter Firmin was born on **December 11, 1928** in Harwich, Essex, England, the son of Lewis Charles and Lila Isobel Firmin. "The sea was a part of my childhood. A walk from our house through the fields brought us to the marshes, to the sea, and to the sandy beach at Dovercourt. Except during the summer, it was fairly remote and deserted, and we could play quietly by the marshes. My mother's family originated from Harwich and were sea-going people. Her father served as a Bosun on the cross-channel ships, and an uncle was a lightship captain.

"My general impression of those early years is of an irresponsible childhood with few worries except perhaps school matters—bullying and worrying about being late. I can remember the bully of the infants school very clearly (I was only four and a half at the time). A friend and I had to pass by his house on the way to school, and we always dreaded that he would catch us. The last straw came when I was cycling home on my own and he tried to stop me. I ended up throwing my bike at him and that was that.

"The most formative influence was my mother who encouraged creativity in her children. She would sit us at a table with pencils and paper to draw and make models. When my brother and I played cowboys and Indians, we would make dollar notes. My mother made us costumes, using the beads off an old lampshade for the fringes on the Indian's costume. I always wanted to be the Indian."

Firmin expressed an awareness of different styles and techniques in illustration at an early age. "Coming from a fairly unsophisticated background, most of the fiction I came across

was either in Christmas books or comics. I tried to make my own comics, drawing strips once or twice. We didn't have any examples of great artists such as Arthur Rackham, but our set of Oldham's *Dickens*—most families owned a standard set—with illustrations by George Cruikshank and Phiz was very powerful. We had plenty of stimulus from pictures in *Picture Post* and *John Bull,* but no pictures on our walls. No art with a capital 'A'.

"The cinema was more exciting than anything at the time. 'Robin Hood' was considered history and culture. I saw the first full-length animated 'Snow White' and Max Fleischer's 'Hoppity Comes to Town,' about a little grasshopper. My father bought us a second-hand, hand-cranked 35mm film projector and managed to get hold of bits and pieces of film off-cuts. These were the bits cut off from films which broke during showings in local cinemas. We were able to project bits of Charlie Chaplin and sections of romantic films.

"We made our first animated film by painstakingly sticking a strip of paper down the middle of a piece of film and drawing pictures. Influenced by 'Hoppity Comes to Town,' they were black and white drawings because there weren't any colour films then. We couldn't actually project it but we were able to look through the front hole, turn the handle and see the little moving picture happen.

"I was asked in elementary school what I wanted to become and I answered, 'an artist or a sculptor'; I didn't know what a sculptor was but my Mum told me to say it. It is always frightening to start at a big school when you're quite small. I was fairly nervous, and I found the rules terribly complicated.

We had a very strict master, an ex-Royal Navy, who expected to toughen us by making us strip to the waist and throw snowballs. It wasn't real misery, you just hoped it would end as soon as possible. I found having to climb ropes more dreadful.''

Great Britain declared war on Germany on **September 3, 1939,** and its cities were heavily bombarded by German air raids. "After six months my brother and I were evacuated to Gloucestershire. I don't remember the travelling or leaving my mother, but I recall arriving in a little village and not being able to understand the people because of their strange accents. We were taken to a tiny, primitive, limestone cottage with chickens in the garden to meet our new caretaker, Mrs. Olpin. I looked up and there against the skyline was the silhouette of an old lady dressed in black with a long skirt, a sack over her back and a cat sitting behind her. She was gleaning corn for her chickens.

"Being evacuees was an adventure and a strange experience. The village was feudal. Next to our cottage was an old farmworker, Dan, who served as local dustman. He took the horse and cart round for the rubbish and collected the cider apples in season. He and his brother kept their cottage in absolute squalor, which we thought was great. They would always have their table laid with a loaf of bread and butter—somehow they managed to get hold of things other people couldn't get during the war—and we would go in and eat thick slices. During the air raids Mrs. Olpin would sit us under the stairs and make us wear her late husband's hats for protection.

"We spent one winter entirely snowed in and unable to go to school.

"Our parents only visited twice. The first time they came, they were horrified at the conditions of the tiny house without electricity. We had to use candles and my mother was shocked to discover that a mouse would chew on them at night. We were very self-sufficient and found life too interesting to be worried about being away from home. It was different for my sister, however, who was only six when she was evacuated to digs that were even more primitive than ours."

In **1942** the family was reunited. "Except for the occasional air raid (Harwich was one of the bases of the Navy Reserve Fleet), the war was pretty remote from us children. We used to listen to the American Forces' Network on the radio and, when my parents went to bed on Saturday nights, we'd sit up and listen to Saturday Night Theatre until midnight. My brother and I would make aircraft models from the latest identification pictures of the Luftwaffe.

"As our school was still evacuated, we attended Colchester Grammar School, an old-fashioned, fee-paying school with a lot of snobbery. It wasn't a happy experience. After a few months I was allowed to go to a high school in Clacton but my brother remained there. He took the first chance to leave and joined the service as an aircraft apprentice when he was fourteen."

At the age of fifteen, Firmin was accepted into an art school in Colchester for three years. "Art school was very exciting, I met people who actually made their living painting and drawing. There were apprentices of typography and typesetting. The school was a very small, old-fashioned facility on the top floor of a girl's high school. It was just three rooms with

(From *The Last of the Dragons* by Edith Nesbit. Illustrated by Peter Firmin)

juniors at one end and seniors at the other. I went into the senior group with sixteen other students."

The curriculum consisted of life drawing, costume designing, perspective, measured drawing, history of art, all culminating to the eventual Intermediate Examination in Arts and Crafts. Happily, Firmin could devote his entire studies to art and forget about math, French, and English. "I did my first wood engraving and illustration there. Someone had brought up a litho press from the basement but no one knew how to work it. The teachers weren't very broad in their talents."

Youthfully reticent, Firmin remembers "falling for one of the girls who posed for the costume life drawing classes, but I was too shy to make any advances." However, he did enjoy a social life and had several girlfriends. As my father did not dance, I went with my mother to Saturday Night Socials down at a church hall in Dovercourt where I would quickstep or do old-time dancing, partnering these rather large old ladies.

"I was called up for National Service in 1947 and went into the navy for a couple of years, broadening my horizons. I met people from Scotland and Yorkshire, and Cockneys, and people from the west country I would never have met otherwise. In the reserve fleet, we were put to work painting, scraping and maintaining the few ships. I was first based in my home town. On night duty as quartermaster I was relieved at midnight and would walk up the quay to see my Dad in the telegraph office and have a cup of tea with him, taking him some duty-free tobacco, so it wasn't like being in the forces at all. Then we were towed up to Newcastle for a refit and then to Rosyth in Scotland and 'put into mothballs.'"

Firmin's brother died at the age of twenty-two in a flying accident while patrolling in a Spitfire between Hong Kong and mainland China. "I comforted my sister and my mother but can't remember what effect the news of Lewis's death had on me personally. It seemed so unreal. When something like this happens so far away, you can't comprehend it; it seems more like fiction. I often wonder what he would be doing now if he had lived. We would have been very interested in each other's work, and probably could have done something together because he had the technical ability to get into films."

1949-1952. Firmin's stint in the National Service made him eligible for a grant to study graphics at Central School of Art in London, which was then in the book production department. "It was mostly an illustration department taught by such luminary painters as Laurence Scarfe, Keith Vaughan, and engraver Gertrude Hermes. There were a lot of little magazines coming out after the war and we all collected examples of people who illustrated in the *Radio Times, Lilliput* and *Leader.*

"An American, John Hoppe, came to Central as a student and developed a technique called 'mobilux' which was a live performance of abstract light. Light projectors and reflective strips were wiggled about in different colours onto a screen in time to the latest jazz music. We went to other colleges demonstrating this amazing invention, and it was eventually used as a method of decor for fashion shows.

"We also worked on Picasso's, 'Desire Caught by the Tail,' at the Watergate Theatre by the River Thames. We were asked to project lights onto a screen while the actors played their strange parts.

"I admired Paul Klee and the Bauhaus group. I didn't go into the Bauhaus ethic, but I wanted to be modern. I wanted to do something a bit out of the ordinary. I used to go to the Tate Gallery in London, where I saw a monumental painting by Picasso. It was a very powerful painting of a big female figure against a blue sky. A Henry Moore Madonna and Child in the chapel of a church at Northampton made a big impression on me, too. I've never forgotten the monumentality of the carving and the feeling that everything about it was right. A painting or a sculpture can have as much power as a large animal. You can never appreciate art by seeing reproductions or photographs. You have to be in the presence of a painting because that's the size and shape and feeling that the artist intended."

With a friend of his from Central, Firmin hitchhiked through France and Spain. "We went to Paris to visit the Louvre, the Impressionist Museum and to view paintings we'd only seen in reproductions before. Then we split; he went to Italy to see the great buildings, and I went to Spain to see the bullfight. Picasso's sculptures of bulls and his etchings of the fights had fascinated me.

"Terence Conran was at Central at the same time as I. He was doing furniture and industrial design and was the first to wear tartan trews—trousers made from material used by the Black Watch [The Royal Highland Regiment] which you could buy at the ex-army stores. It was a very dark tartan with a black background and yellow, green and red lines, quite subdued really. Conran had some made specially to fit him. I had mine for about ten years and they still hadn't worn out. We thought we were very daring wearing corduroys and duffle coats. We were regarded as the depraved young people of the time.

"During my student years, the Festival of Britain was held as the centenary of the 1851 Great Exhibition, showing off all the artistic and scientific achievements of Great Britain. After the war it was felt that Britain needed cheering up, that our morale needed boosting because everything was a bit depressed since we were still rationed and life was pretty dull. The exhibition was built on the south bank of the River Thames. The Dome of Discovery was thought to be a very exciting new development, looking like a space ship and under its great dome displaying all the scientific achievement of the day. The Skylon, the tallest structure in London, represented man's achievements and his ambitions to get into space. There was a strange mixture of futuristic invention and English quirkiness."

Central School of Art was well represented in the Exhibition. "Laurence Scarfe did a mural; Eduardo Paolozzi exhibited sculpture. A friend, who was a typography and design student, assisted with an exhibition of the atom for the Science Hall. Running behind schedule, we stayed up all night putting little atoms in—ping pong balls with fishhooks—and sticking little bits of lettering on glass cases. We were still at it in the morning and had to hide behind a table because the King was coming round to open the exhibition."

1952. Firmin married Joan Clapham, a fellow student at Central whom he met during his last year. "Joan was in the bookbinding department. It was all very quick. We went to an exhibition of wallpaper together in January, got engaged at Easter and were married in July. Her parents were a bit afraid of this awful art student sweeping their daughter off her feet, but they came round to the idea. The local paper reported that, 'The bride and groom left for their honeymoon in the south of France,' which sounds very important but actually we got on a train to Exeter, sent our smart clothes back home, changed into our jeans and duffle coats, went on the boat to Dunkirk with our haversacks, and hitched to the south of France. We stayed for four or five days in a cave by the sea because we couldn't afford anything else. We saw all the castles in France and came back through northern Italy and Switzerland. I financed the honeymoon with the money I had made illustrating

One of "The Clangers," created by Peter Firmin.

a little history book during the last term at Central, for which I was paid about 120 pounds (about $200).

"When we returned, I worked for two years in a stained glass studio painting pictures of saints on glass, cutting the glass, firing it and learning the craft. The boss of the firm, Frances Spear, designed the windows while we craftsmen carried out his directions. I've always had the fault of drawing people with heads that are too big for their bodies, looking slightly humorous; some of the saints in my stained glass windows had rather large noses and funny faces.

"We lived out of London for a while when our first daughter, Charlotte, was born and then moved to a flat in Battersea in Albert Bridge Road within walking distance of the park, and I got a job in a publicity studio on Bond Street doing posters and drawing giant ice-creams and that sort of thing." Firmin decided to take the risk of going freelance, first as illustrator for the *New Scientist* magazine, then illustrating various small magazines. These were lean times.

In **1958** he had the good fortune to meet Oliver Postgate who provided an entree into the world of television. The two men were to become collaborators on many future films and books. "I was teaching at Central School of Art when Oliver came looking for someone to illustrate a television story—someone who was hard up and would do a lot of drawing for very little money. Things clicked between us straight away because he was quite inventive, had lots of ideas and push, and I didn't mind working hard. He was a couple of years older and working as a floor manager for television. He had just gotten married and acquired not only a wife but three stepchildren, so he had to quickly find a better way of earning a living.

"'Alexander the Mouse' was the first program we worked on together. 'Alexander' lived behind the wainscotting of a house in London when he was chosen King of the Mice. His coronation was complete with boat ride down the Thames and a ceremony on Mouse Island. Oliver wrote six episodes and I did all the drawings and the cut-outs.

"'Visimotion,' the live-animation process we used to make 'Alexander the Mouse' was quite expensive and required three tables and mirrors. We needed a storyteller, three animators who worked the pictures with magnets and three people operating the cameras which looked into the mirrors. They used magnets to animate little bits of cardboard on top of pictures. Magnets are rather unreliable and characters jumped easily or turned somersaults by mistake. We did it for six months then Oliver decided to buy a camera and make animated films. I went on drawing using the same process for other people's stories. One of them, 'The Miller and the Magic Trees,' by Robert Bolt introduced the character of Baron Bollingrew."

"The first film that Oliver and I made together was 'Ivor the Engine.' Ivor was a little Welsh engine. The engine driver was based on my Welsh friend, Idris. The stationmaster resembles a signalman who used to work on the railways at Harwich and had a rather long, sad, lugubrious face with a drooping moustache. Oliver wrote and narrated the story for television."

Firmin's luck was beginning to change. He found himself having to hire two more people to handle all of the work, and his income tripled. In 1959 he moved his family into an eighteenth-century farmhouse in Blean, near Canterbury in Kent, his home ever since. His family had grown to include six

Two of Firmin's characters, Fred Barker and Olly Beak.

daughters, and it was decided that the countryside was a perfect spot for child rearing. "Blean is a couple of miles from Canterbury and fifty miles from London so it's quite easy to get into town. It's a lovely part of the country, and Oliver lives just a mile up the road. We turned the cowshed into my studio, Oliver uses the pig-sty, and we restored and tiled the big barn and in it made all our puppet films."

Before they tackle any project, Firmin and his partner conceive the ideas and characters in a joint effort. "Oliver and I make two sorts of films: animated cardboard cartoon films which are a bit like a cheap version of Walt Disney films, and we make puppet films. The animated cardboard films utilize cut-out figures which move on a drawn background. The film is taken frame by frame and a character is moved a little for each frame so that when you see the film running, it all comes to life.

"For me, it was a matter of doing a lot of drawings and cut-outs, always keeping in mind what would be useful for Oliver to animate. Because it's a very simple method of animation, the heads, bodies and legs are all different puppet-like parts."

1959. "The television people asked me to come up with a fifteen-minute programme which could be made for fifty pounds. Joan and I thought of various possibilities and came up with the idea of reviving nursery rhymes. I did the animated cartoons from simple bits of cardboard that could be worked from behind. This developed into 'Musical Box' which I did weekly for eight years, first with Rolf Harris, then with Wally Whyton.

"I was paid about thirty pounds an episode and for that I had to make the puppets, do the animation, and go to the studio and perform. 'Musical Box' was a mixture of singing nursery rhymes and puppets talking. There was no script. I've got some discs of Rolf Harris and me singing in little voices at double speed to sound like little cats and foxes. One day Rolf sang a song and told me that we needed two voices, and that I would have to do the harmony. Without any warning, I was going back to my Sunday school days singing harmony.

"'Noggin the Nog' was my idea although Oliver developed other characters and wrote all the stories. Noggin was a little Viking figure based on the ivory chessmen in the British Museum. I don't know where the word Noggin came from, but when I looked it up I found that it meant either a small barrel or a little block of wood, and I thought that suited a squat little person. The villain was called Nogbad the Bad. Noggin's bride was Nooka, an Eskimo girl. My daughter, Hannah, had seen the film, 'Nanook of the North' about the Eskimos. There was one shot of all the Eskimos getting under their sealskin blankets with nothing on. Hannah went to bed one night and took her pajamas off and said, 'I want to go to bed with nothing on, I want to be a little Nook.' So I thought there should be a race of people called the Nooks.

"In the first story, Noggin went off to find his bride. It was a little love story in which Noggin went to fetch Nooka in his long ship. I had been abroad to Esbjerg, Denmark as a youth. Because Esbjerg is a coastal town similar to Harwich, a club was formed to encourage friendships between the people of both places. I was very keen on Scandinavian people and mythology. There were a lot of links between the Vikings, the Scandinavians, and us.

"The BBC bought the series. Oliver's voice narrated the films, and every year we did six complete stories. In 1965 we did the first of ten Noggin books, based on the series and using very simple language aimed at children learning to read."

In **1962** Firmin created his most famous puppet, Basil Brush, a joke-telling fox. He became so popular that toys, games and wallpaper were based on him. "The Basil Brush television series never went to America. The Americans wanted to change his name for the books. They said Basil wasn't a very good name for a macho character, but I resisted. Most of our films have been seen in Australia, New Zealand, Sweden and Germany.

1964. He contributed drawings to accompany folk songs for the famous BBC series "Blue Peter." The BBC commissioned Firmin and Postgate to make a series of puppet films for small children. In response they made, "Pogle's Wood."

"The world of 'Pogle's Wood' was a hollow tree, complete with a witch and a magic bean plant. The series showed life in different parts of the country—men working in the woods, taking in the harvest, shoeing horses, and building roads. Those scenes were filmed by Oliver and incorporated into the rest of the film with a commentary provided by the puppets. Our children were filmed rushing through the woods for some of the scenes. I think they rather liked their Dad working for television.

"After 'Pogle's Wood' the BBC asked us to do a series to be shown as part of the 'Watch with Mother' lunchtime programmes for younger children. It was shown after the first man had landed on the moon. 'The Clangers' are a race of mice who live on a planet in outerspace. One of Oliver's sons, Dan, gave him the idea for the character of the Soup Dragon when he was telling his father a story. Our children have all given us ideas over the years.

"'Bagpuss' was also created as part of the BBC's 'Watch with Mother' series. I called him Bagpuss because he was fat as a bag. He lived in a shop with a little girl called Emily. (My youngest daughter is seen in the title sequence). Toys in the story are brought to life by magic. There are other characters in the series, such as Madeleine, the rag doll, and Gabriel the singing toad with a banjo. When Emily finds a broken toy or an old object, the characters tell stories and sing songs about it and are able to repair it as good as new. We made thirteen fifteen-minute 'Bagpuss' films—a year's work. We later did a series of reading and picture books about him."

In **1969**, Firmin published his first self-illustrated book, *Basil Brush Goes Flying,* based on his television puppet. "I remember sitting on the lawn writing the first Basil Brush book and finding it easy. I write them very quickly because they're very simple language using simple ideas and repetition. The sketches come easily off my pen, and if I'm working in black and white, I'll probably complete two drawings in a day; if I'm using colour, probably one.

Oliver Postate, with two of Firmin's children, on the set made for filming "The Clangers" at Hillside Farm. ■ (Photograph by Cathy Courtney.)

Peter Firmin sketches Bagpuss.

"I tend not to base characters on real people, and my cartoon characters are not caricatures of anyone. Their shape and looks have to do with their characters rather than an attempt to make them look realistic. Sometimes I worry when I look at published drawings, 'If only I'd worked on it for another day or perhaps gone to the library for some decent reference material.' I'm a perfectionist in some ways, but I'm a bit lazy, too, so I'm not always as exact as I might be. On the whole I work better under pressure and, unless I've got something important to do like cutting the grass, I get on with work first thing in the morning."

1982. Firmin and Postgate collaborated on a series of television films called 'Tottie and the Dolls' House,' based on a book by Rumer Godden. "It's a rather unpleasant story in some ways and it ends up with a celluloid doll going up in flames and a nasty china doll trying to take over the doll house. The story also involves the people who own the doll house. We did the film in two sections. When people were playing with the doll house we used still photography. When the action moved inside the doll house, the picture came to life, and you could see the dolls moving. I made the doll house, the rooms, and all the furniture as well as the dolls themselves. They were quite realistic."

1988. Firmin's most recent project is quite different from his work for children and takes him back to his early training at art school. "I'd been doing some lino-cuts for pleasure and always wanted to illustrate a whole book either with engravings or lino-cuts. I was partly inspired by my daughter Hannah

who does a lot of engraving on vinyl, a finer form of lino-cutting. My wife suggested that I illustrate an edition of Vita Sackville-West's *The Land,* a long philosophical poem about England and its countryside. The original publication was out of print and I found out that someone was interested in reissuing it. I did one or two specimen prints and eventually Webb & Bower, a publisher based in Exeter, backed the project. *The Land and the Garden,* long poems of Vita Sackville-West's have been published in one volume with about fifty illustrations engraved on vinyl.

"I knew that once I started working on the poems, I would have to forget about children's books for the time being. I read the poems several times, and hope to convey the feeling of them without actually illustrating what Vita Sackville-West has said, harmonising, instead, the pictures with the text. Her images are so strong that it's pointless for an illustrator to try to repeat them. I'm not a very literary person, but I get the same sort of pleasure from these poems as I do from some of Shakespeare's sonnets.

"I've always admired the work of Thomas Bewick, a great innovator, who revived the art of engraving on wood and became one of the best illustrators of his day. I have collected his books, and those of his brother, John, since I was at Central. I once spent a whole week's wages from the stained glass studios on a couple of Bewick's books.

"He engraved on boxwood blocks, which is a very fine and difficult process. Boxwood is expensive and you can't afford

Engraving by Peter Firmin. ■ (From *The Land and the Garden* by Vita Sackville-West.)

to make too many mistakes. Lino-cutting is a much broader process and the illustrations would have to be reduced a lot to fit on the page. It's possible to get a much finer effect using the same tools by engraving on vinyl, and ordinary vinyl tiles are easier to get nowadays. You cut into it, taking away the areas that you want to come out white on the page and leaving the surface that you want to print; if you want the branches of a tree, you cut out all the sky between them and leave the branches. I've got an old Albion printing press in the barn and I print from that, but it is possible to print by hand by just rubbing the paper on the surface of the engraving.

The Firmin family circle has grown to include eight grandchildren. Artistic talents and the need to create has been passed on from parents to daughters. "There are children's annuals with published pictures done by Charlotte and Hannah when they were quite young. Charlotte did some of the illustrations for the 'Bagpuss' films. All the girls either went to art school or college, and it was great because they started with me. Charlotte is an illustrator and author of children's books, and Hannah is a book and magazine illustrator for adults. Katie's a cartographer. Josie works decorating hand-painted china with Christopher Stangeways, and Lucy lives in Italy working in fashion and leathercraft. Emily is at Central School, where Joan and I were, and has just made a film herself, so everything's gone full circle."[1]

FOOTNOTE SOURCES

[1]Based on an interview with Cathy Courtney for *Something about the Author.*

FOR MORE INFORMATION SEE:

Books for Keeps, School Bookshops Association (London), July 1980.
Brigid Peppin and Lucy Micklethwait, *Book Illustrators of the Twentieth Century,* Arco, 1984.
"Firmin and Postgate Present. . .'Pinny's House' and 'Tottie,' School Bookshops Association, September, 1986.

FOSTER, Sally

PERSONAL: Born in Baltimore, Md.; daughter of Reuben (a lawyer) and Eleanor (an artist; maiden name, Whiteley) Foster. *Education:* Bennington College, B.A. 1959; attended Maryland Institute College of Art, 1968, and 1978, and Ansel Adams Photography Workshop, Yosemite, Calif., 1972. *Religion:* Episcopalian. *Agent:* Eleanor Roszel Rogers, 1487 Generals Highway, Crownsville, Md. 21032. *Office:* c/o E. P. Dutton, 2 Park Ave., New York, N.Y. 10016.

CAREER: MEDICO, Baltimore Md., girl friday, 1960; *News-American,* Baltimore, feature writer, 1961-63; Peace Corps Headquarters, Washington, D.C., staff member, 1965-66, writer and researcher, 1966-68; free-lance writer and photographer, 1967—; Department of Public Health, Washington, D.C., visual information specialist for the "War on Rats' program, 1969-70. Peace Corps volunteer, Brazil, 1963-65; consultant, Westinghouse Learning Corporation, Health Services Division, Bladensburg, Md., 1971-72; consultant, American Oc-

SALLY FOSTER

cupational Therapy Association, Rockville Md., 1973-74; bicentennial coordinator for the International Visitor's Center, Baltimore, during 'Operation Sail,' 1976-77; member of CARE Committee of greater Baltimore. *Exhibitions:* Third Eye Gallery (solo), Baltimore, Md., 1978; Loyola Gallery, Baltimore, 1980; Three Arts Club of Homeland, Baltimore, 1983; Space Telescope Science Center (solo), Baltimore, 1986; Roland Park Country School Evening School (solo), Baltimore, 1987; Hamilton Street Club, Baltimore, 1989. *Awards, honors:* Children's Choice from the International Reading Association, 1985, for *A Pup Grows Up.*

WRITINGS:

SELF-ILLUSTRATED WITH PHOTOGRAPHS

A Pup Grows Up, Dodd, 1984.
Where Times Stands Still, Dodd, 1987.

ILLUSTRATOR

Linell Smith, *Who's Who in the Zoo,* Oak Tree, 1981.

Photographs have appeared on calendars and post cards. Contributor of cover photographs to *Country Kids, Maryland, Port of Baltimore, Maryland Horse, Horse Play, Project Hope, Peace Corps, Brazilian Business,* and *Africa.* Contributor of

articles and photographs to periodicals, including *Baltimore Sun, Baltimore News-American, Washington Post, Messenger, Towson Times, Los Angeles Times* and *Front Lines.*

WORK IN PROGRESS: Simon Says. . .Let's Play!, a book on old-time games, to be published by Dutton.

SIDELIGHTS: "As a child, I wanted to be an artist when I grew up. I decided to decorate the walls of my room with drawings of clowns. I dumped my crayons on the floor and picked out a blue and then a red. With sweeping gestures, I drew clown faces with big smiles and tall hats. Needless to say, this did not go over so well with my parents.

"On Saturday mornings I used to go to art classes at the Baltimore Museum of Art. The Museum kept one of my paintings. It was of a grasshopper on a railroad track with a pick in his teeth and a carpet tack. I borrowed the idea from an old children's song.

"At some point—when I was around ten—I picked up a camera and my interest changed to photography. I would take pictures of my cat who was extremely patient with me. I would prop him up in a chair, stick a pair of eyeglasses on him, and stuff an index card between his paws. I'd dash back to click the shutter before he moved. I would develop the film in trays spread out in the bathroom. (We only had one bathroom and I always hoped that somebody wouldn't have to use it.) I'd make contact prints in a simple box printer. It had a red light that you could turn on to see what you were doing. The white light is what made the picture. The fun ended when my mother discovered all the thumbtack holes in the window frame, resulting from my tacking up a black cloth to block out the light.

"It seems that I have always taken pictures and I always enjoyed writing compositions in school. I had my first story and pictures published when I was fifteen. The *Maryland Horse* magazine paid me all of five dollars for an article about our school horse show. I xeroxed the cheque and stuck it in a scrapbook.

"When I was growing up, my parents tried to give me the usual 'advantages' that parents like to give to their children: swimming lessons, dance lessons, riding lessons, tennis lessons, modeling lessons and acting lessons. (They knew music was a lost cause. Even now, my dog sings better than I do.) Riding and tennis were the best—but the acting served me well. I ended up going to Bennington College where I majored in drama.

"Bennington had a three month non-resident work term each year and I always looked for particularly interesting things to do during that time. During my junior year I worked for the Baltimore Department of Public Welfare as a caseworker in the foster home division. In my senior year, I worked as a courier for the Frontier Nursing Service in the eastern mountain section of Kentucky.

"After college, I worked as a feature writer for the Baltimore *News-American*. Some stories were glamorous like the one about Buster Keaton. Others were not, like 'Dishes Pose Threat of Lead Poisoning.' On a slow day, my editor sent me out to write a story on what it was like to drive one of those huge road-clearing machines. (I had on a tight skirt. . .not exactly the best attire for that sort of thing.) The workers really cleared everything out of the way. I'm not sure they trusted me!

'Can you guess what this English Setter will do? ■
(From *A Pup Grows Up* by Sally Foster. Photograph by the author.)

"In 1961, the Peace Corps came along. In the spring of 1963, I decided to join. India was my first choice. Latin America was my second. I got Brazil. I spent two years working in a health/community development project in the *favelas* or slums of Rio de Janeiro. The slums stretch out like clumps of fallen cobwebs on the hillsides overlooking the city. Shacks keep popping up overnight like mushrooms. The people who live in these shacks had come, for the most part, from Brazil's often parched northeast. They think they will find work and their lives will be easier. Instead, they discover that jobs are hard to find, food is scarce and crime is rampant. We worked out of a health post, tracking down tuberculosis patients who had failed to pick up their medicine, giving shots against typhoid and polio, or talking to a mother about nutrition.

"After the two year stint in Brazil, I came back and worked at Peace Corps Headquarters in Washington, D.C. as a writer/researcher in the staff training division. The next year I took a leave of absence and spent nine months in eleven countries in Africa. I did some work for the Peace Corps and went on a photographic assignment for the Sisters of Our Lady of Africa (a Catholic missionary organization). One of the pictures that I took in Ngorongoro Crater in Tanzania became a double spread in National Geographic's book on lion cubs.

"Over the years I continued to work largely in writing and photography. For a year I was the visual information specialist for the 'War on Rats' program in Washington, D.C. I had to write a filmstrip to teach people where rats come from and how to get rid of them. The script turned out well, but I made one mistake. I forgot that I would then have to take the pictures. How do you take a photograph of a rat eating a hole in the side of an oatmeal box? My first thought was to get someone to trap a rat for me. Then, we would chloroform the creature just a little. My plan didn't work. The rat died. Furthermore, a local resident in the neighborhood wasn't too happy when we left the rat there. 'We got enough of them there things without you bringing in more,' he yelled. I also remember the day I picked up the freeze-dried rats from the Smithsonian. They were in a shoe box and I rode the public bus.

"For the last several years I have been working on children's books and this is, perhaps, what I like most. I am able to combine both the writing and photography, and largely the focus has been on animals and people. Now I often find that I take the pictures and then write the text. I don't have to worry about posing animals in impossible situations.

"I fell into doing children's books by accident. I had taken some pictures of a friend's Arabian horses. She wanted to sell them and needed the photographs for ads. On the day I delivered the pictures, she showed me some riddle/verses she had written about zoo animals. She wondered whether I could take some pictures and perhaps make riddles out of them, too. The author had already published several books. Her name was Linell Smith and she was the daughter of the poet, Ogden Nash. I went to work right away on the photographs, borrowing some I had already taken in Africa. The result was *Who's Who in the Zoo.*

"We were going to do the book on dogs together—but then her life got too complicated. She didn't have time to write the text. I had already taken the pictures and felt like someone who arrives at the airport, planning to go on a trip with a friend who doesn't show up. Should I continue to my destination or turn back? I decided to go ahead and give it a try. Another friend prodded me by saying: 'Do it yourself. You write those short sentences, anyway!' So I did it.

"My editor knew about my long time interest in the Amish and asked me whether I had considered doing a book about

The cleaning and tidying-up chores for the whole family never end. ■ (From *Where Time Stands Still* by Sally Foster. Photograph by the author.)

them. At first, I completely dismissed the idea. The Amish don't like to be photographed. Still, the idea kept gnawing at me. I wondered whether there was any way this would be possible, without upsetting them. Clearly, there were many who said 'no.' But, surprisingly, some let me take the pictures. Little by little, I was able to gather enough material to put together *Where Time Stands Still.* I have great admiration and affection for the Amish. Even now, I enjoy going to help a family harvest their wheat, bring in their hay, or shell their limas. Sometimes, I'll go into town and buy some ice and we'll make fresh strawberry or peach ice cream in the old wooden hand-crank freezer.

"My favorite poem is Robert Frost's 'The Road Not Taken.' In some respects I feel that I have taken the road 'less traveled by'—and it has 'made all the difference.'"

FOR MORE INFORMATION SEE:

Charles Kupfer, "Rare Photos Capture Unusual Amish Life," *Baltimore Messenger,* March 2, 1988.

FOX, Aileen 1907-

PERSONAL: Born July 29, 1907, in London, England; daughter of W. Scott Henderson (a solicitor) and Alice McLean; married Sir Cyril Fox (director of the National Museum of Wales), July 6, 1933; children: Charles, Derek, George. *Education:* Newnham College, Cambridge, B.A., 1929, M.A.,

1932. *Home:* 2 The Retreat, Topsham, Exeter, Devonshire, England.

CAREER: University College, Cardiff, South Wales, lecturer, 1940-46; University of Exeter, Exeter, England, senior lecturer in archaeology, 1947-72; University of Auckland, Auckland, New Zealand, visiting lecturer, 1973-74; Auckland Museum, Auckland, Edward Vaile archaeologist, 1974-76. *Member:* Society of Antiquaries (fellow). *Awards, honors:* Honorary D.Litt., University of Exeter, 1984.

WRITINGS:

Roman Exeter, Manchester University Press, 1952.
Roman Britain (illustrated by Alan Sorrell), Lutterworth, 1961, Dufour, 1968.
South-West England, Praeger, 1964, revised edition, David & Charles, 1973.
Prehistoric Maori Fortifications in the North Island of New Zealand, Longman (Auckland), 1976.
Tiromoana Pa, Te Awanga: Hawke's Bay, Excavations, 1974-1975, Department of Anthropology, University of Otago, 1978.
Carved Maori Burial Chests, Auckland Museum, 1983.

Contributor of articles to professional journals, including *Antiquaries Journal, Antiquity, Proceedings of the Prehistoric Society, Archaeological Cambrensis, Transactions of the Devonshire Association Proceedings,* and *Devon Archaeological Society.*

SIDELIGHTS: "My first degree was in English at Cambridge which taught me how to write as well as appreciate good literature. I became interested in British archaeology when I went to dig at the Roman fort at Richborough in Kent in 1929. There I learned my trade under J. P. Bushe-Fox. I spent six months at the British School in Rome in 1930, studying the monuments, and I met the artist Alan Sorrell. I married one of the leading archaeologists, Cyril Fox, director of the National Museum of Wales in Cardiff, and with whom I shared many interests. My only book for children, *Roman Britain*, illustrated by Alan Sorrell, was written when my eldest son, Charles was eleven years old and was directed at his age group."

HOBBIES AND OTHER INTERESTS: Gardening, bird-watching, walking, travel.

FRAZETTA, Frank   1928-
(Fritz)

PERSONAL: Born February 9, 1928, in Brooklyn, N.Y.; son of Alfred Frank and Mary (Prinz) Frazetta; married Eleanor Doris Kelly (manager of Frazetta Prints, Inc.); children: Frank, Bill, Holly, Heidi. *Education:* Attended Brooklyn Academy of Fine Art. *Home and office address:* P.O. Box 919, Marshalls Creek, Pa. 18335.

CAREER: Artist. Illustrator of comic strips, including "Johnny Comet" (title changed to "Ace McCoy"), 1952-53, "Flash Gordon," 1953, and "L'il Abner." Also illustrator of numerous covers of books, periodicals, and albums. Formerly associated with comic-book publishers, including Baily, Pines, Fawcett, and National. Founded Frazetta Prints, Inc. Co-animator of "Fire and Ice" (animated film). *Member:* National Cartoonists Association. *Awards, honors:* Two Hugo Awards; four awards from Warren Publishers; and awards from other organizations and periodicals, including *Playboy*.

WRITINGS:

The Fantastic Art of Frank Frazetta, Rufus Publications, 1975.
Frank Frazetta: Book Two, Bantam, 1977.
Frank Frazetta: Book Three, Bantam, 1978.
Frank Frazetta: Book Four, Bantam, 1980.
(With Eleanor Frazetta) *Frank Frazetta: The Living Legend*, Sun Litho-Print/Frazetta Prints, 1980.
Frank Frazetta: Book Five, Bantam, 1985.
(With James Silke) *Death Dealer*, Tor Books, 1988.
Death Dealer: Book Two, Tor Books, 1989.

ILLUSTRATOR

Edgar Rice Burroughs, *Tarzan and the Castaways*, Canaveral, 1965.

FRANK FRAZETTA

E. R. Burroughs, *The Master Mind of Mars,* Doubleday, 1973.

WORK IN PROGRESS: Illustrations for L. Ron Hubbard's science-fiction books.

SIDELIGHTS: **February 9, 1928.** Born and raised in the Sheepshead Bay section of Brooklyn, New York. At a very early age, Frazetta showed exceptional artistic ability, and sold his first crayon drawing at the age of three—to Grandma—for a penny. It was her interest and encouragement that motivated him to continue drawing.

Sheepshead Bay was a tough neighborhood where gang wars and violence were common everyday occurrences, and according to Mike Gross, Frazetta's former editor at *National Lampoon,* "Frank couldn't face the tough Brooklyn street fighters he grew up with, until one day he took on the biggest bully in the neighborhood and beat him; then he became the meanest kid on the block."[1]

1936. Following the advice of one of his teachers, Frazetta's parents enrolled him in the Brooklyn Academy of Fine Arts run with a free hand by a classical Italian artist, Michael Falanga. "We used to sit around and draw anything we wanted to as students. It was *very* informal."[1]

Frazetta continued to draw and paint through his teens but slacked off for a few years to pursue his interest in baseball at which he was so adept he was offered a contract by the New York Giants.

1944. His mentor, Michael Falanga died, and Frazetta entered the world of commercial art as an assistant, doing fill-in work on comic books for John Giunta, a prolific science-fiction cartoonist during the '40s and '50s. He subsequently persuaded Giunta to produce a comic of his own creation starring a character he had originated in grammar school. "Snowman" appeared in the now classic issue of *Tally-Ho* of December, 1944. It was the start of a long career in the comic-strip field.

For the next few years, however, Frazetta was still ambivalent about choosing a career, and he continued to play baseball, receiving more professional offers after batting .487, compiling most hits and more runs scored, and winning the Most Valuable Player Award for the Parade Grounds League in Ebbets Field, home of his favorite team the Brooklyn Dodgers. As he did not take comic books that seriously, he found that he could "bat out a six-pager in two days, leaving the rest of the week to play ball and fool around."[2]

He finally opted for an artistic career, rationalizing that in sports, "You're too old while you're still young! In art, you're as old as your imagination."[2] His second thoughts about baseball ended with an offer from Walt Disney who liked his animal drawings. Frazetta decided to remain in New York, however, but felt encouraged by the recognition of such a renowned Hollywood studio. He began drawing with more confidence, and felt that he had made the right decision. "I think if the Dodgers had moved to Los Angeles before then, I might have gone. But in those days, California was too far removed from Major League baseball for my liking."[2]

"I knew since I was a kid I'd find myself. When I was sixteen and finally saw some professionals at work, I knew I could do that stuff easily. Not technique, not color or drawing—I appeal to the basic feelings. The hamminess in me asks will this audience like it, will the sophisticates think I missed? Is there a little something for everyone?"[1]

Began earning his living by drawing funny animal stories, and a multitude of illustrations for different comic houses. Most of his early work was signed "Fritz," a nickname friends gave him as he grew up. His first major assignment came in 1949 with the publication of the legendary "Shining Knight" series for National's *Adventure Comics.* More strips followed including the popular "Dan Brand" and "Tipi" series, and science-fiction tales in collaboration with fellow artist Al Williamson. The tales involved disproportionate beasts, sensuous women and fantasy landscapes which would become Frazetta's trademark. "I respond to an action, then paint what I *feel* about the action. A woman can be sensuous and erotic in typical, mundane movements, and I try to capture that precise motion or pose when she is at her most sensuous. I do exaggerate a lot in my work, but I find I have to exaggerate least when I paint women. The real thing is often more than enough."[2]

"I see things as they exist but I paint them from the image they've left on my mind rather than how they appear in reality. For instance, if you really examine your fears, you realize how out of proportion they are. Your mind's eye constantly paints pictures far in excess of what's real. I try to capture those images in my work. I'll make the fist coming straight at you larger, bonier, and much more menacing, because I'm dealing with the emotion of fear and not the anatomical proportions of the hand."[3]

1952. Magazine Enterprises published *Thun'da King of the Congo,* the only complete comic book ever realized by Frazetta. The first issue became a classic, and is regarded by experts as the best of his comic work. *Thun'da* chronicled an Edgar Rice Burroughs-type adventure of a bare-chested hero whose airplane crashed in a lost world of prehistoric men and animals. Frazetta, who wanted to draw the Tarzan newspaper strip, had hoped to be noticed by Burroughs. When he did not get the strip, he signed with the McNaught Syndicate to do "Johnny Comet," a newspaper strip about a car racing driver built along the line of Tarzan. He gave it up after a few years, and returned to comic books, producing a collector's item series of Buck Rogers covers. George Lucas claimed that they were the inspiration for his "Star Wars" saga.

1954. Spent several weeks ghosting Dan Barry's *Flash Gordon* before working for cartoonist Al Capp as an assistant on *Li'l Abner,* a position he held for nine years. "I got one hundred fifty dollars a week and had to work only a day and a half. I was always out playing ball—what a life, I thought. Then I saw I was getting nowhere, not growing—and Capp, whom I liked, was gonna cut my salary—so I quit. I'll get back into cover illustration. So I had holes in my shoes and was taking these great covers around to the publishers—and they were too good! These guys would blink and nothing registered. My Buck Rogers covers. So I told them, Hey, I'm the guy whose covers always used to boost your circulation before I left to do *Li'l Abner!* Didn't get through. I was 'old-fashioned.' So I get a job to do a little head of Ringo Starr. And that got me a phone call to do the movie poster of Woody Allen's 'What's New, Pussycat?' My God, suddenly I had a check for five thousand dollars, a whole year's pay, earned in one afternoon! Ho, we had *that* check photographed."[1]

November 17, 1956. Married Eleanor Kelly on Sadie Hawkin's Day.

Went on to illustrate for men's magazines such as *Cavalcade, Gent,* and a series titled "Li'l Annie Fannie" for *Playboy.*

In the early '60s, painted magazine covers for Jim Warren who created a line of black-and-white graphic story magazines modeled on the horror comics of the fifties. Frazetta's paintings for *Eerie, Creepy,* and *Vampirella* magazines were so impressive that James Warren named a corporate award in his

(From *Jungle Tales of Tarzan* by Edgar Rice Burroughs. Illustrated by Frank Frazetta.)

(From Frazetta's portfolio of *Lord of the Rings* by J. R. R. Tolkien.)

Drawing from Frazetta's Kubla Khan portfolio.

honor, and bestowed several upon him. "...[The 'Cat Woman'] painting was done in a day originally. And it was reproduced, for *Eerie,* or *Creepy,* I forget which. The original concept had her with blonde hair in a leopard skin, and it had one or two more leopards and it wasn't quite as moody. And, as I am wont to do, I look at a painting and see possibilities afterwards, and say to myself, maybe this approach was a little silly, maybe I can really work with a nice, serious approach. And so you see what happened. I approached it with some intelligence and made a nice, kinda classy concept out of it. And it seems everyone that comes here and sees it for the first time—I mean I'm talking about a period over a fifteen year span—every time I drag this thing out—BANGO! That's their new favorite. I'm talking about people like Dino de Laurentiis, Sylvester Stallone, George Lucas—anyone who comes here and sees it for the first time. And it's one of my own favorites because I'm very sentimental about the subject matter. I mean, if anything says *Frazetta,* 'Cat Woman' does. See, I don't really—barbarians are a new thing for me, I was never into barbarians. I was always, even as a child, enamoured of beautiful women and pretty cats and trees and vines and mossy-covered things. That's my area. Even in animation, I loved to kinda fondle the vegetation, and the little toadstools that grow up the side of gnarled old trees. And I love women. So I put it all together in one concept. I could probably go on painting

sequel after sequel to this thing and have a *lot* of fun, I mean I really enjoy myself."[4]

Frazetta'a best friend, Roy Krenkel, introduced him to paperback cover paintings. He started with Ace paperbacks, and finally got the chance to do a series of Tarzan and many other characters from Edgar Rice Burroughs' novels. "...I think [my first cover] was the cover for *Tarzan,* the one hanging from a tree limb. I remember I was very excited. It was not particularly good, either, but my oldest fans have a real sense of nostalgia about these things. They'd make a 'discovery': here suddenly was a new guy doing things a little bit different, and they all got excited. Actually, I kid you not, I was better—better talented than what it shows at that stage of the game. But they didn't pay very much in those days and their attitude was kinda negative. So I gave it as much time as it seemed to me the job was worth.

"...I'm your true artist, very sensitive. If you treat me bad, I'm going to give you back what you give. See, for the most part I did a little sketch for each book, not my best work, but I didn't intend it to be, not for those prices.

"I have read [Burroughs] since I was a child. I was really into Tarzan. . . .I'd read *all* the Burroughs books—had a lot of fun

(From the first edition of the comic book *Thun'da*.)

with them. In fact, that was one of my aspirations as a kid. To be an artist and possibly do a Tarzan strip—Oh *boy!* I think it was my dream. And it seems the Burroughs people were never particularly interested. Somehow they never wanted me even though the Frazetta fans were out there plugging away. But they were never interested in it until it was too late. When I finally went on to other things, *then* they suddenly decided they'd do me a big favor and I had to say 'no way.' It was too late, I'd really lost interest. That was the story."[4]

Lancer paperbacks, who planned to publish *Conan*, the heroic fantasy epic of Robert E. Howard, hired Frazetta to illustrate the covers. The books sold more than ten million copies, and many readers bought them just for the cover art. This established Frazetta as a master of sword and sorcery, and led to a painting career. "The minute I discovered another publisher, like Lancer, and they offered me a little more, and more important, a little appreciation, plus I kept the original— BONGO!—I mean my work was suddenly a thousand times better. See, I always had ways of working so that anything I

did would reproduce just dandy, just fine, more than adequate, no matter what the price. But for Lancer, now I started to handle the work with love, because it was *my* art, and I began to really pull out all the stops and do what I was capable of doing. But people see it as some kind of evolution. It's not so, I mean I could show you work that preceded the Ace covers that I did for myself that was far superior. Like the Buck Rogers painting, for instance. And the lion painting—that was done before any Ace cover and that's in league with the stuff I did later.

"...Covers at a certain stage were easier. After all, you sat there and devoted all your energies to creating *one* picture, *a* painting. Whereas a strip is an awful lot of work with a certain sacrifice of quality because you just don't have the time. But it's fun too. A lot of fun. I love telling stories and moving figures from panel to panel, but again, it didn't pay very well then. You could starve to death. But with a cover, suddenly you're noticed overnight, it's such an easy way for an artist to go. You have to remember, even when I was doing comics as a child, telling stories, every once in a while I'd sit down and do a *painting, one* picture that said it all: and I liked *both*. If you ask me if I prefer to paint color or use the black and white media, I *love* black and white, really love it every bit as much. But when you weigh the two it seems that people are just overwhelmed by a full-color painting rather than a black and white drawing, even when the drawing is better. And I guess basically I want the greatest possible reaction. But I will always do black and white drawings because it's *fun*, it's relaxing. Sometimes you don't know yourself what's going to pop out. But basically it's just drawing and design. Now with the other thing you have lighting, color, a few things that make it more difficult."[4]

Because Frazetta's covers sold books, he became more selective about projects he undertook, and also started to retain ownership of all his original art, allowing only first printing rights. His wife Ellie became his business manager and started a publishing venture which distributed Frazetta's signed reproductions, posters and annual calendars. A friend of the couple recalled: "Ellie set a precedent. She protects his work and gets it back from the companies. He was pretty bitter when his early Burroughs covers that were bought for two hundred fifty dollars were resold for five hundred, and then sold again, and so on. It got him. He took one Burroughs cover in to the publisher, who said he was going to keep it, and Frank said he wanted to take it home and touch it up. Then he did a quick rough overnight and handed that in. Ha. He's a street-tough Brooklyn guy from Sheepshead Bay, and it shows. You know: Catholic family, Italian cooking, good smells. But he's completely out of this world. Until recently, few people beyond fantasy collectors knew his work. But he has won some medals as an illustrator and is becoming recognized. He's an incredibly good-looking man and quite a womanizer. I mean, he and some of his buddies would see a girl coming down the street and he'd stop his pals at a window. 'I want to meet this girl!' And she'd walk by, Frank eating her up, and the guys

Frazetta's "Spaceman," circa 1973, echoes his Buck Rogers drawings.

would watch. 'She's a *dog,* Frank!' 'No, no, those ankles, that arm, look at *that neck!'* he'd see something in her, but a dog, you know?...He has done some of his best paintings in forty-eight hours; he uses fast-drying oils, sometimes delivers covers that are still tacky. 'Don't touch it; it just landed.' Today, he's a family man, with a close, loving exchange with his wife. She's a woman of strong opinions—she's not swallowed up by her husband, nor he by her. She's very out front about prices, won't come down. And no compromise; Frank owns everything he does. And it's paying because the *big* breakthrough has been these portfolios and calendars on art racks everywhere. Success comes to deserving people."[1]

1971. Moved to the Pocono Mountains in East Stroudsburg, Pennsylvania, where he devoted himself to painting. "I have to be restrained. Subtle, somber. I'm not a great painter. I know mood and action and concept. It's action that makes the thing erotic, it's the fluid movement of the woman, not the proportions. I love people, I love form, I got to paint lovable monsters, not too much blood, lots of humor, women cute and pudgy. I'm not going to do the great Roman era, I don't have the heart. When I become a bore, I change. I have the freedom now to do whatever I want. No profound message. Just some fine art."[1]

Working from imagination rather than from research, Frazetta paints quickly in oil without any reference other than a mirror he keeps at his side to "check out things. I rely on my concept of how things move rather than look. That's why I don't use photos for reference. Photos distort reality more than I do when they freeze an action and explain nothing about that action [such as] where and how it started, where and how it will end. What's more, I don't want to become a slave to the 'real,' the accurate. I don't want to record history, and I certainly don't paint to capture *realism.* I paint the dramatic, the erotic, the romantic. And I can only do that by painting from imagination, by forcing the figure into extreme actions to achieve drama and impact."[2]

"...I think all these young artists who are imitating me are missing the trick. They don't see I'm just being me.

"I'm very physical minded. Brain, fine, but this body is put here for use. If *anybody* could jump around like my heroes, it's me. Not many artists are physical types. I've been jumped on by twenty guys in a movie theater and got out alive. In Brooklyn I *knew* Conan, I knew guys just like him.

"...I carry around a picture in my dreams I'd like to do...*wolves* out in Kansas. Realistic, but just a touch of Frazetta, *creatures* of the night. I hope to paint it. It would be fine art, I guess.

"I had a few years in the late sixties when I went blah, everything cute and show-offy, too deliberate. I have to work from the unconscious, not too unconscious, but just let the brush start pulling things out I didn't know were in there, use accidents, and go with a focal point, and taste, instinct, without being muddled, just flow over the canvas board, follow the mood, the rhythms. I always do best on departures—something new—the first three or four Conans, *fresh! Silver Warrior* with the polar bears: that's new, that's crazy—love it! *The Sea Witch*—something different, a departure. I think of Hal Foster doing Prince Valiant year in, year out—a great artist—but I couldn't do it. His early work, the Tarzans, the early Prince Valiant, beautiful! brilliant! too many virtues to name. Me, I want new characters, new action, new blood."[1]

Frazetta also referred to his "doodlebooks," filled with sketches in black ink or pencil sometimes with a color wash that might

"The Indian Brave," painting by Frazetta.

later be united in a major painting. "...When you really get down to it I guess the drawing and the doodling, the relaxing fun, are really a sort of preparation. I mean I like the fun but I like the powerful things too. But that doesn't just happen. You have to think, and plan, and work and change and develop. In the end I guess you have to kind of get out of your own way and let the painting speak for itself."[4]

About inspiration and influences, Frazetta said: "'King Kong,' of course, was one of the great influences in my life and in many artists' lives. And then the old monster movies, like the early 'Frankenstein' films, had that magic and mood.

"It has an old-fashioned flavor and a lot of pizazz. It's like my work! It's rugged and primitive and hopefully, very exciting."[5]

"[And also] Howard Pyle maybe, the father of American illustration. His student, N. C. Wyeth, was shallow by comparison. My main influences are the countless European illustrators. There's a fine line between illustration and fine art. I give more of a fine-art approach with a beginning, a middle and an end. You don't really tire of my stuff. Years go by and they don't fade a bit in interest. To me, people are more terrifying than grass and rocks, which don't move me. I can't do what Andrew Wyeth does. I want *feelings*. My fine-arts background, eight years of it, it had nothing to do with the fantastic stuff I do now. My illustrations pop out of my head. Sometimes I only *lure* you into the text and the painting—I literally leave the text unillustrated. To hell with what's expected. I'd be less restrained than anyone before me. I pulled the frustration out of current illustration....But I have a fire I haven't tapped out of sheer laziness. One painting, 'Downward to Earth,' very strange painting, very surreal, I went all out surreal, total barrage—*what's he doing?*—it won an award! The snobs gave me an award. They've been educated to think there's only one school of Art. They forget Rubens and Michelangelo's superheroic figures, but because mine aren't religious...."[1]

"I love the Old Masters for their unquestionable abilities in composition and draftmanship, but they were reserved, restrained by their time. I love the Impressionists for their color and daring. They were obviously less restrained. Today there's *no* restraint, and I'd be a fool to restrict myself in any way to please fans, critics, or peers. I'm an artist of my time; that's the only thing I can be. I find barns boring, so why paint barns? Barns already exist. They don't need me to create them. What I do create *doesn't* exist, and to me that's...more exciting!

"The intellectual proprieties have been ruling art for thirty-five years. Here is the whole irrational boiling away underneath—the id, the red-eyed animal. Nobody's touching it. So it's left to the illustrators to be the vanguard of the unconscious, people with animal powers. God, look at the record jackets! Innately talented artists from universities have been intimidated and steered into fine arts, fearful of leaving their unconscious out of the box—so we *have* to go to the illustrators. The most really interesting stuff today is in unserious art. A lot of it's junk. But look what the twelve-tone music did, the devitalization it brought. Most rock is junk, but whatever *is* powerful is likely to be found there. The commercial arts are now a good decade ahead of the intellectuals, a submerged, turbulent river, ready to break out."[2]

Frazetta's paintings, which have attained critical acclaim, also appeared on posters for such movies as "After the Fox," "The Fearless Vampire Killers," and Clint Eastwood's "The Gauntlet." He also did promotional pieces for ABC's "Battlestar Galactica."

(From *The Silver Warrior* by Michael Moorcock. Illustrated by Frank Frazetta.)

During the summer of **1980,** he became involved in an animated film drawn in the spirit of his pen and ink art. The film was released in 1983 as "Fire and Ice." "The inspiration, the fire, had gone out of me. I was sitting around, resting on my laurels and doing the same thing over and over. I needed a challenge. That's when I made up my mind that I was going to Hollywood to make a movie, although I didn't know how, when or with whom."[6]

"...I've had a number of calls to get involved with films in some capacity or other, either as visual consultant or art director and I considered them. But Ralph [Bakshi, director of 'Fire and Ice'] came out and offered me a 50-50 deal, which is quite another story.

"We co-produced and when I say that I mean we *co*- produced. I did a minimum of drawing, but I did a lot of teaching. I taught the animators how to draw like Frazetta, from the background artists right on down to the figure artists and the colorists. I also worked with the actors and the stuntmen and told them how I wanted them to move and look. I designed the costumes, put on makeup and directed in part with Ralph, and he's a real strong director."[5]

Scenes from the film were first shot with live actors, and rotoscoped by animators to be used as a guide. "The masters all used models. If that isn't a form of rotoscoping, I don't know what is. We're going far beyond the mere duplication of actors on film in this picture. You can't imagine how much

(From the full-length animated movie ''Fire and Ice.'' Co-produced by Frazetta and Ralph Bakshi, 1983.)

we change the live action footage—everything from the flow of the hair, to the placement of an arm or leg, to adding curves or musculature. What we're doing here is pure art. It really is.

''There are limitations, of course. You can't recreate light and shadow like in a fully-rendered painting, unless you have forty years to play with it. We've got 70,000 frames in the film. If I lived to be a thousand, I couldn't paint that many frames. But we've got some techniques in 'Fire and Ice'—approaches to color and movement and character design—that more than compensate for the limitations. You won't miss the light and shadow.''[6]

''Many people came down to see what Ralph was doing and they were very skeptical. 'You're going to do Frazetta. Ha. Ha.' But they were really shocked at how beautiful the work looked. It's quite a first, I think. Some of the artists at Ralph's studio didn't see how it was possible and I guess I encouraged them to reach out and they pretty much surprised themselves with their growth in that period of time. They all learned to draw far better. They learned to paint better and to understand what I was doing in my work. It's incredible. . . .

''I had a number of paintings that fit in. These would be the more primitive of my paintings, the ones with Neanderthals and monkeys to represent the villains and of course, my constant primitive girl, whom I've done a number of times, like in the Pellucidar series, with the black hair and scanty outfits.

''The hero is not very different than my barbarians or my lighter heroes with blond hair; the scrappy but vulnerable hero type. And then there's a second hero, the real standard type not unlike Conan. There are also witches, sorcerers, madmen, wicked queens, ogres, reptiles and wolves. There's everything.

''It is an adult film, not a kiddie film. Certainly, it's visually beautiful and kids should love it to death, and it has enough fast power that everybody should have a good time. It's not a hokey little animated film; it's quite a dazzling film. . . .''[5]

''Unlike some artists, my goal was to captivate a larger audience without any sacrifice in artistic quality.''

FOOTNOTE SOURCES

[1]Donald Newlove, ''The Incredible Paintings of Frank Frazetta,'' *Esquire,* June, 1977.

[2]Nick Miglin, ''Frank Frazetta at Bat,'' *American Artist,* May, 1976.

[3]Betty Ballantine, editor, *Frank Frazetta: Book Two,* Bantam, 1977.

[4]B. Ballantine, editor, *Frank Frazetta: Book Five,* Bantam, 1985.

[5]James Van Hise, ''Frank Frazetta,'' *Comics Scene,* May, 1983.

[6]Kyle Counts, '' 'Fire and Ice,' '' *Cinefantastique,* December, 1981.

FOR MORE INFORMATION SEE:

Fred Nardelli, *Frank Frazetta Index,* Nardelli, 1975.

William Stout, "The Movie Poster Art of Frank Frazetta," *Fanfare*, winter, 1978.

Maurice Horn, editor, *The World of Encyclopedia of Comics*, Chelsea House/Gale, 1980.

"Spectrum: Frazetta," *Questar*, October, 1980.

Guy Delcourt, "Films au Futur: 'Fire and Ice,'" *L'ecran Fantastique* (France), May, 1982.

Kyle Counts, "'Fire and Ice,'" *Cinefantastique*, July/August, 1982.

Cinema (France), May, 1983.

Harry Haun, "'Fire and Ice'—a Brutal Fantasy," *New York Daily News*, November, 23, 1983.

Walt Reed and Roger Reed, *The Illustrator in America 1880-1980: A Century of Illustration*, Madison Square Press, 1984.

Denis Gifford, *The International Book of Comics*, Crescent Books, 1984.

L. W. Wagner, "Heroic Fantasies of Frank Frazetta," *Philadelphia Inquirer*, May 26, 1985.

Chris Henderson, "One Hundred Most Important People in Science Fiction/Fantasy: Frank Frazetta," *Starlog*, November, 1985.

Ron Goulart, *The Great Comic Book Artists*, St. Martin's, 1986.

Jack Sullivan, *The Penguin Encyclopedia of Horror and Supernatural*, Viking, 1986.

FREEMAN, William Bradford   1938-
(Bill Freeman)

PERSONAL: Born October 21, 1938, in London, Ontario, Canada; son of Arthur MacDonald (a teacher and politician) and Margaret Elizabeth (a teacher; maiden name, Graham) Freeman; married Marsha Hewitt (an author and teacher); children: Erik, Peggy, Jessica. *Education:* Acadia University, B.A., 1964; McMaster University, M.A., 1970, Ph.D., 1979. *Home:* 16 Third St., Ward's Island, Toronto, Ontario, Canada M5J 2B2.

CAREER: Writer. Has worked as a probation officer, 1964-68, a lecturer at McMaster University, Hamilton, Canada, a

WILLIAM BRADFORD FREEMAN

sociologist at Vanier College, Montreal, Quebec, Canada, and is presently a limited market dealer for Third Street Funding (his own company). *Member:* Writers Union (Canada), Montreal Citizens Movement. *Awards, honors:* Canada Council Children's Literature Prize, 1976, for *Shantymen of Cache Lake;* Vicky Metcalf Award from the Canadian Author's Association, 1984, for his body of work in the field of juvenile fiction.

WRITINGS:

JUVENILE; UNDER NAME BILL FREEMAN

Shantymen of Cache Lake, Lorimer, 1975.
The Last Voyage of the Scotian, Lorimer, 1976.
First Spring on the Grand Banks, Lorimer, 1978.
Cedric and the North End Kids (illustrated with photographs by Lutz Dille), Lorimer, 1978.
Trouble at Lachine Mill, Lorimer, 1983.
The Harbour Thieves, Lorimer, 1984.
Danger on the Tracks, Lorimer, 1987.

ADULT; UNDER NAME BILL FREEMAN

(Editor, with wife, Marsha Hewitt) *Their Town: The Mafia, the Media, and the Party Machine,* Lorimer, 1979.
1005: Political Life in a Union Local, Lorimer, 1982.

PLAYS

"Ghosts of the Madawaska," first produced in Ottawa, Canada, at the Great Canadian Theatre Company, December, 1985.
"Glorydays," first produced in Hamilton, Ontario, Canada, at Theatre Aquarius, September, 1988.

Shantymen of Cache Lake and *Last Voyage of the Scotian* have been translated into French.

ADAPTATIONS:

"Shantymen of Cache Lake" (play), produced in Canada.

SIDELIGHTS: Freeman was born in London, Ontario, in 1938. His father was a high school teacher and part-time politician and actor; the children were included in political discussions and encouraged to defend their opinions. His mother, also a teacher, passed on a strong sense of history to her family.

Although his family encouraged education, Freeman became disenchanted with school and dropped out in his senior year of high school. He lived in England for three years, and met a group of people who were interested in the arts. This new group of friends inspired him to write in earnest, although his first novel for children was not published until many years later. "When I was a kid I was interested in everything—sports, books, movies, you name it, everything but school."

Freeman grew tired of the unsettled life and returned to Canada, where he entered Acadia University in New Brunswick and studied politics and sociology. Later, he entered the doctoral program at McMaster University in Hamilton. "I studied enough to get a Ph.D. in sociology, but my passion has always been books and politics." Research for his doctoral thesis on local politics and organized crime led to the publication of his first non-fiction book, *Their Town.*

Although he had written stories in high school, it wasn't until 1975 that his first adventure story for Canadian children was published. For several years Freeman developed a successful series of historical novels, for readers from nine to thirteen, about the adventures of the Bains children, a family without a father living in the 1870s. While following the adventures of the resourceful Bains chlidren, his readers get a lot of information about life in Canada during that period. "I became a writer because books have always been important to me. I wanted to write historical novels for young people about the *real* Canada—realistic books describing life the way it really was. I started out to do that over fifteen years ago, and I'm not finished yet."

FOR MORE INFORMATION SEE:

Irma McDonough, editor, *Profiles 2*, Canadian Library Association, 1982.

Joan McGrath, "Freeman and Crook Offer Adventure and Mystery in Serial Form," *Books for Young Readers*, April, 1987.

GAGNON, Cecile 1936-

PERSONAL: Born January 1, 1936, in Quebec, Canada; daughter of Onesime (a lawyer) and Cecile Desautels; married Michel Bergeron (a medical research doctor), August 31, 1963; children: Nicolas, Emmanuelle. *Education:* Laval University, B.A., 1956; attended Boston University, School of Fine and Applied Arts, 1956-59, Ecole Nationale Superieure des Arts Decoratifs, Paris, 1958-59, and Ecole du Louvre, Paris, 1960-61. *Home and office:* 12 avenue de la Brunante, Montreal, Quebec, Canada H3T 1R4.

CAREER: Writer, illustrator and editor. Consultant for Office of the Commissioner for Official Languages, Ottawa, Canada, 1979; chief editor of *Passe-Partout* (magazine for children),

1980; director of Brindille Collection, Heritage Publishers, 1980; chief of children's publications, Pierre Tisseyre Publishers, Montreal, 1982—; director of *Coulicou* (magazine for children), 1983. *Member:* Communication-Jeunesse (president, 1977-79), Union des Ecrivains Quebecois, International Board on Books for Young People (Canada). *Awards, honors:* Grand Jury of Letters Prize, Montreal, 1962, for *La peche a l'horizon;* Award of Merit from the Foire International de Leipzig, and named a Notable Canadian Children's Book, both 1964, both for *O Canada!;* Province of Quebec Literary Prize, 1970, for *Martine-aux-oiseaux;* Raymond-Beauchemin Prize from the Association of Canadian Teachers of French, 1980, for *Alfred dans le metro,* and 1985, for *L'ascenseur d'Adrien.*

WRITINGS:

La peche a l'horizon (title means "Fishing for the Horizon"; self-illustrated), Editions du Pelican, 1959.

Martine-aux-oiseaux (title means "Martine of the Birds"; self-illustrated), Editions du Pelican, 1964.

(Editor) Micheline Desjardins, *Initiation a la geographie urbaine* (title means "Initiation to Urban Geography"), Holt, 1970.

Le voyage d'un cerf-volant (title means "The Journey of a Kite"; self-illustrated), Editions Heritage, 1972.

Le voilier et la lune (title means "The Sailboat and the Moon;" self-illustrated), Editions Heritage, 1972.

Trefle et Tournesol (title means "Clover and Sunflower"; self-illustrated), Editions Heritage, 1972.

La marmotte endormie (title means "The Sleeping Groundhog"; self-illustrated), Editions Heritage, 1972.

La journee d'un chapeau de paille (title means "A Straw Hat's Day"; self-illustrated), Editions Heritage, 1972.

CECILE GAGNON

La bergere et l'orange (title means "The Shepherdess and the Orange"; self-illustrated), Editions Heritage, 1972.

Plumeneige (self-illustrated), Editions Heritage, 1976, translated by Valerie Hepburn Craig, published as *Snowfeather* James Lorimer, 1981.

L'Epouvantail et le champignon (title means "The Scarecrow and the Mushroom"; self-illustrated), Editions Heritage, 1978.

Le paraplui rouge (title means "The Red Umbrella"; self-illustrated), Editions Heritage, 1979.

La chemise qui s'ennuyait (title means "The Lonesome Shirt"; self-illustrated), Editions Heritage, 1979.

Les boutons perdus (title means "The Lost Buttons"; self-illustrated), Editions Heritage, 1979.

Lucienne (illustrated by Fernande Lefebvre), Editions Heritage, 1980.

L'edredon de minuit (title means "The Christmas Comforter"; self-illustrated), Editions Heritage, 1980.

Une nuit chez le lievre (title means "Overnight at the Hare's"; illustrated by Jean-Christian Knaff), Editions Heritage, 1980.

Alfred dans le metro (title means "Alfred in the Subway"; self-illustrated), Editions Heritage, 1980, another edition illustrated by Louise Blanchard, Editions Heritage, 1983.

Le pierrot de Monsieur Autrefois (title means "Mr. Yesterday's Puppet"; illustrated by Josee La Perriere), Editions Mondia, 1981.

Les Malurons, (three books; self-illustrated), Centre Educatif et Culturel, 1981.

Les lunettes de Sophie (title means "Sophie's Eyeglasses"; illustrated by J. L. Perriere), Editions Projets, 1981.

Toudou est malade (title means "Toudou Is Sick"; illustrated by J. C. Knaff), Editions Projets, 1981.

Le roi sans royaume, Editions Projets, 1981.

Zoum et le monstre (title means "Zoom and the Monster"; illustrated by J. L. Perriere), Editions Projets, 1981.

Le roi de Novilande (title means "The King of Everything New"; illustrated by Darcia Labrosse), Editions Pierre Tisseyre, 1981.

Ble d'inde, le lutin (title means "The Corn Elf"; illustrated by Robert Bigras), Editions Heritage, 1981.

Johanne du Quebec (title means "Johanna from Quebec"), Editions Flammarion, 1982.

La vache et d'autres animaux (title means "Cows and Other Animals"), Editions La Courte Echelle, 1982.

Histoire d'Adele Viau et de Fabien Petit (title means "The Story of Amy Green and Jonathan Small"; illustrated by D. Labrosse), Editions Pierre Tisseyre, 1982.

La boule verte (title means "The Green Ball"; illustrated by Martine Bouree), Editions Flammarion, 1982.

Pourquoi les moutons frisent (title means "Why Do Sheep Have Curly Hair"; illustrated by Suzanne Duquet), Editions Pierre Tisseyre, 1982.

Plumeneige, Album (title means "Snowfeather Album"; illustrated by Suzanne Duranceau), Editions Heritage, 1983.

Une grosse pierre (title means "A Big Rock"), Editions Heritage, 1983.

La maison Miousse (title means "The Miousse House"), Editions de l'Amitie, 1983.

Surprises et Sortileges (title means "Surprises and Magic"), Editions Pierre Tisseyre, 1983.

J'invente une histoire, Editions Heritage, 1983.

Operation Marmotte, Editions Heritage, 1985.

Bonjour l'Arbre, Editions du Raton Laveur, 1985.

J'ai chaud!, Editions du Raton Laveur, 1986.

J'ai faim!, Editions du Raton Laveur, 1986.

L'ascenseur d'Adrien, Editions Heritage, 1986.

Le Lutin sans nom, Editions Passe-Partout, 1986.

Les Cachemires, Editions Passe-Partout, 1986.

No one in Europe knew about North and South America or the Pacific Ocean. ■ (From *O Canada!* by Isabel Barclay. Illustrated by Cecile Gagnon.)

L'Oiseau-Vent, La mere des Aigles, Messidor, 1987.

Moi, j'ai rendez-vous avec Daphne, Editions Heritage, 1987.

Un chien, un velo et des pizzas, Editions Quebec-Amerique, 1987.

Chateaux de sable, Editions Pierre Tisseyre, 1988.

Doux avec des etoiles, Editions Pierre Tisseyre, 1988.

Le royaume de la nuit, Editions du Sorbier, 1988.

Le nouveau logis, Editions du Raton Laveur, 1988.

ILLUSTRATOR

Monique Corriveau, *Le secret de Vanille* (title means "Vanilla's Secret"), Editions du Pelican, 1958.

Les extravagances de Ti-Jean, Beauchemin, 1963.

Pipandor, Editions Jeunesse, 1963.

Kilucru, Beauchemin, 1963.

Helene Boulle, Editions Jeunesse, 1964.

Isabel Barclay, *O Canada!,* Doubleday, 1964.

La tulipe blanche (title means "The White Tulip"), Editions de l'amitie, 1967.

Marmitons (title means "Little Cooks"), Editions Jeunesse, 1971.

Romulo sur les Ailes de l'Esperance (title means "Romulo on the Wings of Hope"), Editions du Jour, 1973.

Au jardin de Pierrot, Volumes 2 and 3 (title means "In Pierrot's Garden"), Editions Heritage and Radio-Canada, 1974-76.

Le voilier et la lune (title means "The Sailboat and the Moon"), Editions Heritage, 1972.

The Story of Canada, Pagurian, 1974.

(From *Histoire d' Adele Viau et de Fabien Petit* by Cecile Gagnon. Illustrated by Darcia Labrosse.)

Autour de moi (title means "Around Me"), Centre Educatif et Culturel, 1977.
Goute a tout (title means "Taste All"), Editions Fides, 1978.
Moi et les Miens (title means "Me and My Friends"), Centre Educatif et Culturel, 1978.
Henriette Major, *Kapuk*, Editions Heritage, 1979.
H. Major, *Doudou et les assiettes* (title means "Doudou and the Plates"), Editions Heritage, 1979.
H. Major, *Les 5 freres* (title means "The Five Brothers"), Editions Heritage, 1979.

Contributor to *Lurelu, Hibou, Francofonia, Yakari, Jeunes Annees, Toupie, Toboggan, T'aime Lire,* and *IBBY* Newsletter.

ADAPTATIONS:

"Barnabe les Bottines" (puppet play; based on *Le roi de Novilande*), first performed at Theatre de l'Avant-Pays, Montreal, December, 1983.

WORK IN PROGRESS: Research on North American Indian tales and myths; a series of short texts for small children with a racoon called Miousse as the main character; an historical novel of the period 1895-1920.

SIDELIGHTS: "I am interested in all aspects of creativity, especially in children. I look for creative people and I try to teach youngsters to become creative.

"Concerning my work I must say that my studies in art have helped me enormously in the course of my 'career.' It was in art school that I learned to LOOK and OBSERVE things: people, objects, animals, and environment. After that I spent three years in Paris working with a noted animator (Arno Stern) in his children's workshop (Academie du Jeudi) where I started undoing all I had learned, working the other way, i.e. helping young people find a way with pencil, brush, and colour to express their self as opposed to learning 'how to.'

"Later I started thinking about words as a means of expression. I began inventing stories in words and pictures. Finally I turned all my energy to writing.

"I became president of a group called Communication-Jeunesse whose aim is to promote children's books written in French (in Quebec) in every possible way and place: bookstores, libraries, schools, cultural centers, etc. That prompted trips lecturing or putting up book exhibits and meeting with children or attending book fairs. I travelled throughout Canada, in the United States and Mexico, and in Europe: France, Italy and Switzerland. I lectured in many universities and for school teachers' or librarians' conventions and seminars.

"I also edited a magazine for four-year-olds for the Ministry of Education, wrote various reading material (French) for first, second and third grades and am now co-director of a privately-owned children's magazine for four to eight-year-olds called *Coulicou*.

"What I prize most of all are the meetings with children that I still maintain today in spite of a hectic schedule. During those visits I try to show elementary grade students that writing books is fabulous and inventing stories is a fascinating game that everyone can try. We often invent stories in five minutes that could become best sellers!

"Since I speak French, English, and Italian fluently, I try to visit children wherever I travel. I am at present working on a project to experiment creativity with children in Italy at a school in Siena.

"One of my stories *Plumeneige* was translated into English in Canada and one of my favorite books *Le roi de Novilande* has been transformed into a puppet play by a professional puppet troup in Montreal under the name 'Barnabe les Bottines.'

"I think that writing for children is great but also very, very demanding. To write for children one must be *true*, have mountains of feelings and emotions about things and always be on the side of children, never on the side of adults and grownups 'who know.' Humour is a must. All this means that writing for children is difficult in spite of what is generally thought, and I love Isaac Bashevis Singer for saying that he wrote for the young because only they '. . .still believe in God, the family, angels, devils, witches, goblins, logic, clarity, punctuation and other such obsolete stuff.'

"In the long run I think that the old tales of yesteryear are still the best literature of all. I still do a lot of research on folk and popular tales from early days in French Canada and from the North American Indians: many of my adaptations have been published in magazines in Canada and in Europe."

FOR MORE INFORMATION SEE:

Le Canada francais et sa litterature de jeunesse, Editions CRP, 1981.

GELMAN, Jan 1963-

PERSONAL: Born November 14, 1963, in New York, N.Y.; daughter of Steve Murray (an editor) and Rita (a writer; maiden name, Golden) Gelman. *Education:* University of Colorado, B.S. 1985. *Agent:* Marilyn Marlow, Curtis Brown, 10 Astor Pl., New York, N.Y. 10003.

CAREER: Free-lance writer, 1981—; *Campus Press*, Boulder, Colo., photographer, 1983-84; *Longmont Times Call*, Longmont, Colo., intern writer and photographer, 1984; *Vail Trail*, Vail, Colo., editor and writer, 1987—. *Member:* Society of Children's Book Writers.

WRITINGS:

Summer in the Sun, Archway, 1983.
Boys! Boys! Boys!, Archway, 1983.
Faraway Loves, Archway, 1984.
Take a Chance on Love, Archway, 1984.

JAN GELMAN

Lots of Boys!, Archway, 1985.
Seven-Boy Vacation, Archway, 1986.
Marci's Secret Book of Flirting—Don't Go Out without It, Knopf, 1989.

Contributor of articles to periodicals, including *Sport Style* and *Vail*.

SIDELIGHTS: "I was born and raised in Greenwich Village, New York. At age twelve my family uprooted and headed west to Los Angeles, California, where I experienced culture shock.

"Eventually, I grew to love the bee-bop, beachy lifestyle that I was strewn into and I stored my other lifestyle in the back of my mind. These teenage years were very impressionable to me and I remember them vividly. It is for this reason that I've devoted my book writing to the young adult level, using personal experiences and familiar personalities as the basis for my books.

"The diversity of growing up in a city and a suburb has broadened my horizons and opened a large field of ideas for my writing. My interest in people has led me to an unending desire to travel and learn about different cultures and languages.

"I took a semester off during college and traveled with a friend through Europe in hopes to fulfill this desire. It only expanded it. I have since traveled to Central America, South America, Mexico and more. I have been living in Boulder, and Vail, Colorado for six years, loving the mountains and small town ambiance.

"My interest in writing stemmed from growing up in a family of jouralists including my parents and my brother. For years I submerged my interest in writing because I wanted to be different. 'Are you going to be a writer just like your mother and father?' was a question I loathed.

"But when I left home for college, my interest overrode my stubborn independence and I took a step into the writing world. With my mother's guidance, I published my first book when I was eighteen years old. From there, I continued writing books and have further expanded my career to include newspaper and magazine journalism.

"Currently, I am working as an editor for the entertainment and feature section of a weekly newspaper in Vail, Colorado. I am organizing, writing, editing and laying out the work in my search to learn more about the field. I am concurrently finishing up my latest young adult book and I see only expansion in my future as a journalist."

HOBBIES AND OTHER INTERESTS: Skiing, volleyball, photography, traveling.

GILMAN, Phoebe   1940-

PERSONAL: Born April 4, 1940, in New York, N.Y.; immigrated to Canada, 1972; daughter of John (a salesman) and Hannah (Slatoff) Gilman; married Mani Deligtisch (divorced); married Brian Bender (a computer consultant); children: Ingrid, Melissa. *Education:* Attended Art Student's League, and Hunter College, 1957-59; studied under Ernst Fuchs at Bezalel

PHOEBE GILMAN

Academy, Jerusalem, Israel, 1968. *Religion:* Jewish. *Home:* 30 Edgemore Dr., Toronto, Ontario M8Y 2N2, Canada. *Agent:* Nancy Colbert, 303 Davenport Rd., Toronto, Ontario, Canada M5R 1K5.

CAREER: Free-lance artist, author and illustrator, 1967—; Ontario College of Art, Canada, fine arts instructor, 1975—. *Exhibitions:* Le Theatre du P'tit Bonheur, Toronto, Canada, 1973; Galerie Heritage, Toronto, 1974, Prince Arthur Gallery, Toronto, 1982. *Member:* Canadian Society of Children's Authors, Illustrators, and Performers; Canadian Children's Book Centre, Canadian Writers' Union. *Awards, honors:* Merit Award from the Art Directors Club of Toronto, 1984, and exhibited at the Bologna International Children's Book Fair, 1985, both for *The Balloon Tree*.

WRITINGS:

SELF-ILLUSTRATED

The Balloon Tree, North Winds Press, 1984.
Jillian Jiggs, Scholastic-TAB, 1985, Scholastic, 1988.
Little Blue Ben, North Winds Press, 1986.
The Wonderful Pigs of Jillian Jiggs, Scholastic-TAB, 1988.

WORK IN PROGRESS: Grandma and the Pirates, a picture book, to be published by Scholastic.

SIDELIGHTS: "When I was growing up, my closest friend was my cousin Joel. We were both considered a bit weird by other children. We used to have our 'favorite spot'; a secluded area, under the willow trees that grew on the banks of the Jerome Reservoir in the Bronx. We went there to draw pictures and write stories. I remember the conflict I felt about being considered 'different.' These days, it's an enjoyable feeling, back then it wasn't. Incidentally, Joel grew up to be a writer, too."

Years later, "on the way home from spending the day at the zoo, my daughter, Ingrid, accidentally let go of the helium balloon we had bought as a souvenir. Helplessly, we watched as it floated up and up and up only to get caught on a branch of a tree.

"As I searched for a way to retrieve her treasure, I couldn't help noticing the remnants of many more balloons which had met similar fates. How I wished that tree would sprout balloons which would then drop magically into the waiting arms of all the children who had been similarly disappointed.

"That was the beginning of the idea for *The Balloon Tree.* It was to take fifteen years of writing and re-writing until the story reached its final form.

"First I tried it out with an old king as the hero. He was too grumpy. Then I tried a magical balloon man. He was too tricky. Then I tried a dragon too contrived and besides there were too many dragon stories around. Next, I tried a young prince. This nearly worked...until I asked my youngest daughter, Melissa, if she would mind dressing up as a prince and posing for the illustrations of the book. She did mind. Very much. At last, I thought of a young Princess. That was just right, except for her name which used to be Penelope. It only took fifty or sixty more re-writes to reach the version of the story which was printed.

"These days, the stories seem to be tumbling out faster and easier. It must be all the practice I had writing and re-writing *The Balloon Tree.*"[1]

"About *Jillian Jiggs:* she is me. I'm terribly messy. When you are creating something, you can't stop to clean up all the time. You get caught in the urgency of what you're doing. The idea came from a Mother Goose rhyme: 'Gregory Griggs, Gregory Griggs, had twenty-seven kinds of wigs.' When I began, it was about Gregory Griggs, a boy who turns everything around him into a wig. I wasn't very far into the story when I decided I'd be more comfortable if Gregory was a girl. Searching for a similar three syllable girl's name, I came up with Gillian. So I dropped the 'R' from Griggs and Gillian Giggs was born. Once she was out on paper, she took over; changed the spelling of her name and decided not to limit herself to wigs but to turn everything into costumes and mini-theatricals as well. Like myself, she has trouble knowing when to stop. She gets carried away. When I am in the middle of working on something, everything else has to—JUST HAS TO—be done 'later'. . .whenever that is.

"As my daughter Melissa moaned the other day, 'Mom, you're *always* working on *something.*'

"A book can be a true friend, a source of pleasure and companionship, a re-affirmation of the joys and difficulties of being human.

"Now that my own books are being published, I can be a friend to thousands of children. Perhaps I can be a child's introduction to a love of books which will last a lifetime."

FOOTNOTE SOURCES

¹"Phoebe Gilman: *The Balloon Tree,*" *Our Choice/Your Choice,* 1985-86. Amended by P. Gilman.

GONDOSCH, Linda   1944-

PERSONAL: Born October 25, 1944, in Hinton, W. Va.; daughter of Edgar Vernon (a railroad telegrapher) and Mary Pauline (a homemaker; maiden name, Ellison) Wicker; married Werner Gondosch (a chemical engineer), September 4, 1965; children: Lisa, Stephen, Amy, Katherine. *Education:* Ohio University, B.S. (with honors), 1966; Northern Kentucky University, M.A., 1986. *Religion:* Methodist. *Home and office:* 1020 Fairview Dr., Lawrenceburg, Ind. 47025.

LINDA GONDOSCH

CAREER: South Dearborn High School, Aurora, Ind., English teacher, 1982-83; free-lance author, 1984—. Visiting author/lecturer at schools and libraries. Cub Scout leader, Sunday school teacher and secretary to Pastor/Parish Relations committee at Methodist Church, member of local community theater, the Riverton Players. *Member:* Society of Children's Book Writers, National Association for Young Writers, Children's Authors and Illustrators Critique Group, Laubach Literary Action, Hoosier Hills Adult Literacy League. *Awards, honors:* Kentucky Bluegrass Award from Northern Kentucky University, 1988, for *Who Needs a Bratty Brother?*

WRITINGS:

The Strawberryland Choo-Choo (illustrated by Pat Sustendal), Parker Bros., 1984.
Who Needs a Bratty Brother? (illustrated by Helen Coganch-erry), Lodestar, 1985.
The Witches of Hopper Street (sequel to *Who Needs a Bratty Brother?;* illustrated by H. Cogancherry), Lodestar, 1986.
Who's Afraid of Haggerty House? (sequel to *The Witches of Hopper Street;* illustrated by H. Cogancherry), Lodestar, 1987.
The Monsters of Marble Avenue (illustrated by Cat Bowman Smith), Little, Brown, 1988.
The Best Bet Gazette (illustrated by Pat Henderson Lincoln), Lodestar, 1989.

Some of Gondosch's books have been published in Germany.

WORK IN PROGRESS: Ghost Camp.

SIDELIGHTS: "I was born in the small coal mining town of Hinton, West Virginia, but moved shortly after to Cleveland, Ohio. It was during my growing up years in Cleveland that the idea of becoming a writer took root. First of all, I lived in an ethnic neighborhood and had many friends whose families came from countries all over the world. There were interesting characters and exciting events in my neighborhood which would later be the source of ideas for my books.

"My play was highly imaginative. We created make-believe worlds and filled them with imaginary characters. We acted out plays in the garage and wrote stories for the fun of it on my front porch. I also loved to read and was fortunately allowed to roam one of the Cleveland public libraries. Reading for me was pure pleasure and I enjoyed jumping into a whole new world and becoming a different person every time I opened a book.

"When I was about ten years old, I formed a neighborhood club which met on my front porch, the Triple S Club: stamps, stories, and sewing. Stamp collecting and writing stories I loved. The sewing I could have done without, but three activities sounded better than two. I soon had every kid on Ardmore Avenue in Cleveland writing stories and reading them aloud. We made our own puppets and acted out our stories for neighborhood birthday parties. I was learning that stories and the characters in them could become very real indeed. I didn't know then that I was going to be a writer. I only knew that I loved to read.

"I was encouraged to play the violin when it was discovered that my sense of tone was good. Enjoying music, playing the piano and violin, and listening to the way people talk helped me later as I began to write. I love to write dialogue since I seem to have a feel for language, the rhythm and music of it.

"I attended Ohio University during the sixties with the intent of becoming an English teacher. Reading other writers and studying the English language turned out to be the best background I could have had for writing.

"It wasn't until I read a picture book to my two preschool children that I decided to try my luck at writing a published story. Since then I have written stories and books based on my own childhood adventures and the present day antics of my own four children. I like to explore the way children feel about life, the new discoveries they make, and the humorous everyday experiences that all children can relate to. I try to make my characters real so readers identify with them.

"I have studied German and married a chemical engineer who was born in Romania and lived in Austria. We now travel mainly around the Midwest where we live and south to Florida where my parents live. I also travel to schools all around the country talking with 'young authors' about the writing life.

"As a child, I got so much enjoyment from books. Now I'm giving a little back and enjoying every minute."

HOBBIES AND OTHER INTERESTS: Camping and hiking in the woods, aerobics, singing in a Madrigal group, acting in the Rivertown Players community theater group.

FOR MORE INFORMATION SEE:

Artfocus (Dearborn Highlands Art Council), February/March, 1986.
"Author's Story of Perseverance," *Kentucky Post,* January 28, 1987.

GRAMMER, June Amos   1927-

PERSONAL: Born February 10, 1927, in Woodbury, N.J.; daughter of George Ripley (an accountant and painter) and Edith Marie (a homemaker; maiden name, Wren) Amos; married George Bryant Grammer (an artist and painter), July 9, 1954. *Education:* Attended Arlington State College, 1944-46. *Politics:* Liberal. *Home and office:* 126 East 24th St., New York, N.Y. 10010. *Agent:* Naomi Warner, 327 Central Park West, New York, N.Y. 10025.

JUNE GRAMMER

CAREER: Sears, Seattle, Wash., art director, 1947-49; Wally Williams, Fort Worth, Tex., art director, 1950-51; Battelsteins, Houston, Tex., art director, 1951-54; Franklin Simon, New York, N.Y., art director, 1954-56, 1958-78; *Harper's Bazaar,* New York, N.Y., promotion artist/illustrator, 1956-58; Parsons School of Design, New York, N.Y., instructor, 1968-83; free-lance artist, 1973—. *Exhibitions:* Museum of American Folk Art, New York, N.Y. 1971; Wingspread Gallery, Harbor, Me., 1971, 1973; Hunterdon Art Center, Clinton, N.J., 1972; Julie's Artisan, New York, N.Y., 1972-75; Master Eagle Gallery, New York, N.Y., 1983; Incorporated Gallery, New York, N.Y., 1988. *Awards, honors:* Award of Excellence nomination from *Dolls* magazine, 1988, for "Star," a doll she designed.

ILLUSTRATOR:

Mary Mapes Dodge, *Mary Anne,* Lothrop, 1983.
Abearham and Straus the Mouse, Abraham & Straus, 1984.
Abearham and Straus the Mouse Go to a Birthday Party, Abraham & Straus, 1986.
Antique Doll Calendar, Portfolio Press, 1986.
Abearham and Straus the Mouse and the Magic Mittens, Abraham & Straus, 1987.
Victorian Tea Party (pop-up book), W. J. Fantasy, 1988.

WORK IN PROGRESS: A continuing program of products, dolls, figurines, and music boxes for Schmid in Randolph, Mass.; a line of paper products for Steven Lawrence in Carlstadt, N.J.

SIDELIGHTS: "I started drawing when I was five years old. It always gave me pleasure. It still does. I would have to say it is my *greatest* pleasure.

"I had a long career in fashion illustration and became very bored with it. At Parsons School of Design I met another teacher whose great love was dolls. He had an enormous collection. I went to see his collection intending to draw from it for a couple of hours, and stayed three days. It was a turning point in my life. I then sought doll assignments and began looking for publishers interested in antique doll illustrations. At Lothrop they had been looking for an illustrator for the poem, *Mary Anne.* I did a rough for them and that was it!

"Now I design dolls and do doll illustrations. For two years I designed dolls for Lenox china, and now I have a contract with Schmid. I have done six dolls for them, one of which was nominated for an award of excellence from *Dolls* magazine. I also do other doll-related products for Schmid, musical ornaments, figurines, etc.

"I collect Victoriana and *every* book on the subject and utilize these in my work. I collect antique dolls, Victorian clothes, shoes, hats, everything—toys, too. I spend a good deal of time in museums, not only looking, but drawing collections. It is terribly important to keep renewing your *visual education!*"

HOBBIES AND OTHER INTERESTS: Cooking, sewing, reading, poking in antique stores.

FOR MORE INFORMATION SEE:

Dolls, fall, 1983, May/June, 1988.

GULLEY, Judie   1942-

PERSONAL: Born June 7, 1942, in Minneapolis, Minn.; daughter of Mark Allen (a sales representative) and Jane (a

JUDIE GULLEY

homemaker; maiden name, Wentzel) Bussman; married Bill Gulley (owner of Bill's Heating), February 25, 1961; children: Ron, Jeff. *Education:* Attended State University of Iowa— Iowa City, 1960. *Religion:* Catholic. *Home:* R.R. #1 Box 107-G, Lynn Center, Ill. 61262. *Agent:* Gloria Mosseson, 290 West End Ave., New York, N.Y. 10023.

CAREER: Orion Illinois School District #223, Ill., bus driver, 1973—; author, 1980—. *Member:* National League of American Pen Women (vice-president Quad City branch, 1987). *Awards, honors:* Friends of American Writers Award, 1985, and National League of American Pen Women's National Contest, Second Place, and named one of *School Library Journal*'s Best Horse Books of the '80s, both 1986, all for *Rodeo Summer;* National League of American Pen Women's National Contest, First Place, 1988, for *Wasted Space.*

WRITINGS:

Rodeo Summer, Houghton, 1984.
Wasted Space, Abingdon, 1988.

Author of monthly column, "Stories from the School Bus," in *Companion,* 1983—. Contributor of stories to periodicals, including *Family Circle, Woman's World, Western Horseman, Horseman, Horse and Rider, Runner's World, Capper's Weekly,* and *Sunday Digest.*

WORK IN PROGRESS: First Comes Love, a junior high "coming of age" novel.

SIDELIGHTS: "I was born in Minneapolis, Minnesota in 1942, the older of two girls. From the time I was old enough to hold a pencil, I knew I wanted to be a writer. Since it was so difficult for me to talk to other kids—I gave new meaning to the phrase 'painfully shy'—I loved to write. When I put words on paper, they said exactly what I meant. No stammering or stuttering or putting my foot in my mouth.

"Still, I remember my childhood as a wonderful time. I remember sitting in the backyard under a tree with a new pencil and tablet, writing little stories. My first major undertaking was a novel about a man who tried to kill himself, was rescued by an apprentice angel, and had the opportunity to see what the world would be like if he'd never existed. It was written shortly after I'd seen 'It's a Wonderful Life' on television.

"In school, I considered speaking in front of a class the most horrible torture imaginable, and avoided it at all cost. Teachers eventually gave up trying to wring an oral book report out of me. My writing helped carry me through English classes. I turned in lots of extra-credit fiction stories.

"When I wasn't writing, I was reading. Mostly horse books, since I also knew as soon as I was old enough to say the word, that I wanted a horse more than anything in the world. (I never could understand why we couldn't keep a horse in the middle of South Minneapolis.) Authors like Walter Farley and Will James, who added emotion to the action, were my favorites.

"When my dad was transferred to Rock Island, Illinois in 1957, we were closer to the country. I finally wore my parents down and they helped me get a horse, a sweet-natured cream-colored palomino mare named Dolly. From then on, my whole life revolved around horses. My only friends were those who were as horse-nuts as I was. I met a boy named Bill Gulley who worked for a local riding stable. And at the wise old age of fifteen, I knew I wanted to keep him.

"In 1959 Dad was transferred again, this time to Des Moines, Iowa. I attended a little high school just outside of town in Johnston. Forty-two in my class. The English teacher loved my writing and encouraged me to go on with it. I published my first fiction story in a little paper called the *American Newspaper Boy.* A horse story, of course. They paid me eighteen dollars for it. Big money when you're baby-sitting for thirty-five cents an hour, and supporting a horse. I was delighted with the money. But mostly, I was stunned that someone liked my writing enough to actually PAY me for it. I wrote like mad for weeks after receiving the check. Every so often, I reread those stories and sincerely hope the editors who read them have either retired or lost all memory.

"In my senior year, Dolly was killed in a barn fire, and I learned what pain was. Later, a bit of insurance money brought me another horse, but I knew I would never allow myself to love another one as I had her.

"After graduating from high school I left for college, a journalism major. I lasted a little over a semester at the State University of Iowa in Iowa City. Somehow I even managed to give the required speeches. However, I was assigned to a speech class the second semester. I dreaded it so badly, I was purposely late the first day. I walked to the door and peered through the window at the class already in session. After watching for a few minutes, I turned around and went back to the dorm. A week later, I quit school, and two months later, I married Bill.

"My one regret? Not having the guts to express myself. One morning, my college English teacher was discussing *The Secret Life of Walter Mitty,* and made the comment that Walter slipped into his little daydreams because he was slowly going crazy. My opinion was—and still is—that Walter daydreamed to stay sane, to escape for a while into a kinder, more attractive world. I know because I was a daydreamer, too.

"Bill and I bought a small acreage, and brought my horse over from Des Moines. Soon, we each had one, and a truck and trailer. We spent every free hour with the horses, either riding or at shows. Hauling a trailer to fifty or sixty shows over twenty thousand miles during the summer became a way of life, a glorious fantastic life! I was finally doing the things I'd wanted to do ever since I was old enough to tell a horse from a cow. The night my son, Ron, was born, we were busy getting the horses ready to go. Three weeks later, Ron attended his first horse show. When Jeff was born five years later, he was riding a pony before he could walk.

"During the next twenty years, we built and moved into three different houses. Of course, both Bill and I were more concerned about the type of horse barn that would accompany the house. Once, I worked for a boot factory, and then in 1973, took a job—which I still have and love—as a school bus driver in our small country school district.

"My writing career, however, was always in the back of my mind as I tried, now and again, to write something that might be publishable. Then when I was almost forty, I decided it was now or never. Like all families, my husband and kids were off with interests of their own, the horse business was becoming a chore instead of a joy, and of course, I'd spotted the first gray hair. Time was running out and I'd never really noticed. I enrolled at a local junior college in an adult education writing class. The class, taught by one of our area's finest children's authors, Evelyn Witter, was a turning point in the direction of my life.

She was determined that this September at the Princeton Fair and Rodeo she wasn't going to enter the "Culinary Arts" contests. ■ (From *Rodeo Summer* by Judie Gulley. Jacket illustration by John Gampert.)

"During that class, I sent another story to—who else? the *American Newspaper Boy*. Another horse story? You bet. This time they sent me twenty dollars! A pay hike of two dollars in just over twenty years. This, more than anything else, brought home to me that writers—especially those writing for children—can hardly expect to maintain a mansion and staff of servants on royalties.

"I continued to show up at every writing class offered by Witter, and began to submit my work to magazines. Occasionally, an acceptance and a check showed up in my mailbox, adding fuel to the fire of my enthusiasm.

"In 1981 I submitted a first chapter of a book (about horses) to Betsy Haynes, the juvenile workshop leader at a local writer's conference. She tucked it—and me—under her wing, and after the novel was finished, encouraged me to submit it. In 1983 it was accepted by Houghton Mifflin. In 1985 *Rodeo Summer* won the Friends of American Writers Award. The award was all the more fantastic when I read that my idol, Patricia Calvert, was one of the previous winners.

"In 1986 the book was second in the National Contest sponsored by the National League of American Pen Women. Then it was featured as 'one of the best horse books of the '80s,' in the August, 1986 issue of *School Library Journal*.

"At that time, I was gradually losing interest in writing short fiction and articles, and becoming more excited by book manuscripts. The short things, however, brought 'instant gratification,' in a business where rejection is a fact of life. So even now I continue to send out an occasional piece to a magazine. A ten dollar check in the mail on Monday morning from a tiny publication who praises my work to the skies is just as important to my life as the chapter I finished last Friday.

"I'm a staff writer for the *Companion*, a Catholic magazine in Ontario. My little articles are called 'Stories from the School Bus.' The *Companion*'s editors are marvelous to me. They can't afford to pay much, but they treat me like 'Queen for a Day,' every day! I'll write for them until they fire me! Everyone—especially a writer—needs an occasional pat on the back.

"In 1987, my agent, Gloria Mosseson, sold *Wasted Space* to Abingdon Press. In April, 1988 it received first place in the Pen Women's National Contest. The judge, a book editor for a publishing company in Missouri, stated he considered the book, 'the best by far,' of all the entries.

"I wish I could say I write for noble reasons—because of a deep commitment to the field of children's literature, but I have to admit instead, that I write for myself. . .for the child inside that sat in the corner of the playground and daydreamed while the others jumped rope and played hopscotch. . .for that same kid and others who pretended not to care when chosen last for team events in gym class, or who were passed over when Suzi Anderson, the most popular girl in fifth grade, handed out birthday party invitations. These are the kids that matter to me—the ones I hope read my books—and dream their own dreams.

"My current daydream? To write a Newbery Award winner, of course. Doesn't every children's author have the same thought? As an adult, I've learned dreams CAN come true. But now I know it takes more than sitting under a tree with your eyes closed.

"So I'll open my eyes and write. A few hours a day. A day at a time. But—like good old Walter Mitty—I also know when the going gets really tough, a few minutes under the tree in the backyard doesn't hurt a thing!''

HOBBIES AND OTHER INTERESTS: "I'm wildly enthusiastic about most sports, especially those which take my physical and mental self right to the edge of endurance. Most weekends, I participate in either a long distance foot race, a biathlon, or triathlon. Ultimate goal: to be an Ironman World Championship finisher. On quieter days, I play golf or poke around a park or school yard with my metal detector."

GURKO, Miriam   1910(?)-1988

OBITUARY NOTICE—See sketch in *SATA* Volume 9: Born about 1910 in Union City, N.J.; died of pneumonia, July 3, 1988, in Peekskill, N.Y. Editor and author. A chronicler for young adults of the accomplishments of individuals who have shaped history, Gurko wrote *The Lives and Times of Peter Cooper, Restless Spirit: The Life of Edna St. Vincent Millay, Clarence Darrow, Indian America: The Black Hawk War,* and *The Ladies of Seneca Falls: The Birth of the Woman's Rights Movement.* As early as the fifth grade Gurko knew that she would be a writer; she contributed poems, essays, and short stories to her high school and college publications. While studying at the University of Wisconsin, she met and married a graduate student, Leo Gurko. During their early married years, Gurko worked as an editor for various publications in New York until she began to raise a family. She turned to freelance writing because the "domestic life was not quite enough." Gurko was fascinated by history and famous people, and her books reflected those interests. Her stated aim in writing for young people was, "to disclose their own backgrounds to them and to kindle their interest in further exploration along these lines." Her last book, *Theodor Herzl: The Road to Israel,* was published in 1988.

FOR MORE INFORMATION SEE:

Twentieth-Century Children's Writers, 2nd edition, St. Martin's, 1983.

OBITUARIES

New York Times, July 21, 1988.
School Library Journal, September, 1988.
Times (London), October 13, 1988.

HAMMER, Charles   1934-

PERSONAL: Born August 8, 1934, in Tulsa, Okla.; son of August (a janitorial boss) and Cora (a homemaker; maiden name, Andrews) Hammer; married Lenore Fulhage (a civil engineer), July 6, 1956; children: Julie Ruth, Amy Nan. *Education:* University of Tulsa, B.S., 1956; attended Stanford University, 1972. *Politics:* Democrat. *Religion:* Unitarian. *Home and office:* 4829 Black Swan Dr., Shawnee, Kans. 66216. *Agent:* Ann Elmo Agency, 60 East 42nd St., New York, N.Y. 10165.

CAREER: Daily Leader, Guthrie, Okla., reporter-photographer, 1956; *Kansas Star,* Kansas City, Mo., reporter, 1958-73; University of Missouri, Kansas City, Mo., teacher. Has taught journalism part time at Rockhurst, and Park Colleges. *Military service:* U.S. Army, public information specialist, stationed in Europe, 1957-58. *Awards, honors:* Creative writing fellowship from the National Endowment for the Arts, 1987, for unpublished novel, "Certain Sorrows."

CHARLES HAMMER

WRITINGS:

Me, the Beef and the Bum, Farrar, Straus, 1984.
Wrong-Way Ragsdale, Farrar, Straus, 1987.

Contributor of articles and stories to *Virginia Quarterly Review, Washington Monthly, Kansas Quarterly, Foundation News, Kansas City Star,* and *New Republic.*

WORK IN PROGRESS: A novel about a couple, frustrated but loving; an as-told-to book with Walter Byers, a retired executive director of the National Collegiate Athletic Association.

SIDELIGHTS: "Like many former journalists, I make personal experience the basis of my fiction. Fifteen years of fiction writing have taught me, perhaps too late, that the only subjects deeply worth writing about are the dilemmas of human life—not the problems that can be solved, but the dilemmas that we can only grind away at."

HOBBIES AND OTHER INTERESTS: "I love archaeology, gardening (and have an extensive garden with much shade and little sun). Also love airplanes and read much history and history of war."

HILGARTNER, Beth   1957-

PERSONAL: Born December 7, 1957, in Baltimore, Md.,; daughter of C. Andrew (a theorist) and Carol (an educator; maiden name, Howe) Hilgartner; married Ernest Drown (a church musician), September 16, 1979. *Education:* Harvard University, B.A. 1979; Episcopal Divinity School, Cambridge, Mass., M.Div., 1986. *Religion:* Episcopal. *Home:* 58 Spaulding St., Barre, Vt. 05641. *Office:* Christ Episcopal Church, State St., Montpelier, Vt. 05602.

BETH HILGARTNER

CAREER: Episcopal priest. Free-lance writer, 1979—; Christ Episcopal Church, Montpelier, Vt., curate, 1986—. Member of board of directors, Retired Senior Volunteer Program (R.S.V.P.), Central Vermont; member of Pastoral Team for the Montpelier Emergency Food Pantry. *Awards, honors: A Murder for Her Majesty* was chosen one of Child Study Assocation of America's Children's Books of the Year, 1987.

WRITINGS:

Great Gorilla Grins: An Abundance of Animal Alliterations (illustrated by Leslie Morrill), Little, Brown, 1979.
A Necklace of Fallen Stars (illustrated by Michael Hague), Little, Brown, 1979.
A Murder for Her Majesty, Houghton, 1986.
Colors in the Dreamweaver's Loom, Houghton, 1989.

WORK IN PROGRESS: A sequel to *Colors,* tentatively titled *The Feast of the Trickster.*

SIDELIGHTS: "I can actually pinpoint when I began to write. I was in the fifth grade; my teacher (a great innovator) had come up with the bright (and at that time new) idea to get her students to write a story of their own. I was intrigued with this project, and quickly discovered that the story I had begun had no intention of being stopped after a decent three or four pages. Feeling rather like the sorcerer's apprentice—not sure I could stop what I had started, and not very sure where we were going—I persevered with my story, which grew into a long, rather rambling fantasy account I called 'The War of the Sun and the Moon.' There were far more characters and magical things than any one book could possibly need or use, and the plot suffered from a lack of definition, but I had a great time, and from then on, I was hooked on writing.

"Oddly enough, I never became involved in writing journals or diaries (though I made numerous attempts during my somewhat lonely and difficult adolescent years); in many ways, the books I worked on served as my journal, enabling me to work out things in my life, to finish my unfinished business, without spelling everything out in great, self-absorbed detail. Perhaps, writing novels was a protective gesture—a novel was certainly a safer place than a journal to pour out my heart, since our household was full of other teenaged siblings, none of whom would balk at a little blackmail.

"My books still serve me as a place to finish unfinished business; I call it paying 'karmic debts.' Because of this intensely personal motivation for my writing, some of the books I write are not and never will be published; they are too deeply rooted in my own inner life to have much interest to anyone else. All the same, I have found that a reader does not need to be able to figure out what I was 'working on' in order to enjoy the stories I dream up.

"Another peculiar aspect of my personal muse is that for me, writing must be something I do in addition to everything else. At one point, several years ago, I tried to do writing as a full time occupation. It was a dismal failure, resulting in a blocked period of over a year. I found I simply could not use my writing to do what I needed to do if I were constantly worrying about whether or not the current project was 'marketable.' I gave up in disgust and went to work in a bank—and to my surprise, I found myself writing again. I didn't stay in the bank, as I knew from the beginning that such a career was not for me; instead, I went to seminary and was eventually ordained priest in the Episcopal Church."

HOBBIES AND OTHER INTERESTS: "Besides writing, and my work in the ministry, I amuse myself in a number of ways. I sing (soprano) in a variety of contexts, including solo recitals with my husband playing harpsichord and a vocal quartet, 'Vox Sacra,' which we started in 1987; I play the recorder (even in public) and diddle a bit on the harpsichord; I visit schools and libraries as a guest lecturer; I read avidly; I ride horseback and am training my two thoroughbred horses, Cyprian of Carthage and Peter Abelard; I keep three cats (or rather, they keep me!); and when time permits, I enjoy gardening, hiking, swimming and traveling."

HINTON, S(usan) E(loise)   1950-

PERSONAL: Born in 1950, in Tulsa, Okla.; married David E. Inhofe (a mail order businessman), September, 1970; children: Nicholas David. *Education:* University of Tulsa, B.S., 1970. *Residence:* Tulsa, Okla. *Agent:* c/o Delacorte Press, 1 Dag Hammarskjold Plaza, New York, N.Y. 10017.

CAREER: Author of young adult novels. *Awards, honors: New York Herald Tribune*'s Children's Spring Book Festival Honor Book, 1967, *Media & Methods* Maxi Award, and one of the American Library Association's Best Young Adult Books, both 1975, and Massachusetts Children's Book Award from Salem State College, 1979, all for *The Outsiders; Book World*'s Children's Spring Book Festival Award Honor Book, and one of American Library Association's Best Books for Young Adults, both 1971, and Massachusetts Children's Book Award, 1978, all for *That Was Then, This Is Now; Rumble Fish* was named one of American Library Association's Best Books for Young Adults, and one of *School Library Journal*'s Best Books of the Year, both 1975.

American Library Association Best Book for Young Adults, one of *School Library Journal*'s Best Books of the Year, and one of *Booklist*'s Reviewers' Choices, all 1979, American Book Award finalist for Children's Paperback Fiction from the Association of American Publishers, and one of New York Public Library's Books for the Teen Age, both 1980, Sue Hefly Award Honor Book from the Louisiana Association of School Libraries, and California Young Reader Medal nominee from the California Reading Association, both 1982, and Sue Hefly

S. E. HINTON

Award 1983, all for *Tex;* Land of Enchantment Book Award from the New Mexico Library Association, 1982, for *Rumble Fish.*

WRITINGS:

FICTION

The Outsiders, Viking, 1967, large print edition, G. K. Hall, 1988.
That Was Then, This Is Now (ALA Notable Book; illustrated by Hal Siegel), Viking, 1971, new edition, 1985.
Rumble Fish, Delacorte, 1975.
Tex, Delacorte, 1979.
Taming the Star Runner, Delacorte, 1988.

Teacher's guides are available for *The Outsiders, That Was Then, This Is Now, Rumble Fish,* and *Tex,* all written by Lou Willett Stanek, all published by Dell. Hinton's books have been published in England, Denmark, Finland and Germany.

ADAPTATIONS:

"Rumble Fish" (record or cassette), Viking, 1977.
"The Outsiders" (filmstrip with cassette), Current Affairs and Mark Twain Media, 1978, (cassette), Random House.
"That Was Then, This Is Now" (filmstrip with cassette), Current Affairs and Mark Twain Media, 1978.

FILMS

"Tex," starring Matt Dillon, Walt Disney Productions, 1982.
"The Outsiders," starring C. Thomas Howell and Matt Dillon, Warner Bros., 1983.

"Rumble Fish," starring Matt Dillon and Mickey Rourke, Universal, 1983.
"That Was Then, This Is Now," starring Emilio Estevez and Craig Sheffer, Paramount, 1985.

SIDELIGHTS: **1950.** "I was born in Tulsa, Oklahoma, where I have lived most of my life. There is nothing to do there, but it is a pleasant place to live if you don't want to do anything. . . .

"I started reading about the same time everyone else did, and began to write a short time later. The major influence on my writing has been my reading. I read everything, including Comet cans and coffee labels. Reading taught me sentence structure, paragraphing, how to build a chapter. Strangely enough, it never taught me spelling.

"I've always written about things that interest me, so my first years of writing (grade three through grade ten) I wrote about cowboys and horses. I wanted to be a cowboy and have a horse. I was strange for my era, but feel quite comfortable in this one, when everyone wants to be a cowboy and I have a horse."[1]

In **1967,** while attending Tulsa's Will Rogers High School, Hinton revolutionized the genre of the young adult novel with the publication of *The Outsiders,* the story of a confrontation between a group of "greasers" and their more affluent high school peers, the "socs." Hinton began the first draft of her novel at the age of fifteen, and was published when she was seventeen. "*The Outsiders* took me a year and a half. During that time, I did four complete drafts. The first draft was forty pages; then I just kept rewriting and adding details."[2]

I am a greaser and most of my neighborhood rarely bothers to get a haircut. ■ (Cover illustration from *The Outsiders* by S. E. Hinton.)

While Hinton's first book was acclaimed by book critics and applauded by teenagers, many parents objected to the characters' unruly and often violent nature. Some adults became concerned that the storyline might encourage teens to idolize a life of lawlessness and destruction, while others felt it was wrong for young people to be exposed to violence in literature under any circumstances. "...There was no realistic fiction being written for teenagers. It was all Mary Jane goes to the prom, that kind of stuff. I'd been to a few proms and they weren't anything like that. There weren't any books that dealt realistically with teenage life so I wrote *The Outsiders* to fill that gap."[3]

"I felt the greasers were getting knocked when they didn't deserve it. The custom, for instance, of driving by a shabby boy and screaming 'Greaser!' at him always made me boil. But it was the cold-blooded beating of a friend of mine that gave me the idea of writing a book; I wanted to do something that would change people's opinion of greasers. Some 'socs' (the abbreviation of socials) didn't like the way my friend was combing his hair, so they beat him up! Another friend of mine never got enough to eat and frequently slept in the bus station because his father was always beating him up. The socs teased *him* because of his grades. Grades!"[4]

"It always irritated me that people would make assumptions on the way other people dressed or their economic backgrounds that they didn't have feelings. It drove me nuts that people would set up social rules and social games and never ask where these rules came from or who was saying they *have* to do this or that.

"As a kid, everything is life and death. As you get older, it's harder to get suicidal about a bad haircut. But I have a real good memory for what it was like. And I can't stand it when adults say to teenagers, 'Why are you sulking around with that look on your face, you're in the best time of your life!' If it's the best time of my life, I may as well shoot myself."[5]

"*The Outsiders*, like most of the things I write, is written from a boy's point of view. That's why I'm listed as S. E. Hinton rather than Susan on the book; since my subject was gang fights I figured most boys would look at the book and think, 'What can a chick know about stuff like that?'"[4]

"I started writing before the women's movement was in full swing, and at the time, people wouldn't have believed that girls would do the things that I was writing about. I also felt more comfortable with the male point of view—I had grown up around boys...."[2]

"...Most of my close friends were boys. In those days, girls were mainly concerned about getting their hair done and lining their eyes. It was such a passive society. Girls got their status from their boyfriends. They weren't interested in doing anything on their own. I didn't understand what they were talking about."[6]

"...I found nothing in the female culture to identify with. Sometimes, though, I feel like I spent the first part of my life wishing to be a teen-age boy, and the second part condemned to being one."[7]

"None of the events in the book [*The Outsiders*] are taken from life, but the rest—how kids think and live and feel—is for real. The characters—Dallas, who wasn't tough enough; Sodapop, the happy-go-lucky dropout; Bob, the rich kid whose arrogance cost him his life; Ponyboy, the sensitive, green-eyed greaser who didn't want to be a hood—they're all real to me, though I didn't put my friends into the book. The characters are mixtures of people I know, with a bit of myself thrown in."[4]

"The characters have to be part of yourself, you have to understand them. By the time they go through your head and work their way down on paper, they reflect some aspect of you. Ponyboy Curtis probably comes closest to me—he's absent-minded and quiet and daydreams a lot."[2]

Although Hinton wrote *The Outsiders* about a gang, she was not a part of any group at the time. At the time of publication, seventeen-year-old Hinton remarked: "Many of my friends are greasers, but I'm not. I have friends who are rich too, but nobody will ever call me a soc—I've seen what money and too much idle time and parental approval can do to people. That's why I tried not to be too hard on the socs in the book. The thing is, they are *so* cool. Cool people mean nothing to me—they're living behind masks, and I'm always wondering, 'Is there a real person underneath?'

"It's great when people come up and say, 'I read your book and liked it.' But I've always been a quiet person, the kind who takes her time about things. Schedules and details are beyond me—I nearly flunked creative writing because I couldn't spell and couldn't write under pressure. And I'm shy around

(From the movie "The Outsiders," starring C. Thomas Howell, Tom Cruise and Emilio Estevez. Copyright © 1982 by Pony Boy, Inc.)

older people, which doesn't make publicizing the book much fun. I do the best I can but sometimes I wish I'd never written the thing. Then I remember why I wrote it and I don't mind so much.

"My younger sister hasn't once said she's sick of hearing about the book although I know she must be. My mother, after the first shock of reading it ('Susie, where *did* you pick up all of this?'), is selling it to everyone she meets. But it's the reaction of my greaser friends I'm happiest about. 'Did you put me in it?' is the question they ask most, not 'What could *you* know about the way we feel?' They have confidence in me.

"The gang that inspired my book is gone now, and I'm too old to go around in jeans and carry a knife. But I don't need to anymore; I can still be a friend in dresses and make-up. Maybe not a buddy, but a friend. And if I ever forget how it is to be a teen-ager in a savage social system, I've got it all written down."[4]

The Outsiders was a major success among teenagers, selling more than four million copies in the United States. The book's popularity enabled Hinton to attend the University of Tulsa, where in 1970 she earned an education degree and met her future husband David Inhofe. However, being catapulted into fame and fortune at eighteen was not without problems; Hinton had a writer's block for several years. "I couldn't even write a letter. All these people were going, 'Oh, look at this teenage writer' and you think, God, they're expecting a masterpiece and I haven't got a masterpiece."[5]

1971. Hinton's second book, *That Was Then, This Is Now,* was written with the encouragement of her future husband. The writing was slow—two pages of manuscript a day over a period of three to four months—and deliberate. But the result was a book that Hinton considered better written than *The Outsiders*. "I have no idea why I write. The old standards are: I like to express my feelings, stretch my imagination, earn money. (One you don't usually see on the list is 'total incompetence at anything else,' which certainly applies in my case.) Writing is much easier to do than to talk about.

"I'm a character writer. Some writers are plot writers. . . .I have to begin with people. I always know my characters, exactly what they look like, their birthdays, what they like for breakfast. It doesn't matter if these things appear in the book. I still have to know. My characters are fictional. I get ideas from real people, sometimes, but my characters always exist only in my head. . . .Those characters are as real to me as anyone else in my life, so much so that if I ran into one of them at the laundry I wouldn't be all that surprised.

"There is an interesting transformation that takes place in the beginning of a book. I go straight from thinking about my narrator to being him. Like Lon Chaney becoming the werewolf. Only substitute typewriter for full moon. This can be fun. . . ."[7]

1975. *Rumble Fish,* the story of a boy who struggles to acquire a tough reputation, continued the theme of delinquent youths. "When I was writing *Rumble Fish* I was reading a lot about color symbolism and mythology, and that came through with-

(The 1985 Paramount film ''That Was Then . . . This Is Now,'' starred Emilio Estevez who also wrote the screenplay.)

out my realizing it. It was a hard book to write because Rusty-James is a simple person, yet the Motorcycle Boy is the most complex character I've ever created. And Rusty-James sees him one way, which is not right, and I had to make that clear.

"It's about over-identifying with something which you can never understand, which is what Rusty-James is doing. The Motorcycle Boy can't identify with anything. He's something other than what his neighborhood thinks, but he can't find anything he wants to be or do.

"The Motorcycle Boy's flaw is his inability to compromise, and that's why I made him colorblind. He interprets life 'in black and white,' and he has the ability to walk off and leave anything, which is what ultimately destroys him.

"I did not give the Motorcycle Boy a name because I wanted to emphasize his alienation. Actually, he did not give himself the title, others did. The neighborhood was so bad that the boys needed something to boast about.

"Every time I get a letter from a kid who says that *Rumble Fish* is his favourite book, he's usually in the reformatory. I write about kids who don't fit into the mold; I wouldn't make them up. But the book's readers don't identify with the Motorcycle Boy; they identify with Rusty-James.''[8]

Hinton's next book, *Tex* (the story of two brothers left in each other's care by their rambling father) is also about deliquent youths trying to make it in a world shaped by protest, drugs, violence and family disruption. "I can't say that Tex is a lot

like me. But he was the narrator I most enjoyed being. Capable of thinking, he has to be made to think: he relies on instinct instead of intellect. And basically his instincts are good. Capable of violence, but not malice, he has to learn things the hard way—a basically happy person trying to deal with unhappiness. I envied his total lack of suspicion.

"His brother tells him, 'Tex, you are not stupid, and you're not all that ignorant. But how anybody as simple-minded as you are has managed to survive for fourteen years is beyond me.' A person of action, without much physical fear, Tex does manage to survive situations he brings on himself—but he also survives those he has no control of and can see no justice in. He does so by learning that every action has a reaction—but many times there is a *choice* of reactions.

"Tex McCormick will very likely grow up to be a horse-trainer and live in a rather narrow world. His brother, Mason, however, will go as far as brains and ambition will carry him. I don't think it's impossible these two kinds of people could respect and like each other, without wanting the other's life.

"In trying to say what Tex is about, the best I can come up with is: relationships, which are complicated even for simple people; and maybe love, which can't cure anything but sometimes makes the unbearable bearable; and being a teen-ager, which is problem enough for anybody. Mainly it's about Tex McCormick, perhaps the most childlike character I've ever done, but the one who makes the biggest strides toward maturity. I have to admit he's a favorite child.''[7]

According to librarians, Hinton is one of the most popular authors of "reluctant readers," in the junior-high age group. Her books are read without having to be assigned. One high school teacher, deeply concerned about the drop in reading, pointed out: "The choice is not between an adolescent's reading *Tex* and reading [D. H. Lawrence's] *Sons and Lovers,* but between reading *Tex* and reading nothing."

". . .My stories just pull young readers in. Teachers will read the first chapter of one of my books aloud to a class, then assign the rest for home reading. The kids find themselves finishing the volume in one or two sittings."[9]

"I think the readers identify with the characters so strongly. They either know somebody like that person or they feel they are just like that person. I get letters from kids saying, 'Those aren't my problems, but those are my feelings.' And I get the same kinds of letters today that I got fifteen years ago. The problems are different but the feelings are the same."[5]

"The trouble is, grownups write about teen-agers from their own memories, or else write about teen-agers from a standoff, I'm-a-little-scared-to-get-close-they're-hairy view. Teen-agers today want to read about teen-agers today. The world is changing, yet the authors of books for teen-agers are still fifteen years behind the times.

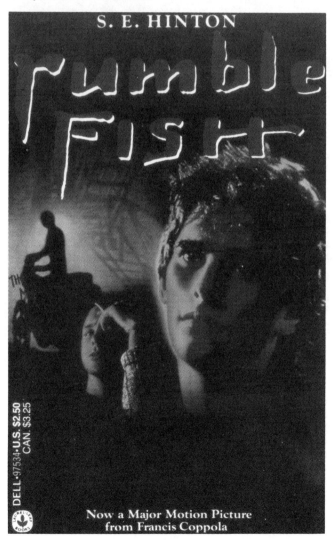

An old fear started creeping up my backbone. ■
(From *Rumble Fish* by S. E. Hinton.)

"In the fiction they write, romance is still the most popular theme, with a-horse-and-the-girl-who-loved-it coming in a close second. Nowhere is the drive-in social jungle mentioned, the behind-the-scenes politicking that goes on in big schools, the cruel social system in which, if you can afford to snub every fourth person you meet, you're popular. In short, where is reality? On the other side of the coin, there are the hair-raising accounts of gangs, motorcycle and otherwise; gangs hold a fatal fascination for adults. Adults who try to write realistically seem to mix up the real with the dirty.

"And speaking of realism, nothing makes a teen-ager blush more than a grown-up writer trying to use 'geer,' 'fab,' 'camp,' 'groovy' in dialogue. The rule is: If you don't say it yourself, don't say it. It comes out fake. And one of the more redeeming qualities of teen-agers is their loathing for anything fake.

". . .We still get books on Mary Jane's big date with the football hero. Why not write it realistically? (I said real, not dirty.) Most kids nowadays date for status. There are cliques and classes and you date so you can say you had a date with so-and-so, the president of the student council. You may loathe him, but personal likes and dislikes don't matter anymore. And the higher up the social ladder you go, the cooler it gets. You say what everyone else says. You wear what everyone else wears. And you are so cool, so scared someone is going to think you're not 'In,' that you don't have time to think about another person. Your date is there to enhance your status. It's a role you're playing for a very cruel audience, and you don't make slips.

"That, friends, would make a realistic romance. Because in spite of everything, you may still make slips.

"Now let's take the business of cars. Teen-agers spend half their waking hours in cars, and yet they are scarcely mentioned in teen-age literature. If they're mentioned at all, it's the story of how Tommy fixed up his jalopy and won the local drags, or lost them and enriched his character: either ending is satisfactory. Yet Tommy is more likely out dragging his SS397 up and down the local strip, impressing girls and risking his life and other people's lives, and if the cops chase him to give him a ticket he (1) stops because he lives on the very 'right' side of town and his parents or friends can fix the ticket; (2) stops because it's the local cop, who probably just wants to say, 'Why don't you take it out to the expressway tonight. I'll match you against my cousin's Vet'; or (3) runs.

"*That* would make a realistic story about cars.

"All we hear is how teen-agers are rebelling against authority, against lack of authority, against country, against parents. This is partly true. It is more true that all we are doing most of the time is asking, 'Why?' and getting as an answer, 'Because it's always been done this way.' If there were more stopping and explaining *why* it's always been done this way, there'd be more understanding. Understanding breeds communication. There we are back at the root of the matter.

"Books for teen-agers portray us as a carefree group, when all we hear is 'The future is in your hands!' Our parents didn't have to worry through their childhood about whose hands the future was in. And when responsibilities did come, they were ready for them. Now, from thirteen on, you worry about the future. No wonder, then, by seventeen, some say, 'You made the world, you fix it,' and retreat into a hazy drug world where there are no responsibilities.

"People are always asking for teen-agers' opinions on things, and writing about them. You've heard of people reading the

(Matt Dillon and Mickey Rourke starred in the Universal film "Rumble Fish," 1983.)

symptoms of a disease, and then suddenly developing the disease? Well, you can't pick up a magazine or a newspaper that doesn't declare that teen-agers are rebellious, over-worked, over-pampered, under-privileged, smart, stupid and sex-crazed. No wonder some develop the symptoms.

"Adults who let small children watch hours of violence, unfunny comedy, abnormal behavior and suggestive actions on TV, scream their heads off when a book written for children contains a fist fight. But violence too is a part of teen-agers' lives. If it's not on television or in the movies, it's a beating-up at a local drive-in. Things like this are going to take place as long as there are kids. Only when violence is for a sensational effect should it be objected to in books for teen-agers. Such books should not be blood and gore, but not a fairyland of proms and double-dates, either. Sometimes I wonder which extreme does the most harm.

"Teen-agers should not be written down to; anyone can tell when his intelligence is being underestimated. Those who are not ready for adult novels can easily have their love of reading killed by the inane junk lining the teen-age shelf in the library. Parents complain of their children's lack of enthusiasm for reading, but if they had to read a 'Jeri Doe, Girl Reporter' series, they'd turn off, too.

"Teen-agers know a lot today. Not just things out of a textbook, but about living. They know their parents aren't superhuman, they know that justice doesn't always win out, and that sometimes the bad guys win. They know that persons in high places aren't safe from corruption, that some men have their price, and that some people sell out. Writers needn't be afraid that they will shock their teen-age audience. But give them something to hang onto. Show that some people don't sell out, and that everyone can't be bought. Do it realistically. Earn respect by giving it."[10]

Hinton continues to speak to teens. All four of her books have been made into major Hollywood feature films; "Tex," the first movie, released in **1982,** was produced by Walt Disney. "At first I said, 'No, thank you, I'm not interested in doing a Disney movie.' I thought they'd really sugar it up, take out all the sex, drugs and violence and leave nothing but a story of a boy and his horse. Then Tom Wilhite, vice president at Disney, landed on my doorstep and convinced me that they wanted to broaden their audience and do a hard PG movie. I liked Tom Wilhite and agreed to sell on the condition that my horse got to play the lead horse. Those two deals happened within a week of each other."[6]

The shooting was done in Tulsa, and Hinton was involved in the casting, scriptwriting, and directing of her own work as a collaborator of director Tim Hunter. "Once I sold the books I expected to be asked to drop off the face of the earth. But that didn't happen. I know that I had extremely rare experiences for a writer. Usually the director does not say, 'Boys, these are important lines, so you've got to know them word for word. . . .' "[6]

"I was just stunned that I liked all these movie people. I thought they'd all be money-grubbing, sex-crazed dope addicts, but they're not money-grubbing at all."[5]

"But, on the other hand, I'm well aware that the writer is usually not the most respected member of the crew."[11]

During the same period, a group of high school students from Lone Star, California sent a petition to Francis Coppola nominating him to make a movie of their favorite book, *The Outsiders*. Coppola's producer, Fred Roos recalled: "The jacket was so tacky. It looked like the book was privately printed by some religious organization. I carried it around with me for weeks, but I didn't open it. One day I found myself on an airplane, and I was tired of carrying it around. I said to myself that I'd give it ten pages. I ended up reading it cover to cover and I agreed with the kids. I thought it was a movie."[12]

Roos highly recommended the project to Coppola who eventually contacted Hinton: "When I met Susie, it was confirmed to me that she was not just a young-people's novelist, but a real American novelist. For me the primary thing about her books is that the characters come across as very real. Her dialogue is memorable, and her prose is striking. Often a paragraph of her descriptive prose sums up something essential and stays with you. . . ."[6]

Hinton, who had turned down previous offers for the movie rights to *The Outsiders*, accepted Coppola's offer after being impressed by his screen adaptation of "Black Stallion." As with "Tex," she was on the set as a creative consultant. "When Francis visited me in Tulsa, he showed me how he was writing the screenplay. He had literally taken the book apart, outlining

DELL•97850•U.S. $2.95 CAN. $3.95

S.E. HINTON
author of THE OUTSIDERS

Now a Major Motion Picture

Cover from a paperbound edition of Hinton's 1979 novel. ∎(From *Tex* by S. E. Hinton.)

in red the sections with action and the passages of introspection in blue.

"Working with that guy is so funny. He can go forever and thinks that everyone else can, too."[11]

"Halfway through 'The Outsiders,' Francis looked up at me one day and said, 'Susie, we get along great. Have you written anything else I can film?' I told him about *Rumble Fish*, and he read the book and loved it. He said, 'I know what we can do. On our Sundays off, let's write a screenplay, and then as soon as we can wrap 'The Outsiders,' we'll take a two-week break and start filming 'Rumble Fish.'' I said, 'Sure, Francis, we're working sixteen hours a day, and you want to spend Sundays writing another screenplay?' But that's what we did."[6]

". . .We were in his office for about twelve hours writing before I finally said, 'I can't go any further, I'm beat.' And he said, 'No, no, no! We'll put some more tapes on the machine. Here's another glass of wine. Stay, stay.'

"He put a tape of the Police on the machine and after a while he looked up and said, 'I really like that drummer. Get me that drummer!' And the next thing I knew Stewart Copeland was sitting in on the 'Rumble Fish' rehearsals playing the drums so we could rehearse to his beat."[11]

"It's the first time I've ever felt at home in a group situation. I've never been a joiner. In Tulsa I have a reputation for being slightly eccentric. Even my close friends think I'm a little nutty. But with the movie people I was accepted instantly.

"Also, when you're making a movie, you feel like an outlaw. Traffic stops for you, and you don't keep the same hours that anybody else keeps. I like that outlaw feeling. And there's one other nice thing about the movies. There's always somebody else to blame. With a novel, you have to take all the blame yourself."[6]

"I really have had a wonderful time and made some very good friends during the filming. Like a lot of authors, I'd heard the horror stories about how they buy the property and then want the author to disappear and not meddle around worrying about what they're doing to the book.

"But that didn't happen at all. They invited me in right from the start, and I helped with the screenplays. The scripts stick closely to the books, and so much of the dialogue is mine, so naturally I'm happy with them.

". . .I guess I thought I'd collect some really funny, cynical Hollywood stories. And that's where I got disillusioned. The movies are damn near as good as my books."[13]

"Rumble Fish" and "The Outsiders" were both released in 1982 starring Matt Dillon, one of America's most successful teenage actors. "Matt identifies with Rusty-James [in *Rumble Fish*]. He told me a long time ago, when we were shooting 'Tex,' that *Rumble Fish* was his favourite book. He said '[We] gotta get somebody to make a movie of it so I can play the part.' And I said that by that time, he might be too old; I asked him if he'd play the Motorycyle Boy. He said, '[Y]eah, and if I'm really old, like twenty-seven, I'll direct.'

"Matt is exactly the kind of kid I write about. Of course, he's a much more complex person than any of my characters, but he has facets of all of them. He has a sweet side, which was good for 'Tex,' and that street-wise thing that got him through Dallas in 'The Outsiders,' and a funny, charming cockiness that's perfect for Rusty-James.

"I love to see Matt walking around reading books. He had read all of mine before we ever met, and I feel I'm partly responsible for the fact that he likes to read now.

"I didn't know Mickey Rourke [Motorcycle Boy in 'Rumble Fish'], but after Francis told me who he was, I remembered seeing 'Body Heat' and thinking, when he came on the screen, 'I know that guy.' It was such a strong recognition factor, I wonder if it was a premonition."[8]

1985. Release of the movie 'That Was Then, This is Now.'' While Hinton enjoyed working for the movie industry, her primary involvement as a writer continued. ''...I still think of myself as a novelist, and with the next book I'm writing, I'm doing everything I can to make it unfilmable.''[6]

"I don't think I have a masterpiece in me, but I do know I'm writing well in the area I choose to write in. I understand kids and I really like them. And I have a very good memory. I remember exactly what it was like to be a teen-ager that nobody listened to or paid attention to or wanted around. I mean, it wasn't like that with my own family, but I knew a lot of kids like that and hung around with them. They were street kids, gang kids, sort of scrounging around, and somehow I always understood them. They were my type."[13]

FOOTNOTE SOURCES

[1]Doris de Montreville and Elizabeth J. Crawford, editors, *Fourth Book of Junior Authors*, H. W. Wilson, 1978.
[2]Lisa Ehrichs, "Advice from a Penwoman," *Seventeen*, November, 1981.
[3]"Tex and Other Teen Tales," *Teen*, July, 1982.

[4]"Face to Face with a Teen-Age Novelist," *Seventeen*, October, 1967.
[5]Carol Wallace, "In Praise of Teenage Outcasts," *Daily News*, September 26, 1982.
[6]Stephen Farber, "Directors Join the S. E. Hinton Fan Club," *New York Times*, March 20, 1983.
[7]"Notes from Delacorte Press for Books for Young Readers," *Delacorte Press*, winter, 1979/spring, 1980.
[8]"Rumble Fish," *Production Notes*, No Weather Films, 1983.
[9]Lisa Robin, "The Young and the Restless," *Media and Methods*, May/June, 1982.
[10]Susan Hinton, "Teen Agers Are for Real," *New York Times Book Review*, August 27, 1967.
[11]Hal Hinton, "Writer of 'Tex' Is Comfortable Dealing with Disney and Coppola," *Chicago Tribune*, December 24, 1982.
[12]Aljean Harmetz, "Making 'The Outsiders,' a Librarian's Dream," *New York Times*, March 23, 1983.
[13]Dave Smith, "Hinton, What Boys Are Made Of," *Los Angles Times*, July 15, 1982.

FOR MORE INFORMATION SEE:

School Library Journal, May, 1967 (p. 64), September, 1971 (p. 174), October, 1975 (p. 106).
Publishers Weekly, May 22, 1967 (p. 64).
Atlantic Monthly, December, 1967 (p. 401).
Saturday Review, January 27, 1968 (p. 34).
English Journal, February, 1969 (p. 295).
Times Literary Supplement, October, 30, 1970 (p. 1258), April 2, 1976 (p. 388).
School Librarian, December, 1970 (p. 455), December, 1976 (p. 335), March, 1977 (p. 21).

Dillon and Hinton on the set of "Tex."

Matt Dillon, star of the movie "Tex."

Horn Book, August, 1971 (p. 389), December, 1975 (p. 601).
D. L. Kirkpatrick, editor, *Twentieth-Century Children's Writers,* St. Martin's, 1978, new edition, 1983.
Variety, May 12, 1982 (p. 445), October 6, 1982, October 6, 1983.
Times-Picayune (New Orleans), July 25, 1982 (section 8, p. 4).
Newsweek, October 11, 1982 (p. 105).
"Cinema," *Time,* October 11, 1982, April 4, 1983, October 24, 1983.
Detroit News, October 15, 1982 (section D, p. 3).
Christian Science Monitor, November 4, 1982 (p. 19).
American Film, April, 1983 (p. 34).
New York, April 4, 1983.
People Weekly, April 4, 1983.
Village Voice, April 5, 1983 (p. 53).
Monthly Film Bulletin, September, 1983 (p. 238).
David Rees, *Painted Desert, Green Shade,* Horn Book, 1984.
Wilson Library Bulletin, September, 1985 (p. 61).
Nation, March 8, 1986 (p. 276).
"Is the Young Adult Novel Dead?," *Society of Children's Book Writers,* November/December, 1987.

HIRSH, Marilyn   1944-1988

OBITUARY NOTICE—See sketch in *SATA* Volume 7: Born January 1, 1944, in Chicago, Ill.; died of cancer, October 17, 1988 (some sources say October 18), in New York, N. Y. Educator, illustrator, and author. Hirsh's career spanned both Jewish and Indian cultures, but she was best known for writing and illustrating children's books on Jewish themes, sometimes inspired by the recollections of her older relatives. Two of her books, *Where Is Yonkela?* and *The Pink Suit,* were about her father. "I was very honored to win the First Annual Association of Jewish Libraries' Sydney Taylor Body of Work Award for my contribution to Jewish children's literature in 1980," she said.

In addition to her Jewish heritage, Hirsh, who was also fascinated with India, wrote and illustrated books on Indian culture. She was exposed to the art of India while working there for the Peace Corps during the 1960s, and her first children's works were on Indian subjects. While in India, she taught English and art to ten- to thirteen-year-old children. "India is a second home to me, and my career in children's books also began there," she once remarked. When she returned to America, Hirsh specialized in Indian and Buddhist art history, teaching at New York University's Institute of Fine Arts and at the Cooper Union School for the Advancement of Science and Art.

During her career, she produced over thirty books, including: *The Elephants and the Mice: A Panchatantra Story* (a Junior Literary Guild selection), *Ben Goes into Business, How the World Got Its Color, Deborah the Dybbick: A Ghost Story, Potato Pancakes All Around,* and *I Love Hanukkah.* Three of her books were adapted into filmstrips, which she also illustrated: "Could Anything Be Worse?," "Ben Goes into Business," and "The Rabbi and the Twenty-nine Witches." She also illustrated books by other authors, including *The House on the Roof* by David Adler and *Wales' Tales* by Susan Saunders, which was a Junior Literary Guild selection.

FOR MORE INFORMATION SEE:

Contemporary Authors: New Revision Series, Volume 16, Gale, 1986.

OBITUARIES

New York Times, October 22, 1988.
School Library Journal, December, 1988.
Horn Book, January-February, 1989.

HISSEY, Jane (Elizabeth)   1952-

PERSONAL: Born September 1, 1952, in Norfolk, England; daughter of Richard Reeve (a naval officer) and Shelagh (Smith) Colls; married Ivan Hissey (a graphic designer), August 1, 1979; children: Owen James, Alison Julia. *Education:* Attended Great Yarmouth College of Art, 1969-70; Brighton College of Art and Design, B.A., 1974. *Home:* Sussex, England. *Agent:* c/o Century Hutchinson Childrens Books Ltd., Brookmount House, 62-65 Chandos Place, Covent Garden, London WC2N 4NW, England.

CAREER: Worthing Sixth Form College, Sussex, England, art teacher, 1974-80; illustrator and designer, 1980—.

WRITINGS:

JUVENILE; SELF-ILLUSTRATED

Old Bear, Philomel, 1986.
Little Bear's Trousers, Philomel, 1987.
Old Bear Tales, Philomel, 1988.
Best Friends, Philomel, 1989.

WORK IN PROGRESS: Little Bear Lost; writing and illustrating another children's book, to be published by Century Hutchinson.

SIDELIGHTS: "After I had produced a number of greeting cards and a large, full-color calendar, I was approached by Century Hutchinson to write and illustrate a children's book. The idea appealed to me because I am able to fit the work into the evenings. This leaves me free in the daytime to be with my children gathering ideas for stories and subject matter for drawings.

"I work in colored pencils in a realistic style; concentrating on accurate representation of form and texture, the well-worn toys that I portray in my children's books lend themselves to this technique. I feel that children enjoy detail and my books bring toys to life in a matter-of-fact way, familiar to children. Everyday objects are portrayed in ordinary settings—the action alone being unexpected!"

HOPKINS, (Hector) Kenneth   1914-1988 (Christopher Adams, Anton Burney, Warwick Mannon, Paul Marsh, Edmund Marshall, Arnold Meredith)

OBITUARY NOTICE: Born December 7, 1914, in Bournemouth, Hampshire, England; died April 1, 1988, in Norwich, England. Educator, publisher, editor and author. Hopkins is credited with writing some sixty books and pamphlets, including detective stories and children's books, often under pseudonyms, and with editing, publishing, and contributing to many more. Among his more notable works are the critical studies *The Poets Laureate* and *Portraits in Satire;* a biograph-

JANE HISSEY

ical tribute to the Powys brothers, John Cowper, Llewelyn, and Theodore; many poetry collections, including *Love and Elizabeth,* lyric poems addressed to his wife; and an autobiography, *The Corruption of a Poet.* As Edmund Marshall he wrote children's books, such as *Tales of Ambledown Airport* and the *Missing Viscount.* He was a contributor to *The Children's Book of Famous Lives,* the *Encyclopedia Britannica,* and *The Dictionary of National Biography.* Hopkins was for many years a regular reviewer for the *Eastern Daily Press* and served as literary editor of *Everybody's* following World War II. Furthermore, he operated his own publishing house and taught English literature and creative writing at several American universities. His manuscripts, a selection of his literary correspondence, and other material relating to his work are at the Humanities Research Center of the University of Texas.

FOR MORE INFORMATION SEE:

Contemporary Authors: New Revision Series, Volume 17, Gale, 1986.

OBITUARIES

Times (London), April 7, 1988.
Guardian (London), April 12, 1988.

KEILLOR, Garrison 1942-

PERSONAL: Surname is pronounced *Kee*-ler; born Gary Keillor, on August 7, 1942, in Anoka, Minn.; son of John Philip (a railway mail clerk and carpenter) and Grace Ruth (a homemaker; maiden name, Denham) Keillor; married Mary C. Guntzel, September 11, 1965 (divorced, May, 1976); married Ulla Skaerved (a social worker), December 29, 1985; children: (first marriage) Jason, (stepchildren) Morten, Malene, Mattias. *Education:* University of Minnesota, B.A., 1966, graduate study, 1966-68. *Politics:* Democrat. *Religion:* Plymouth Brethren. *Home:* New York City, and Copenhagen, Denmark. *Office:* Minnesota Public Radio, 45 East 7th St., St. Paul, Minn. 55101. *Agent:* Ellen Levine, Ellen Levine Literary Agency, 432 Park Ave. S., New York, N.Y. 10016.

CAREER: Writer. KUOM-Radio, Minneapolis, Minn., staff announcer, 1963-68; Minnesota Public Radio, St. Paul, Minn., producer and announcer, 1969-70, 1971-73, host and principal writer for weekly program "A Prairie Home Companion," 1974-87. *Awards, Honors:* George Foster Peabody Broadcasting Award, 1980, for "A Prairie Home Companion"; Edward R. Murrow Award from the Corporation for Public Broadcasting, 1985, for service to public radio; Grammy, 1988,

GARRISON KEILLOR

for best spoken-word recording; Minnesota Book Award, 1988, for fiction.

WRITINGS

Happy to Be Here: Stories and Comic Pieces, Atheneum, 1982, expanded edition, Penguin, 1983.
Ten Years: The Official Souvenir Anniversary Program for a Prairie Home Companion, Minneapolis Public Radio, 1984.
Lake Wobegon Days, Viking, 1985.
Leaving Home: A Collection of Lake Wobegon Stories, Viking, 1987.
Don: The True Story of a Young Person, Redpath Press, 1987.
We Are Still Married: Stories and Letters, Viking, 1989.

RECORDINGS

"News from Lake Wobegon" (cassette), Minnesota Public Radio, 1983.
"Gospel Birds and Other News of Lake Wobegon" (cassette), Minnesota Public Radio, 1985.
"Prairie Home Companion: The Final Performance" (cassette), Minnesota Public Radio, 1987.
"Ain't That Good News" (record; cassette), Minnesota Public Radio, 1987.
"A Prairie Home Companion: The Last Show," (videocassette; also broadcast on the Disney Channel), Disney Home Video, 1987.
"Second Annual Farewell Performance of *A Prairie Home Companion,*" Radio City Music Hall, New York, N.Y., June, 1988.

Contributor of articles and stories to *New Yorker* and *Atlantic Monthly.*

ADAPTATIONS:

"Lake Wobegon Days" (cassette), Minnesota Public Radio, 1986.
"Happy to Be Here" (cassette), Minnesota Public Radio, 1987.

WORK IN PROGRESS: A novel about the death of live radio; a novel entitled, *Lake Wobegon Loose.*

SIDELIGHTS: Born **August 7, 1942** in Anoka, Minnesota, and christened Gary by his parents, John and Grace Denham Keillor. "I've lived all of my life in Minnesota. As a child, the Laura Ingalls Wilder books were special to me because they were set so close by. These stories led me to other books written by Minnesota authors, and later I read Sinclair Lewis and F. Scott Fitzgerald. I've loved all kinds of books—including books that are far better than anything Lewis or Fitzgerald ever wrote—but it amazed me as a boy that people could make books out of the terrain and population where I lived. It just amazed me, to think that you could write books about Minnesota."[1]

"When I was four years old, I fell through a hole in the haymow into the bull pen, missing the stanchion and landing in his feed trough full of hay, and was carried into the house and laid on my grandma's sofa, which smelled like this quilt, and so did a warm shirt handed down to me from my uncle. When I was little I didn't think of grownups as having bare skin; grownups were made of wool clothing, only kids were barenaked; now I'm older than they were when I was little and I lie naked under a quilt made of their clothes when they were children. I don't know what makes me think I'm smarter than them."[2]

"I grew up in the Plymouth Brethren Church. The Brethren were a tiny minority for whom life was strictly an upstream paddle. A great many things that the people of other creeds got to do were forbidden to us. I've felt that restriction as far back as I can remember. Still, being part of a minority—of whatever sort—is not the worst thing that can happen to somebody.

"I still believe what I was brought up to believe. I don't go to a Brethren assembly anymore, but I think that's more my fault than theirs. I doubt I'll ever go back, but you never know. People make some unusual turns in their forties, and so could I.

"I'm uncomfortable with churches more liberal than what I was brought up in. I have a hard time sitting still when a preacher's talking about the value of being a good person. Church is for sinners like me. Good people ought to stay home and read the *Times.*

"Religion *is* rigorous, whether a lot of people see it that way or not. That's not to excuse the cruelties committed in the name of rigor and doctrinal purity. If those people had *really* been rigorous themselves, they wouldn't have been intolerant.

"Most people think of fundamentalists as narrow-minded, unhappy, sexually frustrated, embittered people who are intolerant of everything that's different, hypocrites, to boot. That's a novelist's point of view, though. It's not based on the church I grew up in."[3]

"...The storyteller in our family was my Uncle Lew Powell, who was my great uncle, my grandma's brother, who died only a couple of years ago, at the age of ninety-three. In a

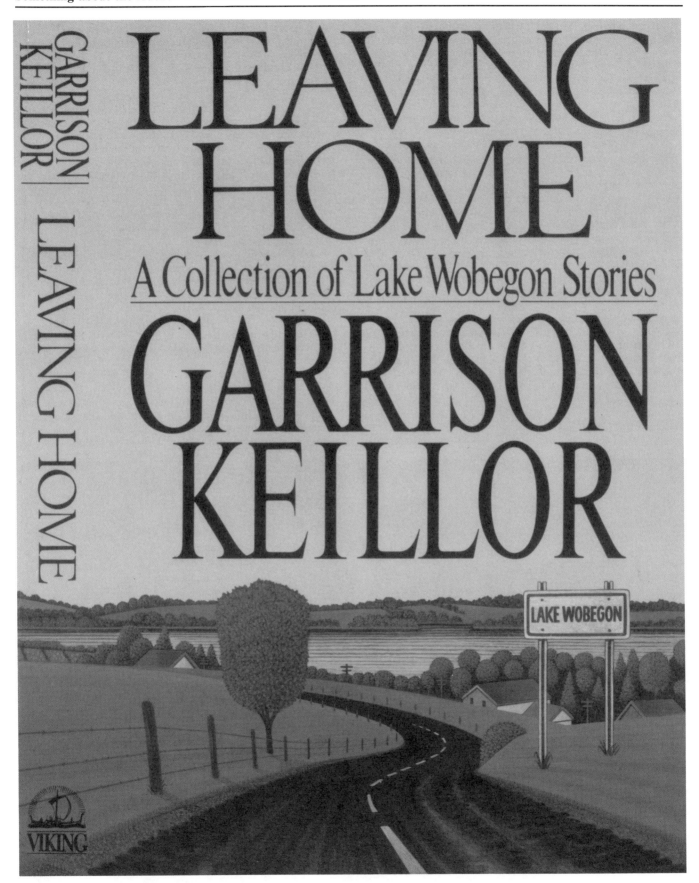

(Jacket illustration by Peter Thorpe from *Leaving Home* by Garrison Keillor.)

family that tended to be a little withdrawn, taciturn, my Uncle Lew was the friendliest. He had been a salesman, and he liked to drive around and drop in on people. He would converse, ask how we were doing in school, but there would be a point when he would get launched, and we would try to launch him. There were two different house-burning stories. I worked in a little bit of one in the book, the one where Great Grandpa came back from the Colorado gold fields, is the legend, and the gold dust was all lost in the blaze.

"My parents would be in the living room, and my Aunt Ada and my brothers and sisters. We would be eating popcorn. I remember lying on the floor when it got late so my mother wouldn't see me and send me to bed. Uncle Lew would stop for a while, and then someone else would spell him, my dad or my Aunt Ruth. And then Uncle Lew would come back. The period he talked about so well was about ten years on either side of the turn of the century. A beautiful time, I still think so. I just wanted him to tell more and more and more. I wanted to know everything. What it looked and smelled like, what they ate and what they wore.

"I remember Uncle Lew's stories not as coming to a moral, really, but to a point of rest, a point of contemplation. As I got older, of course, life was becoming strange. I looked to those stories of his, and to the history of the family, as giving a person some sense of place, that we were not just chips floating on the waves, that in some way we were meant to be here, and had a history. That we had standing."[4]

"As I get older, more and more often I hear my father's voice coming out of me, and I find myself saying things he would say. I write things that seem to me to be something my father would have said, or my Uncle Lew would have said—sort of an apotheosis of what they would have said if they had been writers. I find a satisfaction in doing that, that I don't get from writing funny stories."[1]

"New York was the first place I traveled as a boy. My dad took me. . .and I got to see the Brooklyn Dodgers play at Ebbets Field, to see Coney Island. I never forgot it. Especially because he didn't really want to take me, but he did. And it's the trip of my life, that trip I took. . .to the big city. It's the trip against which all other trips are compared. I could tell you everything about that trip, where we stayed, and almost everything that we did. So if you have eleven- or twelve-year-old kids, keep that in mind. Whatever you do for them may likely turn out to be permanent and memorable."[5]

"When I was fourteen, I was happy to read all day every day and into the night. I hid in closets and in the basement, locked myself in the bathroom, reading right up to the final moment when Mother pried the book from my fingers and shoved me outdoors into the land of living persons.

"She was right to do that. If she hadn't, I would be four feet tall, have beady little eyes and a caved-in chest and a butt like a bushel basket.

". . .Our family subscribed to *Reader's Digest, Popular Mechanics, National Geographic, Boys Life,* and *American Home.* My people weren't much for literature, and they were dead set against conspicuous wealth, so a magazine in which classy paragraphs marched down the aisle between columns of dia-

"It has been a quiet week in Lake Wobegone."

The continuing saga of "Buster the Show Dog," a regular feature on "A Prairie Home Companion."

mond necklaces and French cognacs was not a magazine they welcomed into their home. I was more easily dazzled than they and to me the *New Yorker* was a fabulous sight, an immense glittering ocean liner off the coast of Minnesota, and I loved to read it. I bought copies and smuggled them home, though with a clear conscience, for what I most admired was not the decor or the tone of the thing but rather the work of some writers, particularly the *New Yorker*'s great infield of Thurber, Liebling, Perelman, and White.

"They were my heroes: four older gentlemen, one blind, one fat, one delicate, and one a chicken rancher, and in my mind they took the field against the big mazumbos of American literature, and I cheered for them. I cheer for them now, all dead except Mr. White, and still think (as I thought then) that it is more worthy in the eyes of God and better for us as a people if a writer makes three pages sharp and funny about the lives of geese than to make three hundred flat and flabby about God or the American people."[6]

Submitted poetry to his junior high school newspaper under the byline Garrison Keillor. "It was in a school and at a time when boys didn't write poetry. So I used the name Garrison. It sounded a little stiffer, a little bigger. Flags flying. I think I was trying to hide behind a name that meant strength and 'don't give me a hard time about this.'"[1]

1960. Studied at the University of Minnesota at Minneapolis, working as a parking lot attendant to help pay for tuition. He dropped out for one year, because he was low on funds, but returned when he became employed at the campus radio station, KUOM. "I put myself through school working for the University of Minnesota radio station. I got the job, I think, because I was able to imitate the voice that they were looking

for. I could broaden a few vowels and get a kind of cultivated, funereal tone with a very slight British sound to it.

"Radio announcing is easy indoor work. You sit in the studio and you say, 'We have just heard "Appalachian Spring," by Aaron Copland, and we now turn to the music of Beethoven.' Announcing is much easier than parking cars or washing dishes, and yet it has a kind of status attached to it that I've never understood."[3]

"When I burst upon the radio business in 1963 as the friendly announcer of 'Highlights in Homemaking,' I badly wanted my voice to sound like that of Orson Welles, as rich and smooth as my mother's gravy on Sunday pot roast, and I succeeded so far as to sound at least brown and thick and lumpy, and then the pretense was too hard to keep up, and by the time 'Prairie Home' rolled along, my voice had drifted back toward center and sounded more like my dad's."[2]

That same year he became fiction editor for *Ivory Tower*, the campus literary magazine and interned briefly with the *St. Paul Pioneer Press*. "I loved newspaper writing, I did my share of weather, lots of obits, called hospitals to see if people in traffic accidents had died, and I interviewed authors. That's no way to live. Interviewing celebrities is just a step above calling the morgue."[7]

1965. Married fellow student Mary Guntzel, a music major and sometime contributor to *Ivory Tower*.

1966. Received a B.A. in English from the University of Minnesota. "It was a mistake to have gone to the university, to expend the time I did. . . .It had a corrupting influence on me on what I wrote. It removed me from what I had to write about and what I still have to write about—which is people that I came from and the class of people that I have some feeling about."[7]

Keillor traveled East by bus seeking employment with a nationally known magazine, and interviewed with the *Atlantic Monthly* in Boston. ". . .I rode the bus up from New York City and struck Boston early in the morning. I changed my clothes and washed my face in the Greyhound bus terminal. And I think that during the interviews they could tell that I was somebody who had just changed in a public rest room. I had a kind of hangdog look about me. I looked a little bit stiff, too, because I had to keep my hand on my leg where I had spilled some Orange Julius two days before. Well, they said they didn't have any jobs just then and they would let me know. . . ."[8]

1968. Hosted a three-hour classical music show for Minnesota Public Radio. "Part of this had to do with money—it's not easy to earn a living freelancing humorous fiction—but also with an attraction to radio. There's a wonderful simplicity about radio which cuts through my own pretenses.

"I had an early-morning radio show. You sit at a microphone with your favorite music, talk to people and wish them a happy birthday and try to create something pleasant and happy for them. Seemed to me to be a simple, decent service to mankind. Whereas sitting at a typewriter and writing often seems to me to be particularly ambitious, in sort of a scheming, crafty way. So much in humor and comedy is manipulative. But I love to write, I do it every day and I have since I was a little kid. So I've had to resolve these things somehow."[1]

"Radio makes me feel *competent*. A writer feels like an amateur every morning. He has to relearn his craft every time he sits down. When someone tells a writer, 'Hey, that was a terrific story,' he thinks of all the silly stuff he's written and all the blank paper he's stared at, and he thinks, 'How can that be so?' With radio it's different. When I do a show, I feel competent in something."[9]

1969. Son, Jason, was born. "Being a parent is not something that people ever feel confident or secure about."[10] Keillor told students at Gettysburg College. "When you were tiny children, we started to read about tremendous advances in prenatal education. And when you got a little bit older, we started reading great books about early childhood and fantastic things that parents can do. We've always been a step behind in bringing you up. . . .We wanted to bring you up with information about sex that we never had. Our parents only told us that if we listened to rock 'n' roll, we would have babies—and they were right."[10]

A parody of small town newspaper stories, called "Local Family Keeps Son Happy," about a family that hired a local prostitute to keep their seventeen-year-old son company so he wouldn't leave home was published in the *New Yorker*. It was the first of many Keillor stories published by the magazine. "When you write. . .fiction for the *New Yorker* and you feel as I did then about the *New Yorker,* you tend to be an extremely careful writer. I went through a great many drafts, and I studied every sentence, and it was work that I enjoyed doing, but it was also very difficult."[11]

"I still love the *New Yorker* and love writing for them, and want to write anything I can for them. But there's another style of writing that I cannot do for them, which is to me more Midwestern, more colloquial. My Lake Wobegon monologues, which all start out as writing, are humor that is also sentimental. They have an emotional base you don't have in short, satirical fiction. Satire to me has a moral base but not an emotional base. And the monologues, always do."[1]

Keillor belts out a tune.

March, 1971. Left broadcasting to try writing full time. "I would sell a story and then wait two weeks and call and ask for the money. It bothered me that I was spending so much time doing what seemed like humiliating, adolescent things. . .to look through the *New Yorker* to get ideas on how to write another story they would want. It did me no good and I knew that, but just to be busy and neurotic and try to have a plan about it and go at things straight."[7]

Months later he returned to Minnesota Public Radio, this time to KSJN, the flagship station in St. Paul. He attributed this upgrading to his having been published in the *New Yorker*. "I would never have been able to get away with playing the music I did unless I happened to be associated with a magazine which, although it has changed, still, in the Midwest, stands for being Uptown."[7]

1974. Keillor was assigned by the *New Yorker* to do a feature story on the Grand Ole Opry, and returned with a format in mind for "The Prairie Home Companion." "It occurred to me then that I needed a hobby. . .and I thought I'd like to *talk* for a hobby. I'd like to say funny things that couldn't be edited, that no researchers would examine—and that led me to live radio."[8]

The first live broadcast of "The Prairie Home Companion" took place on July 6th of that year, and included favorite local musicians as well as scripted radio sketches, with Keillor as the host. One Saturday in the summer of 1975, he delivered a monologue, seemingly unscripted, which began "It has been a quiet week in Lake Wobegon. . ." and told of the residents of that mythical town. "I stood at the microphone, looked up into the lights, and let fly. If the crowd got restless, I sat down on a stool, which caught their interest, and if they rustled again, I stood up. After twenty minutes or as soon as the story came to an extremely long pause, I stopped and said, 'That's the news from Lake Wobegon, where all the women are strong, the men are good-looking, and all the children are above average,' and walked off."[2]

"[Lake Wobegon's] residents include almost all of the people I've known in my life. The town also incorporates most of what has ever happened to me. My childhood, my education, my belief, and my disbelief all go back to that place, and from Lake Wobegon I get my voice."[8]

"The place is an invention between myself and the audience and we are all aware of this. I don't really do too much, just draw out a few lines, and the audience fills in everything else. Lake Wobegon is a screen we have set up. We are really looking for something beyond that screen, though. It would be pretentious if we tried to say exactly what that is, but it's always there."[12]

The challenge of performing for a live audience holds a particular significance, since Keillor considers himself a shy person. "Shy is beautiful, for the most part. . . .A lot of people who are not shy think that those of us who are would simply like to be uninhibited. That's not true. What a lot of shy people really dread is talking nonsense."[13]

"An audience is intimidating, really intimidating. . . .But I never want to see the day when it isn't. Sometimes the thing that you dread and are afraid of is the very thing you should do, just in order to not have to think about it."[14]

"As terrifying as getting up in front of an audience was—and still is today—nobody can resist laughter. The chance to make people laugh has a powerful attraction."[11]

1976. Divorced wife.

1978. "A Prairie Home Companion" found a permanent home in the World Theatre in St. Paul. "The World Theater, our home for half of those thirteen years, was the right place for that sort of seance, a classic Shubert two-balcony house from 1905, inhabited by two bats and the ghost of a stagehand, all seats within eighty feet of the stage, closer than first base to home. Standing at stage center with your toes to the footlights, you're as close to a thousand people as you can conceivably be. Out there on the prairie where even close friends tend to stand an arm's length apart, such intimacy on such a grand scale is shocking and thrilling and a storyteller reaches something like critical mass, passing directly from solid to radio waves without going through the liquid or gaseous phase. You stand in the dark, you hear people leaning forward, you smell the spotlights, and you feel invisible.

"No script, no clock, only pictures in your mind that the audience easily sees, they sit so close. You come to be so calm out there, it is more like going to bed than going out to work. It is like crawling under [the] quilt that my grandma Dora Keillor made for me from scraps of clothes worn by my aunts and uncles, which is soft and thin from years of sleep, which comes easily to me when I lie under a smell that goes back to my earliest times lying in bed between my mother and father."[2]

"A Prairie Home Companion" was first heard nationwide in 1980. "I always thought that one of the most wonderful things about the show was that I didn't know many people who listened to it, and they would tell me about their kids and talk about walleye fishing and complain about work and compare automobiles and discuss gas mileage. From this and my memories, I derived a town and populated it. I didn't invent anything. I simply took what I saw around me and put it in another form and came up with fiction.

"I would take a small thing and make it stand for something. To me, that's what a writer does. I think that I was put here on Earth to do that, to write in extravagant praise of common things."[15]

1982. *Happy to Be Here* published. "I can't think of stories in formal terms until they're written. Then I can look at a story that I have written or that someone else has written, and I can describe its form, as I did when I was in school and was asked to write term papers. Every story finds its own form. Finding that form is the great struggle of writing, for which there is no prescription. I would say that the essential element in storytelling is the passion of finding out how to tell it. If you don't have that passion to tell a story, you will settle for telling it not very well, which is almost worse than not telling it at all. But if you have the passion to tell a story, it becomes a wonderful problem in your life like being in love. It becomes an irritation, a splendid misery, that might get some work out of a person to do his little part in adding to the world's knowledge."[16]

"Writing is still a pleasure after all these years. I've stuck an awful lot of paper into typewriters, and still get a little thrill with each fresh sheet. One never knows what might result. It's usually dreary but in writing, unlike teaching, we get to destroy the failures. In teaching, all the failures graduate anyway, as I well know, having been one of them."[17]

"At some point in the writing, I will sit down with a manuscript and go over it, word for word, more than once—sometimes many times. Writing consists of very small parts pieced together into a whole, and if the parts are defective, the whole

Keillor performs before a packed house. ■(Photograph courtesy of Minnesota Public Radio.)

won't work. But that's a mechanical view. What really comes first is feeling and passion and curiosity.

"If the writer is true to personal experience, the reader is offered something recognizable. It's only as you are faithful to the peculiarities and the exact description of personal experience that you create something that other people will be able to take as their own."[16]

1985. *Lake Wobegon Days* published. "I'm more comfortable put into the third person. There's no one character that's more me than another; there are a lot of characters to whom I ascribe what happened to me; there's not one character I'm especially fond of over another. There's not one hero in the piece. In fact, there aren't many heroes around Lake Wobegon at all."[17]

"The book has what I believe to be the longest footnote in American fiction [a twelve-page parody of Martin Luther's ninety-five theses]. I was pleased with the footnotes in the book and that one in particular. I think footnotes have a place in fiction. There is supporting material which can be read in sequence or earlier or just glanced at or eliminated entirely, and that can go into footnotes. It really allows a person freedom of digression that you want in a book. And I like the idea of a book being packed and rich and having layers."[1]

Attended his twenty-fifth high school reunion where he became reacquainted with Ulla Skaerved, a Danish social worker who had been an exchange student in Anoka when he was a senior. They were married months later. "I met my wife Ulla...in 1959 when we were seventeen. She was an AFS exchange student come from Denmark to Anoka, Minnesota, and I was a classmate who admired her and suffered mute ecstasy and unspeakable torment over her, oftentimes simultaneously. I was a writer. Long before I dared say hi to her in

the hallway, I had written poems about her red hair and brown eyes, her stunning smile and grace, her sweetly accented voice, and about my love for her which was spiritual and fine, being secret, was also unrequited. I was 6'3" tall and weighed 150 pounds, all of it pure feeling struggling to get onto paper. It wasn't easy. I felt that I was one of the first people in the world to ever fall in love like that, and it was hard to put such an extraordinary phenomenon into mere English words such as are used by other people.

"Twenty-five years passed, and one warm day in August, 1985, I drove north from Minneapolis along the Mississippi River to a friend's house to meet [her] again who had returned from Denmark for the silver anniversary reunion of our high school class. I got out of the car, walked toward the house, and she opened the door and came down the steps into the sunshine. We embraced each other. We walked along the shore and around our old neighborhood, and on my way home I stopped and got about ten pounds of books about Denmark out of the library. I learned the phrase *jeg elsker dig* for 'I love you' and, in case that made me spill my coffee, *undskyld* for 'Excuse me.' I had gone along all this time knowing nothing about Denmark except Hans Christian Andersen, strong beer, Hamlet, and flat furniture with skinny legs, but what I felt for her was tumultuous and overpowering and the rest of my life became clear to me.

"I wrote her two or three poems that week, nothing so original because—at the age of forty-three you start to understand that love isn't unique or individual but is common as dirt, which is what is most beautiful: to know that our love for each other is the same stuff that other people's lives are made of, an ordinary, mysterious everyday transcendent quality, the stuff of music. So I sang. I sang *'Jeg Fik En Sorg Sa Stor'* to her and the next day after saying goodbye, I drove around Min-

Keillor and Ulla pose with their children after their wedding. ■ (Photograph courtesy of Wide World Photos, Inc.)

neapolis singing 'Lovesick Blues' at the top of my voice—
'That last long day she said goodbye, Lord, I thought I would
die'—and sang it the next Saturday on 'A Prairie Home Companion,' and 'Let Them Talk' and 'Slow Days of Summer.' I
sang 'Tell Me Why' alone in hotel rooms touring with the
show, sang 'The Water Is Wide' to her on the telephone, sang
'Whoopi Ti Yi' on a visit to Copenhagen in September, and
again in October, and 'Ain't That Good News' in November
when she visited me. I sang a love song every Saturday on
the show because I was happy. We married in December at a
little church north of Copenhagen, with great festivity, attended by our four elegant children, in a shower of rice and a
chorus of *Skols,* amid speeches and songs. The organ played
'What a Wonderful World' as we receded, and here we are,
one more husband and wife in the sweet history of marriage,
not so different from all the others."[18]

"My true love doesn't know anything about 'A Prairie Home
Companion,' and she doesn't read English well enough to
know that I am a humorous person. She thinks of me as passionate and sweet and a terrific singer, which is what I have
wanted to be all my life."[19]

"I've had sort of a running disagreement with the two newspapers in town over what constitutes private life, and there
really isn't any way to resolve it. . . ."[20]

"The hometown newspaper decided that, being a published
author, I was a credit to the community and should be paid
close attention, so it announced my romance with my wife and
published a photograph of our house, our address, and interviews with the neighbors. I felt watched. Felt mistaken for
somebody else. It dawned on me that life might be better
elsewhere. That winter it was warm, there was no snow, the
landscape was dry and brown and bleak. We left Saint Paul
in June, as soon as school was out."[2]

"It wasn't the fact of being known that was so hard. I think
a person who does a radio show can expect to be known beyond friends and family. . . .It was the feeling that I had of
being punished, in a way, for having done better than I was
supposed to.

"I had thought for many years that I would live all my life in
Minnesota. I had no particular wish to go elsewhere. But I
couldn't live in my hometown under those circumstances. When
your home is no longer a place you feel secure, a place you're
understood and people respect you, it's like not having a front
door."[21]

Keillor also sensed that his contribution to the show was not
what it had been or could be. "I've simply come to the point
where my material isn't as good as I want it to be. It's time
to pull away, listen to the way people talk. I need the discipline
of reporting to get back my ear for dialogue."[22]

"Then, you see, you lose your ability to gather material. Suddenly people don't talk to you about all these interesting things.
They talk about, 'Isn't this interesting what's happening to
you?' I don't know that it is so interesting, actually."[15]

"You do something for twelve years and maybe you learn how
to do it too well. Then you need something else to come along
to create new problems."[23]

In **1987,** he decided to move his family to Denmark, thus
ending the run of "The Prairie Home Companion." The ad-
justment to life in a new country was one he felt ready to
make. "Some days it seems that I am living the immigrant
dream in reverse, starting with success in America, then the

Dust jacket for Keillor's 1989 book. ■ (From *We Are
Still Married* by Garrison Keillor. Illustrated by
Wendell Minor.)

voyage, then the life of servitude in the Old World. It's hard
work setting up housekeeping in a foreign language. But then
I take my shopping bag down to the open market on Freder-
iksborggade and one look down the avenue of booths heaped
with crates of produce and I'm home in Lake Wobegon, back
in the land of tomatoes and cucumbers. Cucumbers are *agurker*
in Danish, but tomatoes are *tomater* and I see *meloner* and
nektariner, bananer, radiser, broccoli, selleri, and plenty of
aebler (both 'Golden Delicious' and 'Granny Smith'). For
vandmelon, you pay ten kroner, almost $1.50, and they're as
big and thump as well as what I remember from our *vandmelon*
patch at home. *Mais* is ten kroner for three ears, a little expensive, but when it comes to *mais* who counts the cost?

"Sweet corn was our family's weakness. We were prepared
to resist atheistic Communism, immoral Hollywood, hard liq-
uor, gambling and dancing, smoking, fornication, but if Satan
had come around with sweet corn, we at least would have
listened to what he had to sell. We might not have bought it
but we would've had him in and given him a cup of coffee."[2]

". . .In Denmark, a country that I have been trying to figure
out, and a country that I felt so much more certain of my
opinions about it the first week I was there than I did a month
later. I felt after a week in Denmark that I could write a book
about it, then after a month or so I thought I could write a
magazine article about it; and now I'd be satisfied to say three
true things about that country."[5]

Leaving Home, a collection of stories from "A Prairie Home
Companion," published. "It seems to me that in a great many
of these stories, even before I was aware of it, I was showing
signs of being ready to pick up. Some of the characters in the
stories are thinking the same thing. And others are coming to
realize that this is where they'll be the rest of their lives.

"I wrote these as stories and then performed them on the show—not from a script, but from an imperfect memory. I felt that they were better as stories than they were in performance. I want them to appear in the best way they can, which is in print. My aim was not to transcribe a performance and put it in print; some of the best stories that I did on the show really were performances and I've not included them here.

"My fear was that the longer I did the show and talked about Lake Wobegon, the more I would cut corners and not do justice to the characters in the town. But I feel that I did give them my best effort as a writer. If I were to sit down and write another book about Lake Wobegon, I might do many things differently, and it might have a different feeling to it, especially now that I'm so far away, but I was pleased with the way the characters came across in print."[20]

In the fall, Keillor and his wife moved to New York City. He subsequently addressed the National Press Club in Washington, D.C. "It's lovely to come here and break my retirement with you. It's a frightening thing to get up in front of a microphone and be on radio and talk to a roomful of people after months of not doing it; months of being in another country. . .where if an American can say 'Good Morning' and 'Thank You' and 'Where is the railway station,' they think you are just brilliant. Especially your mother-in-law does.

"I've had three months off—more than that, five months—to sit and contemplate all of those people whom I've told stories about; and a storyteller has to keep working. If you ever stop and think about what you've done, you just feel such guilt about not having done better by these people.

"I miss ['The Prairie Home Companion']. I miss it terribly. I could not find any work in Denmark that I was the least bit useful at, except for washing dishes. As we see these headlines in the paper [the stock market crash of October, 1987], we start to think about other career skills we might have, and washing dishes is one of mine. I put myself through a part of college washing dishes, which is why I do it so seldom now that I'm married, because I'm a professional. I can handle large amounts of them, but to do just a few really doesn't interest me that much. Same reason that journalists don't write letters. But I did dishes in Denmark."[5]

Keillor discussed some future plans with *Publishers Weekly,* including a screenplay based on Lake Wobegon. "I've never written a script before and it feels awkward, the times I've given it a try. It came from my interest in doing something I'd never done before, and also being able to see this town. People who listened to the stories on the radio claimed they could see the town, but I only had a hazy view. I wanted to put the characters up on screen so I could take a look at 'em.

"But I'm finding it's hard to move them in and out [of scenes]. Mainly it's hard to move them out. They tend to walk in and just hang around, same as I do in real life. I never know how to leave a party.

"I'm working on a novel that is set in a radio station which I started almost ten years ago. I'm going to throw out the characters and keep the radio station—fire the staff and start over again. They just didn't interest me long enough.

". . .I want to get back to writing fact pieces for the *New Yorker.* I've been fiddling with a piece about coming to Denmark and the experience of feeling stupid.

". . .I'll have to get back to doing something in front of an audience in the near future, or else accept that I couldn't do it anymore. I don't think you can lay off for too long—it's too scary, too terrible. I'd hate to think of not performing again

Front illustration from the boxed set of four audio cassettes.

GARRISON KEILLOR

AIN'T THAT GOOD NEWS

PRODUCED BY CHET ATKINS

Album cover for Keillor's 1987 record.

right now, but it could happen. It's something that you need other people in order to do; it's not like writing. I miss the link with people."[20]

The pull of an audience is indeed strong in Keillor. In **1989** he prepared for a third farewell tour, recounting the doings in faraway Lake Wobegon. His is also preparing twenty-four new broadcasts for the fall. "Perhaps I will move some of the Wobegonians to New York,"[24] he mused.

FOOTNOTE SOURCES

[1]Diane Roback, "PW Interviews: Garrison Keillor," *Publishers Weekly,* September 13, 1985. Amended by G. Keillor.
[2]Garrison Keillor, "A Letter from Copenhagen" (introduction), *Leaving Home,* Viking, 1987.
[3]Peter Hemingson, "The Plowboy Interview," *Mother Earth News,* May-June, 1985. Amended by G. Keillor.
[4]John Skow, "Lonesome Whistle Blowing," *Time,* November 4, 1985. Amended by G. Keillor.
[5]National Press Club Speech, Washington, D.C., 1987.
[6]G. Keillor, "Introduction," *Happy to Be Here,* Atheneum, 1982.
[7]Ira Letofsky, "For Garrison Keillor Fantasy Is a Lot More Fun Than Reality," *Tribune* (Minneapolis), July 29, 1976.
[8]James Traub, "The Short and Tall Tales of Garrison Keillor," *Esquire,* May, 1982.
[9]Paul Judge, "Portrait: Garrison Keillor," *Life,* May, 1982.
[10]"Education: Lake Wobegon Chronicler Garrison Keillor at Gettysburg College, Gettysburg, Pa.," *Time,* June 22, 1987.
[11]*Current Biography,* August, 1985.

[12]Les Lindeman, "In a Lake Wobegon Daze," *Chicago Sun Times*, September 13, 1985. Amended by G. Keillor.

[13]Edward Fishe, "Small-Town America," *New York Times*, October 31, 1982.

[14]Jon Pareles, "Prairie Humor Comes to the Big City," *New York Times*, May 13, 1983.

[15]Peg Meier, "Wobegon and the Burden of Celebrity," *Newsday*, April 20, 1987.

[16]Michael Schumacher, "Sharing the Laughter with Garrison Keillor," *Writer's Digest*, January, 1986. Amended by G. Keillor.

[17]John Bordsen, "All the News from Lake Wobegon," *Saturday Review*, May-June, 1983. Amended by G. Keillor.

[18]"Line Notes" from "Ain't That Good News" (record album), Minnesota Public Radio, 1987.

[19]"Lake Wobegon's Garrison Keillor Finds a Love That Time Forgot and the Decades Can't Improve," *People Weekly*, November 25, 1985.

[20]Alan Bunce, "Denmark-Bound Keillor Chats about His Plans," *Christian Science Monitor*, March 3, 1987.

[21]D. Roback, "Leaving the Shores of Lake Wobegon," *Publishers Weekly*, August 21, 1987.

[22]Dirk Johnson, "With Singing, Satire and Sentiment, Lake Wobegon Fades," *New York Times*, June 14, 1987.

[23]Steve Scheider, *New York Times*, March 1, 1987.

[24]"People," *Time*, June 5, 1989.

FOR MORE INFORMATION SEE:

Time, November 9, 1981, February 1, 1982, September 2, 1985, October 26, 1987, March 28, 1988 (p. 88).
Country Journal, January, 1982.
Washington Post Book World, January 18, 1982.
Chicago Tribune Book World, January 24, 1982.
Chicago Tribune, May 20, 1982.
Christian Century, July 21-28, 1982, November 13, 1985.
Linda Feldmann, "Radio's 'Prairie Home': City Slickers Like It, Too," *Christian Science Monitor*, May 23, 1983.
People Weekly, February 6, 1984, October 12, 1987.
New York Times, July 8, 1984, August 20, 1985, October 31, 1985, November 1, 1987.
Detroit News, September 1, 1985.
Detroit Free Press, September 8, 1985.
Dan Cryer, "America's Hottest New Storyteller," *Newsday*, October 13, 1985.
Michael Walker, "Interview: The Met Grill," *Metropolitan Home*, November, 1985.
"Door Interviews Garrison Keillor," *Wittenberg Door*, December-January, 1985-86.
Wayne Lee Gay, "Voice of the Prairie," *Continental*, February, 1986.
Newsweek, June 15, 1987, July 4, 1988 (p. 30).
"Leaving Lake Wobegon," *Time*, June 29, 1987.
Video, September, 1987.
Daily News, October 25, 1987.
Garrison Keillor, "How to Write a Personal Letter," *Reader's Digest*, November, 1987.
"Garrison Keillor: Beyond Lake Wobegon," National Public Radio, 1987.
Michael Fedo, *The Man from Lake Wobegon*, St. Martin's, 1987.
Variety, March 16, 1988.
Parade, May 29, 1988.

KOVALSKI, Maryann 1951-

PERSONAL: Born June 4, 1951, in New York, N.Y.; daughter of Samuel and Alice (Caputo) Kovalski; married Gregory

MARYANN KOVALSKI

Sheppard (a commercial film director), August 30, 1976; children: Genevieve F., Joanna E. *Education:* Attended School of Visual Arts, 1969-72. *Home:* 138 Balmoral Ave., Toronto, Ontario, Canada M4V 1J4. *Office:* 14 Monteith St., Toronto, Ontario, Canada M4Y 1K7.

CAREER: Vickers & Benson Advertising, Montreal, Canada, art director, 1974-75; free-lance editorial illustrator, 1975-84; free-lance author and illustrator of children's books, 1984—. Co-owner of Dinsmore Gallery, 1984-85. *Exhibitions:* Dinsmore Gallery, Toronto, 1983; Children's Bookstore, Toronto, 1984; McGill Club, Toronto, 1987; Vancouver Art Gallery, British Columbia, 1988. *Member:* Canadian Society of Children's Authors, Illustrators, and Performers; Writers Union; Society of Illustrators (N.Y.); McGill Club.

WRITINGS:

SELF-ILLUSTRATED

Brenda and Edward, Kids Can Press, 1984.
The Wheels on the Bus, Little, Brown, 1987.
Jingle Bells, Little, Brown, 1988.

ILLUSTRATOR

Allen Morgan, *Molly and Mr. Maloney*, Kids Can Press, 1981.
Ted Staunton, *Puddleman*, Kids Can Press, 1983.
Lois Sharon and Bram Sharon, *Mother Goose: Songs, Finger Rhymes, Tickling Verses, Games and More*, Douglas & McIntyre, 1985, Atlantic Monthly, 1986.
Frances Harber, *My King Has Donkey Ears*, Scholastic-TAB, 1986.
Rose Robart, *The Cake That Mack Ate*, Kids Can Press, 1986, Little, Brown, 1987.
Tim Wynne-Jones, *I'll Make You Small*, Douglas & McIntyre, 1986.
Paulette Bourgeois, *Grandma's Secret*, Kids Can Press, 1989.
Alice's Birthday Giant, Scholastic, 1989.

The wheels on the bus go round and round

round and round

round and round

The wheels on the bus go round and round

all around the town.

Grandma, Jenny, and Joanna had so much fun . . .

(From *The Wheels on the Bus* by Maryann Kovalski. Illustrated by the author.)

WORK IN PROGRESS: The Fish 'n Chips Man and His Wife, for Kids Can Press.

SIDELIGHTS: "Because I came to the field as an illustrator first, I've been fortunate to have been allowed a great deal of 'on-the-job' training, observing the writing of others while illustrating their work.

"I've also been encouraged to go beyond decorating text. When I was given the manuscript to *The Cake That Mack Ate* I received no suggestions or instructions except to 'go.' It was easy to see the farmer and his wife as an older couple—no problem. But making Mack a little boy (as was the author's intention) struck me as a bit lacking. After a bit it just seemed to make sense that Mack be their dog. How lucky I was that the author, Rose Robart, was a good sport and was delighted!

"I suppose it's also true that I rely on pictures for visual sub-plots because of my history as an illustrator, even when I write the text. I thumbnail (sketch little pictures) as I write story ideas. It's a habit I don't recommend, though, as it has gotten me into trouble more than once. I develop a fondness for an image, or a scene, that I desperately want to see happen—even if it's at the peril of the story! I've written around it, disguised it only slightly and fooled no one. Finally my publisher gets me to abandon it and remember the point of the exercise—to make a good story with words and pictures.

"If a story is to be good it must be true. That doesn't mean that it must be an actual retelling of a factual event, though many a good story has started out that way. It must be from the heart. It must have a universal emotional truth. Later the

writer can detach emotionally and a good and ruthless editor will polish it. I learned that the hard way. In the beginning I wrote countless bad stories about 'the little people who lived in the forest. . . .' Essentially I was telling some vague rehash of the Brothers Grimm or a story I loved from my childhood. The original writer's story was good and mine were so bad because they were not *my* stories. The person I have become is clearly a city person. The urban sprawl I find myself in is endlessly fascinating to me. Finally I have come to realize that sticking to one's own landscape and heart is really most prac-tical, as well as most satisfying. For me, having two small children hasn't changed me as an author or an illustrator, I don't think. Essentially I want to write what I want to write about. I don't try to please my audience of small children. I don't do 'market research' at home. I tried it once and my kids loved what I wrote. I think they sensed mommy's des-perate need for their approval and they wanted more cookies and they are not fools. Anyway, the publisher hated it. So much for market research. I find trying to please deadly be-cause that's a hop, skip, and jump away from anticipating a reaction. The results are almost always stilted and self-conscious.

"Having children has had one helpful effect on my work, though. It's made me realize how new the world is for them. How few snowfalls they've seen, how rare is a thunderstorm.

"This obvious truth came home to me with a great bang only last Christmas. I was taking my almost three-year-old to see Santa Claus. This was my first child and I was realizing a long held fantasy of this moment. I was terribly excited and was counting the days and talking the whole trip up to my daughter for weeks. She was as excited as I was. Finally the great day arrived and we trooped off to the department store. Every child in the free world was on that line. I jollied her along with 'This is *so* exciting, isn't it Gennie?' I hopped with anticipation and the hope that she wouldn't become exhausted and bored. She was wonderfully energized with the excitement of seeing the great man himself so would only gasp from time to time, 'Oh Mommy, I can't wait to see Santa Claus!' Finally we were getting closer. We were, by this time, shrieking with excitement. Our turn. There was a little bridge we had to cross and Santa's bifocalled assistant with a clipboard in the crook of her arm motioned impatiently for us to come forward. We raced over the little bridge, our coats and packages spilling when Gennie stopped, 'Mommy wait!' She held my arm, 'Who *is* Santa Claus?' I forgot to tell her the obvious. I do that in my writing too.

"Each book affords me another exploration, another chance to strengthen my visual and verbal skills. In one book I may be exploring architecture. In my latest book, *Jingle Bells,* I really wanted to explore mood. It turned out to be a valentine to New York City. When I was doing it I forgot how much I missed it, how much I loved it when it gets hit by those rare great swamping snowfalls. As kids we would stare out the windows, desperate for a snow holiday. As I worked on those pictures I got so deeply involved in the memory I could smell it, I could hear the chains on the cars' tires. It was really quite a remarkable experience. I remembered so many parts of my childhood growing up in the Bronx I thought I'd forgotten in my present rather sedate life here in Toronto.

"Each book requires great concentrated bouts of observation. All this observing has brought an unexpected richness to my life. For the longest time my only passion was to become good at what I did—I didn't know it would make me love life more."

FOR MORE INFORMATION SEE:

Quill & Quire, October, 1985.
Toronto Star, November 1, 1987.
Writers on Writing, Grolier, 1988.

LORD, Bette Bao   1938-

PERSONAL: Born November 3, 1938, in Shanghai, China; came to the United States in 1946; naturalized U.S. citizen, 1964; daughter of Sandys (a Nationalist Chinese government official) and Dora (Fang) Bao; married Winston Lord (president, Council on Foreign Relations), May 4, 1963; children: Elizabeth Pillsbury, Winston Bao. *Education:* Tufts University, B.A., 1959; Fletcher School of Law and Diplomacy, M.A., 1960. *Home:* c/o Bao, 626 Floyd St., Englewood Cliffs, N.J. 07632. *Agent:* Irving Paul Lazar Agency, 211 South Beverly Dr., Beverly Hills, Calif. 90212.

CAREER: University of Hawaii, East-West Cultural Center, Honolulu, assistant director, 1960-61; Fulbright Exchange Program, Washington, D.C., program officer, 1961-63. Taught and performed modern dance in Geneva and Washington, D.C., 1964-73; conference director, National Conference for the Associated Councils of the Arts, 1970-71. Lecturer with the Leigh Bureau; member of selection committee, White House Fellows; member of board, National Committee on United States-China Relations, Inc. *Awards, honors:* National Graphic Arts Prize, 1974, for photographic essay on China; American Book Award nomination, 1982, for *Spring Moon;* honorary LL.D. from Tufts University, 1982; Jefferson Cup Award from the Virginia Library Association, 1985, and one of Child Study Association of America's Children's Books of the Year, 1987, both for *In the Year of the Boar and Jackie Robinson.*

BETTE BAO LORD

WRITINGS:

JUVENILE

In the Year of the Boar and Jackie Robinson (juvenile; ALA Notable Book; illustrated by Marc Simont), Harper, 1984.

OTHER

(With sister Sansan) *Eighth Moon: The True Story of a Young Girl's Life in Communist China,* Harper, 1964.
Spring Moon: A Novel of China, Harper, 1981.

WORK IN PROGRESS: The Middle Heart, a novel of China.

SIDELIGHTS: Born in Shanghai, China, Lord came to the United States with her father when she was eight years old. "What if I had never sailed from Shanghai to Brooklyn in 1946, left the land of my birth as a child? Would I still be I? Sometimes, in humility, I bow to history. Sometimes, in hubris, I shout yes.

"Surely everyone wonders about roads not taken—that other school, that other job, that other love. But there is a difference: Only we immigrants can point to the fork that above all else has shaped our destinies. We know its longitude and latitude. We know the year, the day, the hour we embarked. We know whether the skies then were lit by the sun or salted with stars.

"To me, this journey, be it a single step or across the world, reveals us far better than the cast of our features, the lilt of our speech, or even our metaphysical familiarity with alien ways we have never been taught. Many will scoff at my naivete. Others will call me a fool. Perhaps that is why I have not dared write the story of America and me, except in a children's book. For to do so would risk the credibility of the teller and the realism of the tale.

"Indeed, my life is a fable even the gullible Snow White would find hard to swallow. I docked in Brooklyn on a sleepy Sunday and was enrolled at P.S. 8 in Brooklyn Heights on a sneezy Monday. Dopey and bashful was I because I didn't speak a word of English, but always at hand were people happy to instruct me. And, believe it or not, never once did I hear from anyone in New York a suggestion as grumpy as 'Take a slow boat to China, girl. In America, only we can do it. You can't!'

"On that first day at school, the principal asked, 'How old are you?' My mother translated. Though eight, I stuck up ten fingers. Sociologists explain that the extra two fingers were because Chinese are considered a year old when born, two upon the new year. The novelist in me asserts it was foreshadowing, without which a suspenseful story degenerates into anecdote.

"Meanwhile, I was the shortest fifth-grader in all of the five boroughs. No one gave it a thought. Weren't Chinese known to be small?

"By the time I was a high-school student in Teaneck, my mother dreamed for me the typical Chinese version of the American Dream. It was not to be 'my son, the lawyer'—rather, 'my progeny, the ist.' In other words, chemist, intern-ist, physicist—in short scientist.

"By college, visions of Nobel Prizes danced in my head. And so I signed up to study how to make a better living through chemistry. To me, it mattered not that in the lab I was a bull in a china shop, in class, the empress of bull. To the head of the department, however, it mattered a lot. Therefore, he made

On and on he squawked while she poked at the keys.
■ (From *In the Year of the Boar and Jackie Robinson* by Bette Bao Lord. Illustrated by Marc Simont.)

me an offer I couldn't refuse: 'Major in chemistry and flunk, or transfer out and pass.'

"No doubt in another country this would be the makings of ignominy, for Mother cried, 'What shame! My daughter, the only Chinese American without an ist.' (Unbeknownst to us both, upon reaching middle age, I would at last become an ist—novelist.)

"Again, foreshadowing. But only with hindsight was everything made clear. Had I not emigrated, skipped two grades, failed at chemistry, I would never have met, much less married, the young Wasp in my world-economics class at the Fletcher School of Law and Diplomacy.

"In novels, an interracial marriage must incur melodrama, if not wrath. In reality, the only reservation to ours was voiced by a GS-15 named Mr. Szluk, who informed me of a State Department ruling that limits the careers of foreign-service officers with immigrant spouses. Henceforth, he spouted, your husband is barred from all work concerning China.

"Today, I write from 17 Guang Hua Lu, the residence of the American ambassador to China. Tonight, I share his bed. Do I have the courage to draw the obvious conclusions and say that a dream I never dared to dream has—? Not me. I'm too superstitious a Chinese to tempt the gods. Not me, I'm too sophisticated a New Yorker for rose-colored glasses tinted red, white, and blue. I'll speak, instead, of the heroine of my children's book: 'Here, Shirley Temple Wong was somebody. She felt as if she had the power of ten tigers, as if she had grown as tall as the Statue of Liberty.'"[1]

Lord's first book told the story of her sister Sansan "who grew up in China, [and] was reunited with the family after a separation of sixteen years.

"I stumbled into writing. I wrote *Eighth Moon*, my sister's story, because she only spoke Chinese and I knew of no writers who did. Ignorant of how difficult it was to get into print, I took up the task. When it was published, it did suprisingly well.

". . .It has been on secondary schools' reading lists. . . .Recently when I was interviewed by someone who was adopted, she said that *Eighth Moon* touched her not only because it was about a girl's life in another country, but as the story of an adopted child.

"[It] was an easy book to write, compared to *Spring Moon*. *Eighth Moon* took only nine months from start to finish. Fiction is immensely more difficult a form."[2]

Lord's first novel, *Spring Moon*, was nominated for the American Book Award in 1982. The book is a family saga that takes place amongst the cultural and political upheavals in China during the past century. ". . .Becoming a novelist was not a girlhood dream, but a middle-aged happenstance. Perhaps if I had known what I know now about the agony of the blank page, the imperative of endless revision, the rigors of technique, I would never have begun a first novel. Blissfully ignorant, I was driven by the idea that I had something to say about China to a Western audience. I learned by trial and error. Writing and rewriting, some chapters as many as twenty times. I compounded my problems when I chose to write in the third person, with many viewpoints, covering almost eighty years. Painfully, I learned to throw out the research that I had painstakingly gathered. With the help of my excellent editor, Corona Machemer, I reworked each part until all contributed to the whole.

Bette Bao Lord with Barbara Walters.

"The success of *Spring Moon* has naturally enriched my life. I love the letters I receive from my readers who say that I have touched them through my characters, that they have enjoyed this journey to China. I marvel at the many doors that have opened since the novel has become a best-seller."[2]

Spring Moon was published in eleven countries, including ". . .being published in Chinese without my permission in Taiwan because that country is not a party to any international copyright convention. Recently I have read this unauthorized translation, and I am shocked and angry. The Crown Company of Taipeh has completely distorted my work. The translator has not only reinterpreted certain phrases and twisted meanings, he has cut out entire sections. And he actually *rewrote* crucial portions of the last part of my book so that it is unrecognizable and nonsensical. He has mutilated my characters and my philosophical outlook. Throughout, his clear intent is propagandistic. I plan to seek amends to this flagrant assault upon my artistic integrity and my personal reputation."[2]

FOOTNOTE SOURCES

[1]Bette Bao Lord, "China Doll," *New York*, May 12, 1986.
[2]Jean W. Ross, "CA Interview," *Contemporary Authors*, Volume 107, Gale, 1983.

FOR MORE INFORMATION SEE:

Best Sellers, September 15, 1964.
New York Times Book Review, September 27, 1964, October 25, 1981.
New York Times, August 30, 1981, December 2, 1981.
Saturday Review, October, 1981.

Washington Post Book World, October 11, 1981.
Los Angeles Times Book Review, October 18, 1981.
Publishers Weekly, October 20, 1981.
Christian Science Monitor, November 9, 1981.
Chicago Tribune Book World, November 22, 1981.
People Weekly, November 23, 1981.
New Yorker, November 23, 1981.

LORD, Patricia C. 1927-1988

OBITUARY NOTICE: Born March 8, 1927, in Attleboro, Mass.; died July 2, 1988, after a long illness, in Sharon, Conn. Children's book editor. Lord began her publishing career with Oxford University Press as a children's book editor. She later worked for Henry Z. Walck as editor and vice president, and also as a free-lance editor for Franklin Watts. She was a past president of the Children's Book Council.

FOR MORE INFORMATION SEE:

OBITUARIES

Publishers Weekly, August 5, 1988.
School Library Journal, September, 1988.

MATHIS, Sharon Bell 1937-

PERSONAL: Born February 26, 1937, in Atlantic City, N.J.; daughter of John Willie (a longshoreman) and Alice Mary (Frazier) Bell; married Leroy Franklin Mathis, July 11, 1957

SHARON BELL MATHIS

(divorced, 1979); children: Sherie, Stacy, Stephanie. *Education:* Morgan State College (now Morgan State University), B.A. (magna cum laude), 1958; attended D. C. Teachers College; Catholic University of America, M.L.S., 1975. *Religion:* Roman Catholic. *Residence:* Fort Washington, Md. *Agent:* Marilyn Marlow, Curtis Brown Ltd., 10 Astor Place, New York, N.Y. 10003.

CAREER: Children's Hospital of District of Columbia, Washington, interviewer, 1958-59; Holy Redeemer Elementary School, Washington, D.C., teacher, 1959-65; Bertie Backus Junior High School, Washington, D.C., special education teacher, 1965-66; Charles Hart Junior High School, Washington, D.C., special education teacher, beginning 1966; Stuart Junior High School, Washington, D.C., special education teacher; author of children's books; Benning Elementary School, Washington, D.C., librarian, beginning 1975; Friendship Education Center, Washington, D.C., library media specialist, beginning 1976. Howard University, Washington, D.C., writer-in-residence, 1972-74. Writer in charge of children's literature division, Washington, D.C. Black Writers Workshop, 1970-73. Member of board of advisers, Lawyers Committee of District of Columbia Commission on the Arts, 1972—; member of Black Women's Community Development Foundation, 1973—.

AWARDS, HONORS: Award for a children's book manuscript from the Council on Interracial Books for Children, 1969, and chosen one of Child Study Association of America's Children's Books of the Year, 1971 both for *Sidewalk Story;* Bread

Loaf Writers Conference Fellow, 1970; *Teacup Full of Roses* was chosen one of Child Study Association of America's Children's Books of the Year, one of *New York Times* Best Books of the Year, and one of the American Library Association's Best Young Adult Books, all 1972, and Coretta Scott King Award, runner-up, 1973; Coretta Scott King Award, 1974, for *Ray Charles; Listen for the Fig Tree* was selected one of American Library Association's Best Young Adult Books, 1974; *Boston Globe-Horn Book* Honor Book for Text, one of Child Study Association of America's Children's Books of the Year, Notable Children's Trade Book in the Field of Social Studies from the National Council of Social Studies and the Children's Book Council, and one of *New York Times* Outstanding Books, all 1975, and Newbery Honor Book, 1976, all for *The Hundred Penny Box;* Arts and Humanities Award from Club Twenty, 1975.

Award from the District of Columbia Association of School Librarians, 1976; Arts and Humanities Award from the Archdiocese of Washington, D.C., 1978; Wallace Johnson Memorial Award, 1984, for "Outstanding Contributions to the Literary Arts"; Arts and Letters Award from the Boys and Girls Clubs of Greater Washington, 1984; Arts and Letters Award from Delta Sigma Theta Sorority, 1985; Outstanding Writer Award from the Writing-to-Read Program, D.C. Public Schools, 1986.

WRITINGS:

Brooklyn Story (young adult; illustrated by Charles Bible), Hill & Wang, 1970.

Sidewalk Story (juvenile; illustrated by Leo Carty), Viking, 1971.

Teacup Full of Roses (young adult; ALA Notable Book), Viking, 1972.

Ray Charles (juvenile biography; illustrated by George Ford), Crowell, 1973.

Listen for the Fig Tree (young adult; ALA Notable Book), Viking, 1974.

The Hundred Penny Box (juvenile; ALA Notable Book; *Horn Book* honor list; illustrated by Leo Dillon and Diane Dillon), Viking, 1975.

Cartwheels (young adult), Scholastic, 1977.

Author of "Ebony Juniors Speak!," a monthly column in *Ebony, Jr!*, 1972-85, and "Society and Youth," a bi-weekly column in *Liteside: D.C. Buyers Guide*. Work included in anthology *Night Comes Softly: Anthology of Black Female Voices*, edited by Nikki Giovanni. Contributor of stories and articles to periodicals, including *Negro History Bulletin*, *Black America*, *Essence*, *Encore*, *Black World*, *Black Books Bulletin*, *Acorn*, and *Horn Book*.

ADAPTATIONS:

"Teacup Full of Roses" (record; cassette), Live Oak Media, 1977.

"The Hundred Penny Box" (cassette; record; filmstrip), Random House.

WORK IN PROGRESS: Sammy's Baby, a children's book; a book on voter registration.

SIDELIGHTS: "The evening before I was born, my parents, Alice Frazier Bell and John Willie Bell, walked along the boardwalk in the winter weather. My mother, after suffering two previous miscarriages, was about to give birth to her first child. There were only small pinches of pain. Harsh labor was hours away and there was time to talk, time to be alone with their plans and hopes. They might have spoken of a thousand things, or just a few. Were they, perhaps, a wee bit frightened now that the birth was imminent? How would they manage if something went wrong? The couple didn't have a place of their own but lived with my maternal grandparents, Richard (Dick) Frazier and Mary Frazier, in the house at 203 N. Virginia Avenue.

"After a time, the long, slow walk was terminated. A dear young friend, Festus (Fes) Braithwaite, drove the couple to Atlantic City Hospital in a somewhat worn-out black and yellow Chrysler taxicab that he used for both personal and business purposes. At the hospital, Dr. J. Hurlong Scott, a highly successful and popular Black doctor. . .was waiting."

February 26, 1937 "I was born at 8:10 in the morning, squalling—indignant at having been thrust from my own private paradise/space into a brightly lit theater. On the stage, a small place was made for me.

"Ten days later, my parents and I went home in Fes Braithwaite's yellow and black cab. This time, my father drove. My father, who was never to know his true parents (He was born in New Orleans, Louisiana—and reared by Abraham and Emma Gaskins), had his first real family at last. He was to say to me many times over the years, 'You were the first person I could truly call my own.'

"Although my mother was a housewife and my father a waiter at the Chelsea Hotel at the Boardwalk and Illinois, I had a fine English carriage and was an infant clotheshorse.

"Sunshine streamed into the upstairs front bedroom the three of us shared. I must have loved being held in their arms, listening to their gentle speaking voices and their beautiful singing voices. Alice was a fine soprano all of her life and John sang three times a week on WFPG-Radio. He sang classics on Wednesdays and black spirituals every Friday from 9:00 to 9:15 every evening. He was not paid. Although he is seventy-five, his voice is smooth and melodic. Daddy's voice is still strong and he sings without strain."[1]

"There was my maternal grandmother, Mary Frazier. Quiet, she was, like the light breeze of a perfect summer morning. Grandma was ever tranquil. Serene. She was our Calm Place. I don't think that she ever raised her voice. Not even when she scolded us. And if we—the children—were really being very horrible at any given time, it was necessary to stop and listen now and then for her light steps. Grandma baked picturebook rolls every Sunday morning, and cooked dumplings so delicious that we took them for granted and never thought about them until she was gone from us. This extraordinary Mother/Grandmother/Quiet Friend.

"And finally my beloved paternal grandfather, Richard Frazier. A true patriarch if ever there was one. He seemed always to know what was right and what was wrong, and young marriages—faltering—often made it through because of his influence. The men in the family respected him, and the women respected him. He was so proud of all of us and I would give almost anything to have him be a part of all that has happened to me in the last five years. He was a bookman, my grandfather. He believed in books and newspapers and read them constantly. And woe to the grandchild without a working knowledge of the major issues of the day. There was an air about him, and it affected you, and you wanted so to please, to have him say—'Well done.'"[2]

"My grandfather. . .was a sanitation employee who sought to give his family every opportunity to succeed. Blind in one eye, he swept the streets of Atlantic City with dignity and by doing so he was able to provide a lovely home, furniture, high-school educations, books, and family trips.

"When my mother graduated from Atlantic City High School, in 1934, the ceremony was held at Atlantic City Convention Center. My grandfather was required to perform his sanitation duties, downstairs in the Center. He could hear the music upstairs and could sense the excitement of his family gathered above. Grandpop knew how beautifully my mother was dressed, that she had been—and always was—a fine student. A proud man, he wanted to be upstairs in the crowd with all the other parents celebrating. His entire family was gathered for the joyous occasion, his precious daughter Alice—graduating. Grandpop had been told earlier, when he requested permission to attend the graduation, that to insist that he be able to attend his daughter's graduation—even though he was already in the building—would be grounds for instant dismissal, even though he had worked many years for the sanitation department.

"A few hours of joy would have meant the end of what he had been able to provide for his family.

"But a racist, corrupt machine could only control his movement—not his spirit. Thus the quiet patriarch tidied up the belly of the huge building while believing the edifice was there this day—merely *to honor his daughter*.

"All of my life, whenever I have looked at the Atlantic City Convention Center, I have thought of it as a place that exists to salute one Black girl's triumph and her father's great cour-

His father and brother were already dead. Ray Charles Robinson was alone. ■ (From *Ray Charles* by Sharon Bell Mathis. Illustrated by George Ford.)

age. Of all the graduations in this family, none will ever equal that one—at least for me.

"A year after I was born, my parents were able to afford a home of their own. The house, at 714 Drexel, contained a four-room apartment with parquet floors and a coal furnace that provided steam heat. It cost my young father twenty-four dollars each month. My mother, needing more money for her family, worked part-time at Truxton's Variety Shop (next to Truxton's Hollywood Grill) where she sold candy and other items at the popular Black-owned establishment. Later, my father was able to secure a better series of jobs as timekeeper, bookbinder, and recreation (sports) head for the WPA."[1]

Her father was offered work as a blacksmith's helper at the Brooklyn Navy Yard. After six months of work, the family was able to move to the Bedford-Stuyvesant section of Brooklyn, at 570 Hancock Street. "Immediately, I missed my plump grandmother's soft arms and dimpled cheeks. I missed her rolls and biscuits—always smeared with sweet butter. I missed her chicken dumplings. I missed helping my grandfather 'read' his newspaper. I missed his wide smile and his shoulders—with enough room to hug me and Bubba and Pat, at the same

time. Gone were his stories. Mini-tales of my mother's growing-up years."[1]

A year later the family moved to 283 Halsey Street. "Daddy was becoming increasingly dissatisfied at the Brooklyn Navy Yard where he had to continually train young white men who then went on to become mechanics—with better pay—while he remained locked into the *helper* position without any hope of upward mobility or advancement. He had simply traded New Jersey's racism for the New York variety.

"The situation at home became strained, and my mother, pregnant, could do little to help.

"What I really remember about Halsey Street was my birthday party, at five, and of Daddy holding a camera and doing silly things to make his shy firstborn smile so that he could take my picture. I remember the kitchen was crowded with people, and there was laughter all around.

"In the midst of World War II, Daddy became a longshoreman—loading ammunition and supplies for soldiers.

"Months later, my parents separated—never again to live as man and wife.

"My father took Momma to dinner at their favorite Chinese restaurant, with the hope of reconciliation. But my mother was badly disillusioned, and frightened. She would depend not on him but on herself.

"Momma never removed her wedding rings, however. And my father was never too far away, although he seemed to prefer living in Queens. My brother and I, when we were older, enjoyed riding the El to Queens—and then a bus—to visit my father and bring back desperately needed money. As the saying goes, Daddy was never more than 'a telephone call away.'

"With the help of God, my mother managed to move herself—and her four children (I was five, Bubba was three, Pat two years old, and Marcia was only six months) to a lovely apartment governed by rent-control laws—at 219 Bainbridge Street, between Reid and Patchen Avenues, where the fire escape awaited my discovery.

"I don't remember when I actually realized how very special was this private playground/haven/sanctuary of mine. This iron patio jutting out into open space. Other tenants, all around, ignored theirs. I appreciate their generosity because I was always alone on my wrought-iron balcony—outside my kitchen window. Sometimes I would sit on the window sill itself with my bare feet against the gridiron floor, textbooks and paper there beside me. Other times, I would sit at the edge of the square balcony and dangle my feet out and over the world below, a book pressed against the bars.

"In the years that were to come, at 219 Bainbridge Street, I would sit on my fire escape in any weather (except thunder and lightning—mostly lightning) and read and do my homework (P.S. 70, Holy Rosary Elementary School, and St. Michael's Academy—a high school), talk with my mother while she cooked, or just think. I believed in knights and princes and princesses and castles and instant rescues. Everything was possible while I sat and imagined on my fire escape. I wrote little poems and short stories that my mother was proud of. I listened to poems she wrote and watched her sketch her drawings. As I grew older, my favorite books in the whole world were read over and over: Richard Wright's *Black Boy,* Betty Smith's *A Tree Grows in Brooklyn* (my father, too, had been a singing waiter like Francie's), and Willard Motley's *Knock On Any Door.*"[1]

Helped by her neighbors, Mrs. Bell raised her four children, despite the fact that she was often sick. As World War II continued, she was able to obtain work as a welder at Brooklyn Naval Yard. At the end of the war she lost her job. "Momma, like so many other women who had contributed to the war effort, found herself without employment. Welding, however, had taken its toll on her health and she was ill and steadily losing weight (a petite five feet, four inches, she had never weighed more than 103 pounds—except when she was pregnant). Sick and exhausted, she managed to work at two jobs and daily seemed to lose more flesh from her bones. Friends and neighbors tried to advise her to accept public assistance.

"I retreated into my library books and watched her and worried. Although I was eight years old chronologically—I was a hundred years old spiritually. Few of her moments escaped my scrutiny. Once I saw her crying. She was sitting at the kitchen table, head down, 'Why don't you pray?' I pleaded, not realizing that perhaps she had. My mother reminded me of that moment, many times over the years. I believed then, as I do now, that God is a reality—a kind of marvelous force. I believed that He would make an immediate difference in our lives, if only my mother would ask Him. As an adult, I now

know how fervently my mother did petition her God—to make a way out of no way.

"As much as I read when I was growing up—and I read all the time, my mother read more. Images: My mother curled up in a comfy chair, usually near a window—natural light flooding her lovely hair, the book, and the room; my mother so immersed in a book (she loved Frank Yerby) that she didn't hear her children squabbling—or realize that the meal she was cooking had already burned; my mother painting her long, lovely fingernails—and reading a book at the same time; my mother sitting by the open kitchen window, reading—while I sat on the fire escape—also reading; my mother clutching her book and making her delicious baked beans—cooked from scratch, as the old folks say—cinnamon, bacon, and molasses smells wafting from the kitchen, out over the fire escape and clear over to Ms. Lucy's window—another great cook, southern style and any other style one could name.

"The sharing of books and reading and writing was always very precious between my mother and me. It was a most wonderful focal point. When I became a published writer, it was perfect only because I could share it with her."[1]

As Mathis grew into adolescence, her mother began to suffer heart attacks. "I grew up praying that my mother wouldn't die and leave us alone. I knew that the four of us would have a very difficult time if something were to happen to Momma. I agonized that she might die even while she slept. It was wonderful to hear her stirring, moving about, in the morning. This was a situation understood, perhaps, only by youngsters in similar situations. I couldn't really communicate it to my friends—and I did not.

"An introverted teenager, I grew more inward. I kept my circle extremely small."[1]

(From *The Hundred Penny Box* by Sharon Bell Mathis. Illustrated by Leo and Diane Dillon.)

(Jacket illustration by Leo and Diane Dillon from *Listen for the Fig Tree* by Sharon Bell Mathis.)

At school, she began to write. "My English teachers, at Saint Michael's Academy, encouraged me to continue to write my stories and provided an early showcase of what skills I had. . . .

"The nuns, in English classes, always allowed me to read my compositions aloud. I'm sure my stories were quite amateurish but because I knew I would have to read them to the class— I rewrote and polished my images as best I could, given my limited skills at the time. English classes were bright moments, during a time of well-defined worries."[1]

Most summers were spent with her grandparents in Atlantic City, while her mother worked in New York. "Summers were special. Summer meant that my brother and my sisters and I had an opportunity to visit Grandmom and Grandpop in Atlantic City. It meant that we could pack sandwiches and stay at the beaches most of our day. It meant we had a chance to listen to Grandpop tell his stories. It meant that we could eat Grandmom's biscuits at will, and her lemon meringue pies! Summer meant that my mother could get some rest, with the four of us gone—or if her health held up, work an extra job. Momma worked in a laundromat on Reid Avenue. She placed the dingy clothes and linens of other families in the commercial washers and dryers and—if the service was paid for— folded and ironed the laundry.

"My mother's health broke again. At the time, she was working at the laundromat and at a candy store and in a small business office. This time, after a lengthy stay in the hospital, she applied for public assistance and was accepted."[1]

During the summers of **1950-1951** the children went to Lynchburg, South Carolina, with Mrs. Mattie Jenkins, a woman who had helped to raise Mathis' father. "I was excited to visit a real farm but was dumbstruck when we finally arrived at the house where we were to spend the summer. The house stood on four cinder blocks and there, lying coiled beneath it, was a friendly snake (a king snake, he kept rats out of the chicken house). Instead of indoor plumbing, there was a nearby outhouse—usually with a snake—or two—inside.

"The only reason that I could tolerate the idea of living near a creek, with a resident water moccasin, was that it was helping my mother to get some needed rest. Crossing the logs, over that creek, while keeping my eyes peeled on a coiled cottonmouth would be an everlasting image. 'He's always there,' Jacob (one of Aunt Mattie's sons) said. 'He's not thinking about you.'

"My fire escape seemed especially far away.

"I can still remember, though, that when I saw my father striding across the field to fetch us for the journey back to Brooklyn, I was a little sad about having to leave. . .reluctant. The summer had been different from any other I had ever known. I had learned to string tobacco (and dodge fat, green tobacco worms), picked cotton and pushed the puffs down into a burlap sack (making small sums of money, based on the weight of the cotton), ironed with a cold iron that had to be heated atop a wood-burning stove. I had been *re*baptized in a

Sidewalk Story
By Sharon Bell Mathis

(Cover illustration by Daryl Zudeck from *Sidewalk Story* by Sharon Bell Mathis.)

river, wept at a mourner's bench in a small country church, drank raw milk, and sat on a mule. I had eaten redeye gravy over hominy grits for breakfast, and watched a hog slaughtered and barbecued over a hole dug in the ground and filled with glowing ashes."[1]

1952. An invitation was extended by her godmother, Bertha Reed Lee McDonald, to spend the summer with her in Baltimore, Maryland. "That summer, at 1003 Wheeler Avenue, was grand indeed. My godmother, whom I began to call G'Mom, also loved to write. . . .Her husband, Jesse, didn't write poetry but he was a ready listener. So was my pal Rusty, a dog they owned with the hint of German shepherd genes. Rusty would listen to the results of my scribbling with what seemed like profound concentration—moments before he padded away without even a backward glance. Well, occasionally, I would get the backward glance.

"G'Mom insisted that I keep writing my poems, on demand, sometimes at 2:00 A.M., if we were still awake and talking. She seemed to marvel that I could create a poem so speedily. G'Mom never criticized my writing but accepted it wholly. She had been a teacher in the Baltimore city schools for fifteen years at that time, and was certainly no stranger to the creative writing of children. At every opportunity, she encouraged me to express myself. Clearly, she was pleased with my rudimentary skills. To further impress her, I clarified and compressed my images. . .willingly editing my words. My godmother insisted that I keep all of my stories in a spiral notebook that

she would ask to see from time to time—either to read herself, or to show to visiting relatives and friends, many of whom were also teachers in the city's schools.

"Although the house on Wheeler Avenue didn't have a fire escape, there was a fine front porch where I could sit for hours—in the shade—and write and read."[1]

Graduated from high school in **1954** in a beautiful dress sewn by her mother. Unknown to Mathis, her mother had arranged for Bertha McDonald to take Mathis home to Baltimore to attend Morgan State College there. "Packing to go away was different this time and I was excited. I think my mother knew that I would never really come back, but, thank God, I didn't realize it."[1]

July 11, 1957. During her sophomore year she eloped with LeRoy Franklin Mathis. They were married in Arlington, Virginia by a Justice of the Peace and went to live with LeRoy's cousin in Washington, D.C., where LeRoy worked as a psychiatric forensic technician at St. Elizabeth's Hospital. Mathis commuted to Morgan State College and graduated magna cum laude in 1958. Dr. Martin Luther King was the commencement speaker.

She temporarily abandoned her dream of becoming a writer. "I was told that black writers could not really make a living, not even as journalists. Frank Yerby and Richard Wright were superstars. I could not see my work in their class and so limited my dreams and followed a more traditional course."[3]

"I was anxious to work and supplement Leroy's income so that we could live in a place of our very own.

"My first position was as an interviewer at the Children's Hospital of the District of Columbia, an ancient building—and two smaller ones—in the vicinity of Thirteenth Street in the northwestern section of the city. My daily caseload of sick children and their struggling indigent parents left me feeling drained, and very often depressed. Try as I might, I couldn't detach myself emotionally.

"It was a relief to discover that I was pregnant. Ecstatic, I was only too happy to resign and come home to wait for a baby I fervently prayed would be healthy. I had more knowledge than I needed about dreadfully ill infants."[1]

Her first daughter, Sherie, was born September 23, 1959. Three weeks later she began work as a fifth grade teacher at the Holy Redeemer Elementary School in Washington, D.C., where she worked until 1965.

1963. May 16, her second daughter, Stacy, was born. Two years later, her third daughter. The family moved into their first home with their growing family. Mathis continued to teach. "It was during the years that I taught remedial math in a special education program at Hart that I began to think about writing for publication.

"I began by subscribing to magazines for writers: the *Writer* and the *Writer's Digest*. I borrowed books on writing from the public library. I bought books on writing that were advertised in the writers' magazines. My reading became highly selective. I would read only one genre for months at a time. At night, when my children were sleeping, I *sketched* short stories, edited the life out of my images, discarded and retrieved characters. Agonized.

"I began to notice that my stories for, and about, children began to develop more frequently. The characterization of chil-

Mathis with grandson, Thomas Kevin Allen II.

dren were superior to my depiction of adults. Although my stories centered more and more around juvenile protagonists, the thought of writing solely for children never entered my mind.

"If I was aware of anything, it was that the desire to write became increasingly overwhelming. If I didn't write for a whole day, I wasn't happy (whatever *happy* meant). Day after day, for hours—no matter what else had to be done—I developed my manuscripts. I rented a typewriter. Two weeks later, I bought a typewriter. Final copy had to be typed on 100 percent cotton rag, long grain. Drafts were also written on expensive paper—I thought the manuscripts looked more crisp, professional.

"My family and my best friends watched and wondered. Sure, they knew that I had always loved to write a few poems—but this was something else entirely.

"All I knew was that the more I wrote, the more I wanted to write."[1]

1969. Her first children's story, "The Fire Escape," was published May 2 in *News Explorer*. "Two extraordinary events occurred for me before the end of 1969: I signed my first children's book contract (*Brooklyn Story,* a high-interest, low-vocabulary novel for teenagers with reading deficiencies, to be published by Hill & Wang), and Annie R. Crittenden, an award-winning playwright, founded the D.C. Black Writers Workshop for professional and aspiring writers. Free seminars

were conducted in poetry, drama, fiction, and nonfiction. When a number of writers expressed interest in learning to write for children, Crittenden developed a children's literature division and named me as its director.

"The year **1970** went on to become even more wonderful. Two of my poems, 'Ladies Magazine' and 'R.S.V.P,' were anthologized in Nikki Giovanni's *Night Comes Softly: Anthology of Black Female Voices* (from Langston Hughes 'Night comes softly black like me'). . . .

"The first time I held that book in my hand, I just cried and cried. Some of the most poignant images I would ever read were there on those pages. So many Black women bent over typewriters, hearts overflowing—and I was one of them."[1]

1974. Mathis took a sabbatical from the Washington, D.C. public schools to attend Catholic University to earn a Masters of Science in library science. Soon after she was assigned to Benning Elementary School in Washington as a librarian.

1975. *The Hundred Penny Box* was chosen as a *Boston Globe-Horn Book* Honor Book. Like the main character of the book, Aunt Dew, Mathis' grandfather kept a collection of pennies, unknown to Mathis. After the book's publication, and three weeks before the awards ceremony, she discovered the connection between her beloved grandfather and her main character. "Grandpop was ninety-two years old when he died, as dignified and as proud as ever. Among his personal belongings was a small well-worn leather pouch. Inside were ten pennies

Lilly Etta laughed to see a round earring on one side and a flat one on the other side. ■
(From *Sidewalk Story* by Sharon Bell Mathis. Illustrated by Leo Carty.)

covered with green mold. My mother told me of the existence of this purse only three weeks ago. Momma did not know the significance of the ten pennies. I saw the pouch and the pennies this morning for the first time, on the plane into Boston.

"So when I think—as I sometimes do—that nothing fits, I'm always proven wrong. Everything fits. And fits perfectly. Just like Aunt Dew.

"Aunt Dew came unbidden but not unwelcome into my consciousness and I must say that I loved her immediately. But along with this love came the recognition that I lacked the skill to portray her as beautifully as she appeared in my mind. She was so perfect.

"I not only loved her, I respected her. She took over my mornings and my afternoons and my nights, and I was proud to have her company. When I thought about *The Hundred Penny Box* becoming an Honor Book, I realized that the best person to talk with about it would be Aunt Dew herself. And Michael—if he was around. He wasn't.

"When I saw her this time, in some special place within me, she was rocking in the chair that they had given to her—by the window that they had also given her. She did not look out of this window very often. She wasn't looking out of it now.

"Quiet Rocking. Light Chair Sounds. As if the movement was not actually there, not actually heard.

"'Aunt Dew,' I asked. Standing nearer, wishing to touch her. 'What do you want me to tell the people?'

"I kissed her.

"'Tell them to carry on,' she said. 'Dewbett, herself, is doing that—carrying on.'"[2]

"Trouble was brewing. . . .Although my book-writing world was intact, my personal life was fast disintegrating. A twenty-one-year-old marriage was nearing its end. Although my husband gave me flowers, our life together was not the same.

"On **July 29, 1978** (while I was a Fellow at the MacDowell Colony in Peterborough, New Hampshire), Loyola Federal Savings approved the mortgage loan for a townhouse I was purchasing in Fort Washington, Maryland—a suburb near Washington, D.C. I left the Colony immediately, gathered my children from the home of my mother and brother in Brooklyn, and went to settlement. After several weeks of trying to live in two homes, I quietly gathered my daughters and left. The divorce decree was awarded to me in 1979. Sadly, my husband died on October 2, 1980."[1]

Mathis began to suffer writer's block. "Each day, I made a million promises to write something. Anything. After all, I had never really believed in writer's blocks.

"Months turned into years. If I could write, the results were shallow and quickly discarded. I spoke with John Oliver Killens and followed his advice religiously—write something each day, he advised.

"My mother listened to me carefully and understood how fearful I was of never writing again. My father said, 'Get a tape recorder and write my story, that would be something different!' Linda Zuckerman, my editor, invited me to her Brooklyn home to relax. 'Let's talk about it Sharon,' she suggested.

"I couldn't talk about it.

"There was in my life a dark Moses. His name: John Theodore Whitney. Handsome and tall, with skin like polished ebony, he has salt and pepper hair. He has the ability to snatch me away from worry—or, if he cannot do that, lends his impressive shoulders to lean on."[1]

Mathis began to write again, and when her mother came to live across the street from her in Fort Washington, she was ecstatic. "No day could have been more perfect than the day my mother moved across that little street from me. There she was, to hug and to talk with forever!

"Momma and I went everywhere together, to theaters. . . , parties, and book affairs. I promised her that I was writing. She believed me, because she knew I was trying. She didn't talk about writing unless she was sure I wanted to."[1] Her mother lived for three more years, and died on May 25, 1983. "Our family is honoring my mother's last wish—that her children remain as close (spiritually and physically) as possible and to take care of one another. She had looked forward—so much—to the time when we would be in close proximity to one another."[1]

Now a grandmother herself, Mathis enjoys writing for children. "I feel very secure with children. That might sound psychotic, but I enjoy children. I'd like to have a children's TV show. I know that sounds bold, but there should be a show oriented toward children's books."[4]

"The Black child is usually portrayed as lacking street wit in books written by whites. I teach—and I see textbooks that have painted a few faces brown. But they still haven't added any fact about Blacks. Parents, teachers and librarians primarily are responsible for the books children read. And it's their duty to inspect these books more carefully and not buy or order them just because the faces are Black."[5]

"Black children will leave my books with a feeling that I know they *live*."[3] For she considers her work "a salute to black kids."[6]

Mathis is daughter, mother, grandmother, teacher, writer. ". . .I'm not alone. . . .What I have been given by the black community I now give back."[3]

FOOTNOTE SOURCES

[1]Adele Sarkissian, editor, *Something about the Author Autobiography Series,* Volume 3, Gale, 1987.

[2]Sharon Bell Mathis, "Ten Pennies and Green Mold," *Horn Book,* August, 1976.

[3]Frances Smith Foster, "Sharon Bell Mathis," *Dictionary of Literary Biography,* Volume 33, Gale, 1984.

[4]Hollie I. West, "A Dream Career," *Washington Post,* March 21, 1971.

[5]Liz Gant, "'That One's Me!'—New Books for Black Children That Mirror Their World," *Redbook,* August, 1972.

[6]Janet Harris, "*Teacup Full of Roses,*" *New York Times Book Review,* September 10, 1972.

FOR MORE INFORMATION SEE:

New York Times, March 27, 1970 (p. 22).

Horn Book, August, 1971, February, 1973, April, 1974, June, 1974.

Alleen Pace Nilsen and Kenneth L. Donelson, *Literature for Today's Young Adults,* 2nd edition, Scott, Foresman, 1985.

LUCINDA McQUEEN

McQUEEN, Lucinda (Emily)   1950-

PERSONAL: Born March 8, 1950, in Springfield, Mass.; daughter of Carroll Gates and Elizabeth (Leonard) McQueen; married Jeremy Guitar (an illustrator) 1975. *Education:* Rhode Island School of Design, B.F.A., 1972. *Home and office:* Pumpkin Hill Farm, Warner, N.H. 03278.

CAREER: Illustrator, 1972—. *Exhibitions:* Society of Illustrators Show, New York, N.Y., 1975, 1977, and 1978. *Awards, honors:* Judges' Gold Seal Award from the Society of Illustrators Show (Boston), 1978, for illustrations "Aunt Rose" and "Rat to the Rescue."

WRITINGS:

Baby Farm Love, Grosset, 1988.
What Does Sunny Bunny Love? Grosset, 1988.
Baby Zoo Animals, Grosset, 1989.
Counting Bears, Grosset, 1989.
(With husband, Jeremy Guitar), *Tidy Pig: Just Right for Fours and Fives,* Random House, 1989.

ILLUSTRATOR

Miriam Morton, *Zoo Babies,* Ginn, 1973.
Patty Wolcott, *The Cake Story,* Addison-Wesley, 1974.
P. Wolcott, *Beware of a Very Hungry Fox,* Addison-Wesley, 1975.
Adelaide Holl, *Let's Count,* Addison-Wesley, 1976.
Betty Boegehold, *The Garden at the End of the World,* Harcourt, 1976.
Alma Gilleo, *The Mystery of the Missing Valentines,* Society for Visual Education, 1977.
Irene Herz, *Hey! Don't Do That!,* Prentice-Hall, 1978.
Graham Tether, *Skunk and Possum,* Houghton, 1979.
Jay Williams, *The Water of Life,* Four Winds, 1980.
Michaela Muntean, *Theodore Mouse Goes to Sea,* Golden Press, 1983.
Claude Clayton Smith, *The Gull That Lost the Sea,* Golden Books, 1984.
Dorothy M. Kunhardt, *Kitty's New Doll,* Golden Books, 1984.
Jan Wahl, *Cheltenham's Party,* Golden Press, 1985.
Linda Hayward, *Snowy Day Bear,* Grosset, 1985.

L. Hayward, *Windy Day Puppy,* Grosset, 1985.
The Little Red Hen, Scholastic, 1985.
L. Hayward, *Rainy Day Kitten,* Grosset, 1986.
L. Hayward, *Sunny Day Bunny,* Grosset, 1986.
Patricia Scarry, *Patricia Scarry's Little Willy and Spike: The Adventures of a Rabbit and His Porcupine Friend,* Golden Books, 1986.
M. Muntean, *Theodore Mouse Up in the Air,* Golden Press, 1986.
Mary L. Tufts, *The Wee Kitten Who Sucked Her Thumb,* Grosset, 1986.
Dina Anastasio, compiler, *Bedtime Stories,* Grosset, 1987.
Charles Perrault, *Puss in Boots,* translated by Eric Suben, Golden Books, 1987.
J. Wahl, *Little Dragon's Grandmother,* Golden Books, 1988.
David Werner, *The Silly Sisters,* Golden Books, 1989.
Lucille Hammond, *New Boots for Rabbit,* Lady Bird Books, 1989.
Margo Lundell, *The Wee Puppy Who Wet His Bed,* Grosset, 1989.
M. Lundell, *It's Bedtime,* Grosset, 1989.

"CABBAGE PATCH KIDS" SERIES

Roger Schlaifer, *Xavier's Fantastic Discovery,* Childrens Press, 1984.
(With J. Guitar) *Otis Lee,* Parker Brothers, 1984.
(With J. Guitar) *Sybil Sadie,* Parker Brothers, 1984.

MUNRO, Roxie   1945-

PERSONAL: Born September 5, 1945, in Mineral Wells, Tex.; daughter of Robert Enoch (an automotive shop owner and boat

ROXIE MUNRO

The Supreme Court of the United States. ■ (From *The Inside-Outside Book of Washington, D. C.* by Roxie Munro. Illustrated by the author.)

builder) and Margaret (a librarian; maiden name, Bissey) Munro; married Bo Zaunders (an artist and photographer), May 17, 1986. *Education:* Attended University of Maryland, 1963-65; Maryland Institute College of Art, 1965-66; University of Hawaii, B.F.A., 1969, graduate work, 1970-71; attended Ohio University, 1969-70. *Home:* 20 Park Ave., New York, N.Y. 10016. *Office:* 41 Union Square West, #806, New York, N.Y. 10003.

CAREER: Roxie (dress company), Washington, D.C., dress designer and manufacturer, 1972-76; television courtroom artist in Washington, D.C., 1976-81; free-lance artist, 1981—. *Exhibitions*—Group shows: New York Public Library, New York, N.Y., 1986; Detroit Institute of Art, Mich., 1987; Hign Museum, Atlanta, Ga., 1987; Boston Atheneum, Mass., 1987; Corcoran Gallery of Art, Washington, D.C., 1988; Victoria and Albert Museum, London, England, 1988; Art Gallery of Ontario, Canada, 1988; Fine Arts Museum of San Francisco, Calif., 1988. One-woman shows: Foundry Gallery, Washington, D.C., 1977-79, 1983, 1986; Delaware Museum of Art, 1980; Gotham Book Mart, New York, N.Y., 1986. Works are included in many private and public collections. *Member:* Artists' Equity. *Awards, honors:* Yaddo Painting Fellowship, 1980; *The Inside-Outside Book of New York City* was named one of *New York Times* Best Illustrated Children's Book, and one of *Time*'s Best Children's Book, both 1985.

WRITINGS:

SELF-ILLUSTRATED

Color New York, Arbor House, 1985.
The Inside-Outside Book of New York City, Dodd, 1985.
The Inside-Outside Book of Washington, D.C., Dutton, 1987.
Christmastime in New York City, Dodd, 1987.
Blimps, Dutton, 1989.

The Inside-Outside Book of London, Dutton, 1989.

ILLUSTRATOR

Diane Maddex, *Architects Make Zigzags: Looking at Architecture from A to Z,* Preservation Press, 1986.

Cover artist for *New Yorker.* Contributor of illustrations to *Washington Post, U.S. News & World Report, Gourmet, Historic Preservation,* and *New Republic.*

WORK IN PROGRESS: A series of oils called "City Light."

SIDELIGHTS: "I am essentially a painter; I do big oils of cities primarily and am interested in space and light.

"After college I did dress design and manufacturing for small boutiques. I started working as a courtroom artist in 1976 for television and newspapers (my first trial was Watergate in Washington, D.C.), but continued doing a lot of oils (exhibited widely, including a solo show at the Delaware Museum of Art) and free-lance illustration. In 1981 I sold my first cover painting to the *New Yorker* and immediately moved to New York City. By 1987 I had sold sixteen cover paintings. My first book published by Arbor House in 1985 was *Color New York.* My first children's book in color was *The Inside-Outside Book of New York City.* I have since done five others.

"Unlike many children's book creators, I don't have a lot of specific memories of my childhood. I remember mainly sensuous impressions: water running across rocks in a ditch, the dried fall leaves, the splash of waves across a boat's bow.

"I lived in a small town in a more or less rural area and didn't have close friends nearby. Much of my spare time was spent reading and daydreaming. My parents encouraged their children (my older sister is also a professional artist) to make their own toys, to draw, and of course to read. We also traveled a lot. From the late forties to the mid-sixties we took family vacations by car. We drove through the South, Northeast, and West, visiting the cities and the countryside.

"My work is therefore, I think, an art developing from perception. It is very visual, spatial. Ideas develop from a kind of active seeing. When I walk down a street, ride a bus, or go up an escalator, I FEEL the changing space. I see patterns, paintings everywhere. My mind organizes reality. I'll notice two gray cars, a red car, a black car, and two more red cars—aha!—a pattern.

"When I am working on a painting, perhaps a fantasy landscape, perhaps a real view from atop a building, I sometimes have a shift of consciousness. Suddenly I am IN the tiny car on the winding road, or swinging down the big city avenue.

"I think that children relish rich, complex, and interesting images. Not until I had published my first children's book did I go back to my home library and look again at books that had affected me as a child. I was amazed to find that every line, shape, and color, every figure and setting of the exquisite illustrations by Arthur Szyk in *Andersen's Fairy Tales* were totally familiar to me. It was as if I had seen them yesterday, rather than over thirty years ago. I remember pouring over the book many times, drinking up the richness of the paintings, never tiring and always fascinated.

"I am certain that my work is influenced by those early impressions of rich color, ornate patterns, and dynamic use of space. I do paintings that excite me while I am working on them. Perhaps my books will give children something to engage their interest and stimulate their imaginations.

"My husband, Bo Zaunders, is from Sweden. He illustrated *Max, the Bad-Talking Parrot*, which was published by Dodd, and is working on a book of photographs for E. P. Dutton.

"Bo and I travel three to six months a year; he does travel photography and I do illustrations for my books and magazine work. I have a great studio overlooking New York City; the view is of the Empire State Building and the Metropolitan Life Tower."

HOBBIES AND OTHER INTERESTS: Travel, reading.

FOR MORE INFORMATION SEE:

Washington Post, July 2, 1972, November 21, 1981, April 21, 1987.
New York Times, October 20, 1985, December 2, 1985, February 26, 1989.
Washington Post Book World, November 10, 1985, June 14, 1987.
Time, December 23, 1985.
Philadelphia Inquirer, November 6, 1988.

OLSEN, Violet (Mae) 1922-

PERSONAL: Born May 8, 1922, in Spencer, Iowa; daughter of Peter (a farmer) and Johannah (a homemaker; maiden name, Villadsen) Larsen; married William Donald Olsen (an industrial specialist), January 28, 1950; children: Jennifer Olsen Lamphere, Patricia Olsen Mitchell, William, Matthew, Melissa Olsen McBride, Barbara Olsen Lipnick, John. *Education:* Attended American Institute of Business, Des Moines, Iowa, 1940; University of Iowa, B.A., 1949; graduate study at Ro-

VIOLET OLSEN

sary Graduate College of Art, Florence, Italy, 1982. *Politics:* Independent. *Religion:* Roman Catholic. *Home and office:* 1010 West 15th St., Davenport, Iowa 52804. *Agent:* Dorothy Markinko, McIntosh and Otis, Inc., 310 Madison Ave., New York, N.Y. 10017.

CAREER: Art and English teacher in Davenport, Iowa, 1962-78; Iowa Annie Wittenmyer Home for Children, Davenport, special education teacher, 1966-69; Vera French Community Mental Health Center, Davenport, volunteer art therapist, 1978—. *Military service:* U.S. Navy, Women Accepted for Volunteer Emergency Service (WAVES), 1943-46. *Member:* National League of American Pen Women, Association of Community Organizations for Reform Now, Writers Studio, Women Writers Workshop, United Neighbors, Friends of Art, Friends of the Library, Quad Cities Writers, Danish Sisterhood. *Awards, honors:* Founder's Award from the Indiana Writers Conference, 1974, for "Another Warsaw;" named Writer of the Year by the Writers Studio, 1974, and by Quad Cities Writers, 1982, for *The Growing Season;* Juvenile Fiction Award from the Mississippi Valley Writers Conference, 1975, and Notable Book in the Field of Social Studies from the National Council of Social Studies and the Children's Book Council, and Midland Authors Award for Best Children's Fiction Book, both 1987, all for *View from the Pighouse Roof;* Juvenile Fiction Award from the Iowa Wesleyan Writers Conference, 1983, for "The Big Catch and the Cover-up."

WRITINGS:

The Growing Season (juvenile novel), Atheneum, 1982.
Never Brought to Mind (young adult novel), Atheneum, 1985.
View from the Pighouse Roof (sequel to *The Growing Season*), Atheneum, 1987.

Contributor to periodicals, including *Reader's Digest* and *Our Family.*

WORK IN PROGRESS: Sequels to *The Growing Season* and *View from the Pighouse Roof,* entitled *A Short Season of Peace* and *For the Duration;* a non-fiction book under the direction of the head of the University of Iowa's art department entitled *The Inspiration and Faith of Great Christian Artists;* a young adult biography, *Frances Perkins, Stateswoman, the Story of FDR's Secretary of Labor.*

SIDELIGHTS: "When I was very young, my big ambition was to become an artist, not an author. I majored in art education in college and became an art teacher. During this time, in the late sixties and throughout the seventies, I began selling free-lance articles and short stories to magazines and newspapers. The first articles I sold were written about famous artists such as Leonardo da Vinci and Michelangelo. It seemed to me that people who have never had the chance to study art in college would like to know more about the great art masters who painted or sculpted famous works of art that were inspired by the Bible. These articles were easy to write and sell.

"My childhood on an Iowa farm during the thirties was never one of sorrow and deprivation. I grew up in a big, close-knit, Danish-American family in which we had more happy times than sorrowful ones. It was when I became a teacher at the Iowa Annie Wittenmyer State Children's Home that I began writing serious fiction for juveniles and young adults. The children I taught had been removed from their homes by the courts under tragic circumstances, often victims of child abuse and neglect. I wanted youngsters who have childhoods that are happy and free from conflict to have a better understanding of children who are not so fortunate. So I began writing the stories of troubled children. These were hard to publish. It seems that many editors do not like fiction in which children are shown to have unhappy lives over which they have very little control or hope of changing. I also wanted to show in fiction that through education and the determination not to be defeated by an unhappy childhood, a person can still achieve a good life and should always look to the future with hope.

"Because I was very close to the children I taught, many who were mentally retarded, emotionally disturbed, or both, I decided to use historical fiction, setting my stories in the past (the 1930s) when I was growing up. My characters in *The Growing Season* are fictional people who are often drawn from my own family, friends, and neighbors but changed in such a way to reflect the kind of people I want to reveal in the theme of my books. Anton Myrer, author of *The Last Convertible*, taught a novel workshop at the Indiana University Writers' Conference and I learned a lot about writing fiction from him. He said, '*Fiction takes the raw material of life and distills it into a higher truth* (theme).' I believe all good writers do this.

"Although my books, *The Growing Season* and its sequel *View from the Pighouse Roof*, are about Marie Carlsen who is growing up in Iowa during the Great Depression, the theme is universal. Children of every time period, geographic location, economic condition, and family situation can identify with Marie's fears—of growing up, losing a loved one, making friends, developing confidence and self-esteem, and perhaps most of all, searching for sunshine and hope in a dark and dreary everyday life. I think people who write for children and young adults should always preserve the element of hope in novels. I suppose the most fascinating thing about writing for young people is that they do grow and change and have great capacity to hope, extend love, and make the world a better place in which to live.

"The idea for *Never Brought to Mind* came to me when four teenage boys from our city were killed in a one-car accident during Christmas vacation. It was 1973 and I was a substitute teacher in the English classroom which one of the boys had attended before his death. I kept thinking about his empty desk and how his closest friends must be suffering his loss. At that time, not many young adult novels had been written about depression when sudden death ends the relationship between

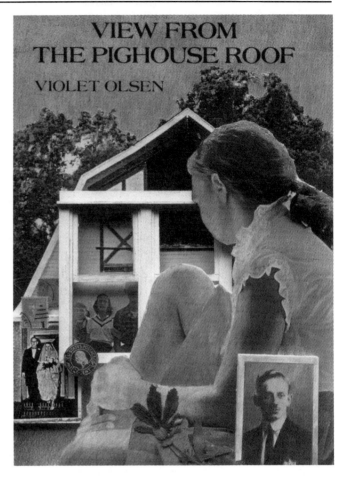

It wasn't fair! She'd wanted to go to Katie's house for Christmas dinner. ■ (Jacket illustration by Viqui Maggio from *View from the Pighouse Roof* by Violet Olsen.)

best friends or young teenage boyfriend and girlfriend. Even though all the characters in *Never Brought to Mind* are fictional, the book was difficult to write because the characters soon took over the story and became very real to me.

"I now spend a lot of time as an author in the schools through the Iowa and Nebraska Arts Councils' Artist in the Schools program. It is extremely rewarding to work with young writers. I'm convinced that everyone has a story to tell and the younger they start the better writers they will become and the higher quality of literature will be available to children and young adults in the future. Writing is an excellent way to have a voice in what kind of world we wish to live. I shall always believe that the pen (or in the modern world—typewriter or word processor) is mightier than the sword."

HOBBIES AND OTHER INTERESTS: Drawing, painting, creative writing workshops and seminars.

FOR MORE INFORMATION SEE:

"Olsen Novel: A Touching Book for Young Adults," *Des Moines Register*, July 21, 1985.
"Vi's Pen Is Her Past," *Quad-City Times*, July 13, 1986.
"Midland Authors Honor Olsen's *Pighouse Roof*," *Des Moines Register*, July 3, 1988.
"Author Writes Portrayals," *Ledger* (Fairfield, Iowa), October 26, 1988.
"Author's Advice—Build on Your Experience," *Valley Voice* (Creston, Iowa), December, 1988.

ORLEV, Uri 1931-

PERSONAL: Surname legally changed, 1958; born February 24, 1931, in Warsaw, Poland; son of Maksymilian (a physician) and Zofia (a homemaker; maiden name, Rozencwaig) Orlowski; married; children: Lee, Daniella, Itamar, Michael. *Home:* 4 Ha-berekha St., Jerusalem 94 112, Israel.

CAREER: Member of Kibbutz in Lower Galilee, Israel, 1950-62; writer, 1962—. *Military service:* Israeli Army, 1950-52. *Member:* Hebrew Writers Association. *Awards, honors:* Awards from the Israeli Broadcasting Authority, 1966, for "The Great Game," 1970, for "Dancing Lesson," 1975, for "The Beast of Darkness," and Television Prize, 1979, for youth program "Who Will Ring First?"; Prize from Youth Alia, 1966, for *The Last Summer Vacation;* Prime Minister Prize (Israel), 1972, and 1989, for body of work; Ze-ev Prize from the Israel Ministry of Education, 1977, International Board on Books for Young People (IBBY) Honor List (Israel), 1979, both for *The Beast of Darkness;* Haifa University Prize for Young Readers, 1981, IBBY Honor List (Israel), 1982, Sydney Taylor Book Award from the Association of Jewish Libraries, Mildred L. Batchelder Award for Translation, Edgar Allan Poe Award runnerup from the Mystery Writers of America, and Jane Addams Children's Book Award Honor Book from the Jane Addams Peace Association, all 1985, Silver Pencil Prize, for the best translated book to Dutch, 1986, and Honor Award from the Ministry of Youth, Family, Women and Health of the Federal Republic of Germany and West Berlin, 1987, all for *The Island on Bird Street.*

URI ORLEV

WRITINGS:

JUVENILE

The Beast of Darkness (novel), Am-Oved, 1976.
The Little-Big Girl, Keter, 1977.
Noon Thoughts, Sifriat-Poalim, 1978.
Siamina, Am-Oved, 1979.
The Lion Shirt, Massada, 1979.
Hole in the Head, Keter, 1979.
It's Hard to Be a Lion (novel), Am-Oved, 1979.
The Good Luck Passy, Am-Oved, 1980.
Granny Knits, Massada, 1980.
Mr. Mayor, Let Us Sing, Massada, 1980.
Wings Turn (short stories), Massada, 1981.
The Island on Bird Street (novel; ALA Notable Book), Keter, 1981, translated by Hillel Halkin, Houghton, 1984.
Big Brother (novel) Keter, 1983.
Journey to Age Four, Am-Oved, 1985.
The Wrong Side of the Bed, Keter, 1986.
Shampoo on Tuesdays, Keter, 1986.
The Dragon's Crown (novel), Keter, 1986.
The Man from the Other Side (novel), Keter, 1988.

TITLES IN ENGLISH TRANSLATION

The Lead Soldiers (novel), Sifriat-Poalim, 1956, translated from the original Hebrew by H. Halkin, P. Owen, 1979, Taplinger, 1980, new edition, Keter, 1989.
Till Tomorrow (novel), Am-Oved, 1958.
The Last Summer Vacation (short stories), Daga, 1967.

TRANSLATOR FROM POLISH

Henryk Sienkiewicz, *In the Desert and Jungle,* Y. Marcus, 1970.
The Stories of Bruno Schulz, Schocken Publishing House (Israel), 1979.
Janusz Korczak, *King Matthew I,* Keter, 1979.
Stanislaw Lem, *Eden,* Massada, 1980.
S. Lem, *Invincible,* Schocken, 1981.
S. Lem, *Pirx the Pilot,* Schocken, 1982.
J. Korczak, *Little Jack's Bankruptcy,* Hakibbutz Hamenchad, 1985.
J. Korczak, *Kajtus the Wizard,* Am-Oved, 1987.
S. Lem, *Back from the Stars,* Keter, 1988.
S. Lem, *Stars' Diarys,* Keter, 1989.

SCRIPTS

"The Great Game" (juvenile), Israel Broadcasting Authority, 1966.
"Dancing Lesson," Israel Broadcasting Authority, 1970.
"The Beast of Darkness" (juvenile), Israel Broadcasting Authority, 1975.
"Who Will Ring First" (juvenile), Israel Broadcasting Authority, 1979.

Author of television and radio plays for adults and children. Some of Orlev's books have been published in England, Holland, Poland, West Germany, East Germany, France, Denmark, and Japan.

WORK IN PROGRESS: A juvenile novel tentatively titled *The Lady with the Hat,* for Keter.

SIDELIGHTS: "When I was little I wanted to be a policeman. Later, I wanted to be a tramcar driver. The trams didn't use horns but had bells instead, and I thought it would be a very dignified and interesting profession to operate the tram bell with my foot. When I was eleven I knew that I would be a poet, and I did indeed begin to write poems. All this happened

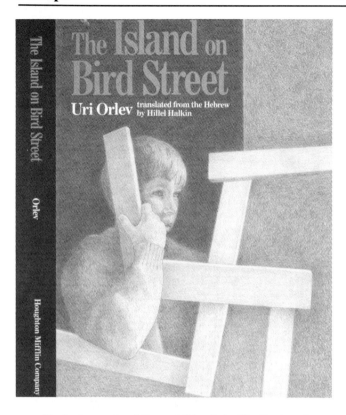

She had gone to visit some friends in Ghetto A and never returned. ■ (Jacket illustration by Jean Titherington from *The Island on Bird Street* by Uri Orlev.)

in Poland and therefore the poems were not in Hebrew. I still have the notebook. In it I find dates like January 20th, 1944 or May 13th, 1945, and on the cover, in large letters, 'Perhaps.' Only to my brother did I reveal the meaning of 'Perhaps.' I was referring to what we said constantly to each other, 'Perhaps we'll be saved.' Only in a time of disaster, or fire or earthquake, or flood do children think in such terms. And, of course, in wartime.

"The war we went through lasted not six days but six years, from when I was eight until I was fourteen. This was World War II, which many call the Holocaust.

"A woman once called to speak to me about one of the books I had written on this subject. At one point she asked, 'Did writing this book enable you to "finish" with the Holocaust?' I replied that I cannot 'finish' with it because I went through it as a child. It is perhaps possible that adults, adult writers, are able to 'finish' with the Holocaust, though I find it difficult to believe. I certainly cannot, because I don't wish to, because what other people call the Holocaust was, for me, my childhood.

"Like any childhood, there were many beautiful and exciting things in it, and, in my case, many painful and frightening things. I have memories of my mother enveloping us with love in difficult situations, treating us with great patience and some spanking—reading to us and telling us stories about her childhood. I remember many adventures that came our way because of the strange places we played in and the strange objects we found there—all sorts of things that one finds in the street only in wartime, like the barrel of a cannon which we exploded by mistake. Or a dead horse that opened its mouth. Or crazy Rubinstein who ran through the ghetto shouting in Yiddish, 'Everyone's equal,' as we ran around after him. I asked my mother what he meant and she answered that perhaps he was

saying that all are equal in the face of death. That was when I wrote my first poem.

"When I came to Israel after the war I learned a new language and lost the language of my childhood. And when I tried to write poetry I found that I was no longer able to. So I began to write stories, and later, books for adults. Only when I was forty-five did I write my first children's book, *The Beast of Darkness.*

"I once asked some school children whether they thought *The Beast of Darkness* was real or imaginary. One child replied, 'It's partly imaginary, partly not, because you can create such a beast only in your imagination but you can rely on it as though it were real.' And that is what I do when I write. I invent things and then I find that they are real and that I can rely on them and live with them."

FOR MORE INFORMATION SEE:

New Statesman, June 7, 1979.
Daily Telegraph, June 21, 1979.
New York Times Book Review, March 23, 1980.
Chicago Sun-Times, March 23, 1980.
Boston Globe, March 30, 1980.
Chicago Tribune Book World, April 27, 1980.
Booklist, March 15, 1984.
Horn Book, April, 1984.
Publishers Weekly, April 13, 1984.
Christian Science Monitor, May 4, 1984.

PHILLIPS, Elizabeth Louise (Betty Lou Phillips)

PERSONAL: Born in Cleveland, Ohio; daughter of Michael and Elizabeth (Materna) Suvak; married John S. Phillips, January 27, 1963 (divorced, January, 1981); married John D. C. Roach, August 28, 1982; children: (first marriage) Bruce, Bryce, Brian. *Education:* Syracuse University, B.S., 1960; Case Western Reserve University, graduate work, 1963-64. *Politics:* Republican. *Religion:* Roman Catholic. *Home:* 1923 Olympia Dr., Houston, Tex. 77019.

CAREER: Teacher in Shaker Heights, Ohio, 1960-66; Cleveland Press, Ohio, sportswriter, 1976-77, *Pro Quarterback* (magazine), New York, N.Y., special features writer and editor, 1976-79; free-lance writer, 1976—. *Member:* Society of Children's Book Writers, International Platform Association, Delta Delta Delta.

WRITINGS:

UNDER NAME BETTY LOU PHILLIPS

Chris Evert: First Lady of Tennis (juvenile), Messner, 1977.
Picture Story of Dorothy Hamill (juvenile), Messner, 1978.
The American Quarter Horse (illustrated by Marce Olsen and with photographs by Francis Shepherd), McKay, 1979.
Earl Campbell, Houston Oiler Superstar (juvenile), McKay, 1979.
The Picture Story of Nancy Lopez (juvenile; ALA Notable Book), Messner, 1980.
Go! Fight! Win! The National Cheerleaders Association Guide for Cheerleaders (juvenile; illustrated by Lawrence R. Herkimer and with photographs by F. Shepherd), Delacorte, 1981.
(With Roblyn Hendon) *Something for Nothing: Give-Aways and Near Give-Aways for Teenage Girls,* Ace, 1981.

Brush Up on Hair Care (juvenile; illustrated by Lois Johnson), Messner, 1982.
(Editor, with son, Bryce Phillips) *Texas. . .The Lone Star State* (juvenile), F. Watts, 1987.

Contributor to *New Book of Knowledge,* and of articles to young adult and sports magazines.

FOR MORE INFORMATION SEE:

COLLECTIONS

De Grummond Collection at the University of Southern Mississippi.

PIENKOWSKI, Jan (Michal) 1936-

PERSONAL: Born August 8, 1936, in Warsaw, Poland; came to England, 1946; son of Jerzy Dominik and Wanda (a chemist; maiden name, Garlicka) Pienkowski. *Education:* King's College, Cambridge, B.A. (with second class honors), 1957, M.A., 1961. *Religion:* Catholic. *Home:* London, England. *Agent:* Angela Holder, Gallery Five Ltd., 121 King St., London W6 9JG, England. *Office:* Gallery Five Ltd., 121 King St., London W6 9JG, England.

CAREER: J. Walter Thompson (advertising agency), London, England, art director, 1957-59; William Collins Sons & Co. (publisher), London, art director in publicity, 1959-60; *Time and Tide,* London, art editor, 1960-61; McCann Erickson (ad-

JAN PIENKOWSKI

vertising agency), London, England, television producer, 1962-63; Gallery Five Ltd. (publisher), London, co-founder and art director, 1961-78, consultant art director, 1978—; author and illustrator of children's books, 1967—. Consultant on mechanical books, Walker Books Ltd. *Member:* Society of Authors. *Awards, honors:* Kate Greenaway Medal Honor Book from the British Library Association, 1971, for *The Golden Bird;* Kate Greenaway Medal, 1972, for *The Kingdom under the Sea and Other Stories,* and 1980, for *Haunted House;* Kurt Maschler Award runnerup from the Book Trust (England), 1984, for *Christmas: The King James Version.*

WRITINGS:

SELF-ILLUSTRATED CHILDREN'S BOOKS

Numbers, Heinemann, 1973, Harvey House, 1975.
Colours, Heinemann, 1973, published in America as *Colors,* Harvey House, 1975.
Shapes, Heinemann, 1973, Harvey House, 1975, Simon & Schuster, 1981.
Sizes, Heinemann, 1973, Harvey House, 1975, Messner, 1983.
Homes, Heinemann, 1979, Messner, 1983.
Weather, Heinemann, 1979, Messner, 1983.
Haunted House, Dutton, 1979.
ABC, Heinemann, 1980, Simon & Schuster, 1981.
Time, Heinemann, 1980, Messner, 1983.
(With Anne Carter) *Dinner Time,* Gallery Five, 1980, published in America as *Dinnertime,* Price Stern, 1981.
(With Helen Nicoll) *The Quest for the Gloop,* Heinemann, 1980.
Robot, Delacorte, 1981.
Gossip, Price Stern, 1983.
(With H. Nicoll) *Owl at School,* Heinemann, 1984.
Christmas: The King James Version, Knopf, 1984.
Farm, Heinemann, 1985.
Zoo, Heinemann, 1985.
Little Monsters, Price Stern, 1986.
I'm Cat, Simon & Schuster, 1986.
I'm Frog, Simon & Schuster, 1986.
I'm Mouse, Simon & Schuster, 1986.
I'm Panda, Simon & Schuster, 1986.
Faces, Heinemann, 1986.
Food, Heinemann, 1986.
Small Talk, Orchard Books, 1987.
Easter: The King James Version, Random House, 1989.

"MEG AND MOG" SERIES; WITH HELEN NICOLL

Meg and Mog, Heinemann, 1972, Atheneum, 1973, revised edition, Heinemann, 1977.
Meg's Eggs, Heinemann, 1972, Atheneum, 1973, revised edition, Heinemann, 1977.
Meg on the Moon, Heinemann, 1973, Penguin, 1978.
Meg at Sea, Heinemann, 1973, Penguin, 1978, revised edition, Heinemann, 1979.
Meg's Car, Heinemann, 1975, David & Charles, 1983.
Meg's Castle, Heinemann, 1975, David & Charles, 1983.
Mog's Mumps, Heinemann, 1976, David & Charles, 1983.
Meg's Veg, Heinemann, 1976, David & Charles, 1983.
Meg and Mog Birthday Book, Heinemann, 1979, David & Charles, 1984.
Mog at the Zoo, Heinemann, 1982, David & Charles, 1983.
Mog in the Fog, Heinemann, 1984.
Mog's Box, Heinemann, 1987.

ILLUSTRATOR

Jessie Gertrude Townsend, *Annie, Bridget and Charlie: An ABC for Children of Rhymes,* Pantheon, 1967.
Joan Aiken, *A Necklace of Raindrops and Other Stories,* J. Cape, 1968, Doubleday, 1969, revised edition, 1972.

(From *Meg's Castle* by Helen Nicoll. Illustrated by Jan Pienkowski.)

Nancy Langstaff and John Langstaff, compilers, *Jim Along, Josie: A Collection of Folk Songs and Singing Games for Young Children* (ALA Notable Book; *Horn Book* honor list), Harcourt, 1970, new edition published as *Sally Go Round the Moon*, Revels, 1986.

Edith Brill, *The Golden Bird*, F. Watts, 1970.

J. Aiken, *The Kingdom under the Sea and Other Stories*, J. Cape, 1971, revised edition, 1975, Penguin, 1986.

Agnes Szudek, *The Amber Mountain and Other Folk Stories*, Hutchinson, 1976.

Dinah Starkey, *Ghosts and Bogles*, Hutchinson, 1976, reissued, Heinemann, 1985, David & Charles, 1987.

J. Aiken, *Tale of a One-Way Street and Other Stories*, J. Cape, 1978, Doubleday, 1980.

J. Aiken, *Past Eight O'Clock* (stories), J. Cape, 1986, Viking Kestrel, 1987.

Also illustrator of Gloria Fuertes' *Aurora Brigida y Carlos*, Editorial Lumen (Barcelona).

"JAN PIENKOWSKI'S FAIRY TALE LIBRARY" SERIES

Jacob Grimm and Wilhelm Grimm, *Jack and the Beanstalk*, Heinemann, 1977.

J. Grimm and W. Grimm, *Snow White*, Heinemann, 1977.

J. Grimm and W. Grimm, *Sleeping Beauty*, Heinemann, 1977.

Charles Perrault, *Puss in Boots*, Heinemann, 1977.

C. Perrault, *Cinderella*, Heinemann, 1977.

J. Grimm and W. Grimm, *Hansel and Gretel*, Heinemann, 1977.

Designer of wallpaper, murals, fabrics, cards. Graphic illustrator for "Watch!," a British Broadcasting Corp. television series, 1969-71; created design for "Meg and Mog Show,"

Arts Theatre, London, 1982 and 1983, and for "Chips Comic" television show.

ADAPTATIONS:

Meg and Mog (play; first produced in London, England at the Unicorn Theatre, 1981), Samuel French, 1984.
"Meg and Mog" and "Meg's Eggs" (cassette), Cover to Cover, 1985.
"Meg at Sea" and "Meg on the Moon" (cassette), Cover to Cover, 1985.

WORK IN PROGRESS: Two new titles in the "Meg and Mog" series.

SIDELIGHTS: Pienkowski was born on **August 8, 1936** in Warsaw, Poland, the son of Jerzy Dominik and Wanda Maria Pienkowski. "I was born before the war and I had three years which were, so to speak, 'normal'—not that I remember very much of that. I'm never sure whether I really remember or whether I've fabricated it because somebody told me about it. My earliest memory is of my father's house, like a Dufy painting. I've been back to the place and it is the most beautiful sight. Of the house not a trace remains, not a stone, nothing. You can see where the house must have stood on a bluff above a wide river on what is now the Russian border. It was the most spectacular run of land with huge trees in the park. I remember the garden, then the park, then the river at the bottom, and a wonderful early summer day with people in summer clothes walking about, and I remember a wonderful, carefree feeling.

"I remember the terrace in front of the house, the circle of the drive where the carriages drove up and the flower bed in the middle. I'd been given a tricycle. I remember my nanny pushing me and I was terribly angry and saying, 'No, no, you must let me do it myself,' and I couldn't. I was hopeless and my feet slipped off the pedal. I was obviously no good at it, but was frightfully cross that she was trying to help me.

"I remember my mother's mother, who was a doctor, sitting under a dark tree, a larch, I think, doing embroidery. That was rather out of character, but I still have the item she made. She said, 'What shall I embroider?' and I said, 'Me,' and she

did. That's all I remember from before the war: those three things.

"My mother studied science and has a degree in metallurgy and chemistry. My father read estate management which was going to be his occupation."[1]

Pienkowski had a half-sister, his father's daughter by his first marriage, who succumbed to scarlet fever at the age of five. "I'd rather have had a dead sibling than none at all, it gives you a bit of competition which is a probably a good thing. Of course, in some ways she was unfair competition, as all dead people are, because she was perfect and could not be proven otherwise because she wasn't there.

"Because of my sister's death, my father was perhaps over protective of me as a child. I had a very strong constitution and was seldom ill, but when I was, it was made into a major drama. I was extremely fond of my father, particularly in his later years, but I think this was a barrier between us in my childhood."[1]

Pienkowski moved with his parents to western Poland during the early part of World War II. "My father had been in the army until the fall of Poland, and afterwards worked as a bailiff managing an estate.

"We were only allowed to kill a pig once a year. More than one was a crime punishable by death; everything had to go to the German front. Making butter was punishable by death, too. It all sounds medieval, but that's how it was. Because we lived in the country, we were allowed to have poultry. I used to go with another boy to get pond weed to feed the ducks. He would stick his arm into the bucket and pull the weed out, and half a dozen leeches with it. I could never bring myself to do that and thought him terribly brave. His name was Tadek, and we were great chums, doing all the Tom Sawyer things that boys do, climbing trees and falling into ponds.

"I always enjoyed making things out of every conceivable type of material, especially paper, which may be why I work with cut paper now. Making things out of paper, especially Christmas decorations, is a Polish tradition. My father gave me a Fret saw and we would make letter racks and other

(From *Meg's Castle* by Helen Nicoll. Illustrated by Jan Pienkowski.)

things. And we had off-cuts of wood from the carpenter to make palaces or other buildings.

"Many of my family are architects. I can remember making a kind of house by setting stakes in a circle in the ground and weaving branches in between, like a hurdle. And Tadek and I would make dams across the stream. I enjoyed watching the blacksmith at work and loved all the beautiful, rusty things lying about outside the forge.

"I wore shorts and had bare feet all summer long, and I had my head shaved or my hair cut very short to prevent lice. In the winter I wore lots of clothes and looked like a bundle. Once we found some baby foxes in the woods whose mother had been killed. They were very hungry, so we took them home in our pockets. Three died fairly soon. Much later, when the fourth one died I had this wonderful hat made out of him. It was so cold in the winter that hats were very important. When you live in the country you become used to the idea of life being limited.

"I remember the frost patterns of beautiful fern leaves on the windows. There was a lot of snow every year. We didn't go skating because we didn't have any skates, but we went sliding on the ice and made snowmen and had snowball fights. Once I fell through a hole in the ice. There were two reasons why there were holes. One was for the fish to breathe, and the other was that we had an ice house, like a little cellar with a vault and earth on top. It was next to the pond, the source of the ice, and all sorts of game—mainly hares—was stored in

And the four plain bedposts stretched up higher and higher. ■ (From *Past Eight O'Clock* by Joan Aiken. Illustrated by Jan Pienkowski.)

it. Ice and salt were thrown in on top, and in the summer it worked like a freezer.

"My mother ran a little school for the local children in our glazed porch, which was against the rules and quite risky. She would read *Dr. Doolittle* and *Tom Sawyer* to me. My favourite was Kipling's *The Jungle Book*. Kingsley's *Heroes* made an impression on me before I learned to read myself.

"I drew quite a lot. There wasn't much paint around so I tended to use coloured pencils and cut things out. I can remember trying to draw horses, failing, and feeling very frustrated. I drew castles and palaces—I had only the vaguest idea of what they looked like. I was fixated on the idea that a palace had to have a tower. Most of my drawings were heroic type of things.

"I used to have terrible nightmares about a witch. They came very regularly. Like all nightmares when you describe them, they're not very frightening, it's just the atmosphere. There were a variety of scenarios and they all involved the witch. She would chase me and I would run slower and slower and not be able to get away. Sometimes, she had a house made of mirrors and a huge pot into which she would try to pop me. I was scared of the dark and still am. I could see light coming from under the door, and I could hear the comforting noise of grown-ups talking. I would lie there and hope that eventually whatever it was that was in the room with me would go away."[1]

Pienkowski's idyllic country childhood came to an abrupt end in 1944. "My father was involved in the Resistance and many people were being arrested. He had to go away, or sooner or later, they would have caught him. One day he went to the station and didn't come back. I remember he sent me a toy train—I didn't want a toy train. I wanted my father. My mother told me he would come back, but I remember feeling abandoned, let down, and that it was somehow his fault.

"The estate we lived on had been given to a German, who lived in the big house. I didn't see very much of him, but I knew he was there and I knew he was German. Obviously the Germans were people like any other, some were all right and some were not. He happened to be a very decent sort. That's why my father got away, because I think he probably knew what my father was up to and he let him go.

"After a few months, we followed. It wasn't really explained to me what was happening. I remember having breakfast with the lamp lit because we had to catch an early train. I have always hated having the lights on at meals during the day because it reminds me of that time.

"Although all of Poland was under German occupation, some of it was actually annexed into the Reich and was treated as part of Germany while some was treated as a separate place under occupation. There was a frontier between the two and you couldn't really communicate. By going to Warsaw we almost went into another country.

"We moved to the city, met my father again, and had an apartment on the fifth floor. It was the summer of 1944. I went to school briefly, for the first time. No schools were allowed in Poland. The Germans had closed them because they wanted the Poles to be a source of physical labour and not to be educated. Schools, universities—they all were shut. I went to a secret, underground school where I didn't know any of the kids. They were town children and thought my country accent was very silly, and because I didn't know about city things they thought I was a bit simple. I was very intimidated and they were very sophisticated.

"In the late summer of 1944 the Russians came closer and closer until they were actually on the other side of the river. The Polish Resistance rose up against the Germans who were by then in full retreat. Rather than wait to be liberated by the Russians, the Poles wanted to liberate themselves. The Russians then withdrew and allowed the Germans to bring back their troops and their airforce. The Germans systematically flattened the place.

"I remember the visual images, but not the sound of destruction. I remember seeing all the fires but I don't remember people screaming. I found the explosions very exciting, beautiful in their way. The Germans were so systematic, they destroyed the city street by street. So there was no point in panicking because they weren't going to suddenly drop a bomb on you. There was no defense of any kind.

"My mother carried on teaching me very methodically. I think my parents managed not to show their anxiety. What my mother was extremely good at was keeping the structure of the day going, whatever happened. Even if we were being bombed we would have a bath in cold water, at the proper time, on the fifth floor because things had to be done in a certain way. It is tremendous to have the feeling that everything is all right even in the midst of chaos, and that you mustn't give into it. Rather a British idea in a way.

"All this has left me with a strong sense of the impermanence of things, but at the same time losing everything has made me work terribly hard in order to regain a secure base."[1]

Next minute they were far away. ■ (From *The Kingdom under the Sea and Other Stories* by Joan Aiken. Illustrated by Jan Pienkowski.)

After the destruction of Warsaw, the Pienkowski family moved to Austria. "Leaving Warsaw was very sad because it was so thoroughly destroyed in a way that's almost impossible to imagine—just a lot of rubble with the odd wall and chimney sticking out.

"We went to Austria by train in the late autumn of '44, in open trucks with very high walls made for cattle. I remember terrified, crying children who had lost their parents being passed from carriage to carriage in the hope that they would find their relatives. That made an impression on me, and I have never forgotten it. I was lucky because I was with both my parents, although my father was nearly shot getting across to my mother and me.

"The Germans needed people to work the land because their men were either dead or at the front. My mother worked in the kitchen of a big house for a rather dreadful Czech-Austrian woman, and my father worked on a farm. We spent the winter in Austria but in the early spring the Russians advanced so we moved on.

"We managed to move to Bavaria which was about a hundred miles away. Austria and Bavaria were incredibly beautiful, I'd never seen hilly country before. Suddenly there were these blue hills and lakes and wonderful churches with onion domes. We were not there for very long before the Germans lost the war and the American army came and liberated us in May, 1945."[1]

The family moved to Italy where Pienkowski's father joined other liberated Polish officers. "Italy was smashing. I remember the American soldiers in Italy as very large and terribly rich—wonderful cars and watches and shiny objects of every kind.

"I was taken to see 'The Barber of Seville' in Rome. All I remember about it is the set—two bits of palazzo, one on the right and one on the left, and a real fountain coming out of the wall.

"I had always assumed that one day we would go back to our home in the country in Poland. It was while I was in Italy that I realized we were never going back. My parents couldn't decide whether to go to Australia, where my father had a relative, or to England."[1]

Like many other Polish families, the Pienkowski's chose Britain. "I was ten years and three months old. We went to a camp in Herefordshire in the middle of England. It was a very hard winter, that legendary winter of '46 and '47, with tremendous snow and ice and cold. It was just like Poland except that everyone was terribly unprepared for this weather. Unlike Poland, there was no double glazing, insufficient heat, and no proper clothes. People were extremely kind to us. They gave us clothes and held parties for the children. One woman gave my mother a beautiful patchwork quilt; it was the first time I'd seen that kind of work and I used to look at the patterns for hours.

"After my father was demobilized, we bought a small farm on the Welsh border in Radnorshire with some friends. It was a beautiful place. I was sent to a boarding school in Herefordshire which was a terrific shock, since I wasn't used to being away from my parents at all, and I was the only foreigner in the school. I didn't cope with it terribly well and begged my father to take me away, but he wouldn't."[1]

It was a difficult transition for young Pienkowski, but he learned English quickly and moved on to a state school in Prestigne.

He enjoyed being there and made friends. Later, the family moved to London where he continued his education at a Catholic grammar school. His art exposure increased considerably, much to his delight.

1954. Studied classics at King's College, Cambridge. He spent time with his first love—designing posters and sets for university drama groups. "I was not happy reading classics. I had a delightful series of tutors and supervisors who were sympathetic to my predicament, including F. L. Lucas [editor of Penguin classics], who used to say, 'Hello Pienkowski, have you done anything this week?' And I used to say, 'No sir, I'm afraid I haven't, I've been so busy.' 'Never mind,' he'd say, 'the Poles and the Irish are the children of chaos. What shall we talk about today?' Then we'd talk about life in general because I hadn't done my essay.

"I was involved with all forms of design. My major thing was posters; I seemed to corner the market in that. They were hung all over the place with my name on them so my teachers could see perfectly well what I was doing. Nobody had ever done such spectacular posters before, and I seemed to have an ingenious talent for getting the printers to do things they hadn't done before because I was technically interested in the production. The good posters were stolen immediately. . .it was exciting.

"The first stage set I did was a terrible botch-up because the person who was doing it slammed out in a rage—a typical theatrical experience—and I had to take over at the last minute in great haste with few ideas."[1]

1957. "After Cambridge I joined an advertising agency, J. Walter Thompson in Berkeley Square, and they offered me work in the copywriting department. I told them I didn't want to write copy. The personnel officer said, 'But you've got a degree in English and classics.' 'I know,' I said, 'but I want to be in the art department.' They didn't like this one little bit. I had to see the assistant head of the art department, a very nice man who painted watercolours. (My work is the opposite of watercolours.) I showed him all the stuff I'd done at Cambridge and he was indifferent to it. He asked if he could see some paintings, and mercifully I'd done some portraits and nudes. Reluctantly he agreed to give me a job.

"After university I lived with my parents again. I used to trot down to the tube every morning, very excited. I had all these paints and was enjoying myself, and I was being paid for it. I was so thrilled it was unbelievable. I've never had that feeling of elation about going to work since. As a beginner, I was doing everything that was 'non-press' and didn't get into the newspapers or magazines or onto the hoardings. We did dreadful leaflets, every kind of free give-away, the odd back of a cornflakes packet, all that sort of thing. My designs always went through. I felt that this was what I was born to do. I never questioned it.

"After J. Walter Thompson, I went to Collins Publishing to do their publicity material, then to *Time and Tide*, a weekly magazine, as art director. When it sold, I got a golden handshake, and went to the Greek Islands for six months. After that I joined another advertising agency, McCann Erickson, my last permanent job.

"I was not really happy in an office situation. I didn't like the meetings, I didn't like the diplomacy, the politics. I always wanted to get on with the designs. A Cambridge friend of mine, Angela Holder, and I had started making our own Christmas cards in our last year at Cambridge. I designed them, got them printed, and she sold them. The company gradually grew, and I was able to make enough money from it not to have to work for anyone else."[1]

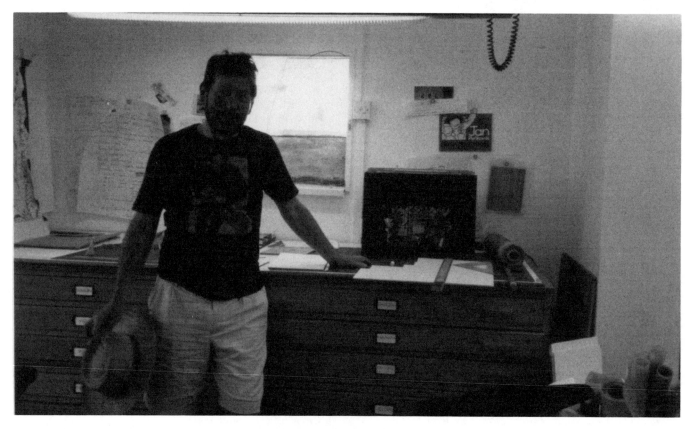

Pienkowski in his workroom. ■ (Photograph by Cathy Courtney.)

His designs for greetings cards, bright carrier bags, and stickers came to dominate fashionable London, particularly its thriving King's Road. "It was a very innocent, exciting time when King's Road, a little high street in West London, became a sort of artistic Mecca. It was a small street on a very human scale, not like the West End at all. It had a buzz about it at the beginning of the sixties which was the beginning of the design revolution. It was a new world. Suddenly there was a different kind of style—beautiful girls with corpse make-up, big black eyes, long hair, and very tight clothes. Bazaars [boutiques] opened and Mary Quant and all that sort of thing. Suddenly an English style emerged.

"My designs were right for the moment: I did very bright paper bags, paper clothes were all the rage, and stickers."

"I bought an Austin Healy Sprite with an open roof on impulse and remember driving with a friend of mine down King's Road, and she said to me, 'Do you know, Jan, one day this will be considered the Golden Age. It will be this mystical time that people will ask you about.' She was right. From then on, I started to look at it from the outside.

"I think a period of great success is very dangerous. Somebody once asked me to draw a line of my career as I see it, showing the ups and downs. I drew a line which went a bit like a plaited rope, up and down, but then another line intersecting it did something different. He was very startled by this, and I asked what most people did. 'They draw a straight line going slightly uphill,' he said. That's ridiculous, no natural process is ever like that. It's very dangerous to get caught on a point of success because it's very hard to get down, you must always have something else. Unless you're a genius like Roald Dahl, it's better to lurk in the shadows and emerge into the sunshine every now and then wearing a different hat."[1]

"Helen Nicoll was director of a children's educational programme for the BBC called 'Watch!,' and she asked me if I would design the credits and titles for it. It was a lot of fun. For each show I would do a drawing. It was me drawing but you couldn't see me so it was like animation. You saw the picture growing like magic, somewhat like Paul Keels' idea of 'a line going for a walk.' The skill of it was to keep the children guessing what it was going to be for as long as possible—that was the clever part. It was quite popular.

"I had to dress in black—black jumper, black trousers, black beret with a veil over my face and black gloves. I became terribly allergic to something in the studio because of the heat and the dust. My nose kept running, and I kept blowing it and forgetting about the blasted veil. It was awful.

"Then Helen married and left BBC to look after babies. We started the 'Meg and Mog' books which we still do. I had very firm ideas about what the books should look like. I once saw a television programme by Kenneth Clark about Japanese culture. He explained that in Japanese there is one word which means both drawing and writing and that there is no difference in concept. This appealed to me enormously and in my nursery books and 'Meg and Mog' books the idea is that there is no essential difference between the drawing and the writing, they both convey information and fight for supremacy. Sometimes the writing is important, sometimes the drawing.

"The latest book, *Mog's Box*, is all about sibling rivalry and jealousy. One of the animals has a lunch box, the other one doesn't and is frightfully jealous. So, Mog casts a spell and an enormous box appears. Mog is frightfully pleased, opens it and peers inside, but then he's disappointed because there's only a strange green thing there. Eventually it becomes a cater-

pillar and the word caterpillar *is* the caterpillar itself, so the word and the image are fused into one. In that book we have actually achieved what I wanted to do.

"The next book is going to be about going into hospital. We're trying to have something which exorcises terror. Possibly some of my own childhood feelings about doctors will feed it. Helen and I have lots of wild ideas and then Helen pares and prunes and puts them into economically good, plain English. We fight so much; it's a really good working relationship. She lives some way off and we meet to work in a motorway service station."[1]

Pienkowski has developed a special way to interact with school children. He prefers participation over giving talks. "Children vary tremendously from school to school. It depends on the staff and the tradition. I remember going to one school in the Highlands where they had no art teacher at all. The children were sitting in this Dickensian classroom with little pieces of paper, rulers and hard pencils. They didn't know what was going to happen; it was amazing. They just sat there. I don't know what they thought they were going to do with their rulers and their pencils, but anyway we got on and painted on the gothic windows of this rather grim building. We painted on the inside with bright transparent paints and they got more and more wild and very excited when we used colour. It was wonderful to see them, they'd never had access to that before.

"It's fair to say that deaf children are usually very good at self-expression, and Downs Syndrome children usually extremely good. You discover ways of working with them. It's fairly easy to work with deaf children because you can communicate with them through movements, once you've learned the names of the colours. Downs Syndrome and mentally handicapped children have problems with communication, but if there is a high adult-child ratio, it works well. If you have too many children, it becomes chaotic and the result might not be very satisfactory. They have a wonderful freedom of expression if you can actually spend time with them.

"I never discuss my books with children and I don't believe in market research. The most important thing is that it must entertain me, then it's got a chance of entertaining someone else."[1]

Pienkowski began using silhouette, which has become an important element in his work quite by accident. In order to get a commission, he had to submit a sample. ". . .I really slaved over it but the figures were dreadful. . .I had to set off with this dreadful picture. In despair I blacked in the face of the worst figure. It looked a bit better, so I did them all."[2]

"When I did the silhouettes I discovered inadvertently that all children could identify with all the characters. Gradually it dawned on me that the greatest advantage of having everybody black is that it doesn't matter what colour you are. You can be the princess or the prince or the wicked witch. I think that is a positive thing and I try to do it deliberately now. Because I was an immigrant myself I feel a certain bond with people who did not originate here. I think that's an important element in my picture books.

"Joan Aiken is probably the best writer I have worked with. We talked about *The Kingdom under the Sea* in general terms and then she sent me the text. If, for example, I thought a tower would make a better picture than a palace of ivory, she would very graciously change it in the text."[1]

"When I did *The Kingdom under the Sea* I laid out the text line by line and put in the pictures so the whole thing was

THE KING WHO DECLARED WAR ON THE ANIMALS

Once there was a poor young nobleman who had nothing in the world but a ruined castle in the forest, a horse, and a hound. So he was obliged to go hunting every day, in order to get his food. However he looked after his animals with great care, brushing and combing them every evening, giving them the same food as he had himself, and chopping wood to make a fire so that they should be warm at night. In consequence of this they loved him dearly.

One day the young lord went hunting with his hound in a densely thicketed part of the forest. He tied his horse to a tree outside this bushy patch and left him grazing.

Presently a fox came by and stopped to admire the horse.

"My word, brother, you seem fat and glossy! Your

(From *The Kingdom under the Sea and Other Stories* by Joan Aiken. Illustrated by Jan Pienkowski.)

welded together. I made a chart of the whole book, too, so that I could work out where the colour fell. That way I got colour on twenty pages instead of only twelve and I could do the coloured initials."[2]

1979. Produced his first pop-up books, *Haunted House, Robot,* and *Dinner Time.* "Judith Elliott at Heinemann told me there was a revival of interest in paper mechanics and would I like to do one? I didn't know whether I could, but I would as long as I could work with the engineers. I went to Los Angeles where the pop-up king, Wally Hunt, lives. He is a man with a blazing passion for paper. He has two or three people working with him who are very clever at making paper jump through hoops, one of whom is Tor Lokvig.

"Tor came to London and we worked together. I wanted to do a horror book. We thought of a ghost train, but the trouble is that you would have had to have the train in every picture. Then I came up with the idea of a house and a person shown around room by room. There were no people in the house, only two little mice. Usually when you open a pop-up book something spectacular happens, but on the first spread of *Haunted House* you open it and things disappear, leaving you with a slightly uneasy feeling that something has disappeared. The book came slowly and painfully.

"Then the engineer came in and we went through it in a week and improved it. For example, the monster coming through the bathroom wall wasn't nearly as good as it is now. The

man who was in charge of the money used to stand over us like a vulture saying, 'You can't have that, too much expense.' I remember one Wednesday when he had to go to Newton Abbot and I said to Tor, 'Wednesday we do the bathroom!' The bathroom got twice as much paper as the rest!"[1]

"[I flew] out to Los Angeles to check the colour proofs, and then went on to Columbia to see the factory. I was very impressed. All the work is done by girls, and conditions are no worse then they'd be in an English printing works. In some ways they're even better. They don't get paid very much, which is why we can afford to do these books at all, but on the other hand it's very warm, there's a constant pleasant temperature and daylight, food is plentiful and not expensive. It's a very attractive place and the girls seem to enjoy their work.

"When I went to Popayan for *Haunted House* there were about 200 or more girls working there. This year when I went back for *Robot* there were nearly 500. They have had an absolute explosion. These books have brought wealth and prestige and self respect to Popayan—it's the only industry there. That's very pleasing.

"Ines Calvache [is] Miss Fixit on the production line and she translates my work and the engineer's work into reality. She's extremely experienced, and trained as a jeweller—so she's got the skill in her hands (all the girls seem to have very delicate hands and fingers which is why I think they're so good at doing these books), and Ines figures out ways of putting these

'I thought I saw a saucer
on the roof last night'
said the cat

'I
must
just
tell
my
friend...

(From Pienkowski's pop-up book *Small Talk*. Illustrated by the author.)

things together, of getting the bugs out. She worked incredibly hard on *Haunted House* and *Robot* and deserves a medal.

"I would like to go on record as saying that with these mechanical books, although they may have my name in big bold type or lettering on the cover, they're really a team effort, and they're the work of a. . .lot of people. I may have the original idea, but the actual doing of it is a very complicated business, and *Robot* was the most complicated of all. There we probably had a dozen people who worked on that and put it together."[3]

1984. *Christmas* published. It look three years to plan. "It was a daunting task to approach a story so familiar and so important. The King James Version is acknowledged as the greatest translation of the Bible and I felt that no retelling could equal it for the beauty of its language or its narrative force.

"Just as the original scholars translated the Christmas story into a familiar language, so the pictures must attempt to translate it into familiar settings. What settings though will match the magical archaic words, so well-known to children from many well-loved carols and Nativity plays?

"I have set the pictures in the country which is the heritage of every child—the land of legend.

"The castle of King Herod is fit for a villain. Full of gloomy dungeons and bristling with armed men, it looms menacingly over the humble little town where we discover Mary in her back garden doing her washing and hanging it up, as the Angel Gabriel appears with the great news.

"The silhouettes of the pictures allow the children's imagination free rein to identify with characters, whatever their ethnic background. They can dress the three kings in the richest colours and paint the houses of the crowded street to match the town they know.

"The pictures are married to the text by illuminated capital letters and gold foliage, a traditional embellishment for the words of the Gospels. The plants are chosen to help tell the story: the holly and the ivy form a rustic bridge to carry the running deer to the lowly cattle shed standing surrounded by the trees of a winter forest. This is not the Palestine of 1 A.D. but the landscape of the Christmas Carol, where the snow lies deep and crisp and even.

"The wise men are portrayed as the three kings of fable, forming an innocent link between the scheming King Herod and the child in the manger. They visit both in turn and deliver their precious gifts of gold, frankincense, and myrrh as Joseph and Mary are working to make a shelter for the baby. In the tropical moonlight we see them embark on their voyage home together with their menagerie of pack animals.

"The book was printed in an appropriately exotic setting. Only Singapore could provide a book decorated with gold and I enjoyed working with the printers to get it right.

"The drama of the story was challenging as well as rewarding: the most difficult scene was perhaps Herod's cruel horsemen galloping through autumnal brambles in pursuit of the innocent babies of Bethlehem, as the Holy Family makes their escape under cover of darkness lit up by a flash of lightning.

"As the rainbow follows the storm we find the child in his father's workshop surrounded by the carpenter's tools which we can recognise, and holding the nails which we can also recognise.

"Working on this book has been an enriching experience and I hope children everywhere will enjoy following the story in words and pictures, be it on their own or with their family."[4]

1988. "The *Easter* book has a tremendous effort of every sort; it was a physical marathon trying to get it finished for the Bologna Book Fair, an endurance test of working every day, seven days a week and into the night. I worked with several assistants and my editor. These are all well-known themes and the subjects of many great paintings, so it was a question of finding my own approach. It was fairly obvious what the set pieces had to be, 'The Last Supper,' 'The Betrayal,' and 'Christ before Pilate.'

"The book was a very big number for me, and it's still going round in my head quite a lot. It lasted about a year from start to finish and I was thinking about it for three years before that."[1]

Pienkowski has been designing stage sets since his Cambridge days. In 1988 he worked on two, "Beauty and the Beast" for London's Royal Opera House, and a production by Theatre Complicite.

In the 1980s painting took up an increasing amount of Pienkowski's thoughts and time. "Just as in the early seventies, when I had a mounting sense of unease I now have perhaps an analagous feeling of discomfort, so I'm moving towards a completely useless activity—drawing from life, drawing from landscape, painting the landscape, painting the figure, working in cut paper, and working for the theatre. I think it's unhealthy to stay with books exclusively.

"I've started to have my paintings and cut paper work exhibited. At the moment it has the attraction of novelty. It's a fairly unnerving experience, but exciting because you get an immediate reaction. My first exhibition was at the Oxford Gallery, and I didn't go back after the private view. I've just had one at the Lyric Theatre, Hammersmith, and I did go back a couple of times just to make sure the pictures were hanging straight. The artwork for *Easter* has been exhibited in the crypt of St. Martin in the Fields, in Liverpool Cathedral, and in Belfast, and this pleases me enormously."[1]

Despite his enormous and sustained success, Pienkowski has feelings of self-doubt. "Sometimes I think I'm a total failure."[1]

"All creative people need reassurance. When you show what you've done, every single thing you've got is there. And if you've had a little success it gets worse because there's more

at stake. When the first books came out I thought I was lucky to be published at all. I still do."[2]

"I think it's good to feel insecure. There's a part of me that thinks I would like to sit in a landscape, preferably with water in it, wearing a straw hat, and be this dear old man who paints hopeless landscapes. I don't think I will ever be like that because I am driven from within by an energy that makes me try harder. I have had some awful failures and learned to avoid some mistakes.

"I like working with other people, I get much better ideas when I do. I don't think I'm as good on my own as when I'm part of a group. I have a terrible wish to please—a dreadful fault, but it's also the engine which drives me. I can get depressed about any subject you care to mention and be melancholy for ages, which is why I have to be with other people."[1]

FOOTNOTE SOURCES

[1]Based on an interview by Cathy Courtney for *Something about the Author.*
[2]*Books for Keeps,* November, 1981.
[3]Tony Bradman, "How Girls with Nimble Fingers in Columbia Have Helped in a Publishing Success," *Publishing News,* October 16, 1981.
[4]Jan Pienkowski, "Christmas," *Bookcase,* winter, 1984.

FOR MORE INFORMATION SEE:

Junior Bookshelf, August, 1972.
Books for Young Children, Volume 9, number 4, 1974.
Lee Kingman and others, *Illustrators of Children's Books: 1967-1976,* Horn Book, 1978.
Doris de Montreville and Elizabeth D. Crawford, editors, *Fourth Book of Junior Authors and Illustrators,* H. W. Wilson, 1978.
Times Educational Supplement, October 30, 1981, October 2, 1987.
Instructor, September, 1982.
Publishers Weekly, April 29, 1983, November 16, 1984, May 30, 1986.
School Library Journal, September, 1983, May, 1986, September, 1987, October, 1987.
"An Interview with Jan Pienkowski," *Puffin Post,* summer, 1984.
New York Times Book Review, November 11, 1984.
Arts Review, January 29, 1988 (p. 50).

POLESE, Carolyn 1947-

PERSONAL: Surname is pronounced Poe-*less*-a; born December 26, 1947, in Berkeley, Calif.; daughter of James (an inventor) and Esther Miriam (a teacher; maiden name, Holman) Polese; married Peter Alan Lehman (a professor), August 11, 1976; children: Jacob, Benjamin. *Education:* University of California, Berkeley, B.A., 1972; attended University of California, Los Angeles, 1976; Simmons College, M.A., 1987. *Home:* Arcata, Calif. *Agent:* Ruth Cohen, P.O. Box 7626, Menlo Park, Calif. 94025.

CAREER: Free-lance writer, 1975—; Deep Springs College, Deep Springs, Calif., lecturer, 1976-79; Gateway Community School, Arcata, Calif., founding librarian, 1987—. Artist-in-residence, Gateway School, Calif., 1988—. *Member:* Society of Children's Book Writers. *Awards, honors:* Mary Tinkham-Broughton Fellow at Bread Loaf Writers' Conference, 1979; Christopher Award, 1986, for *Promise Not to Tell.*

CAROLYN POLESE

WRITINGS:

Something about a Mermaid (juvenile; illustrated by Gail Owens), Dutton, 1977.
Promise Not to Tell (juvenile; illustrated by Jennifer Barrett), Human Sciences Press, 1985.

Contributor of articles and reviews to national magazines and newspapers, including *Christian Science Monitor, Los Angeles Times, Washington Post News Service, Mothering, Utney Reader,* and *School Library Journal.* Children's book review editor, *Union* (Arcata, Calif).

WORK IN PROGRESS: Several children's book manuscripts; a young adult novel set in the redwood country of California; research on indigenous cultures and mythic studies.

SIDELIGHTS: "I grew up in a family of adventurous people. As a child, my favorite times were backpacking in the wilderness with my parents, two sisters, older brother, and our dog, Puck. My great-great grandmother was born in California before the Gold Rush. From my grandmother, I heard family stories about the westward movement, immigration, and frontier life. From her, I also got my love of beautiful books. I'd sit for hours on the couch or in the garden of her lovely old Berkeley home and pour over books she had collected when my mother was little. I read *Little Lord Fauntleroy* with the Reginald Birch illustrations, many wonderful books illustrated by Arthur Rackham and Kay Nielsen, and *At the Back of the North Wind* by George MacDonald with Jessie Willcox Smith's dreamy end papers. My grandfather—who died long before I was born—had been a botanist. I loved to sit at the old desk in his study reading the books on his shelves, drawing with

his gold-tipped fountain pen, and imagining myself to be a scientist, writer, and traveller like he had been.

"Through grade school and high school I wrote poetry, essays, and stories, and received several prizes for my writing. Even though I majored in fine arts at college, I continued to write. For a while, I was a reporter and editorial assistant on the *Berkeley Barb* and later wrote feature stories and held an editing position at the *Daily Californian.* I wrote about the human side of news events from soup kitchens to student riots. After graduating, I founded a small newspaper in the South Gate area of Sacramento.

"In college, I took up rock climbing and canoeing. It was on a canoe trip on California's Eel River that I met Peter Lehman, who became my husband. Together, we have travelled throughout the wilds of North America. In 1975 we crossed the sub-arctic Barren Lands by canoe, recording geographic information for the Canadian government and taking photographs of wild animals for magazine articles. Soon after, I wrote my first children's book, *Something about a Mermaid,* which not surprisingly has a wilderness related theme. For three years Peter and I lived on a cattle ranch in the eastern High Sierra and taught at a tiny college not far from the setting of *Promise Not to Tell.*

"Now we live in Arcata, a small town in the rugged northwestern corner of California. Here I write, raise our two sons, teach creative writing, and review children's books. My study, on the top floor of our Victorian home, is piled with books

The secret was over; she felt relieved and tired. ∎
(From *Promise Not to Tell* by Carolyn Polese. Illustrated by Jennifer Barrett.)

and papers because I keep several research and writing projects going at once.

"In 1986 my family moved with me to Boston for a year while I completed graduate school in children's literature at Simmons College. I also worked at *Horn Book* magazine and Joy Street Press, getting an insider's view of the children's book publishing world before coming back home. Since then, writing about children's books has become an important part of my work.

"In 1988, the California Arts Council awarded me an artist-in-residence grant. The school where I work is a three-room, rural schoolhouse with a total of forty students in kindergarten through sixth grade. The school children and I have been writing, reading, and exploring the hero theme. We published an anthology of their work and recently appeared on television.

"Courage in childhood interests me. I see it daily in the lives of my sons and my students. When I wrote *Promise Not to Tell* I had in mind the heroism of children who speak out when adults are wrong. At the time, I was told I was taking a big risk to write about sexual assault. But I knew, from my own experiences, that many children have to deal with this. I wanted young readers to realize that they were not alone in facing this kind of problem and I wanted them to see that—like Meagan—they have a lot of strength to draw on."

PRIMAVERA, Elise 1954-

PERSONAL: Born May 19, 1954, in West Long Branch, N.J.; daughter of Jerry (a builder) and Corrine (a housewife; maiden name, Miller) Primavera. *Education:* Moore College of Art, B.F.A., 1976; attended Arts Students League, 1980-84. *Home:* 343 East 74th St., 14M, New York, N.Y. 10021.

ELISE PRIMAVERA

CAREER: Free-lance fashion illustrator, 1976-79; free-lance children's book illustrator, 1979—. *Awards, honors: Make Way for Sam Houston* was selected one of *New York Times* Notable Books, 1986.

WRITINGS:

Basil and Maggie (Junior Literary Guild selection; self-illustrated), Lippincott, 1983.

ILLUSTRATOR

Joyce St. Peter, *Always Abigail*, Lippincott, 1981.
Dorothy Crayder, *The Joker and the Swan*, Harper, 1981.
Margaret K. Wetterer, *The Mermaid's Cape*, Atheneum, 1981.
Eila Moorhouse Lewis, *The Snug Little House*, Atheneum, 1981.
M. Wetterer, *The Giant's Apprentice*, Atheneum, 1982.
Art Buchwald, *The Bollo Caper: A Furry Tail for All Ages*, Putnam, 1983.
Natalie Savage Carlson, *The Surprise in the Mountains*, Harper, 1983.
Delia Ephron, *Santa and Alex*, Little, Brown, 1983.
Miriam Anne Bourne, *Uncle George Washington and Harriot's Guitar*, Putnam, 1983.
Elaine Moore, *Grandma's House*, Lothrop, 1985.
Margaret Poynter, *What's One More?*, Atheneum, 1985.
Jean Fritz, *Make Way for Sam Houston* (Junior Literary Guild selection), Putnam, 1986.
Jamie Gilson, *Hobie Hanson, You're Weird*, Lothrop, 1987.
Patricia Lee Gauch, *Christina Katerina and the Time She Quit the Family* (Junior Literary Guild selection), Putnam, 1987.
J. Gilson, *Double Dog Dare*, Lothrop, 1988.
E. Moore, *Grandma's Promise*, Lothrop, 1988.
Jane Yolen, *Best Witches*, Putnam, 1989.

WORK IN PROGRESS: Illustrations for *Christina Katerina and the Great Bear Train* by Patricia Lee Gauch, for Putnam; writing and illustrating children's books.

SIDELIGHTS: Primavera began her career as a fashion illustrator and changed to children's book illustration in 1979, because fashion illustration proved too unfulfilling for her creativity. To boost her confidence, she attended an illustrator's workshop. "I felt very encouraged after three weeks. I spent the summer of 1979 putting a portfolio together to show publishers. At the time I had an agent who took my work around to fashion people. I decided to leave her and take my children's book portfolio around myself.

"I saw everybody and anybody who would give me an appointment and once I got in the door I'd always ask if there was anyone else that could see me while I was there."[1]

Primavera's first break was a book jacket for Harper & Row. "A few months later I got a picture book from Margaret McElderry.

"I've always admired the artists associated with Howard Pyle and the Brandywine School. I love the way children's books were illustrated in the early 1900s. I especially like N. C. Wyeth, Jessie Willcox Smith, and Charlotte Harding. I became familiar with these artists from visiting the Brandywine Museum in Chadd's Ford, Pennsylvania."[1]

Primavera's work day begins at seven a.m. "I work straight through until three o'clock or so. Then I go look after my horse and run. And then do errands. That's pretty much the day for me.

"As far as my work time goes I spend much of it working out the sketches and dummy and the 'look' of the book. I try to

"That's all right, Basil," Maggie said, trying to look at the bright side. ■ (From *Basil and Maggie* by Elise Primavera. Illustrated by the author.)

capture its mood through an appropriate style. This takes a good deal of time because I'm not always comfortable or facile in a particular style. So I spend a lot of time not only on sketches, composition, and characterization (and the dummy in general), but also on the finishes because I'm working in an unfamiliar medium.

"The one thing I do keep in mind is to make the most bizarre thing seem possible and real to the reader. It's sort of like watching a good magician perform: you know he really can't be pulling that rabbit out of the hat, but it all looks so real that for a moment something magical really is happening. This is the response that I try to work for through my illustrations."[1]

"With all the different types of books that I have done, I have to say that the most fun has been *Best Witches*. For research, I spent a lot of time in the local costume store. When I actually finished *Witches* (nine months later), my studio was crammed with witches' hats, rubber skeletons, fright wigs, plastic frogs, and black hairy spiders. At the time I was selling my house, and I used to love to watch my real estate agent show prospective buyers the studio—I don't think they knew whether to laugh or report me to the local authorities!"

FOOTNOTE SOURCES

[1]Jim Roginski, *Behind the Covers: Interviews with Authors and Illustrators of Books for Children and Young Adults,* Libraries Unlimited, 1985.

REID, Meta Mayne   1905-

PERSONAL: Born January 23, 1905, in Woodlesford, Yorkshire, England; daughter of Marcus Andrew (a farmer) and Elvina (Moody) Hopkins; married Ebenezer Mayne Reid (chairman, Ulster Museum), August 7, 1935; children: Mark McClean, David Mayne. *Education:* University of Manchester, B.A. (with honors), 1926. *Religion:* Presbyterian. *Home:* 8 Malone View Park, Belfast BT9 5PN, Northern Ireland. *Agent:* A. P. Watt & Son, 26-28 Bedford Row, London WC1R 4HL, England.

CAREER: Poet and author of children's books. Has also worked as a broadcaster of tales, poems, and talks for the British Broadcasting Corp. (BBC). *Member:* P.E.N. (president of Irish branch, 1970-72). *Awards, honors:* Listowel Festival Trophy, 1974, for poetry.

WRITINGS:

JUVENILE

Phelim and the Creatures (illustrated by Sydney Passmore), Chatto & Windus, 1952.
Carrigmore Castle (illustrated by Richard Kennedy), Faber, 1954.
All Because of Dawks (illustrated by Geoffrey Whittam), St. Martin's, 1955.
Tiffany and the Swallow Rhyme (illustrated by R. Kennedy), Faber, 1956.

Dawks Does It Again (illustrated by G. Whittam), St. Martin's, 1956.

Dawks on Robbers' Mountain (illustrated by G. Whittam), St. Martin's, 1957.

The Cuckoo at Coolnean (illustrated by R. Kennedy), Faber, 1957.

Strangers in Carrigmore (illustrated by R. Kennedy), Faber, 1958.

Dawks and the Duchess, Macmillan, 1958.

The McNeils at Rathcapple (illustrated by Brian Wildsmith), Faber, 1959.

Storm on Kildoney (illustrated by G. Whittam), St. Martin's, 1961.

Sandy and the Hollow Book (illustrated by R. Kennedy), Faber, 1961.

The Tombermillin Oracle (illustrated by R. Kennedy), Faber, 1962.

With Angus in the Forest (illustrated by Zelma Blakely), Faber, 1963.

The Tinkers' Summer (illustrated by Peggy Fortnum), Faber, 1965.

The Silver Fighting Cocks, Faber, 1966.

The House at Spaniard's Bay, Faber, 1967.

The Glen beyond the Door, Faber, 1968.

The Two Rebels, Faber, 1969.

Beyond the Wide World's End (illustrated by Antony Maitland), Lutterworth, 1972.

The Plotters at Pollnashee (illustrated by Gareth Floyd), Lutterworth, 1973.

Snowbound at the Whitewater (illustrated by Peter Dennis), Abelard, 1975.

The Noguls and the Horse (illustrated by Tony Morris), Abelard, 1976.

A Dog Called Scampi (illustrated by John Laing), Abelard, 1980.

ADULT

The Land Is Dear (novel), Melrose, 1936.

The Far-Off Fields Are Green (novel), Melrose, 1937.

No Ivory Tower (verse), Outposts Press, 1974.

WORK IN PROGRESS: A book about children and the Northern Irish "troubles."

SIDELIGHTS: During her long and distinguished literary career, Reid has penned over twenty fantasy books and historical novels for children, as well as numerous poems. In her writings, she frequently uses Ulster, Ireland as the setting for her fiction. "Although all the literary tradition is on my husband's side of the family I have written since I was very young. I am fortunate in being able to write any time and any place—at the station, on the bus, with my back to the TV set, among family talk.

"Poetry, perhaps, gives the greatest pleasure, but writing for children aged eight to twelve is a kind of poetry. It must transfix the moment, heighten the sense of wonder, and all the time allow the narrative to leap ahead on the backs of firmly drawn characters. I have written straightforward adventure stories, but I prefer fantasy or history as they present the challenge of making a new world.

"My tales move on an Irish country background, and, since my family has lived in Northern Ireland for centuries, much of my detail springs from family stories. To be happy I must write something every day, which accounts for the 400-500 letters I send every year, most of them based on daily minutiae—a rich source of material since both fantasy and history demand practical foundations. My own favourites are *With Angus in the Forest*...and *The Silver Fighting Cocks*...."[1]

When not writing, Reid also enjoys anything Irish (but especially the country), gardening, and walking.

FOOTNOTE SOURCES

[1]D. L. Kirkpatrick, editor, *Twentieth-Century Children's Writers*, St. Martin's, 1978.

FOR MORE INFORMATION SEE:

COLLECTIONS

De Grummond Collection at the University of Southern Mississippi.

RICHARDSON, Carol 1932-

PERSONAL: Born December 25, 1932, in Orlando, Fla.; daughter of Thomas A. (a salesman) and Nina (a homemaker; maiden name, Hurst) Richardson; divorced; children: James Hurst. *Education:* Attended Earlham College, 1950-51, University of New Mexico, 1951-53, and Harris School of Advertising Art, 1954-57. *Home:* 142 N. Beach St., Ormond Beach, Fla. 32074. *Office:* Daytona Beach *News Journal,* 901 Sixth St., Daytona Beach, Fla. 32014.

CAREER: Block's (department store), Indianapolis, Ind., fashion artist, 1959-60; Davison's (department store), Atlanta, Ga., fashion artist, 1961-62; *News Journal,* Daytona Beach, Fla., staff artist, 1962-76; Universal Productions, Daytona Beach,

CAROL RICHARDSON

art director, 1976-78; free-lance illustrator, 1978—; *News-Journal*, Daytona Beach, editorial illustrator, 1981—. *Exhibitions:* "Three Women/Three Themes," Daytona Beach Museum of Arts and Sciences, Fla., 1978; "Shapes and Shadows," Joan Ling Gallery, Gainesville, Fla., 1980; (one-person show) Ormond Memorial Gallery, Ormond Beach, Fla., 1981; Deland Museum, Deland, Fla., 1984. *Member:* Florida Watercolor Society, Southern Watercolor Society. *Awards, honors:* Editor and Publishers Award from *Editor and Publisher,* 1974; First Prize from the Newspaper Color Awards Competition, 1974, for editorial color section front; Top Award from the Florida Watercolor Society, 1976, for "Generation," and 1977, for "Other Voices"; Patrons Award from the Southern Watercolor Society, 1977, for "Generation"; Grumbacher Award from the Florida Watercolor Society, 1982, for "10 A.M."; Wayne Sessions Award from the Florida Watercolor Society, 1988, for "Self-Portrait."

ILLUSTRATOR:

Janice Hale Hobby and others, *Staying Back,* Triad, 1982.

SIDELIGHTS: "I've always drawn since I was a child. Something about being able to put an idea, thought, or reason down on paper—not in words but visually—is exciting to me.

"I love illustration—drawing people and trying to imagine their feelings. That's why I went back to newspaper work—editorial illustration as opposed to advertising. This is a small area and my free-lance advertising work turned out to be mostly designing brochures. Once a year a really nice illustration or architectural interior assignment came along, if I was lucky. I needed a steady paycheck with a son in college!

"Serious illustrative work such as *Staying Back* is a challenge. It is the only book I have illustrated. I want to do more but am concentrating on my watercolors at this time. Also, I do cartoons, funny people doing a myriad of funny things. For instance, a full-color page on the last shopping night before Christmas (with all my friends doing what they would do) or using a vacation trip to Chicago or New Mexico and making a cartoon book of what happened—something funny *always* does. These are not the sort of cartoons where one laughs uproarously—just a small smile when one recognizes a situation.

"Since I'm a watercolorist, I enjoy traveling—New Mexico, New England, Washington, California—and sketching and painting."

RITTER, Lawrence S(tanley) 1922-

PERSONAL: Born May 23, 1922, in New York, N.Y.; son of Irving (a teacher) and Bella (a housewife; maiden name, Gerwitz) Ritter; married second wife, Elisabeth Fonseca (a psychologist), October, 1979; children: Stephen. *Education:* Indiana University, B.A., 1942; University of Wisconsin, M.A., 1948, Ph.D., 1951. *Politics:* Liberal Democrat. *Religion:* Jewish. *Home:* 270 West End Ave., New York, N.Y. 10023. *Agent:* Joan Raines, 71 Park Ave., New York, N.Y. 10016. *Office:* Graduate School of Business Administration, New York University, 100 Trinity Place, New York, N.Y. 10006.

CAREER: Michigan State University, East Lansing, instructor, 1949-50, assistant professor of economics, 1951-55; Federal

LAWRENCE S. RITTER

Juan Marichal. ■ (From *The Story of Baseball* by Lawrence S. Ritter.)

Reserve Bank of New York, New York City, economist, 1955-60; New York University, Graduate School of Business Administration, New York City, professor of finance, 1960—, chairman of department, 1961-69, 1973-80, John M. Schiff Professor of Finance, 1984—. Visiting associate professor, Yale University, 1960. Consultant to United States Treasury, Board of Governors of Federal Reserve System, American Bankers Association, Association of Reserve City Bankers, and Federal Deposit Insurance Corp. *Military service:* U.S. Navy, 1941-45; became lieutenant junior grade.

MEMBER: American Economic Association, American Finance Association (president, 1970), Royal Economic Society, Authors Guild, Authors League of America, Society for American Baseball Research. *Awards, honors:* Lindback Foundation Award for Distinguished Teaching at New York University, 1963; Award of Excellence from the Investment Bankers Association of America, 1968, for *A Marshall Plan for the Cities; The 100 Greatest Baseball Players of All Time* was named one of New York Public Library's Books for the Teen Age, 1982; *The Story of Baseball* was selected one of *School Library Journal*'s Best Books, 1983; Excellence in Teaching Award from New York University, 1984.

WRITINGS:

Money and Economic Activity, Houghton, 1952, 3rd edition, 1967.
The Glory of Their Times: The Story of the Early Days of Baseball Told by the Men Who Played It, foreword by John K. Hutchens, Macmillan, 1966, new enlarged edition, Morrow, 1984.
A Marshall Plan for the Cities, Goodbody, 1968.
(With William L. Silber) *Money,* Basic Books, 1970, 5th revised edition, 1984.
(With W. L. Silber) *Principles of Money, Banking, and Financial Markets,* Basic Books, 1974, 6th edition, 1989.

(With Donald Honig) *The Image of Their Greatness: An Illustrated History of Baseball from 1900 to the Present,* Crown, 1979, updated edition, 1984.
(Editor) *Selected Papers of Allan Sproul,* Federal Reserve Bank of New York, 1980.
(With D. Honig) *The 100 Greatest Baseball Players of All Time,* Crown, 1981, revised and updated edition, 1986.
The Story of Baseball (ALA Notable Book), foreword by Ted Williams, Morrow, 1983.
(With Thomas J. Urich) *The Role of Gold in Consumer Investment Portfolios,* Salomon Brothers Center for the Study of Financial Institutions, Graduate School of Business Administration, New York University, 1984.
(With Mark Rucker) *The Babe: A Life in Pictures,* Ticknor & Fields, 1988.

Managing editor, *Journal of Finance,* 1964-66; book reviewer for *New York Times Book Review* and other periodicals. Contributor to economic journals.

ADAPTATIONS:

"The Glory of Their Times" (recording), *Sporting News,* 1966, (videocassette) *Sporting News,* 1986.

SIDELIGHTS: "To do the interviews for *The Glory of Their Times,* I traveled 75,000 miles searching for the heroes of a bygone era. They were not easy to find. The teams they played for had lost track of them decades ago, and there was no central source of information. Modern players are relatively easy to locate. Since they are entitled to pension benefits, the Players Association keeps track of their whereabouts. But there were no pensions for those I was seeking, and often no Social Security either.

"In desperation, I consulted old baseball record books, which usually contained information on date and place of birth. Then I went to the New York Public Library's collection of up-to-date municipal telephone directories. I reasoned that many of these men might well have returned to their home towns after their playing days were over, and even if they hadn't, relatives might still be living there who could help me.

"Surprisingly, this worked. More often than not the hometown telephone book had a listing for the last name of the person I was looking for, and generally it was a close or distant relative of the old ballplayer. If they didn't know where he was, they at least knew some other member of the family who did.

"Not that it was any bed of roses from there on in. Far from it. As a case in point, for example, consider the tracking down of Sam Crawford, the top long-ball hitter of the early 1900's. I was told that Sam lived in Los Angeles, but when I arrived at the address, his wife, somewhat startled, said he hadn't been there in months. Sam didn't like big cities, she said, so she seldom saw him. Well, then, where could I find him? Oh, she couldn't tell me that; he'd be furious. Sam loved peace and quiet. . .and, above all, he wanted privacy.

"After I pleaded for hours, Mrs. Crawford relented somewhat. She wouldn't tell me exactly where he was, but there was probably no harm in giving me 'one small hint.' If I drove north somewhere between 175 and 225 miles, I'd be 'warm.' Oh yes, she inadvertently dropped one more clue—Sam Crawford, the giant who had once terrorized American League pitchers, enjoyed two things above all: tending his garden and watching the evening sun set over the Pacific Ocean.

"A long drive and inquiries at post offices, real-estate agencies, and grocery stores placed me, two days later, in the small town of Baywood Park, California, halfway between Los Angeles and San Francisco. For the next two days, however, I made no further progress. On the morning of the fifth day, frustrated and disappointed, I took some wash to the local laundromat and disgustedly sat watching the clothes spin. Seated next to me was a tall, elderly gentleman reading a frayed paperback. Idly, I asked if he had ever heard of Sam Crawford, the old ballplayer.

"'Well, I should certainly hope so,' he said, 'bein' as I'm him.'

"I sometimes wonder what could have prompted me to embark on such a strange crusade, searching the highways and byways of America for old ballplayers, a quest that preoccupied me for the better part of six years. For a long time I thought my travels had been inspired by the death of Ty Cobb in 1961 and that I was pursuing a social goal, recording for posterity the remembrances of a sport that had played such a significant role in American life in the early years of the twentieth century.

"But now, on reflection two decades later, I don't think my journey had much to do with social purposes. Deep down, it was a quest of a more personal nature. It so happens that my own father died at about the same time as Ty Cobb. Still vivid in my memory is the day, when I was nine years old, that my father took me by the hand to my first big-league baseball game. It seems to me now that I was trying to recapture that unforgettable ritual of childhood and draw closer to a father I would never see again—and I think that, through *The Glory of Their Times,* I somehow succeeded."

HOBBIES AND OTHER INTERESTS: Watching baseball on television; reading detective novels.

FOR MORE INFORMATION SEE:

Nation, January 30, 1967.
New York Times Book Review, June 12, 1983.
Washington Post, August 15, 1984.
Baseball History, spring, 1986.
"The Ultimate Baseball Library," *Total Baseball,* Warner, 1989.

ROSENBERG, Jane   1949-

PERSONAL: Born December 7, 1949, in New York, N.Y.; daughter of Abner Emmanuel (a real estate developer) and Lily (a homemaker; maiden name, Quittman) Rosenberg; married Michael B. Frankel, February 17, 1974 (divorced, 1978); married Robert F. Porter (an artist and writer), May 30, 1982; children: (second marriage) Melo (stepdaughter), Ava Hermine, Eloise Pearl. *Education:* Attended City of London College, and Sir John Cass College of Art, 1970; Beaver College, B.F.A., 1971; New York University, M.A., 1973. *Home and office:* 2925 Nichols Canyon Rd., Los Angeles, Calif. 90046.

CAREER: Artist, 1971—; Daniel & Charles Associates, New York City, commercial artist, 1973; Ethical Culture School, New York City, art teacher, 1974-75; free-lance illustrator and designer, 1975—; art director of *New York News for Kids,* 1979-80. *Exhibitions:* International House, Philadelphia, Pa.,

JANE ROSENBERG

1971; New York University Galleries, New York City, 1973, Museum of Modern Art Lending Gallery, New York City, 1977; Fuller Gallery, Glenside, Pa., 1979; Judith Christian Gallery, New York City, 1981; 55 Mercer Gallery, New York City, 1982; Master Eagle Gallery, New York City, 1985. *Member:* Graphic Artists Guild.

WRITINGS:

Dance Me a Story: Twelve Tales from the Classic Ballets (juvenile; self-illustrated), Thames & Hudson, 1985.
Sing Me a Story: The Metropolitan Opera's Book of Opera Stories for Children (juvenile; self-illustrated), Thames & Hudson, 1989.

ILLUSTRATOR

Gloria Rothstein, *A Scholastic Skills Program: Vocabulary Skills,* Scholastic, 1980.
Rose Beranbaum, *Romantic and Classic Cakes,* Irena Chalmers, 1981.

Contributor of illustrations to magazines.

WORK IN PROGRESS: Writing and illustrating *The Memoirs of Harlequin,* the story of the clowns of the *commedia dell'arte.*

SIDELIGHTS: "Trained as a fine artist in New York City and exhibiting my paintings in downtown galleries, I turned to free-lance illustration for income. I preferred illustrating to teaching or full-time commercial art, both of which demanded too much time away from the studio. The more my work appeared in magazines, newspapers, and books, the more appealing the notion of illustrating a project of my own became. After two unpublished collaborations with established authors, I was persuaded by my husband, also an artist and writer, to work on a text alone.

"Turning to a lifelong interest—the ballet—I retold the stories of the great classical ballets in the manner of fairy tales, attempting to offer the reader more than a program synopsis. The result, according to Tessa Rose Chester in the *Times Educational Supplement,* is that 'the total impression is possibly the closest one can get to transforming the excitement of a real dramatic performance onto the printed page.' The illustrations, depicting scenes of the ballets, are set on a stage behind the proscenium arch, offering the viewer an accurate interpretation of choreography, costume, and set. In her introduction to *Dance Me a Story,* Merrill Ashley, the New York City Ballet principal dancer, writes, 'the beautiful illustrations, based on actual productions and rich in fanciful detail, together with an evocative, eminently readable text, vividly recreate each ballet.'

"Since childhood, illustrated books have held an irresistible attraction for me. Now I find myself painting and writing for children, telling tales of the ballet, opera, or classical theatre; combining my art with my love of the performing arts into one of the most satisfying of all forms, the illustrated book.

"In my second book, *Sing Me a Story,* I wish to introduce children to the delights of opera. Open to foreign language, poetry, music, and art, young children are the perfect audience for opera."

FOR MORE INFORMATION SEE:

"Three Artists" (videotape), Mannuci Productions, 1978.
Art Diary, Giancarlo Politi Editore, 1985.
Times Educational Supplement, April 11, 1986.

SAGAN, Carl 1934-

PERSONAL: Surname is pronounced *Say*-gun; born November 9, 1934, in New York, N.Y.; son of Samuel (a cloth cutter and factory manager) and Rachel (Gruber) Sagan; married Lynn Margulis (a biologist), June 16, 1957 (divorced, 1963); married Linda Salzman (an artist), April 6, 1968 (divorced, May, 1981); married Ann Druyan (a writer), June 1, 1981; children: (first marriage) Dorion Solomon, Jeremy Ethan; (second marriage) Nicholas; (third marriage) Alexandra. *Education:* University of Chicago, A.B. (with general and special honors), 1954, S.B., 1955, S.M., 1956, Ph.D., 1960. *Politics:* Independent. *Religion:* Independent. *Office:* Laboratory for Planetary Studies, Space Science Building, Cornell University, Ithaca, N.Y. 14853. *Agent:* Scott Meredith Literary Agency, 845 Third Ave., New York, N.Y. 10022.

CAREER: University of Chicago, Chicago, Ill., lecturer, 1956-57; Armour Research Foundation, Chicago, physicist, 1958-59; University of California, Berkeley, Miller research fellow in astronomy, 1960-62; Harvard University, Cambridge, Mass., lecturer and assistant professor of astronomy, 1962-68; Smithsonian Institution, Astrophysical Observatory, Cambridge, astrophysicist, 1962-68; Cornell University, Ithaca, N.Y., associate professor, 1968-70, director of Laboratory for Planetary Studies, 1968—, professor of astronomy and space sciences, 1970—, associate director of Center for Radiophysics and Space Research, 1972-81, David Duncan Professor of Astronomy and Space Sciences, 1976—, Carl Sagan Productions, Inc., president, 1981—; writer.

Visiting professor of astronomy, Stanford University Medical School, 1962-68; National Science Foundation-American Astronomical Society visiting professor at various colleges, 1963-

CARL SAGAN

67; Condon Lecturer, University of Oregon and Oregon State University, 1967-68; National Aeronautics and Space Administration (NASA) lecturer in astronaut training program, 1969-72; Holiday Lecturer, American Association for the Advancement of Science, 1970; Vanuxem Lecturer, Princeton University, 1973; Smith Lecturer, Dartmouth University, 1974, 1977; Wagner Lecturer, University of Pennsylvania, 1975; Philips Lecturer, Haverford College, 1975; Jacob Brownowski Lecturer, University of Toronto, 1975; Anson Clark Memorial Lecturer, University of Texas at Dallas, 1976; Danz Lecturer, University of Washington, 1976; Stahl Lecturer, Bowdoin College, 1977; Christmas Lecturer, Royal Institution, London, 1977; Menninger Memorial Lecturer, American Psychiatric Association, 1978.

Carver Memorial Lecturer, Tuskegee Institute, 1981; Feinstone Lecturer, United States Military Academy, 1981; Class Day Lecturer, Yale University, 1981; George Pal Lecturer, Motion Picture Academy of Arts and Sciences, 1982; Phelps Dodge Lecturer, University of Arizona, 1982; H. L. Welsh Lecturer in Physics, University of Toronto, 1982; Distinguished Lecturer, U.S. Air Force Academy, Colorado Spring, 1983; Adolf Meyer Lecturer, American Psychiatric Association, 1984; Lowell Lecturer, Harvard University, 1984; Jack Distinguished American Lecturer, Indiana University (Penn.), 1984; Distinguished Lecturer, Southern Methodist University, 1984; Keystone Lecturer, National War College, National Defense University, Washington, D.C., 1984-86; Marshall Lecturer, Natural Resources Defense Council, Washington, D.C., 1985; Johnson Distinguished Lecturer, Johnson Graduate School of Management, Cornell University, 1985; Gifford Lecturer in Natural Theology, University of Glasgow, 1985; Lilenthal Lecturer, California Academy of Science, 1986; Dolan Lecturer, American Public Health Association, 1986; Distinguished Lecturer, The Japan Society, 1987; Cohen Lecturer, Moravian College, 1987; Barrack Lecturer, University of Nevada, 1987; Commonwealth Lecturer, University of Massachusetts, Amherst, 1988.

Member of committee to review Project Blue Book (U.S. Air Force), 1956-66. Investigator, Mariner mission to Mars, 1962, Mariner and Viking missions to Mars, 1969—, Voyager missions to the outer planets, 1979; designer of *Pioneer 10* and *11* and *Voyager 1* and *2* interstellar messages; member of advisory council, Smithsonian Institution, Washington, D.C., 1975-80; judge, National Book Awards, 1976; member of Usage Panel, American Heritage Dictionary of the English Language, 1976-82; fellow, Committee for the Scientific Investigation of Claims of the Paranormal, 1976—; member of fellowship panel, John S. Guggenheim Memorial Foundation, 1976-81.

Member of board of directors, Council for a Livable World Education Fund, 1980—; commissioner, President's Commission for a National Agenda for the '80's (McGill Commission), The White House, 1980; member of National Advisory Board, American Civil Liberties Union, 1981—; elector, National Women's Hall of Fame, 1981—; member of advisory board, American University, Washington, D.C., 1982—; member of advisory panel, Civil Space Station Study, Office of Technology Assessment, U.S. Congress, 1982; member of advisory panel, Civilian Space Stations and the U.S. Future in Space, Office of Technology Assessment, U.S. Congress, 1982-84; chairman, Conference on the Long-term Global Atmospheric and Climatic Consequences of Nuclear War, American Academy of Arts and Sciences, Cambridge, Mass., 1982-83; member, American Committee on U.S.-Soviet Relations, Washington, D.C., 1983—; member, American Committee on East-West Accord, 1983—; sponsor, National Campaign to Save the ABM Treaty, Washington, D.C., 1984; member of advisory board, Educators for Social Responsibility, 1984.

Member of visiting committee, The College, University of Chicago, 1986—; member of national advisory board, Mothers Embracing Nuclear Disarmament (MEND), 1986—; member of national advisory board, Illinois Mathematics and Science Academy, 1986—; member of international advisory board, Institute for International Peace Studies, University of Notre Dame, 1986—; member of advisory board, Samantha Smith Foundation, 1987—; member of national advisory board, Americans for Religious Liberty, 1987—; member of advisory board, National Center for Science Education, 1987—; member of board of directors, Spacewatch, Washington, D.C., 1987—.

MEMBER: International Astronomical Union (member of organizing committee, Commission of Physical Study of Planets), International Council of Scientific Unions (vice chairman; member of executive council, committee on space research; co-chairman, working group on moon and planets), International Academy of Astronautics, International Society for the Study of the Origin of Life (member of council, 1980—), P.E.N. International, American Astronomical Society (councillor; chairman, division of planetary sciences, 1975-76), American Physical Society, American Geophysical Union (president, planetology section, 1980-82), American Association for the Advancement of Science (fellow; chairman, astronomy section, 1975-76), American Institute of Aeronautics and Astronautics (fellow), American Astronautical Society (fellow; member of council, 1976), Federation of American Scientists (member of council, 1977-80, 1985—), Planetary Society (president, 1979—), Society for the Study of Evolution, British Interplanetary Society (fellow), Astronomical Society of the Pacific, Genetics Society of America, Authors Guild, Authors League of America, Phi Beta Kappa, Sigma Xi, Explorers Club, American Academy of Arts and Sciences (fellow), World Association of International Relations, World Academy of Arts and Sciences (fellow).

AWARDS, HONORS: National Science Foundation Pre-doctoral Fellowship, 1955-60; Alfred P. Sloan Foundation Research Fellowship at Harvard University, 1963-67; A. Calvert Smith Prize from Harvard University, 1964; Apollo Achievement Award, 1969, Medal for Exceptional Scientific Achievement, 1972, and Medal for Distinguished Public Service, 1977, and 1981, all from the National Aeronautics and Space Administration (NASA); Prix Galabert (international astronautics prize), 1973; Klumpke-Roberts Prize from the Astronomical Society of the Pacific, 1974; John W. Campbell Memorial Award for "Best Science Book of the Year" from the World Science Fiction Convention, 1974, for *The Cosmic Connection;* Golden Plate Award from the American Academy of Achievement, 1975; Joseph Priestley Award from Dickinson College, 1975, for "distinguished contributions to the welfare of mankind"; D.Sc. (honorary) from Rensselaer Polytechnic University, 1975, Denison University, 1976, Clarkson College, 1977, Whittier College, and Clark University, both 1978, American University, 1980, University of South Carolina, 1984, Hofstra University, 1985, Long Island University, 1987; D.H.L. from Skidmore College, 1976; Pulitzer Prize for Literature, 1978, for *The Dragons of Eden;* Washburn Medal from the Boston Museum of Science, 1978; LL.D. (honorary), University of Wyoming, 1978, Drexel University, 1986.

Rittenhouse Medal from the Franklin Institute/Rittenhouse Astronomical Society, 1980; The Explorer's Club 75th Anniversary Award for "achievement in furthering the spirit of exploration," 1980; *Cosmos* was named one of American Library Association's Best Books for Young Adults, 1980; *Broca's Brain* and *Murmurs of Earth* were both selected one of New York Public Library's Books for the Teen Age, 1980; D.H.L. (honorary), Lewis and Clark College, 1980, Brooklyn Col-

Sagan and crew with miniature set of the interior of the Alexandrian library.

lege, 1982; Academy of Family Films and Family Television Award for Best Television Series of 1980, American Council for Better Broadcasts Citation for Highest Quality Television Programming of 1980-81, Silver Plaque from Chicago Film Festival, President's Special Award from Western Educational Society for Telecommunication, and three Emmy Awards from the Television Academy of Arts and Sciences, all 1981, and Ohio State University Annual Award for Television Excellence, 1982, all for "Cosmos" series; George Foster Peabody Award for Excellence in Television Programming, University of Georgia, 1981; Glenn Seaborg Prize for Communicating Science from the Lecture Platform, American Platform Association, 1981; Ralph Coats Roe Medal from the American Society of Mechanical Engineers "in recognition of contribution to planetary physics," 1981; American Book Award nomination for *Cosmos* (hardcover), and *Broca's Brain* (paperback), both 1981; Humanist of the Year Award from the American Humanist Association, 1981; Stony Brook Foundation Award (with Frank Press), 1982, for distinguished contributions to higher education; John F. Kennedy Astronautics Award from the American Astronautical Society, 1983, for "outstanding contributions to public service through leadership in promoting. . .the exploration utilization of outer space."

Honda Prize from the Honda Foundation, 1985, for "contributions toward. . .a new era of human civilization"; Arthur C. Clarke Award for Space Education from the Students for the Exploration and Development of Space, 1984; S.Sc. (honorary), University of South Carolina, 1984; Peter Lavan Award for Humanitarian Service from Bard College, 1984; New Priorities Award from the Fund for New Priorities in America, 1984; Sidney Hillman Foundation Prize Award for "outstanding contributions [to] world peace," 1984; SANE National Peace Award, 1984; Regents Medal for Excellence from the Board of Regents, University of the State of New York, 1984; Physicians for Social Responsibility Annual Award for Public Service, 1985; Leo Szilard Award for Physics in the Public Interest (with Richard P. Turco and others) for the discovery of nuclear winter from the American Physical Society, 1985; Distinguished Service Award from the World Peace Film Festival, Marlboro College, 1985; NASA Group Achievement Award, Voyager Uranus Interstellar Mission, 1986; Nahum Goldmann Medal "in recognition of distinguished service to the cause of peace and many accomplishments in science and public affairs" from the World Jewish Congress, 1986; Brit HaDorot Award from Shalom Center, 1986; Annual Award of Merit from the American Consulting Engineers Council, 1986; Maurice Eisendrath Award for Social Justice from the Central Conference of American Rabbis and the Union of American Hebrew Congregations, 1987; In Praise of Reason Award from the Committee for the Scientific Investigation of Claims of the Paranormal, 1987.

WRITINGS:

(With W. W. Kellogg) *The Atmospheres of Mars and Venus*, National Academy of Sciences, 1961.

(With I. S. Shklovskii) *Intelligent Life in the Universe*, Holden-Day, 1963, reissued, 1978.

(With Jonathan Leonard) *Planets*, Time-Life, 1966.

At 42, Sagan became the leading spokesman and salesman for the new science of exobiology, the search for extraterrestrial life.

Planetary Exploration: The Condon Lectures, University of Oregon Press, 1970.

(Editor with T. Owen and H. J. Smith) *Planetary Atmospheres,* D. Reidel (Amsterdam), 1971.

(Editor with K. Y. Kondratyev and M. Rycroft) *Space Research XI,* two volumes, Akademie Verlag (Berlin), 1971.

(With R. Littauer and others) *The Air War in Indochina,* Beacon Press, 1971.

(Editor with Thornton Page) *UFOs: A Scientific Debate,* Cornell University Press, 1972.

(Editor) *Communication with Extraterrestrial Intelligence,* MIT Press, 1973.

(With Ray Bradbury, Arthur Clarke, Bruce Murray and Walter Sullivan) *Mars and the Mind of Man,* Harper, 1973.

(With R. Berendzen, A. Montagu, P. Morrison, K. Stendhal and G. Wald) *Life beyond Earth and the Mind of Man,* U.S. Government Printing Office, 1973.

(Editor) *The Cosmic Connection: An Extraterrestrial Perspective,* Doubleday, 1973.

Other Worlds, Bantam, 1975.

The Dragons of Eden: Speculations on the Evolution of Human Intelligence, Random House, 1977.

(With F. D. Drake, A. Druyan, J. Lomberg, and T. Ferris) *Murmurs of Earth: The Voyager Interstellar Record,* Random House, 1978.

Broca's Brain: Reflections on the Romance of Science, Random House, 1979.

Cosmos, Random House, 1980.

(With R. Gawin and others) *The Fallacy of Star Wars,* Vintage Books, 1984.

(With P. R. Ehrlich and others) *The Cold and the Dark: The World after Nuclear War,* Norton, 1984.

"The cosmic explainer."

Contact (novel), Simon & Schuster, 1985.
Comet, Random House, 1985.

Also contributor to several books on science. Author of radio and television scripts, including "Cosmos," Public Broadcasting System, 1980, and scripts for Voice of America, American Chemical Society radio series, and British Broadcasting Corp. Contributor to *Encyclopedia Americana, Encyclopaedia Britannica* and *Whole Earth Catalog,* 1971. Contributor of more than 350 papers to scientific journals, and of articles to periodicals, including *National Geographic, Saturday Review, Discovery, Washington Post, Natural History, Scientific American* and *New York Times. Icarus: International Journal of Solar System Studies,* associate editor, 1962-68, 1980—, editor-in-chief, 1968-79; member of editorial board, *Origins of Life,* 1974—, *Climatic Change,* 1976—, and *Science 80,* 1979-83.

Author of more than 600 published scientific papers and popular articles. Several of Sagan's books, including *The Cosmic Connection, The Dragons of Eden, Broca's Brain,* and *Cosmos* have been translated into numerous languages, including French, Spanish, Portuguese, German, Chinese, Hebrew, Greek, Japanese, Dutch, Russian, and Serbo-Croatian.

WORK IN PROGRESS: Nucleus for Random House; *Global Consequences of Nuclear War* (with R. P. Turco and others) for Random House; *The Search for Who We Are: The Gifford Lectures in Natural Theology.*

SIDELIGHTS: "We start out a million years ago in a small community on some grassy plain; we hunt animals, have children and develop a rich social, sexual and intellectual life, but we know almost nothing about our surroundings. Yet we hun-

(Dust jacket illustration by Jon Lomberg from *The Cosmic Connection: Am Extraterrestrial Perspective* by Carl Sagan.)

ger to understand, so we invent myths about how we imagine the world is constructed—and they're, of course, based upon what we know, which is ourselves and other animals. So we make up stories about how the world was hatched from a cosmic egg, or created after the mating of cosmic deities or by some fiat of a powerful being. But we're not fully satisfied with those stories, so we keep broadening the horizon of our myths; and then we discover that there's a totally different way in which the world is constructed and things originate.

"Today, we're still loaded down, and to some extent embarrassed, by ancient myths, but we respect them as part of the same impulse that has led to the modern, scientific kind of myth. But we now have the opportunity to discover, for the first time, the way the universe is in *fact* constructed, as opposed to how we would wish it to be constructed. It's a critical moment in the history of the world."[1]—Carl Sagan

November 9, 1934. Sagan was born in the Bensonhurst section of Brooklyn, N.Y. where his Russian-immigrant father was a cutter who rose to foreman in the garment industry. "It was during the Depression, and we were kind of poor. When I was very little, the basic thing for me was stars. When I was five years old, I could see them at whatever time bedtime was in winter, and they just didn't seem to belong in Brooklyn. The sun and the moon seemed perfectly right for Brooklyn, but the stars were different. I had the sense of something interesting, distant, strange about them. I asked people what the stars were, and I mostly got answers like 'They're lights in the sky, kid.' I could tell they were lights in the sky; that wasn't what I meant. After I got my first library card, I made a big expedition to the public-library branch on Eighty-sixth Street in

Brooklyn. I had to take the streetcar; it was some big distance. I wanted a book on the stars. At first there was some confusion; the librarian mentioned all kinds of books about Hollywood stars. I was embarrassed, so I didn't explain right away, but finally I got across what I wanted. They got me this book, and I read it right there, because I wanted the answer.

"The library book had this stunning, astonishing thing in it—that the stars were suns, just like our sun, so far away that they were only a twinkle of light. I didn't know how far away that was, because I didn't know mathematics, but I could tell only by thinking of how bright the sun is in the daytime and how dim a star is at night that the sun would have to be very far away to be just a twinkle, and the scale of the universe opened up to me."[2]

"My parents always encouraged me to read. Every now and then I would think, gee, wouldn't it be terrific if I had a friend to talk to about the stars, but there wasn't one."[3]

"It must have been a year or two after this that I learned what the planets were. Then it seemed absolutely certain to me that if the stars were like the sun there must be planets around them. And they must have life on them. This was an old idea, of course. Christiaan Huygens, the Dutch astronomer, I found out later, had written about it in the sixteen-seventies. But I thought of it before I was eight. And once I reached that point, I got very interested in astronomy. I spent a lot of time working on distances, coordinates, and parallaxes."[2]

"By the time I was ten I had decided—in almost total ignorance of the difficulty of the problem—that the universe was full up. There were too many places for this to be the only inhabited planet. And, from the variety of life on earth (trees looked pretty different from most of my friends), I figured life elsewhere would seem very strange. I tried hard to imagine what that life would be like, but despite my best efforts I always produced a kind of terrestrial chimaera, a blend of existing plants or animals.

"About this time a friend introduced me to the Mars novels of Edgar Rice Burroughs. I had not thought much about Mars before, but here, presented before me in the adventures of John Carter, was another inhabited world, breathtakingly fleshed out: ancient seabottoms, great canal pumping stations and a variety of beings, some of them exotic. There were, for example, the eight-legged beasts of burden, the thoats.

"These novels were exhilarating to read. At first. But slowly, doubts began to gnaw. The plot surprise in the first John Carter novel which I read hinged on his forgetting that the year is longer on Mars than on Earth. But it seemed to me that if you go to another planet, one of the first things you check out is the length of the day and the year. Then there were incidental remarks which at first seemed stunning but on sober reflection proved disappointing. For example, Burroughs casually comments that on Mars there are two more primary colors than on earth. Many long minutes did I spend with my eyes closed, fiercely contemplating a new primary color. But it would always be something familiar, like a murky brown or plum. How could there be another primary color on Mars, much less two? What was a primary color? Was it something to do with physics or something to do with physiology? I decided that Burroughs might not have known what he was talking about, but he certainly made his readers think. And in those many chapters where there was not much to think about, there were satisfyingly malignant enemies and rousing swordsmanship—more than enough to maintain the interest of a city-bound ten-year-old in a long Brooklyn summer.

A view of Titan, one of Saturn's moons, as created for "Cosmos." ■ (Photograph courtesy of Edwardo Castaneda.)

"The following summer, by sheerest accident, I stumbled upon a magazine called *Astounding Science Fiction* in a neighborhood candy store. A glance at the cover and a quick riffle through the interior showed me it was what I had been looking for. With some effort I managed to scrape together the purchase price, opened the magazine at random, sat down on a bench not twenty feet from the store and read my first modern science-fiction short story, "Pete Can Fix It" by Raymond F. Jones, a gentle account of time travel into a postnuclear-war holocaust. I had known about the atom bomb—I remember an excited friend explaining to me that it was made of atoms—but this was the first I had seen about the social implications of nuclear weapons. It got you thinking."

"I found I was hooked. Each month I eagerly awaited the arrival of *Astounding*. I read Verne and Wells, read, cover-to-cover, the first two science-fiction anthologies that I was able to find, devised scorecards, similar to those I was fond of making for baseball, on the quality of the stories I read. Many ranked high in asking interesting questions but low in answering them."[4]

When he turned twelve, Sagan was asked by his aged grandfather what he planned to be when he grew up. "An astronomer," he replied. 'Fine,' said the old man, 'but how will you make a living?' "[5]

"I didn't make a decision to pursue astronomy; rather, it just grabbed me, and I had no thought of escaping. But I didn't know that you could get paid for it. I thought I'd have to have some job I was temperamentally unsuited to, like door-to-door salesman, and then on weekends or at nights I could do astronomy. That's the way it was done in the fiction I read, in which space science was practiced by wealthy amateurs. Then, in my sophomore year in high school, my biology teacher. . .told me he was pretty sure that Harvard paid [noted astronomer] Harlow Shapley a salary. That was a splendid day—when I began to suspect that if I tried hard I could do astronomy full time, not just part time."

"I had been receiving catalogues from various colleges, and I wanted one with good mathematics and physics. The University of Chicago sent me a booklet entitled 'If You Want an Education.' Inside was a picture of football players fighting on a field, and under it the caption 'If you want a school with good football, don't come to the University of Chicago.' Then there was a picture of some drunken kids, and the caption 'If you want a school with a good fraternity life, don't come to the University of Chicago.' It sounded like the place for me. The trouble was that it had no engineering school, and I wanted an education not only in astronomy and physics but also in rocket engineering. I went down to Princeton to ask Lyman Spitzer, the astronomer, his advice; he was involved in some early rocket studies. He told me that there was no reason an astronomer had to know every nut and bolt of a spacecraft in order to use it. Up until then, I had thought this was necessary—another holdover from the fiction I'd been reading, in which the rich amateur built his own spaceship. Now I realized that I could go to the Unversity of Chicago, even though it had no engineering school. I applied, and entered in the fall of 1951. In the early nineteen-fifties, the University of Chicago was a very exciting place to be. It was strong in the humanities—which I wanted—but it was also very strong in the sciences. Enrico Fermi and Harold Urey were both there, in physics and in chemistry. And it had a superb astronomy department, which operated the Yerkes Observatory."[2]

Through a friend, Sagan was introduced to Indiana University's Dr. H. J. Muller, who had won the 1946 Nobel Prize in Medicine and Physiology for discovering that X-rays caused

mutations in genes. Since X-rays are produced by exploding stars, Muller's findings were linked to astronomy. Interested in those pursuits, Sagan spent the summer of his freshman year working for Muller at Indiana University. "Muller had me doing routine things, such as looking at fruit flies for new mutations. But he ran a real research group, and for the first time I got a feeling of what scientific research was like. Moreover, Muller was interested not only in the origins of life but in the possibility of life elsewhere; he didn't think the idea was the least bit silly. Muller encouraged me to learn genetics. Later, he sustained me through years of studying biology and chemistry, which I had thought were far removed from my main interest, astronomy. I always kept in touch with him. A few years before his death, he gave me a book about space flight by Arthur C. Clarke, and inscribed it, 'Perhaps we'll meet someday on the tundras of Mars.' "[2]

With Muller's letter of introduction to Dr. Urey, who had won the 1934 Nobel Prize in Chemistry for discovering hydrogen and who had gone on to study origins of life, Sagan returned to the University of Chicago to begin his sophomore year. "[Urey] was extremely kind to me when I was an undergraduate. I did an honors essay on how life began. I was very naive, and I remember Urey's comment: 'This is the work of a very young man.' I had the idea that in one fell swoop I could understand the origins of life, though I had not had much chemistry or biology. It was an attempt to learn by doing. Some other people at Chicago were more effective at this than I was. It was a time of great excitement, for this was when Stanley Miller was doing his work, under Urey, on the origins of life. He had filled a flask with methane, ammonia, water, and hydrogen—things you would expect to find in the primitive atmosphere of a young planet—and had passed an electrical discharge, like lightning, through it. The result was amino acids, the first step toward life. Miller had shown that the beginnings of life were not a matter of chance but could happen in any place where the conditions were right.

"Urey showed me through Miller's laboratory. Later, Miller was forced to defend his work before the University of Chicago's chemistry department. They didn't take it very seriously; they kept suggesting that he had been sloppy, leaving amino acids all over his laboratory. I was outraged that something as important as that could be received in such a hostile way. Urey was the only one who spoke up for him. He said, 'If God didn't create life this way, He certainly missed a good bet.' "[2]

Sagan received his master's degree in physics, and went on in 1956 to the University of Chicago's graduate school of astronomy at Williams Bay, Wisconsin, where he worked under the tutelage of Dutch astronomer Dr. Gerard Kuiper. "Kuiper was a respected man, and if he said it was possible for *any* sort of life to exist on Mars that was important. It was a tremendous boost to exobiology."[2]

In **1956** he spent the summer with Kuiper at the McDonald Observatory in Fort Davis, Texas, where he had his first opportunity to see what Mars looked like through a big telescope. "As it turned out, there were dust storms in both places—Mars and Texas. I didn't find any canals. I was satisfied just to be able to see light and dark markings. The seeing was poor, even through the eighty-two-inch telescope at McDonald. There Mars was, though shimmering, squashed, distorted. Then, for an instant, the atmosphere steadied, and I caught a glimpse of the southern polar cap. I saw no fine details. It was no big deal. I realized that the telescopic technique, while interesting, was limited: Sitting under a blanket of air forty million miles from the target was not going to tell me much."[2]

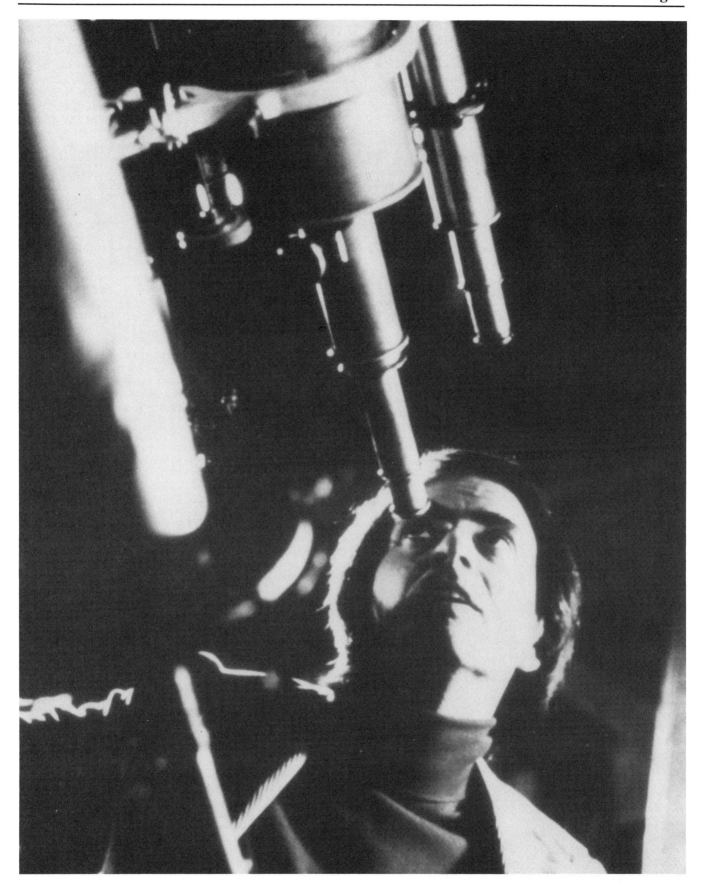

Sagan peering through a telescope at Arizona's Lowell Observatory. ■ (Photograph courtesy of William R. Ray/*Time Magazine*.)

At the age of twenty-one, he published his first paper, "Radiation and the Origin of the Gene," in *Evolution*. It was during this time that Sagan met mentor Joshua Lederberg, then professor of genetics at the University of Wisconsin, an honored Nobel laureate and the inventor of the word 'exobiology' for the study of extraterrestrial life. It was Lederberg, as chairman of the Space Science Board committee studying ways of searching for life in space, who asked Sagan to become a member.

While Sagan was working for his doctorate under Kuiper, he married biologist Lynn Margulis. Two sons were born before the marriage ended in divorce in 1963. He received his doctorate in astronomy and astrophysics from the University of Chicago in 1960. His oldest son, Dorion recalled: "My father used to make up stories about black holes and tell them to my brother and me night after night. In fact, I was probably one of the first people that he experimented on in his attempts to popularize science."[6]

During his years at Chicago, Sagan organized a highly successful campus lecture series on science, including himself as one of the speakers. Some faculty members dismissed it as "Sagan's circus."

He went on to become a research fellow at the University of California at Berkeley, and then, spent a year as visiting assistant professor of genetics at the Stanford Medical School. From 1962-68 he held a joint appointment as astrophysicist at the Smithsonian Astrophysical Observatory in Cambridge, Mass., and lecturer and later assistant professor of astronomy at Harvard. Sagan's flamboyant style did not go over well

Sagan with wife, Ann Druyan.

with old-line astronomy professors at Harvard, so when he was denied tenure in 1968, he moved on to Cornell. With one of his graduate students, James Pollack, Sagan concluded that the bright and dark patterns detected on Mars were not due to seasonal changes in vegetation, as some had theorized, but to winds swift enough to whirl up dust storms in the thin atmosphere and sculpt huge variations in surface elevations. Three years later, *Mariner 9* confirmed his theory of the Martian winds. In his doctoral thesis, he argued that the observed radio emission from Venus was due to a very hot surface, the heat held in by a massive carbon dioxide/water vapor greenhouse effect. The Soviet *Venera* probes, and the American *Pioneer Venus* spacecraft confirmed his theory in the late '60s and '70s.

Sagan was asked about his quest to find life beyond Earth. "I think it's because human beings love to be alive, and we have an emotional resonance with something else alive, rather than with a molybdenum atom. Why are people interested in other animals? Why are we interested in the life history of the armadillo? Why do we go to Antarctica to find out what the emperor penguins have been doing lately? It's fun, because we are primarily drawn to things that are alive."[2]

"Life on Earth is the same, despite some external differences in form. In the essential biochemistry, every one of us—from bacterium to human being—is composed of the same proteins and the same nucleic acids, all put together in the same way. Therefore, the biologists have no idea what is possible in living systems—what ranges of biologies can exist. We have only one example.

". . .We are all descended from a single instance of the origin of life. We're similar because we're related—we bacteria and we people.

"On another planet, the statistical factors work differently, the physical environment is different, evolution follows other pathways, and one would expect that the organisms, if any, would be astonishingly different—not just in their internal appearance, but more fundamentally in their internal make-up. The discovery of life on Mars—even very simple life—would work a fundamental revolution in biology which would have a wide range of practical implications for us here on Earth.

"If we find life on Mars, we will have looked at two planets and found life on both of them—the Earth and Mars. That would go a long way toward arguing for the grand conclusion of an inhabited cosmos. If so, it seems very likely that on many planets in other solar systems life would have evolved into advanced forms. The conclusion naturally presents itself that we might be able to communicate, using radio telescopes, with intelligent beings on planets of other stars. That's why it will be so exciting if we do find life on Mars. On the other hand, if we do not find life on Mars, that would hardly foreclose the possibilities of life on other planets."[7]

A typical weather report on Mars in Earth terms would go like this: "In the Chryse Basin today, the wind was from the northwest at twelve miles an hour, changing at midnight to the south at nineteen miles an hour. The temperature just before dawn was -122 Fahrenheit, rising to -20 Fahrenheit at 2 p.m. The barometric pressure is constant at 7.7 millibars. Chances for rain: zero."[7]

"There is nothing about science that cannot be explained to the layman," says Sagan. However, the purists among his colleagues shudder at such popularization and simplification. His flamboyant style, the speculative nature of some of his work, and his celebrity profile (as a regular on the Johnny

Carson show) further fuel the controversy. "There are at least two reasons why scientists have an obligation to explain what science is all about. One is naked self-interest. Much of the funding for science comes from the public, and the public has a right to know how their money is being spent. If we scientists increase the public excitement about science, then there is a good chance of having more public supporters.

"The other is that it's tremendously exciting to communicate your own excitement to others. It's satisfying. I find the letters I get from kids who have been excited by science extremely rewarding.

"We have a society which is built on science and technology and which uses science in every one of the interstices of national life and in which the public, the Executive, the Legislative and the Judiciary have very little understanding of what science is about. That is a clear disaster signal. It has to be suicidal."[8]

American scientific illiteracy begins around the age of ten and twelve, according to Sagan. "Virtually every kid has an interest in science. It is an essential part of the nature of a human being—the sense of curiosity, discovery, understanding, manipulation of the environment. All kids are born with it, but then something happens in late grade school or junior high school that turns it off."[8]

"The most effective agents to communicate science to the public are television, motion pictures, and newspapers—where the science offerings are often dreary, inaccurate, ponderous, grossly caricatured or (as with much Saturday-morning commercial television programming for children) hostile to science."[1] Sagan's books, frequent appearances on television talk shows, and 'Cosmos,' his thirteen-part series for public television are attempts at restoring balance.

"In the summer and fall of **1976,** as a member of the *Viking Lander* Imaging Flight Team, I was engaged, with a hundred of my scientific colleagues, in the exploration of the planet Mars. For the first time in human history we had landed two space vehicles on the surface of another world. The results. . .were spectacular, the historical significance of the mission utterly apparent. And yet the general public was learning almost nothing of these great happenings. The press was largely inattentive; television ignored the mission almost altogether. When it became clear that a definitive answer on whether there is life on Mars would not be forthcoming, interest dwindled still further. There was little tolerance for ambiguity. When we found the sky of Mars to be kind of pinkish-yellow rather than the blue which had erroneously first been reported, the announcement was greeted by a chorus of good-natured boos from the assembled reporters—they wanted Mars to be, even in this respect, like the Earth. They believed that their audiences would be progressively disinterested as Mars was revealed to be less and less like the Earth. And yet the Martian landscapes are staggering, the vistas breathtaking. I was positive from my own experience that an enormous global interest exists in the exploration of the planets and in many kindred scientific topics—the origin of life, the Earth, and the Cosmos, the search for extraterrestrial intelligence, our connection with the universe. And I was certain that this interest could be excited through that most powerful communication medium, television."[9]

Hence, "Cosmos," the thirteen-part television series oriented toward astronomy with a broad human perspective, was born. The program, by 1987, had a world-wide viewing audience of one-third of a billion people. It was "dedicated to the proposition that the public is far more intelligent than it has generally been given credit for; that the deepest scientific questions on the nature and origin of the world excite the interests and passions of enormous numbers of people. The present epoch is a major crossroads for our civilization and perhaps for our species. Whatever road we take, our fate is indissolubly bound up with science. In addition, science is a delight; evolution has arranged that we take pleasure in understanding—those who understand are more likely to survive. The. . .series. . .represents a hopeful experiment in communicating some of the ideas, methods and joys of science."[9]

1977. Pulitzer-Prize-winning *The Dragons of Eden,* Sagan's first popular book to delve outside the study of astronomy, examines the premise that "a better understanding of the nature of evolution of human intelligence just possibly might help us to deal intelligently with our unknown and perilous future."[10] To help achieve this understanding Sagan traces the evolutionary process of the intelligence of lower animals. He describes the brain evolution of three distinct brains of modern man. The reptilian brain (the oldest) plays a distinctive role in aggressive behavior, territoriality, ritual, and the establishment of social hierarchies. The mammalian brain which generates strong or vivid emotions and the neocortex, common to most higher primates at least in humans. The neocortex is most notably the recorder of culture which does not complement the functions of the earlier two brains but serves to obstruct, deny, repress, and frustrate them. Much of the book's attention is focused on the neocortex, especially the right and left hemispheres.

". . .Unless we destroy ourselves utterly, the future belongs to those societies that, while not ignoring the reptilian and mammalian parts of our being, enable the characteristically human components of our nature to flourish; to those societies that encourage diversity rather than conformity; to those societies willing to invest resources in a variety of social, political, economic and cultural experiments, and prepared to sacrifice short-term advantage for long-term benefit; to those societies that treat new ideas as delicate, fragile and immensely valuable pathways to the future."[11]

The inspiration for Sagan's next work, *Broca's Brain,* came during a tour of the Musee de l'Homme in Paris, where he came upon a collection of jars containing human brains. Examining one of the jars, he found he was holding the brain of Paul Broca, a distinguished nineteenth-century anatomist. *Broca's Brain* is a compilation of essays ranging in topic from ancient astronauts to mathematically-gifted horses.

1981. Married third wife, novelist Ann Druyan. Druyan was one of the writers on the "Cosmos" series and was creative director of the *Voyager* record. She had been Sagan's constant companion for two and a half years. "We were friends and collaborators for several years," said Druyan, "and suddenly we fell in love. At first we didn't allow ourselves to think about it. Once it was out, we moved heaven and earth to be together."[3] Added Sagan, "Until I met Annie I thought love was a hype to sell movie magazines to teenage girls. The idea that it really could be the kind of feeling that popular songs claim was a revelation."[3]

1983. Suffered a near-fatal condition as a consequence of an appendectomy that caused massive internal hemorrhaging. His blood was replaced twice and he had ten hours of surgery in the Upstate Medical Center in Syracuse.

1985. *Contact,* his first novel published. He tried writing fiction "for the same reason I've gone on the 'Tonight' show: to reach a different audience, millions of people."[6]

Approaching Earth in episode one of the television series "Cosmos."

In recent years, Sagan has devoted much of his time to writing and lecturing about the long-term effects of nuclear warfare. He played a major role in the discovery of nuclear winter, the widespread cold and dark likely to be brought about by even a small nuclear war. The scientists' vision of the total devastation and widespread death made him a leading spokesman in the nuclear disarmament movement. In 1986 he was arrested for misdemeanor criminal trespass at the Nevada Test Site, seventy miles northwest of Las Vegas. He and 138 other protesters, most of them doctors, nurses and public-health professionals, were taken into custody after crossing security barriers to demonstrate against continued U.S. nuclear testing in the face of a Soviet moratorium. An underground bomb, the tenth that year, was set off while the protest was in progress. All of the charges were subsequently dropped. With his wife, Ann, he organized in 1987 the largest demonstration at the Nevada Test site ever held, with the largest number of arrests in non-violent civil disobedience in U.S. history.

"The nuclear issue really worries me because we discover, unexpectedly, that we've created a doomsday machine. Yes, there are assurances: 'Trust me—we won't use it.' But that's like giving a loaded revolver to a child.

"Precisely the same technology that we use to destroy our global civilization—nuclear and rocket technology—can also be used to take us to the planets and stars. We can choose either fork in the road. It's like a morality play from the Middle Ages."[12]

"Overall, the human species spends almost $1 trillion a year, most of it by the United States and the Soviet Union, in preparations for intimidation and war....We are at risk. We do not need alien invaders. We have all by ourselves generated sufficient dangers. But they are unseen dangers, seemingly far removed from everyday life, requiring careful thought to understand, involving transparent gases, invisible radiation, nuclear weapons that almost no one has actually witnessed in use—not a foreign army intent on plunder, slavery, rape and murder. Our common enemies are harder to personify, more difficult to hate than a Shahansha, a Khan or a Fuhrer. And joining forces against these new enemies requires us to make courageous efforts at self-knowledge, because we ourselves—all the nations of the Earth, but especially the United States and the Soviet Union—bear responsibility for the perils we now face...."[13]

Sagan's fantasy is to hole up with piles of photographs of the Saturn system. "I have this image of long winter nights with the snow falling outside and there I am lost in the haze layer of Titan [Saturn's largest moon]."[3]

He is currently the David Duncan Professor of Astronomy and Space Sciences and director of the Laboratory for Planetary Studies at Cornell. In addition to the commissions and conferences on extraterrestrial life, Sagan has participated in the work of an enormous number of boards and committees having to do with space exploration, including the groups that formulated the international procedures for sterilizing spacecrafts and several committees for NASA—most notably the imaging teams of *Mariner 9, Viking,* and *Voyager.* He has also become involved in the flights of *Pioneers 10* and *11.* Sagan and Cornell colleague Frank Drake designed plaques to be installed on the crafts depicting the time of launch in relation to the history of our galaxy and pictures of those who launched the crafts—delineations of a nude man and woman. He was also responsible for the Voyager interstellar records aboard the *Voyager 1* and *2* spacecrafts.

FOOTNOTE SOURCES

[1]Jonathan Cott, "The Cosmos," *Rolling Stone,* December 25, 1980.

[2]Henry S. F. Cooper, Jr., "Profiles: A Resonance with Something Alive—I," *New Yorker*, June 21, 1976.

[3]"His 'Cosmos' a Huge Success, Carl Sagan Turns Back to Science and Saturn's Rings," *People*, December 15, 1980.

[4]Carl Sagan, "Growing Up with Science Fiction," *New York Times Magazine*, May 28, 1978.

[5]David Gelman, and others, "Seeking Other Worlds," *Newsweek*, August 15, 1977.

[6]Glenn Collins, "The Sagans: Fiction and Fact Back to Back," *New York Times Biographical Service*, September 30, 1985.

[7]"Beyond Viking: Where Missions to Mars Could Lead," *U.S. News & World Report*, August 30, 1976.

[8]Boyce Rensberger, "Carl Sagan: Obliged to Explain," *New York Times Book Review*, May 29, 1977.

[9]C. Sagan, "Introduction," to *Cosmos*, Random House, 1980.

[10]Richard Restak, "The Brain Knew More than the Genes," *New York Times Book Review*, May 29, 1977.

[11]Charles Weingartner, "A Dragon in Your Head: Carl Sagan's *The Dragons of Eden*," *Media & Methods*, September, 1978.

[12]"Today's Technology May Find E. T. If He's Out There," *U.S. News & World Report*, October 21, 1985.

[13]C. Sagan, "The Common Enemy," *Parade*, February 7, 1988.

FOR MORE INFORMATION SEE:

Christian Science Monitor, November 15, 1965, November 19, 1980.

Current Biography, 1970, H. W. Wilson, 1971.

Arthur Fisher, "Close-Up Photos Reveal a Turbulent Mars: A PS Interview with Carl Sagan," *Popular Science*, September, 1972.

Edward Edelson, "Star Struck," *Washington Post Book World*, November 25, 1973.

Time, January 24, 1974, September 29, 1980, December 14, 1981, October 13, 1986.

Richard Berendzen, "The Solar System and Beyond," *Bulletin of the Atomic Scientists*, April, 1975.

"The Authors," *Scientific American*, May, 1975.

"Lots of Space Mysteries Still Left to Explore," *U. S. News & World Report*, May 19, 1975.

"The Authors," *Scientific American*, September, 1975.

New York, September 1, 1975.

Henry S. F. Cooper, Jr., "Profiles: A Resonance with Something Alive—II," *New Yorker*, June 28, 1976.

Joseph F. Goodavage, "An Interview with Carl Sagan," *Analog Science Fiction/Science Fact*, August, 1976.

Meet the Press, September 19, 1976.

"The Vikings on Mars Provide Vicarious Adventure for a Would-Be Space Explorer," *People*, January 3, 1977.

Carl Sagan, "In Praise of Science and Technology," *New Republic*, January 22, 1977.

John F. Baker, "PW Interviews: Carl Sagan," *Publishers Weekly*, May 2, 1977.

New York Times, May 17, 1977.

Chicago Tribune, May 20, 1977.

Peter Stoler, "Brain Matter," *Time*, May 23, 1977.

Detroit News, May 27, 1977.

Washington Post Book World, May 27, 1977, November 17, 1980.

New York Review of Books, June 9, 1977.

Newsweek, June 27, 1977, August 22, 1977, October 6, 1980, November 23, 1981.

Atlantic, August, 1977.

R. J. Herrnstein, "Psycho-Physiology," *Commentary*, August, 1977, May, 1981.

John Updike, "Who Wants to Know?," *New Yorker*, August 22, 1977.

David Gelman and others, "Seeking Other Worlds," *Newsweek*, August 15, 1977.

C. Sagan, "'Miss Universe,'" *New York Times Magazine*, October 23, 1977.

New York Times Book Review, June 10, 1979, July 19, 1979, January 25, 1981.

R. Berendzen, "Astronomy and Other Subjects," *Science*, July 6, 1979.

Judy Klemesrud, "Behind the Best Sellers," *New York Times Book Review*, July 29, 1979.

National Review, August 3, 1979.

Astronomy, October, 1979.

Roger Bingham, "The New Scientist Interview," *New Scientist*, January 17, 1980.

Science Books and Films, March, 1980.

New Statesman, April 4, 1980.

Bruce Cook, "Carl Sagan's Guided Tour of the Universe," *American Film*, June, 1980.

J. Kelly Beatty, "Carl Sagan's 'Cosmos': Prime-Time Astronomy," *Sky and Telescope*, September, 1980.

David Roberts, "Carl Sagan's *Cosmos*," *Horizon*, October, 1980.

Isaac Asimov, "Isaac Asimov on *Cosmos* Star," *Horizon*, October, 1980.

"The Cosmic Explainer," *Time*, October 20, 1980.

Alvin P. Sanoff, "A Conversation with Carl Sagan," *U. S. News & World Report*, December 1, 1980.

Frederic Golden, "Carl Sagan: Astronomical Superstar," *Reader's Digest*, February, 1981.

William J. O'Malley, "Carl Sagan's Gospel of Scientism," *America*, February 7, 1981.

Jeffrey Marsh, "The Universe and Dr. Sagan," *Commentary*, May, 1981.

William J. Harnack, "Carl Sagan: Cosmic Evolution Vs. the Creationist Myth," *Humanist*, July-August, 1981.

David Paul Rebovich, "Sagan's Metaphysical Parable," *Transaction: Social Science and Modern Society*, July-August, 1981.

William J. Broad, "A Star Fades for Entrepreneur Sagan," *Science*, January 8, 1982.

Science Digest, March, 1982.

Judi Kesselman-Turkel and Franklynn Peterson, "The Marketing of Dr. Carl Sagan," *Omni*, June, 1982.

C. Sagan, "Can We Know the Universe?" *Saturday Evening Post*, July-August, 1982.

Constance Holden, "Scientists Describe 'Nuclear Winter,'" *Science*, November 18, 1983.

Contemporary Issues Criticism, Volume II, Gale, 1984.

"Notes in an Interplanetary Bottle," *Harper's*, November, 1986.

C. Sagan, "Why We Must Continue to Be Explorers," *Parade*, November 22, 1987.

Daniel Cohen, *Carl Sagan: A Biography*, Dodd, 1987.

C. Sagan and Ann Druyan, "Give Us Hope," *Parade*, November 27, 1988.

SHEFELMAN, Janice (Jordan) 1930-

PERSONAL: Born April 12, 1930, in Baytown, Tex.; daughter of Gilbert John (a professor and writer) and Vera (a homemaker; maiden name Tiller) Jordan; married Thomas Whitehead Shefelman (an architect and illustrator), September 18, 1954; children: Karl Jordan, Daniel Whitehead. *Education:* Southern Methodist University, B.A., 1951, M.Ed., 1952; University of Texas at Austin, Library Certificate, 1980. *Home and office:* 1405 West 32nd St., Austin, Tex. 78703.

CAREER: John Neely Bryan Elementary School, Dallas, Tex., teacher, 1952-54; St. Andrews Episcopal School, Austin, Tex., teacher, 1955-57; writer, 1978—; Lake Travis Independent School, Austin, librarian, 1980-84. School library volunteer,

JANICE JORDAN SHEFELMAN

1967-74; speaker at public schools in Texas. *Member:* Society of Children's Book Writers, Austin Writers League, Authors Guild, Heritage Society of Austin. *Awards, honors: A Paradise Called Texas* was included on Texas Library Association's Bluebonnet Award Master List, 1985-86.

WRITINGS:

A Paradise Called Texas (juvenile novel; illustrated by husband, Tom Shefelman, and sons, Karl Shefelman and Dan Shefelman), Eakin Press, 1983.
Willow Creek Home (juvenile novel; sequel to *A Paradise Called Texas;* illustrated by T. Shefelman, K. Shefelman, and D. Shefelman), Eakin Press, 1985.
Spirit of Iron (sequel to *Willow Creek Home;* illustrated by T. Shefelman, K. Shefelman, and D. Shefelman), Eakin Press, 1987.
Victoria House (fiction; illustrated by T. Shefelman), Harcourt, 1988.

WORK IN PROGRESS: Several books illustrated by husband: *A Mare for Young Wolf,* an easy-to-read book, *Country Girl,* a picture book, *Sophie's Indian,* a picture book, and *Farewell, Anna,* a picture book telling a story of two friends about to be separated by the emigration of one's family; *Brother of the Wolf,* a juvenile novel.

SIDELIGHTS: "My childhood was spent in a tree-lined neighborhood of University Park, in Dallas, Texas. We lived only a few blocks from the campus of Southern Methodist University where my father taught German and I rode my tricycle during evening walks with my parents. Daddy read *Winnie-the-Pooh* to me when I was five years old which began a love affair with children's books that has never cooled.

"When at last I entered this university as a student, my favorite courses were children's literature and comparative literature—even though I was an art major.

"Coming out of a protected and idyllic childhood, I yearned to see the rest of the world and have some adventures such as were in books. Soon after graduating, then, I became a campus representative for a student travel organization and earned

summer trips for myself—bicycling around Europe, traveling to North Africa and the Middle East.

"Later, teaching school allowed me generous vacations to travel, and it was on a ski trip to Aspen, Colorado that I met Tom. We discovered we shared the dream of seeing the world—he from a young architect's point of view and I from the sheer love of adventure.

"So, we decided to marry and go around the world together. We sold all our material possessions, and set out aboard a Japanese freighter for the Far East. In Japan we lived for a time in the guest room of a Japanese architect and then in a Buddhist temple. The *Asahi Shimbun,* Tokyo's major newspaper, did a story on our trip and dubbed us the 'Honeymooning Hobos,' a fairly accurate description of our travel style. And fortuitously, they asked us to do a series of articles about our impressions of Japan. I did the writing and Tom did pen and ink illustrations—our first experience at being published.

"After a year of travel that took us to Hong Kong, Thailand, India, and Egypt, we returned home to Austin, Texas, where I soon turned my energies to rearing a family of two sons and sharing with them my love for children's books. When they entered school I volunteered to work in the school library, carding and shelving books, storytelling, and generally staying involved with children and books. So much did I enjoy the library work that I went back to school and became a librarian. When I had a library of my own, I considered the first priority was to get the right book to the right child.

When they rode under a low branch, he pushed her down roughly, over the horse. ■ (From *Willow Creek Home* by Janice Jordan Shefelman. Illustrated by Karl Shefelman.)

"It was only after our two sons had grown up that it occurred to me to try writing a book of my own. I enrolled in a correspondence course in creative writing and began sending in assignments. I knew I wanted to write a children's novel, but about what?

"All during our travels I had been fascinated with visiting ancient ruins of other civilizations. I tried to imagine what it was like to live there hundreds or thousands of years ago. I remember standing on the terrace of the king's palace in the ruined city of Angkor in Cambodia, looking out over a weedy field that had once been the parade grounds. It was a hot, humid day in the jungle and the air shimmered with heat. In my mind's eye the field came astir with rippling banners, bejewelled elephants, bright red parasols, and soldiers carrying lance and shield. And they were parading before me, the queen of Angkor!

"Yes, it was historical fiction I wanted to write, but for my first book I wanted a subject closer to home. I remembered a true story Daddy had told me many times of how my great-grandfather left Germany with his wife and young daughter and sailed to Texas in 1845 to make a new life for hiimself and his family. They had been told Texas was the 'paradise of North America.' But the journey did not turn out as expected—the paradise became a nightmare. And this ready-made plot became my first book, *A Paradise Called Texas*. Since there was more to their story I wrote two sequels, *Willow Creek Home* and *Spirit of Iron*.

"Another reason that I choose to write historical fiction (though not exclusively) is that I love doing research. The University of Texas is in Austin where I live, and their extensive libraries are a gold mine. Not only does research give me knowledge of the times and places I am writing about, it also gives me ideas for many of the incidents in my books. The kidnapping of my heroine in *Willow Creek Home* was inspired by a true story found in an old, old book, *Indian Depredations in Texas*.

"I also like to research the places I write about by going there. It was a powerful experience to walk along a beach on the Texas Gulf Coast one December, the place and month my great grandfather landed—as desolate now as it was in 1845.

"There are several writing techniques that help me get words on paper. First, I stick to a regular, daily writing schedule, nine to five, just like any other job.

"Another technique is that I write whatever comes to mind whether it is good or bad. Sometimes my first draft is *very* bad and sometimes it is only bad. Rarely is it good. I call it the garbage draft. Many people, I think, do not like to write for fear they will be disappointed. I am nearly always disappointed. But I have learned that by rewriting many times, changing, adding, layering on richness of detail, that I can make something good out of something bad.

"Probably the most productive technique of all for me is visualization. During research I collect pictures—photographs, xerox copies, maps—and before beginning to write I stick these up on the walls of my study. So, when I sit down at my desk each morning I am surrounded by images of the past—sailing ships, Indians dressed in buckskin, log cabins, a drawing of Galveston in 1845, and on and on. As I put pen to paper I make pictures in my mind, moving pictures. I see my characters in action, hear them talk, see the wind fill the sails, and all I have to do is write it down.

"The pictures on my wall are also used as visual references by the illustrators of my books who are not only Tom but also

our two sons, Karl and Dan, both artists living in New York City. Karl is a filmmaker, Dan, an editorial cartoonist.

"A dominant force in my life is the idea that one must dream and then go about making dreams come true. Perhaps this belief is the reason the story of my German ancestors' immigration to Texas was so appealing to me. The only way to realize a dream is to *begin*—to write the outline of a book, then the first paragraph.

"I work from an outline, but a flexible one. Often my characters begin to act on their own, forgetting the outline, and that's fun. Still an outline helps, because I can concentrate on one scene at a time and not think about writing a whole long book.

"To be a writer you must read. The rhythm of the words will become a part of you, so be sure to choose the best books. It is also important to make yourself keenly aware of everything around you, and how the scenes and events of life affect you and others. Open up to life and keep a journal of what you see, hear, smell, touch, taste, and think."

Victoria House came about from a book Shefelman read to her sons when they were small. "The idea came from a book called *The Little House*. It was an old, old picture book that won the Caldecott Award in the 30s or 40s. It was a story about a house that sat out in the country, up on a hill, with apple trees all around. But the city grew up and surrounded it, and one day, a descendent of the owners found it and had it moved from the crowded city back to the country—up on a hill, with apple trees all around.

"We read that story to our sons when they were young, but every time Tom and I read it, we were disturbed by the fact that the house had to be moved out of the city. We have always liked living in the city and we decided to do a book where we did just the opposite—move a house from the country to an inner-city neighborhood."[1]

"Now that our sons have left home, Tom and I find that our nest is not empty at all, for we have discovered that making a book is rather like rearing a child. In fact, when we sent off the final watercolor paintings for our first picture book, *Victoria House*, it felt something like sending a child off to college. There was an emptiness in our house, and I remarked, 'Tom, we need another book in our lives.' Happily we now have one and look forward to always having one crawling around underfoot."

FOOTNOTE SOURCES

[1]Becky Knapp, "A House of Tales," *Austin American-Statesman,* August 28, 1988. Amemded by J. Shefelman.

FOR MORE INFORMATION SEE:

"Librarian's Book Opens Up Writing Career," *Hill Country Living* (Austin, Tex.), October 20, 1983.
"Thinking Like a Child," *Austin American-Statesman,* November 1, 1983.
"Child's Book Brings History to Life," *Houston Post,* April 8, 1984.
"Writing Keeps Students Spellbound," *Arlington Daily News* (Tex.), November 17, 1987.
"Reading Key to Author's Success," *Daily Tribune* (Bay City, Tex.), May 11, 1988.

SHEFELMAN, Tom (Whitehead) 1927-

PERSONAL: Born October 3, 1927, in Seattle, Wash.; son of Harold Samuel (an attorney) and Lily Madolene (a singer; maiden name Whitehead) Shefelman; married Janice Jordan (an author), September 18, 1954; children: Karl Jordan, Daniel Whitehead. *Education:* University of Texas—Austin, B.Arch., 1950; Harvard University, M.Arch., 1951. *Home:* 1405 West 32nd St., Austin, Tex. 78703. *Office:* Shefelman, Nix & Voelzel Architects, 105 West 8th St., Austin, Tex. 78701.

CAREER: Kuehne Brooks & Barr, Austin, Tex., designer and project architect, 1951-54; Fehr & Granger, Architects, Austin, associate, 1955-59; School of Architecture, University of Texas, Austin, instructor, 1959-67, associate professor, 1968-72; Taniguchi, Shefelman, Vackar, Minter, Inc., Architects, Austin, partner, 1970-76; Shefelman, Nix & Voelzel, Architects, Austin, partner, 1977—. *Military service:* U.S. Navy, 1945-46; U. S. Army Reserve, Corps of Engineers, 1948-52. *Member:* Heritage Society of Austin, American Institute of Architects (Austin chapter; president, 1981-82), Texas Society of Architects, Austin Natural Science Association (president of the board, 1974-75), Austinplan (steering committee, 1986-88), Society of Children's Book Writers. *Awards, honors:* *Progressive Architecture* Annual Design Awards Program, citations, 1949, 1978; American Institute of Architects (Austin chapter) Biennial Design Awards, 1970, 1974, 1980, 1982; First Award from the Austin Municipal Office Complex Design Competition, 1984; *A Paradise Called Texas* was included on Texas Library Association's Bluebonnet Award Master List, 1985-86.

ILLUSTRATOR:

JUVENILE; ALL WRITTEN BY WIFE, JANICE JORDAN SHEFELMAN

(With sons, Karl Shefelman and Dan Shefelman) *A Paradise Called Texas,* Eakin Press, 1983.

(With K. Shefelman and D. Shefelman) *Willow Creek Home* (sequel to *A Paradise Called Texas*), Eakin Press, 1985.

(With K. Shefelman and D. Shefelman) *Spirit of Iron* (sequel to *Willow Creek Home*), Eakin Press, 1987.

Victoria House, Gulliver Books, 1988.

TOM SHEFELMAN

Author with Robert Harris of *Austin Community Renewal Program, Architectural Studies, for the City of Austin,* Austin Planning Department, 1968.

WORK IN PROGRESS: Illustrating an easy-to-read book, *A Mare for Young Wolf,* and picture books, *Country Girl, Farewell, Anna,* and *Sophie's Indian,* all by wife, Janice Shefelman.

SIDELIGHTS: "My mother was first a singer and pianist and second a painter. Failing to make a musician out of me she settled for an artist. While growing up it seemed that my ticket to social acceptance was my drawing and cartooning ability. I was mediocre in elementary school until teachers learned to let me illustrate my papers and reports, and mediocre in mathematics until I discovered plane geometry in high school.

"Our home in Seattle was blessed with a library well-stocked with beautifully illustrated classics—*Robin Hood, Mysterious Island, Last of the Mohicans*—and I knew them through the pictures before I began to read them. On my ninth birthday I was given a set of *Compton's Picture Encyclopedia.* I remember, vividly, opening one of the volumes to a picture of the Temple of Karnak and marvelling at the mighty columns that dwarfed the man standing between them. At age thirteen my mother enrolled me in a sculpture class in Tucson, Arizona. The instructor happened also to be building, on consignment, a model of an ancient Greek agora surrounded by gracious colonnaded buildings. So, by the time an architect had visited my Seattle high school on career day with his wonderful drawings, it seemed inevitable that I would become an architect. My father, a prominent attorney, was relieved. He was afraid I might become an *artist!*

"During my final year of high school at Schreiner Institute in Kerrville, Texas, one of my favorite activities was drawing cartoons for the school newspaper. It was a short distance to the University of Texas, so I visited the School of Architecture and viewed with awe the large Beaux Arts watercolor and ink renderings on the walls. Later, as a student there, I was privileged to study with Professor Raymond Everett who in the 1940s unabashedly taught us in that grand old medium—watercolor.

"My study at the School of Architecture was interrupted by a year in the Navy. Even there my duties frequently were as artist, varying from sign and poster painter to base newspaper cartoonist.

"While a student at the Harvard Graduate School of Design, the urban design emphasis of the Walter Gropius master class, student life in Cambridge, and visits to Boston and its Beacon Hill, all opened my eyes to what urban living could be.

"I returned to Austin to begin my architectural apprenticeship. During a ski trip to Aspen I met Janice. We married a few months later and went traveling for a year in the Far and Middle East, earning our way as, yes, a writer-illustrator team for newspapers and magazines, writing about places, people, experiences, and perceptions along the way. The final impact of that trip was our walk between the giant columns of the Temple of Karnak.

"I returned to continue as an architect, then a teacher of design and graphics at the University of Texas. Teaching was a learning experience that opened me up to a new level of awareness and understanding. I discovered that design and drawing are a rigorous, selective process of thinking and looking. Appropriately one of my first readings then was Paul Klee's *The Thinking Eye.*

"During this period of awakening, my design studio was at home, a blessing for my two young sons. They, quite naturally, grew up viewing and responding to the world as artists. When Janice began in earnest her latent career as a writer, there was no question that our two sons, then completing college as artists, would join me in a collaboration as illustrators for her first published children's novels.

"It is another fitting cycle that Janice and I began our first draft and sketches of *Victoria House* during a week of skiing, this time in Taos."

Victoria House is about an old Victorian house in disrepair which is moved to an inner-city neighborhood. "The inner-city neighborhood the house was moved to originally was based on the Fan District of Richmond, Va., a totally restored urban neighborhood. But then we decided that Victoria House needed more space, where the houses weren't so close together. So the inner-city neighborhood in the book is a kind of a combination of Richmond and Austin, with more of the character of [Austin's] Hyde Park. Some of the houses in the drawings are from Dallas and some are from Hyde Park and some came from a book on houses that I have."[1]

FOOTNOTE SOURCES

[1] Becky Knapp, "A House of Tales," *Austin American-Statesman,* August 28, 1988.

FOR MORE INFORMATION SEE:

"Waller Creek Plan. . . .," *Austin American-Statesman,* November 10, 1975.
"House of Words," *Texas Architect,* March/April, 1979.

SLATER, James (Derrick) 1929-
(Jim Slater)

PERSONAL: Born March 13, 1929, in Wirral, Cheshire, England; son of Hubert (in the building business) and Jessie (Barton) Slater; married Helen Wyndham Goodwyn, 1965; children: two sons, two daughters. *Education:* Attended schools in England. *Home:* High Beeches, Blackhills, Esher, Surrey, England.

CAREER: Slater Walker Securities Ltd. (investment firm), London, England, founder, managing director, 1964-72, chairman, 1964-75; author. Has worked in an accounting firm, as an accountant and general manager for a metal finishing company in the early 1950s, as secretary for Park Royal Vehicles Ltd. in the mid-1950s, as director of A.E.D. Ltd., 1959, as deputy sales director of Leyland Motor Corporation, 1963, and previously owned the Children's Book Centre in Kensington, England.

WRITINGS:

UNDER NAME JIM SLATER

Return to Go: My Autobiography, Weidenfeld & Nicolson, 1977, new edition, Futura, 1978.
Goldenrod (juvenile; illustrated by Christopher Chamberlain), J. Cape, 1978, new edition, Heinemann Educational, 1981.
Goldenrod and the Kidnappers (juvenile; illustrated by C. Chamberlain), J. Cape, 1979, new edition, Penguin, 1980.
The Boy Who Saved Earth (illustrated by Ron Logan), Hodder & Stoughton, 1979, Doubleday, 1981.
Grasshopper and the Unwise Owl (juvenile; illustrated by Babette Cole), Granada, 1979, Holt, 1980.

Grasshopper and the Pickle Factory (juvenile; illustrated by B. Cole), Granada, 1980.
The Boy Who Found Atlantis, Hodder & Stoughton, 1980.
Grasshopper and the Poisoned River (juvenile; illustrated by B. Cole), Granada, 1982.

"A. MAZING MONSTER" SERIES; JUVENILE; ALL ILLUSTRATED BY SON, CHRISTOPHER SLATER

The Great Gulper, Granada, 1979, Random House, 1981.
Bignose, Random House, 1979.
The Tricky Troggle, Granada, 1979.
Dimmo, Granada, 1979.
Webfoot, Granada, 1979.
Greeneye, Granada, 1979.
The Winkybird, Granada, 1979.
Wormball, Granada, 1979.
Snuggly, Dragon Books, 1980.
Kleenum, Dragon Books, 1980.
Swiggo, Dragon Books, 1980.
Big Snowy, Dragon Books, 1980, Random House, 1981.

Also author of "Roger Robot" series, for children: *Roger the Robot at the Circus, . . .at the Safari Park, . . .at the Seaside, . . .Goes Fishing.*

SIDELIGHTS: "My childhood and early training in accountancy were not unusual in any way, and it was only when I took on my first industrial job that my experience became very different from the norm.

"We were not hard up, but on the other hand I was always made aware of the fact that money did not grow on trees. When I was about twelve I had only one pair of long trousers and I can well remember falling over and tearing them on one knee. They were 'invisibly' mended by a neighbour in a lighter cotton than the rest of the trousers, and I had to make do with them for a long time after that.

"I was educated first of all in a small preparatory school and then, from the age of five, at the local school, Preston Park, which was about a mile away. When I was ten years old the war started [World War II] and as a result I did not have to sit for a scholarship at the age of eleven. During the war, exemptions based upon term work were granted in certain cases, and I was lucky enough to be given one. This meant that I could go to the local secondary school, Preston Manor, which was co-educational. I was fortunate in being able to go to Preston Manor because it was a school that was built just before the war and had very high standards. It was a show-piece for foreign visitors, the educational standards were high, and its amenities included a biology laboratory, chemistry and physics laboratories, extensive playing fields and an excellent gymnasium.

"A large number of children from our area and others nearby were being evacuated to Edmonton in Canada, and my parents decided at one stage that I should join them. I was all ready to go when my mother had an instinctive feeling that it would be wrong, and she withdrew my name from the list at the last moment. The ship sailed and was sunk by a German submarine. Out of ninety children only thirteen survived, and one of my school friends was killed, as well as the daughter of a neighbour who lived opposite us. If we all have nine lives— I reckon that was one of mine.

"My mother always used to insist that I did my homework properly and both my parents gave me every encouragement to try to do well at school. I took it quite seriously at first but when I was about fourteen my attitude became more light-

Suddenly he reached out and tried to slash the boy with his claws. ■ (From *Grasshopper and the Unwise Owl* by Jim Slater. Illustrated by Babette Cole.)

hearted, perhaps because I began to realize that girls were girls. In a sense that was the time when I should have made a real effort, but instead I started to get comments in my school report like 'Irresponsible and a bad influence upon others in the class.' I have a fond recollection of Mr. Kernut, who was my English master at school and a particularly good teacher, but the other teachers did not really register with me, and the headmaster was a very remote figure. My best subjects were chemistry and physics, and I converted part of our garage at home into a laboratory. I remember once making some gunpowder and exploding it in a small thick glass bottle in our garden to the consternation of our neighbours. Looking back I regret not having worked harder when I was at school, but fortunately, just before I took the General Schools Certificate Examination at the age of sixteeen, I worked really intensively for a few months. As a result, I obtained a credit in all the subjects I sat for, with Matriculation exemption and a distinction in mathematics.

"I qualified as a chartered accountant in 1953 at the age of twenty-four. Shortly afterwards I decided that it was time for me to obtain industrial experience.

"I have always been a great believer in what I call the Zulu principle. By this I mean that if you take a relatively narrow subject and study it closely you can become expert in it compared with other people. This is of course a truism, but a very important one, and I use Zulus to illustrate the principle as they do it very well. If you picked up the *Reader's Digest* one month and in it there was an article of, say, four pages on Zulus, after reading that article you would be one of the few people in your town who knew anything about them. If this made you quite interested in the subject, and you noticed two books about Zulus in your local library and read them, you would probably by then be the leading authority in your county on Zulus. If you had now become so interested in the subject that you read all the other books you could find about it, and even visited South Africa to do some research on the spot, you might well find yourself recognized as one of the leading authorities on Zulus in Great Britain. The important point is that Zulus are a fairly narrow subject and you would be putting a relatively disproportionate amount of effort into it. It is the same principle as using a laser beam rather than a scatter gun, and is analogous to Montgomery's excellent strategy of concentrating the attack.

"I applied the Zulu principle to the Stock Exchange. Instead of tackling asset situations,. . .I decided to work on earnings situations, and in particular those of small-to medium-sized companies as opposed to the very large ones. Here was a narrow area of stock market upon which to concentrate my attack."[1]

Slater was a partner in the British investment management service Slater Walker until it closed in the mid-1970s. "There was a sharp contrast between the first seven and the last three years of my time with Slater Walker. In its early years Slater Walker made a very substantial number of acquisitions and became from very small beginnings, one of the largest companies in Britian.....Since then,...Slater Walker has been through the worst bear market of this century and I...resigned from the company; I have been the subject of very considerable criticism, and the Singapore authorities have made an attempt to extradite me; my personal fortune...has gone....

"I can, therefore, claim to have experienced in a very short time exceptional heights and depths in terms of both good fortune and reputation. Obviously, in the early days particularly, I must have done a large number of things right, and equally,...I must have made a number of major mistakes. Certainly in recent years my philosophy has changed—looking back I can see much more clearly both my own strengths and weaknesses and those of the company I was directing at the time."[1]

Slater began to write books in the late seventies. "I had always had it in mind to write a book, but I used to see it as something to be kept for retirement or the last years of my life."[1]

Today British financier and children's author Jim Slater lives in London, England with his wife and four children. One of his sons, Christopher, is the illustrator of the author's "A. Mazing Monster" series. Slater tries out all his books on children before publication, and compiles questionnaires to test their reactions. He feels that far too little research has gone into why children like certain books, and believes stories can be much improved with their help. His other "window" on the children's book world is the Children's Book Centre in Kensington, which he owned. Slater has written a substantial number of children's books, including _Goldenrod_ and _Goldenrod and the Kidnappers. The Boy Who Saved Earth,_ originally published in England, is the first of Slater's books to be published in the United States.

FOOTNOTE SOURCES

[1]Jim Slater, _Return to Go: My Autobiography,_ Weidenfeld & Nicolson, 1977, new edition, Futura, 1978.

FOR MORE INFORMATION SEE:

"Young Lions of Europe," _Time,_ September 25, 1972.
R. Ball, "Jim Slater's Global Chess Game," _Fortune,_ June, 1973.
D. Pauly and P. R. Webb, "Slater under Fire," _Newsweek,_ November 10, 1975.
"Fallen Idol," _Economist,_ September 18, 1976.
Charles Raw, _Slater Walker: An Investigation of a Financial Phenomenon,_ Deutsch, 1977.
Current Affairs, October 28, 1977.
Times Literary Supplement, October 28, 1977.
"Jim Slater on Jim Slater," _Accountancy,_ November, 1977.
B. Page, "Jim Slater Rides Again...and Again," _New Statesman,_ May 5, 1978.
L. Minard, "Return of the Minus Millionaire," _Forbes,_ September 15, 1980.

SLOAN, Carolyn   1937-

PERSONAL: Born April 15, 1937, in London, England; daughter of Robert Gordon (a stockbroker) and Lottie Clemmey (a housewife; maiden name, Waugh) Sloan; married David Hollis, May 15, 1961; children: Peter, Rupert. _Education:_ Attended schools in Newcastle, Harrogate, and Guildford, England. _Home and office:_ 7 Dapdune Rd., Guildford, Surrey GU1 4NY, England. _Agent:_ Murray Pollinger, 4 Garrick St., London WC2E 9BH, England.

CAROLYN SLOAN

CAREER: Queen (magazine), London, England, editorial assistant, 1956-60; free-lance journalist, 1960—; co-proprietor of village shop in Send Marsh, Surrey, England, 1968-72; Unwins (printers), Old Woking, Surrey, photo-typesetter, 1973-75; Yvonne Arnaud Theatre, Guildford, Surrey, press and public relations officer, 1976-80; press representative for Emlyn Williams, 1980; free-lance press consultant, 1980—. _Member:_ Society of Authors.

WRITINGS:

JUVENILE

Carter Is a Painter's Cat (illustrated by Fritz Wegner), Kestrel, 1971, Simon & Schuster, 1973.
Victoria and the Crowded Pocket (illustrated by Peter Bailey), Kestrel, 1973.
The Penguin and the Vacuum Cleaner (illustrated by Jill McDonald), Kestrel, 1974, published in America as _The Penguin and the Strange Animal,_ McGraw, 1975.
Sam Snake (illustrated by Barbara Swiderska), Kestrel, 1975.
Mr. Cogg and His Computer (illustrated by Glenys Ambrus), Macmillan, 1979.
Further Inventions of Mr. Cogg (illustrated by G. Ambrus), Macmillan, 1981.
Shakespeare, Theatre Cat (illustrated by Jill Bennett), Macmillan, 1982.
Skewer's Garden, Chatto & Windus, 1983.
Mr. Cogg and the Exploding Easter Eggs (illustrated by G. Ambrus), Macmillan, 1984.
Helen Keller (illustrated by Karen Heywood), Hamish Hamilton, 1984.
The Friendly Robot (illustrated by Jonathan Langley), Octopus, 1986.
An Elephant for Muthu, Bodley Head, 1986.

(From *Das Kanguruh Viktoria* by Carolyn Sloan. Illustrated by Peter Bailey.)

The Sea Child (Junior Literary Guild selection), Bodley Head, 1987, Holiday House, 1988.
Don't Go Near the Water, Scholastic, 1988.
T-Boy's Weekend (illustrated by Chris Winn), Ginn, 1988.

"MALL" SERIES

Setting Up Shop, Hippo Books, 1989.
Open for Business, Hippo Books, 1989.
Gangs, Ghosts and Gypsies, Hippo Books, 1989.
Money Matters, Hippo Books, 1989.

Contributor to magazines and newspapers, including *Sunday Telegraph, Daily Telegraph,* and *Radio Times.*

WORK IN PROGRESS: Revision of a children's musical and an adult play; developing several ideas for children's books, including a sequel to *Skewer's Garden;* planning various words and music ventures with composer/musician cousin, Nigel Stanger.

SIDELIGHTS: "I was writing one-plot girl-and-pony stories as an eight-year-old. Later it was poetry—light animal verses to dreadful kitsch about little dead children and lonely shepherds. I wasted my pocket money on stamps, sending the manuscript to adult literary periodicals signed 'by Carolyn Sloan, aged 12 yrs. 4 mths.' After school I went to Geneva for a year to learn French and work as an *au pair,* then returned to London and a series of short-lived office jobs where I taught myself shorthand and typing.

"By sheer luck I became editorial secretary on *Queen* magazine at a time of total chaos. Its image and staff changed weekly. I typed, made tea, recklessly cut distinguished authors' copy, and checked proofs before anyone realized I was a complete amateur. After four years I had worked for several editors, written features and captions, put the magazine to bed during a printing strike, and was still making tea. Ever since, when I have written anything from a press release to a controversial newspaper story, a theater program to a book, I have been indebted to the writing discipline learned during those chaotic years.

"I married an English tea planter and lived in South India for seven years, where my two sons were born. My book, *An Elephant for Muthu* is set in a working elephant camp there. It is the only one of my books that is set in India, and it was not written until I had been away from the country for fifteen years. One reviewer, Nicholas Tucker, wrote in *Books for Your Children* that at times it invited comparison with Kipling at his best. That was highly satisfying to me.

"After returning from India we lived in a seventeenth-century cottage and ran a village shop for four years. A large and colorful gypsy family were among our customers, and I based *Skewer's Garden* on them. My interest in theater developed when I shared a flat with my aunt, the late Norah Waugh. She was an expert on historic costume, and for over thirty years lectured and taught practical work in the theater department of the Central School of Art and Design in London. Her three books on the subject are now standard works on both sides of the Atlantic. I wrote *Shakespeare, Theatre Cat* after working at the Yvonne Arnaud Theatre in Guildford. It is basically a child's introduction to the theatre, told in fictionalized form by a theatre cat.

"*The Sea Child* may have been subconsciously inspired by Matthew Arnold's poem 'The Forsaken Merman,' which I learned at school. My only nonfiction book so far is a biography of Helen Keller. I had to read everything she wrote and reams that were written about her and reduce it all to 10,000 relevant words in three months. *That* took journalistic training! I love delving for rare nuggets of fact in books and libraries. I have to stop myself before research becomes an excuse for not writing the book."

HOBBIES AND OTHER INTERESTS: "My interests are reading, theatre, and gardening. I like tracing my family history, in particularly the line believed to go back to the Barretts of Wimpole Street, which would make Elizabeth Barrett Browning my great-great-great aunt!"

SOPKO, Eugen   1949-

PERSONAL: Born March 25, 1949, in Brno, Czechoslovakia; son of Eugen (a railway official) and Bozena (a personnel manager; maiden name, Safarik) Sopko; married Brigita Rabel (an administrative official), November 27, 1970; children: Oliver. *Education:* Fine Art's School, Bratislava, Czechoslovakia, Art Graduate, 1968; Academy of Art, Munich, West Germany, Academic Painter, 1980; further study at University

EUGEN SOPKO

of Munich, 1983. *Religion:* Catholic. *Home:* Zeppelinstrasse 16A, 8000 Munich 90, West Germany. *Agent:* Brigita Sopko, Zeppelinstrasse 16A, 8000 Munich 90, West Germany.

CAREER: Painter, author and illustrator of children's books. Television of Czechoslovakia, Bratislava, Czechoslovakia, painter, 1968-69; Photo-Quelle, Nuernberg, West Germany, painter and art designer, 1969-73; art educator in secondary schools, Nuernberg and Munich, West Germany, 1980-82; author and illustrator of children's books, 1980—. *Exhibitions:* International Exhibition of Illustrations for Children's Books, Bologna, Italy, 1980, 1981; International Exhibition of Illustrations for Children's Books, Otani Memorial Art Museum, Nishinomiya City, Japan, 1980, 1981, 1984; International Exhibition, Sarmede, Italy, 1983-87; Metropolitan Museum of Art, New York City, 1983; Exposicion de libros para minos, Museo Espanol de Arte Contemporaneo, Madrid, Spain, 1984; Biennale of Illustrations Bratislava, Czechoslovakia, 1985; Premi Catalonia d'Illustracio, Barcelona, Spain, 1986, 1988. *Awards, honors:* Illustrator prize from the Museum for Picture Book Art (Troisdorf, West Germany), 1983, for *Townsfolk and Countryfolk; The Miller, His Son and Their Donkey* was selected one of Child Study Association of America's Children's Books of the Year, 1985.

WRITINGS:

SELF-ILLUSTRATED

Drei Staedter auf dem Land, Nord-Sued (Switzerland), 1982, published as *Townsfolk and Countryfolk,* Faber, 1982.
Der verlorene Schluessel (title means "The Lost Key"), Bohem Press (Zurich), 1983.
Der Nikolaus Niklaus (title means "Nick the Nicholas"), Bohem Press, 1987.

ILLUSTRATOR

Branko V. Radicevic, *Lieber Mond komm leuchte mir* (title means "My Friend the Moon") Nord-Sued, 1983.
Aesop, *Mueller, sein Sohn und ihr Esel,* Nord-Sued, 1984, published as *The Miller, His Son and Their Donkey,* Holt, 1985.
Brothers Grimm, *Die Sterntaler,* Nord-Sued, 1985, translated by Rosemary Lanning, published as *The Falling Stars,* Holt, 1985.
F. Huebner, *Der gruene Elefant* (title means, "Little Green Elephant"), Bohem Press, 1985.
Brothers Grimm, *Hans im Glueck,* retold by Jock Curle, Nord-Sued, 1986, published as *Lucky Hans: A Fairy Tale,* Holt, 1986.

WORK IN PROGRESS: Television sketches for children; picture books.

SIDELIGHTS: "I was born in the fine old city of Brno, Czechoslovakia. Shortly thereafter we moved to Bratislava, another fine old city located on the blue Danube. I was a very quiet child, and for as long as I can remember enjoyed a love for music and drawing. I would sit for endless hours in a nearby train station studying the big, black steam locomotives and run home to draw them.

"I began elementary school at the age of six. An active lad, I participated in ice hockey and soccer. My teachers seemed to notice almost immediately my talent for painting and recommended that I visit an art school for talented children. It was clear to me that I would attend a school of fine arts and make the arts my life's work.

"In art school I learned everything from commercial art to graphic art from the ground up. My instructor was (and still is) a famous artist himself. Abstract art and composition were of special interest.

"After school I landed a position as graphic artist with Czechoslovakian television. Here I met my future wife, Brigita, and subsequently emigrated to West Germany, where I taught art design and painting in a Munich high school.

"I later studied at an art school in Munich. My works varied from abstract to landscapes, to humor, to poetic until in 1980 when my interests turned to picture book illustration. I wrote and illustrated my first book and received an award in West Germany for the effort.

"Eight of my picture books have presently reached a worldwide market, and I have two works in progress with many more ideas brewing. My son, Oliver, is at a perfect picture-book age and seems to enjoy his father's book very much.

"My best advice for all children is to try their hand at painting, drawing, and creating stories—and I wish them much fun and happiness in the process."

SWINFORD, Betty (June Wells) 1927-
(Linda Haynes, Kathryn Porter, Bob Swinford, June Wells)

PERSONAL: Born June 21, 1927, in Cartersburg, Ind.; daughter of John Boaz (a railroad foreman) and Dora (a housewife; maiden name, Price) Wells; married Robert Swinford (a sales

BETTY SWINFORD

supervisor), December 28, 1944 (died November 25, 1980); children: Stephen Ramar, Jennie Lynn, Carolyn Renee. *Education:* Attended Arizona Bible Institute, 1947-48. *Religion:* Protestant. *Home:* Rt. 4, Box 884B, Flagstaff, Ariz. 86001.

CAREER: Free-lance writer, 1945—; evangelist.

WRITINGS:

The Adventures of Bobby Keen, Moody, 1961.
Mystery of the Vanishing Horses, Moody, 1962.
Mystery of the Bronzed Buddha, Moody, 1962.
Thunder of Triple R Ranch, Zondervan, 1963.
Dark Is the Forest, Gospel Publishing, 1963.
Drums in the Night, Moody, 1963.
Scotty and the Horse That Wouldn't Die, Moody, 1963.
Mystery of Whispering Sands Island, Moody, 1964.
Beyond the Night, Moody, 1964.
Secret of Picture Rocks Canyon, Moody, 1964.
The White Panther, Zondervan, 1964.
Cry from the Dungeon, Moody, 1965.
Scotty and the Mysterious Message, Moody, 1965.
Driven Afar, Moody, 1965.
Shadow across the Sun, Moody, 1966.
Mystery of the Gold Nugget, Moody, 1966.
Mystery of the White Monkeys, Moody, 1967.
Shadow of the Hammer, Gospel Publishing, 1967.
Mystery of Galley Slave Point, Moody, 1967.
Scotty and the Lost Dutchman Mine, Moody, 1969.
One Day a Stranger, Moody, 1970.
Scotty and the Hijackers, Moody, 1971.
Scotty and the Phantom Monster, Moody, 1972.
Scotty and the Mysterious Mr. J., Moody, 1973.
Scotty and the Mystery of the Dark Angel, Moody, 1973.
The Taste of Wild Honey, Moody, 1973.
Broken Fetters, Moody, 1973.
The World of Knowledge, privately printed, 1976.
He's Taking Me to Glory!, privately printed, 1977.
Terry and the Legend of Indian Joe (illustrated by James Converse), Gospel Publishing, 1978.
Come Away with Me, privately printed, 1979.
Mystery of the Whispering Totem Pole, Moody, 1981.
Mystery at Pier Fourteen, Gospel Publishing, 1988.

Author of more than three thousand published short stories. Some of Swinford's works have been published in German, Finnish, Swedish and Norwegian.

WORK IN PROGRESS: A juvenile book entitled *Stranger in the Hayloft;* an adult non-fiction book entitled *Last Day Deception;* a juvenile book tentatively titled *Man in a Black Sedan,* about a boy whose family moves to another part of the state, leaving the past and friends behind.

SIDELIGHTS: "I was born in 1927 in the tiny farming town of Cartersburg, Indiana. From my earliest recollections, I was taken up with words and loved English and literature. Though a born tomboy who spent much of my time climbing trees, there was usually a book in my hands. When someone gave me a copy of *Elsie Dinsmore,* I read it over and over. And when my parents gave me a toy typewriter for Christmas at age eight—the old *dial a letter and poke* system!—I began to write stories from my own mind. Many times my mom would catch me with the light on in the wee hours and make me go to bed. At age nine my first story appeared in the school paper. There was never a doubt in my mind that I was going to be a writer.

"Also at age nine I contracted tuberculosis from a family in my little town. Actually, it was called 'galloping consumption' because it took the lives of its victims so quickly. Six of us had the disease, but I was the only one who survived. Many mornings I would waken to find my pillow covered with blood and many times I hemorrhaged until all hope was gone. It was a year before I could walk on my own once more.

"I met Bob Swinford when I was fifteen and married him when I was seventeen. We moved to Tucson, Arizona and the dream of my life was fulfilled, that of living on a real, working ranch. This became the base for many of my books, including nearly all the 'Scotty' books.

"But the greatest joy of my life occured just after we had moved west, when I received a check for my very first story. It was only $7.50, but it was wonderful! Since that time I have had published more than 3,000 short stories and articles.

"My husband died in 1980 and since then I have lived alone and still travel extensively as an evangelist.

"I like writing for adults and have a book in the works at the present time. However, I find that writing for children sets my mind free to roam and discover my own adventures. Becoming absorbed in the story makes it real to me, hence it becomes real also for those who read it.

"Other times there is a 'springboard' for a story, such as *The White Panther*. This idea came when my husband and I took a walk through a dry riverbed one Christmas Eve. We looked up to see—not a white panther, but a black one stalking us on the bank just above our heads. So it became a white panther for the story and the rest just evolved as I wrote it. Sometimes my books do simply roll out before me as I write them—without any kind of outline or definite plot in mind. Other times I carefully execute a plot in my mind and detail out each chapter before beginning.

"I see words as being very powerful tools with which we wield our trade. Writing, to me, is an awesome responsibility, for through the power of words I can bring people to tears and anguish, to depression and near despair. I can make people laugh and soar, feel compassion and tolerance. . .cause those who are hanging on the brink of cashing it all in to know that life is worth living after all. I suppose, for those reasons, words seem almost sacred to me. My personal feeling about it is this: I have to write, for that is the only way I can truly express myself. But I must say something somehow that will benefit my readers, otherwise they are words ill spent.

"One of the reviews of *Shadow across the Sun* said that it was 'a story told with love and compassion.' It had been a difficult book to write from the emotional standpoint, for as the writer, I *lived* the story. My lead character had gone to the depths and back, and that short review told me that I had hit my mark. That's reward enough for me.

"I have never taken a writer's course or had any training. Writing is something God gave me and I highly treasure it."

HOBBIES AND OTHER INTERESTS: Horses, the outdoors.

FOR MORE INFORMATION SEE:

Tucson Daily Citizen, July 13, 1963.

COLLECTIONS

De Grummond Collection at the University of Southern Mississippi.

It looked eerie. Haunted. ■ (From *Mystery at Pier 14* by Betty Swinford.)

WEBER, Debora   1955-

PERSONAL: Born March 21, 1955, in Cleveland, Ohio; daughter of Howard F. (an antique dealer) and Charlotte (an antique dealer; maiden name, Monck) Weber; married Eric Miller (a video producer), June 20, 1981; children: Spencer Drew, Emily Rebecca. *Education:* Lake Erie College for Women, B.A. (cum laude), 1977; attended Moore College of Art, 1979. *Home:* 518 Brookhurst Ave., Narberth, Pa. 19072. *Office:* P.O. Box 663, Narberth, Pa. 19072.

CAREER: Drexel University, Philadelphia, Pa., graphic artist, 1980-83; free-lance illustrator, 1980—; Westminster Press, Philadelphia, Pa., part-time free-lance in house graphic artist and illustrator, 1983-85. *Member:* Pennsylvania Horticultural Society, Philadelphia Children's Reading Roundtable. *Awards, honors: Last Names First. . .and Some First Names Too* was chosen one of Child Study Association of America's Children's Books of the Year, 1986.

ILLUSTRATOR:

Mary Price Lee and Richard S. Lee, *Last Names First. . .and Some First Names Too* (Junior Literary Guild selection), Westminster, 1985.

DEBORA WEBER

Margaret O. Hyde and Elizabeth Forsyth, *Know about AIDS,* Walker, 1987.

WORK IN PROGRESS: A series of four board books in full color for children aged two to four, to be published by Stoneway.

SIDELIGHTS: "I proudly supported myself in college through scholarships and by waitressing and received my degree in fine art drawing and watercolor. My interest in illustration was inhibited by the fine art environment. Commercial art was not highly regarded there. I graduated with the skills of drawing and painting but with no practical knowledge of how to make a living at it. After a while, I moved to Phildelphia and enrolled in a commercial art school where my illustration style was valued. My instructor, Beth Krush, insisted that I waste no more time and money as a student and simply take my portfolio and 'hit the pavement.' I've been happily illustrating ever since.

"At first I worked primarily in black and white line art. I gradually introduced watercolors and colored pencil, developing a full-color portfolio. My current goals are to illustrate and write children's books and develop greeting cards and prints.

"My family and I enjoy sailing every weekend on our 'Catalina 22' on the Chesapeake Bay. We have gone on a cruise every year since 1982, the longest trip lasting two weeks. I have fallen in love with English gardens and have cultivated my own cutting garden.

"Working at home as an illustrator is a wonderful way to combine a career and motherhood. Every time I meet a working mother with a child in day care, I realize how fortunate I am to have the ability to work *with* my children nearby. It's still a juggling act but I can work and not experience the guilt of leaving my small children."

HOBBIES AND OTHER INTERESTS: Sailing, gardening, camping, antique collecting, sewing. "I am currently looking into membership in the Daughters of the American Revolution. My mother is a member and I am interested in the family genealogy."

FOR MORE INFORMATION SEE:

Diana Martin-Hoffman, editor, *1986 Artists Market,* F & W Publications, 1985.

WEES, Frances Shelley   1902-1982 (Frances Shelley)

PERSONAL: Born April 29, 1902, in Gresham, Ore.; died in 1982; daughter of Ralph Eaton and Rose Emily (Shelley) Johnson; married W. R. Wees, 1924; children: Margarita Josephine Wees Smith, Timothy John. *Education:* Saskatoon Normal School, Teacher's Certificate, 1923. *Residence:* Stouffville, Ontario, Canada. *Agent:* Curtis Brown Ltd., 10 Astor Place, New York, N.Y. 10003.

CAREER: Writer. Director, Canadian Chautauquas, 1924-31; Company of Public Relations, Toronto, Ontario, account executive, 1941-45; United Nations Relief and Rehabilitation Administration, Ottawa, Ontario, executive director of national clothing collection, 1946. Public relations consultant for Toronto Art Gallery, Lever Brothers, and other companies and organizations. Lecturer to Canadian women's organizations. *Member:* Canadian Women's Press Club, Daughters of the American Revolution, Canadian Authors' Association, Mystery Writers of America, National Genealogical Society, British Genealogical Society, New England Historical and Genealogical Society, Heliconian Club (Toronto).

FRANCES SHELLEY WEES

WRITINGS:

The Maestro Murders, Mystery League, 1931.
The Mystery of the Creeping Man, Macrae Smith, 1931.
Detectives Ltd., Eyre & Spottiswoode, 1933.
Romance Island, Macrae Smith, 1933.
Honeymoon Mountain, Macrae Smith, 1934.
It Began in Eden, Macrae Smith, 1936.
Untravelled World, Eyre & Spottiswoode, 1936.
"Pathways to Reading" series, Gage, 1937-38, Volume I: *Baby, Sally, and Joe,* Volume II: *Home and Round About,* Volume III: *The Open Door,* Volume IV: *Storyland,* Volume X: *Golden Windows.*
Lost House, Macrae Smith, 1938.
(With J. E. Poirier) "J'Apprends a Lire" Series, Gage, 1939.
A Star for Susan, Macrae Smith, 1940.
Someone Called Maggie Lane, Macrae Smith, 1947.
Under the Quiet Water, Macrae Smith, 1949.
Melody Unheard, Macrae Smith, 1950.
M'Lord, I Am Not Guilty, Doubleday, 1954.
The Keys of My Prison, Doubleday, 1956.
This Necessary Murder, Jenkins, 1957.
Where Is Jenny Now?, Doubleday, 1958.
The Country of the Strangers, Doubleday, 1960.
Dangerous Deadline, Ward, Lock, 1961.
The Treasure of Echo Valley, Abelard, 1964.
Mystery in Newfoundland, Abelard, 1965.
Faceless Enemy, Doubleday, 1966.
The Last Concubine, Abelard, 1970.
The Mystery of the Secret Tunnel (illustrated by J. Merle Smith), Scholastic Book Services, 1977, revised edition, Scholastic-TAB, 1979.

Contributor to Canadian, British, and American periodicals including *MacLean's, Saturday Night, Chatelaine, Woman's Home Companion, Argosy,* and *Ladies' Home Journal.*

SIDELIGHTS: "My mystery story, *Lost House,* published in 1938, is the first novel published about marihuana. It was published in 1938 after having been rejected four or five years earlier by my agent because 'nobody will read a book about an unknown drug.' My information about marihuana came from a book on Central America by W. Lavallin Puxley, published by Dodd, Mead in 1928. When marihuana became known, my agent asked what I had done with my old script. I had kept it—all but the last eleven pages, which I rewrote. Our country place, also known as 'Lost House' was bought with the proceeds of the book."

Wees visited the Soviet Union in 1957 and Red China in 1959, traveling on a Canadian passport. Many of her mystery novels have been translated into German and Scandinavian.

FOR MORE INFORMATION SEE:

Martha E. Ward and Dorothy A. Marquardt, *Authors of Books for Young People,* Scarecrow, 1971.

WERSBA, Barbara   1932-

PERSONAL: Born August 19, 1932, in Chicago, Ill.; daughter of Robert and Lucy Jo (Quarles) Wersba. *Education:* Bard College, B.A., 1954; studied at Neighborhood Playhouse with Martha Graham, and at the Paul Mann Actors Workshop. *Home:* P.O. Box 1892, Sag Harbor, N.Y. 11963. *Agent:* McIntosh & Otis, 310 Madison Ave., New York, N.Y. 10017.

CAREER: Actress in radio and television, summer stock, off-Broadway, and touring companies, 1944-59; full-time writer,

BARBARA WERSBA

1960—; Summer lecturer at New York University, 1976, writing instructor at Rockland Center for the Arts, 1978-83. *Awards, Honors: Run Softly, Go Fast* was chosen one of American Library Association's Best Young Adult Books, 1970, *Tunes for a Small Harmonica,* 1976, and *The Carnival in My Mind,* 1982; German Juvenile Book Prize, 1973, for *Run Softly, Go Fast;* National Book Award Finalist, Children's Book Category, 1977, for *Tunes for a Small Harmonica;* D.H.L. from Bard College, 1977.

WRITINGS:

The Boy Who Loved the Sea (juvenile; illustrated by Margot Tomes), Coward, 1961.
The Brave Balloon of Benjamin Buckley (juvenile; illustrated by M. Tomes), Atheneum, 1963.
The Land of Forgotten Beasts (juvenile; illustrated by M. Tomes), Atheneum, 1964.
A Song for Clowns (juvenile; Junior Literary Guild selection; illustrated by Mario Rivoli), Atheneum, 1965.
Do Tigers Ever Bite Kings? (juvenile; verse; illustrated by M. Rivoli), Atheneum, 1966.
The Dream Watcher (young adult; ALA Notable Book), Atheneum, 1968.
Run Softly, Go Fast (young adult), Atheneum, 1970.
Let Me Fall Before I Fly, Atheneum, 1971.
Amanda Dreaming (illustrated by Mercer Mayer), Atheneum, 1973.
The Country of the Heart (young adult), Atheneum, 1975.
Tunes for a Small Harmonica (young adult; ALA Notable Book), Harper, 1976.
Twenty-Six Starlings Will Fly Through Your Mind (verse; illustrated by David Palladini), Harper, 1980.
The Crystal Child (illustrated by Donna Diamond), Harper, 1982.
The Carnival in My Mind (young adult), Harper, 1982.
Crazy Vanilla (young adult), Harper, 1986.
Fat: A Love Story (young adult), Harper, 1987.

Love Is the Crooked Thing (young adult), Harper, 1987.
Beautiful Losers (young adult), Harper, 1988.
Just Be Gorgeous (young adult), Harper, 1988.
Wonderful Me (young adult), Harper, 1988.
The Farewell Kid (young adult), Harper, 1989.
The Best Place to Live Is the Ceiling (young adult), Harper, 1990.

ADAPTATIONS:

"The Dream Watcher" (play) starring Eva Le Gallienne, first produced at White Barn Theater, Westport, Conn., August 29, 1975, later produced by the Seattle Repertory Theatre, 1977-78.

WORK IN PROGRESS: "A trilogy centering on Heidi Rosenbloom who lives on Manhattan's Upper East Side with her divorced, chic, status- and clothes-conscious mother. Heidi and her mother see life very differently, the cause of a lot of conflict between them. Heidi is everything her mother wishes she were not. Heidi buys her clothes in thrift shops, is passionate about dogs, picking up every stray on the street. The series deals with Heidi's growing up through important relationships. The first book deals with a twenty-year-old homeless man she befriends. He is homeless because of circumstance, not because he is a bum. In fact, he is trying, in quite a naive way, to break into show business."

SIDELIGHTS: "I was born in 1932, to a father whose parents were Russian-Jewish, and to a mother who was a Kentucky Baptist. The only child of this stormy marriage, I grew up in almost total solitude. I thought I was lonely when I was simply

(Jacket illustration by Ronald Himler from *The Carnival in my Mind* by Barbara Wersba.)

a loner—and spent much of my childhood daydreaming, writing poems, and creating dramas for my dolls. We lived in California, in a suburb, on a hilltop, and I would spend hours sitting in an almond tree in the back yard—gazing at the glittering city of San Francisco, miles away. I wanted to be a musician, or a dancer, or a poet—anything that would lift me out of what I considered to be a sad life. At night, lying in bed, I would hear the sound of trains passing in the valley, and imagine that I was on one of them. Get away, get away, said the wheels of the trains. Get away, get away, I echoed.

"Family photos show me, as a young child, happy and obviously loved. But around the age of seven or eight there was a change, and I became a somber person whom people were always telling to *smile*. Grammar school was a quiet, unspoken torture. Children's parties were a torture, too. In those days little girls were supposed to look like Shirley Temple, with tight curls and starched dresses. For reasons that I have never understood, I looked more like a German refugee—my mother choosing to dress me in knee socks, Oxfords and dark wools. My long hair was skinned back into two tight, unforgiving braids.

"I remember a blue bicycle with balloon tires, which I rode like a fury up and down the California hills. I remember the wonderful scrape of new roller skates on smooth pavements. The fields of wildflowers were being turned into developments, and there was always the skeleton of a house to climb. . . .

"Then the evening came when a grownup, a friend of my parents, turned to me at the dinner table and asked the inevitable question. 'What do you want to be when you grow up?' 'An actress,' I said without blinking, and the minute the words were out of my mouth, they had the ring of truth. I would be an actress. Like Bette Davis and Joan Crawford. Or even— like Greta Garbo.

"There was a community theatre in the town where I lived, and it seemed the logical place to begin. So one Saturday I walked through the door and asked them for a job. Running errands, going for coffee, handing out programs. I would work for nothing, I said, as long as I could watch rehearsals. Unable to turn down such a sweeping offer, the directors gave me the job and my heart soared. I was now a part of the American theatre and had a place in the world. I was eleven years old.

"Within six months the theatre had given me a part in a play, and from that day on I was stagestruck. No matter that I did not like to act, that it frightened me, and made me almost sick. I had a purpose in life and no longer felt alone. 'I am going to be a great actress,' I would say to myself over and over, as though words could make truth. I memorized my lines until I could say them in my sleep. I went to the library and did research, for the play was set in Russia, and learned how to use stage makeup. Was I any good on opening night? I cannot say. Like many of the important moments in my life, this one is shrouded.

"That year my mother told me that she and my father were getting a divorce. Without knowing what had gone wrong, I watched like a distant observer as my father departed, the house and furniture were sold, and my two cats were taken away to be put to sleep. I loved animals more than people in those days (and still do) so that the loss of the cats was worse than the loss of my father. On the day they were taken away, I crawled into a little space under the house, near the furnace room, and wept.

"The next thing I remember is my mother and me on a train heading East—sitting in a small compartment playing gin

Dust jacket art by Viqui Maggio for the Harper & Row hardcover edition. ■ (From *Just Be Gorgeous* by Barbara Wersba.)

rummy. My father's relatives, to whom she was still close, lived in New York City. We would start over there.

"My mother and I set up housekeeping in a hotel near the Broadway theatre district, and the first thing I did in New York was to go out and buy a ticket to a play. I had never heard of the playwright or the star, but when the matinee was over, I sat in my seat paralyzed by emotion. Ushers were picking up discarded programs, the work-light on stage had gone on, but I could not move. Finally, an usher led me from the theatre and deposited me on the sidewalk outside. The play was *The Glass Menagerie* by Tennessee Williams, and the star was Laurette Taylor.

"I forgot about movie stars and concentrated my attention upon Broadway actresses. Lynn Fontanne, Katharine Cornell, Eva Le Gallienne. I sat in the last row of theatre balconies, holding a small flashlight and writing in a notebook, and watched these women act. I was in love with all of them, but one, Eva Le Gallienne, captured my heart with her steady pursuit of excellence in the theatre—classics, repertory. Thirty years later I would write a play for Eva Le Gallienne called *The Dream Watcher*.

"For me, having come out of a small California town, New York was a revelation. There were museums, and opera and ballet, and more book stores than I knew existed in the world. From nine to three each day I went to private school, but after three o'clock the city was mine. By age fifteen, I was taking acting classes at the Neighborhood Playhouse. By sixteen, I was studying dance with Martha Graham.

"I look back on these days with a kind of sadness, for I, on my way to becoming an actress, did not like to act. What I really liked was being alone, reading and writing, and collecting books. A loner from birth, I felt uneasy in the social atmosphere of the theatre, and suffered from stagefright so severely that I once went to a hypnotist to be cured. Every spare moment I had was spent writing stories and poems, but I did not take this seriously. My writing seemed terrible to me, awkward, imitative, trite.

"I was now disguised to myself as an adolescent, and did all of the things that young girls in the late 1940s did. Wore blazers and bobby socks, stuck new pennies in my loafers, swooned over Frank Sinatra, sat by the phone waiting for boys to call. I wore taffeta formals to proms and received gardenia corsages, fought with my mother over curfews, wore pale lipstick and nylons, went away on my first overnight date to West Point. But the person who did these things was not real to herself. It was as though I felt an obligation to be a 'teen-ager' for a certain number of years. After prep school, this obligation was over.

"My father insisted that I go to college, his choice being Vassar. Instead, I boarded a train one day and traveled up the Hudson to apply at a small liberal arts college called Bard. To my surprise, my entrance exam was an audition on stage. I did a scene from Shaw's *Saint Joan* and was accepted. My father was furious when he found out, via the mails, but I persisted, and at the age of eighteen packed my trunks and went off to school. Save for brief vacations, I never returned home.

"If each life has a pattern, and if the meshing of inner and outer events—synchronicity—does exist, then I was fated to

(Jacket illustration by Deborah Healy from *Beautiful Losers* by Barbara Wersba.)

go to Bard College. From my first day there until my last, I was happy and fulfilled. I acted in all the plays and took all the English courses. I played the piano far into the night in a little glass observatory on a hill. I kept stray cats in my room, ran a donuts and coffee enterprise that traveled from dorm to dorm, made friends, got crushes on professors, fell in love. Applying for a Fulbright Scholarship to England, to study acting, I suddenly developed cold feet and wrote a letter to Eva Le Gallienne, asking her advice. Amazingly, she wrote back—suggesting that I study in my own country rather than abroad. I took her advice and did not go.

"Bard College was small in those days, just three hundred students, and the teachers taught on a one-to-one basis. . . .In the summers, I went off to act in small summer stock companies. In the winter field periods, I worked at off-Broadway theatres in New York. My friends were actors, my mentors were actors—but I did not like to act. Rehearsals over, homework done, I would hole up in my dormitory room around midnight and write stories. I could not stop writing, and yet my writing caused me anguish. It wasn't any good. I never finished anything.

"I graduated from college one June, and a week later was in rehearsal in Princeton, New Jersey. The stock company was a good one, and it was said that producers and directors from New York would be coming down to see the plays. I had the lead in every one of these plays—long, difficult parts. I was exhausted from the last year of college. And my stagefright was now chronic. The first production was *Camino Real* by Tennessee Williams. I played Marguerite Gautier, the legendary 'Camille,' and on opening night, after the curtain had come down, a famous director came backstage and said that

(Jacket illustration by Deborah Healy from *Fat: A Love Story* by Barbara Wersba.)

he had a part for me on Broadway. After he left the dressing room, my fellow actors crowded round me, but where my happiness should have been was an empty space. I knew that I would never call the man, but did not know why. As far as my acting career was concerned, the journey downward had begun.

"That autumn, independent for the first time in my life, I took a cold water flat in the East Village, got a series of part-time jobs, and began to make what in those days were called 'the rounds.' These rounds consisted of going to numerous theatrical offices, trying to see someone important, never being allowed to see someone important, and departing in anger—leaving behind a photo and resume that always ended up in the wastebasket. The tenement building I lived in on Ninth Street was crowded with young actresses, and since among us there was only one good coat—a fur—we would take turns wearing it. . . .I worked in book shops and department stores, ran a projector for a film company, typed in offices. . . .My worst job was waiting tables at Schrafft's, where I dropped a poached egg into a woman's bodice and was promptly fired. My best job was as the head of the correspondence department in a government housing agency. A secret acting student, I worked there by day, getting more and more promotions, while I went to acting school at night.

"The house on East Ninth Street has figured in several of my books, most recently in *The Carnival in My Mind,* because the building and its inhabitants were themselves like a character in a novel. In the basement lived Dennis, who was five feet tall and wanted to be an opera singer. On the top floor lived Samantha, who was a harpist, but whose room was too small for her harp. She kept the harp in the hallway. Next door to my apartment, on the second floor, was Beryl, a shady type who had a stream of gentlemen callers. In the winters all of us froze in our rooms—in the summers we roasted. Rats and roaches were common, but what I remember most from those days was the sunlight on my windowsill and the straw chair in which I would sit reading. I had painted the floors brick red, had built bookcases from floor to ceiling, and played Bach and Mozart on a dilapidated phonograph. The bathtub resided in the tiny kitchen—which meant that it was possible to bathe and cook at the same time.

"After college I had attended acting school for three years, under the guidance of a brilliant, temperamental teacher. His insistence that his students provide themselves with employment by forming their own companies was so strong, and so believable, that upon graduating seven of us did just that. Putting together a staged reading of famous stories about childhood, we hired a booking agent and went on the road. It was my job to adapt the stories into acting form, as well as act in them, and though I did not know it at the time, this work was my first real work as a writer. The stories were wonderful—by people like Dylan Thomas and Virginia Woolf—and as I shaped and cut them, and turned narrative into dialogue, I knew the first pleasure in working at a typewriter that I had ever known. The program was called *When I Was a Child,* and one day in winter, in a rented Volkswagen bus, the seven of us headed West.

". . .Stuffed into the little bus with our suitcases and guitars, stage lights and costumes, we spent three wild months traveling across America, playing in college auditoriums and sleeping in run-down motels. By the time we returned, all of us worse for wear, plans were afoot to put the show on Broadway. But I had fallen ill.

"The diagnosis was hepatitis—and so, leaving the company behind, I went to a friend's house on Martha's Vineyard to

heading for town."
Watchful ran. Through
thickets and pastures
and hillocks and copses.
He woke the Mayor and
he woke the Constable.
He woke the Justice and
he woke the Town Crier,
who put on his hat and
ran through the streets
crying, "Moon mon-

ster," and "All men to the
Square."

The Baker armed him-
self with a wooden spoon.
The Tailor grabbed his
longest needle. The
Candlemaker brought a
bag of candles to set the
monster afire, and all

(From *The Brave Balloon of Benjamin Buckley* by Barbara Wersba. Illustrated by Margot Tomes.)

recuperate. Lying there in bed day after day, staring at the ocean, free of responsibility for the first time in years, I knew that I would never return to the theatre. Something had broken in me that could no longer be repaired, and I was glad. . . .I did not know where I was going, but after fifteen years of struggle I was free. It was then that my hostess said, 'Barbara, why don't you write something?'

"I asked her what she thought I could possibly write, and by way of answering she brought a pad of paper and a pen to my room and left me alone. I looked at the pad of paper, and then I looked at the sea and began to write. A few weeks later I had completed a story called *The Boy Who Loved the Sea*. I didn't know it was a children's story because I knew nothing about children's literature. All I knew was that this was the first piece I had ever been able to finish. It was a fantasy about a child who goes to live in the sea, and I was rather proud of it. Beyond that, I thought nothing.

"A few nights later, the chief copy editor of a New York publishing house came to dinner, and without telling me, my friend and hostess put my manuscript into the editor's purse. The editor read the manuscript, and took it to the children's book editor at the firm where she worked. . . .

"Suddenly I was about to have a book published, and it gave me pause for thought. What was life all about, when fifteen years in the theatre bore no fruit, but one small manuscript did? What was fate trying to tell me? I was not a good writer, but something told me that I had the temperament of a writer, that I could teach myself to write, and have more joy in doing so than I had ever had acting. Thus, at the age of twenty-six, I began a new career.

"The second book, a fantasy about ballooning in the eighteenth century, was harder to do, but I stuck at it. . . .It was clear to me that the form in which I wanted to work was the children's book, and so I began to read children's books by the dozens, trying to understand the difference between picture books and story books and novels. I worked as hard as I had ever worked in my life, sat at the typewriter for eight hours a day, and produced a third book—this time a fantasy about mythical animals.

"I moved to Rockland County in New York, and rented a small house. The fourth book appeared, and then the fifth, as I worked steadily to improve what I was doing, to clarify what I wanted to say. I knew so little about story-telling, and yet in some ways story-telling had been the basis of my life. Reading and writing and collecting books had been my occupations since childhood.

"In 1967, I was working on an historical novel set in eighteenth-century London when a voice came into my head. This voice, that of a young boy, was so strong and insistent that I put the historical novel away, sat down at the typewriter, and did not get up again for seven months. The voice which would not stop speaking belonged to a boy named Albert Scully, and the book in which he told the story of his life was *The Dream Watcher.* On the day that I finished this book I burst into tears, for I knew it to be a milestone in my life. Little did I realize, however, the paths down which Albert Scully and I would walk.

"*The Dream Watcher,* published by Atheneum, was the first of my books to have any length and develop any real characters. Told in the first person, it is the story of a fourteen-year-old boy, a misfit and a loner, who meets a beautiful old woman who tells him that she has been a famous actress. Taking him into her home and her life, Mrs. Orpha Woodfin develops such a sense of integrity in Albert that by the time she dies, he has come into his own. No matter that she lied to him about having been an actress. What she has given him is himself.

"From the day it was published, *The Dream Watcher* changed my life. To begin with, the book sold well and received fine reviews. People all over the country began to write me about their identification with the characters, about an older person

who had changed their direction in life. And it was only then that I realized that this theme of older person helping younger person had been the underlying theme of my own life. Unable to relate to my parents, I had sought parent substitutes everywhere. . . .In friends who were always older than I, and who gave of themselves generously.

"During the next few years I wrote several picture books, became a book reviewer for the *New York Times,* and began to write articles for magazines. I taught fiction writing at New York University. But *The Dream Watcher* would not go away. People connected with the movies came to see me, to inquire if the book couldn't be turned into a film. Others suggested that I do a sequel. I was well into my second novel for young people, a story set in the drug culture of the sixties called *Run Softly, Go Fast*—but *The Dream Watcher* persisted.

"The book went into paperback and kept bringing in mail. Again and again I was told that the story should be turned into a play or a film, but those possibilities seemed remote. What I wanted was to move on, to leave the book behind me and do something different.

"It was not to be—for in the early 1970s a friend of mine gave *The Dream Watcher* to Eva Le Gallienne to read, and one evening this friend called to say that Miss Le Gallienne wanted to play the part of the old woman. Although I was only forty, I felt that my life had come full circle.

"The next five years were a kind of detour, as Eva Le Gallienne and I struggled to make *The Dream Watcher* a reality.

(Jacket illustration by Jerry Pinkney from *The Country of the Heart* by Barbara Wersba.)

The Palisades Country Store.

I had been so moved by meeting this actress that I had been rather mute, but when she turned to me in front of the fireplace of her Connecticut home, an old woman now, not the actress I remembered, but the personality I remembered—the vibrancy, the vitality, the beautiful voice—when she turned to me and said, 'Why don't you write me a play?' I was done for. All plans for children's books and children's novels were swept from my mind as by a great invisible broom. 'I don't know how to write a play,' I said to her. 'Learn,' she advised.

"For the next eight months I read two plays in the morning and two in the evening—to learn this difficult form—and in between I struggled to dramatize my book. As each act was completed, I would take it over to Miss LeG's house, she would give criticism, and then I would head back to my typewriter in Rockland County. . . .

"Within a year I had turned *The Dream Watcher* into a play. I had also become friends with one of the great stars of the twenties and thirties. To my surprise the glamorous woman I had admired in my childhood was herself a loner—a person who fed animals from the woods every night from her kitchen door, whose main interest in life was her garden, and whose library was the finest I'd ever seen. . . .

"We opened at the White Barn Theatre in Connecticut in 1975, and that night I had a sudden understanding of why people write plays, of why in the midst of so much difficulty and pain, playwrights persist. For at the evening's end, as the curtain calls began, and as Miss LeG was led onto the stage

by the young actor who played opposite her, a kind of thunderstorm broke. People cheered, and wept, and applauded, and stamped their feet, as she took curtain call after curtain call. As the applause continued, I ran into the lobby where refreshments were being served, grabbed a glass of champagne, and, without spilling a drop, ran up the back stairs of the theatre and handed the glass to Miss LeG when she came offstage. It was one of the happiest moments of my life.

"The production at the White Barn Theatre had been a summer tryout, a preparation for what we hoped would be a Broadway production. And in the summer of 1977 that production materialized. The play was re-cast, re-designed, and a large group of us flew out to Seattle, where the play would be produced in partnership with the Seattle Repertory Theatre. . . .But just as the White Barn production had been destined to succeed, so this new version was destined to fail. A boy who was much too old had been cast in the part of Albert. An insecure young director had been hired. Ornate, revolving sets had been designed—sets that almost swallowed up the play—and I had been asked to do countless rewrites, none of which I believed in. Opening night was a disaster, and the following day Miss LeG gathered the cast together in the theatre's green room. 'We have failed,' she told them. 'Our butterfly has been cloaked in iron.'

"I came home to Rockland County, went to bed with my two cats, and slept. For some years home had been a nineteenth-century country store, with stained glass windows, marble counters, and gas lamps—and so I walked through the house

He lay down on the ground. Above his head the summer day swarmed like bees, like butterflies. ■ (From *Let Me Fall Before I Fly* by Barbara Wersba. Illustrated by Mercer Mayer.)

for days, staring at the books in my library and watching the sunset turn the stained glass into something evangelical. In the early 1960s, a partner and I had bought this building and restored it to its former beauty. And since it had always been a country store, we decided to operate it as one again—selling penny candy and tobacco, Vermont cheese, homebaked goods, jams and jellies, housewares, toys. It was a marvelous store, and though it never earned a penny, it received constant publicity. . . .Theatrical people from New York drove out to sample its wares—Noel Coward, Katharine Cornell, Mary Martin, Ginger Rogers. During the seven years that we ran the store, I was a writer in the mornings and a storekeeper in the afternoons. It was a good combination.

"In order to do something after Seattle, in order to heal myself, I took a step that surprised me—I opened a school. A small school. Ten students. All women. I called it The Women's Writing Workshop, held the classes in my home, and found a new door opening. . . .There is an old saying to the effect that the only way to learn something is to teach it—so that now, after many years of writing, I was beginning to understand writing for the first time. Guiding the students away from any need to prove themselves, to be good, to shine, I also guided myself away from these goals—and soon I was doing the assignments with them, learning to write naturally, from feeling rather than expectation. . . .

"From the day I began writing professionally, I have worked at the same desk—a large craftsman's table that I bought for ten dollars. And after ruining dozens of typewriters with my pounding, I now type on a solid, indestructible IBM. I begin

work around five in the morning, when I know it will be quiet, work for six hours, and return to work in the afternoon if I am deep in a book. For every manuscript that succeeds there are five that fail, but I can never bring myself to throw the failures away, and they are all kept in a trunk labeled *In Progress*. I have had my share of rejections and disappointments, and a certain number of calamities—like the play—but the impulse to write persists. What keeps it alive is simple curiosity. There is no literary form that cannot be explored more deeply, whether it be novel, short story, or poem, and this is what interests me.

"The first thing that comes when I am about to write a book is the title. Indeed, titles often appear far in advance of the book itself, so that I write the title on a piece of paper, paste it up over my desk, and wait. One of my favorite titles, *Let Me Fall before I Fly,* arrived so many months before the actual story that I found myself repeating the words over and over, as though they were a mantra or a prayer. Let me fall before I fly, let me fall before I fly. . . .Then, suddenly, I knew what the words meant and began to write a story about a little boy who owns an imaginary circus. Of all the books, this one is my favorite. It says what I believe, and it reflects my life.

"I have been blessed with many things. With awards and honors, with books published abroad, and, since 1980, with the friendship of my fine editor Charlotte Zolotow. I have spent the last twenty-five years doing what I like to do, leading the kind of life I think is right for me—and for these things, I am grateful. My career has allowed me to meet people whose talents have influenced me profoundly. Eva Le Gallienne, Janet Flanner, Irwin Shaw, Carson McCullers. . . .

"I look back on my life and ask myself questions. When have I been the happiest? Walking in the Swiss Alps, all worldly cares left behind, all values altered by the enormity of nature. When have I been the most sad? During those moments when human cruelty has been apparent to me, especially if the cruelty is directed towards animals. What do I hope for now? In a conventional sense, very little.

"I have loved being on this earth and feel grief at the thought of leaving it some day. I have been moved to the depths by the natural world, by the passionate desire of plants and animals to reproduce themselves and carry their genes into the future. A flock of Canada geese passing over my house, their honking almost like the barking of dogs, a lone male bird leading the formation—this sight can reduce me to tears. And only yesterday a great swan flew over my head on a passage unknown, its wings making a humming sound on the winter air.

"The journey continues."

FOR MORE INFORMATION SEE:

Library Journal, September, 1968, February 15, 1973 (p. 620).
Young Readers' Review, November, 1968.
Horn Book, December, 1971.
Martha E. Ward and Dorothy A. Marquardt, *Authors of Books for Young People,* 2nd edition, Scarecrow Press, 1971.
Doris de Montreville and Donna Hill, editors, *Third Book of Junior Authors,* H. W. Wilson, 1972.
Top of the News, June, 1975 (p. 427).
English Journal, November, 1976 (p. 20).
Children's Literature Review, Volume III, Gale, 1977.
D. L. Kirkpatrick, *Twentieth-Century Children's Writers,* St. Martin's Press, 1978.
Los Angeles Times Book Review, August 24, 1980.
Bulletin of the Center for Children's Books, July-August, 1982.

(Eva Le Gallienne starred in the Seattle Repertory Theatre production of "The Dream Watcher," 1977-1978.)

Washington Post Book World, August 8, 1982, September 12, 1982.
Best Sellers, October, 1982.
New York Times Book Review, October 24, 1982.
Contemporary Literary Criticism, Volume XXX, Gale, 1984.

WILHELM, Hans   1945-

PERSONAL: Born September 21, 1945, in Bremen, West Germany; came to the U.S.; son of Heinrich (a bank executive) and Hanna (a homemaker; maiden name, Jurgens) Plate. *Education:* Attended business and art schools in Bremen, West Germany. *Home and office:* 7 Berkeley Rd., Westport Conn. 06880.

CAREER: HAG, Bremen, West Germany, commercial apprenticeship, 1963-65; VOLKS, Johannesburg, South Africa, office manager, 1965-67; BASF, Johannesburg, marketing manager, 1967-77; actor, artist and telephone counselor in Johannesburg, 1967-77; world traveller, 1977-79; writer, illustrator, and lecturer, 1977—. *Member:* Authors Guild, Society of Children's Book Writers. *Awards, honors: The Trapp Family Book* was named Best Book of the Year by the West German publication *Eltern,* 1983, and *Tales from the Land under My Table* was selected one of *Time* magazine's Best Children's Book of the Year, 1983; International Reading Association Children's Book Award, 1986, for *A New Home, A New Friend; Blackberry Ink* was chosen one of Child Study Assocation of

America's Children's Books of the Year, 1986, *The Funniest Knock-Knock Book Ever!* and *Let's Be Friends Again!,* 1987; Gold Medallion Book Award from the Christian Publishers Association, 1988, for *What Does God Do?*

WRITINGS:

JUVENILE; ALL SELF-ILLUSTRATED

The Trapp Family Book, Heinemann, 1983, David & Charles, 1984.
Tales from the Land under My Table, Random House, 1983.
Our Christmas 1985, Grolier, 1985.
Bunny Trouble, Scholastic, 1985.
I'll Always Love You, Crown, 1985.
Let's Be Friends Again! (sequel to *I'll Always Love You*), Crown, 1986.
Waldo and the Desert Island Adventure, Random House, 1986.
Mother Goose 1986, Sterling, 1986.
Waldo 1986 for Old and Young, Heye, 1986.
Waldo 1986 with Love, Heye, 1986.
Waldo 1986 between Friends, Heye, 1986.
What Does God Do?, Sweet Publishing, 1986.
Pirates Ahoy!, Parents Magazine Press, 1987.
Mother Goose 1987, Sterling, 1987.
Waldo 1987 for Old and Young, Heye, 1987.
Waldo 1987 with Love, Heye, 1987.
Waldo 1987 between Friends, Heye, 1987.
Best Friends, Otto Maier, 1987.
Oh, What a Mess, Crown, 1988.

HANS WILHELM

Tyron, the Horrible, Scholastic, 1988.
Waldo and the Christmas Surprise, Random House, 1988.
Waldo, Tell Me about Guardian Angels, Gibson, 1988.
Waldo, Tell Me about Me, Gibson, 1988.
Waldo, Tell Me about God, Gibson, 1988.
Waldo, Tell Me about Christ, Gibson, 1988.
Waldo and the Giant Splash, Carlsen, 1988.
Waldo and the Boattrip, Carlsen, 1988.
Waldo and the Orchestra, Carlsen, 1988.
Waldo and the Forest Party, Carlsen, 1988.
One, Two, Three with Waldo, Carlsen, 1988.
In the Zoo with Waldo, Carlsen, 1988.
In the Morning with Waldo, Carlsen, 1988.
Green, Green Are All My Colors, Carlsen, 1988.
Waldo 1988 Datebook, Heye, 1988.
Waldo 1988 with Love, Heye, 1988.
Waldo 1988 between Friends, Heye, 1988.
The Three Robbers and the Moon, Carlsen, 1989.
More Bunny Trouble, Scholastic, 1989.
Mother Goose on the Loose, Sterling, 1989.
Waldo, Tell Me about Christmas, Gibson, 1989.
Schnitzel's First Christmas, Simon & Schuster, 1989.
Waldo 1989 Datebook, Heye, 1989.
Waldo 1989 with Love, Heye, 1989.
Waldo 1989 Friendship, Heye, 1989.

"MERRITALES" CHILDREN'S BOOKS SERIES; ALL SELF-ILLUSTRATED

A New Home, A New Friend, Random House, 1985.
Don't Give Up, Josephine, Random House, 1985.
Totally Bored Boris, Random House, 1986.
Not Another Day Like This, Carlsen, 1988, Grolier, 1989.

The Runaway Giant, Grolier, 1989.
Teaming Up Together, Grolier, 1989.
Here Comes Trouble, Grolier, 1989.
Never Lonely Again, Grolier, 1989.
I Want More, Grolier, 1989.
Friends Are Forever, Grolier, 1989.
I Would Never Tell a Lie, Grolier, 1989.

OTHER

Your Chinese Horoscope (self-illustrated), Avon, 1980.
Fun Signs (self-illustrated), Simon & Schuster, 1981.

ILLUSTRATOR

Yoshihiko Funazaki, *King Raven*, Yugakusha, 1983.
Pat Boone, reteller, *Pat Boone's Favorite Bible Stories for the Very Young*, Random House, 1984.
William Furstenberg, *Stone Soup*, Weekly Reader Family Books, 1984.
Eve Merriam, *Blackberry Ink*, Morrow, 1985.
Joseph Rosenbloom, *The Funniest Riddle Book Ever!*, Sterling, 1985.
Sven Nordqvist, *Pancake Pie*, Morrow, 1985.
J. Rosenbloom, *The Funniest Joke Book Ever!*, Sterling, 1986.
David L. Harrison, *Wake Up, Sun*, Random House, 1986.
J. Rosenbloom, *The Funniest Knock-Knock Book Ever!*, Sterling, 1987.
Emily Little, *David and the Giant*, Random House, 1987.
J. Rosenbloom, *The Funniest Dinosaur Book Ever*, Sterling, 1987.
Jane Gerver, *Piggy's Wig*, Random House, 1989.
J. Rosenbloom, *The Funniest Haunted House Book Ever!*, Sterling, 1989.
Kathryn Cristaldi, *Little Squirrels Christmas Ride*, Random House, 1989.

Illustrator of posters for "Reading Time Encore!" produced by the Children's Book Council, 1987. Wilhelm's books have been published in many languages, including Japanese and German. Designer and illustrator of calendars, greeting cards, and other items related to his various books and animal characters.

ADAPTATIONS:

Tales from the Land under My Table (braille book), Random House, 1983.
"Bunny Trouble" (read-along cassette), Scholastic, 1985.
"Mother Goose on the Loose," Cablevision, 1987.

WORK IN PROGRESS: More books, video and audio cassettes, and television series with Waldo, who is the main character of the "Merritales" series.

SIDELIGHTS: "In the making of books, the important issue is the authenticity and honesty of the artist. Children's books are a very revealing form of art. If handwriting can give us an idea of the character of the writer, our drawings and the type of stories we choose reveal so much more. You cannot be afraid of showing your true self if you wish to become an author or illustrator for these books. Each page and each word can reveal your emotions and fears. But these are also the very foundations with which I can relate to the reader and often share common ground. There is probably a tear on every page of my book—even if it is nicely camouflaged by outrageous humor and fun. The fun and joy are merely the bridge on which we can meet. They are also the symbols of hope which we need so desperately in the many stages of our earthly existence. Giving and sharing hope, joy, and confidence with others are the main reasons I create books. I have no illusions

Most of the time Franklin was alone. (From *Oh, What a Mess* by Hans Wilhelm. Illustrated by the author.)

that my books will change the world or greatly influence the minds of future generations. If I can only bring a little light into the darkness and fears in the lives of children and adults alike, I am a very happy person. The more I am able to give this light, the more light I experience in my own life.

"I am a 'morning person,' and that's the best time for me to have creative ideas and thoughts. I am very serious about attempting to align myself with the highest source of Love and Energy, and I am always grateful for any inspiration that I receive. This inspiration combines with my personal experiences in life and provides the basis for my stories.

"I never really liked the words 'children's book.' Why should they be for children only? In Germany a large portion of all children's books are bought by people without children. Why? Is it because the beautiful art or the subject appeals as much to the adult as to the child? There are no 'typical' childhood problems or situations. Peer pressure, cheating, fighting, fear

of loneliness and rejection, and pains of all kinds do not stop with adulthood. Originally Grimm's fairy tales were told for adults. Therefore, I think that a children's book is an adult book which is so good that it even satisfies children.

"I don't think there are 'bad' and 'good' books. A book either speaks to you or it does not. But then it may very well still speak to somebody else.

"I share with Maurice Sendak a common appreciation for the wonderful world of Walt Disney. We both grew up with Disney's Mickey Mouse, and I loved every story and every page! By literary standards they may never be regarded as great works. But who cares! I still admire the plots, the pacing, and the wonderful selection of characters. To me, Walt Disney is one of the greatest artists of this country.

"In spite of all the joy and fun of making books, there is the sad element that one is never happy with the end result. My

Wilhelm's "wonderful shaggy dog," Waldo.

imagination is far beyond that which I am able to produce on paper. But I think that I share this frustration with many artists. Therefore, I often prefer the loose and free style of water colors which lets the viewer 'fill in' the rest with his or her own imagination.

"I do not work through an agent, but always deal directly with my publishers. This also applies to my overseas publishers because I usually keep all foreign rights of my books. Speaking a few languages is very helpful in this business, particularly when it comes to translations. I also find the direct contact with my editors very important and gratifying, as many editors have become pesonal friends. I wouldn't like to have somebody 'between us.'

"Maybe it is a blessing that I still struggle a little with the English language. This struggle forces me to express the feelings, the fine nuances, and subtleties more in my illustrations. The visual does not have language barriers. In my pictures I can converse and say all the things that I wish to communicate. And children—who are less hurried than adults—can appreciate and 'read' my drawings. After all 'a picture is worth a thousand words.'

"Each new book is another challenge. But when the topic is unusual or very difficult, then the challenge becomes even more exciting. Unfortunately, publishers are not always ready to handle such a book. For instance, *I'll Always Love You* was originally done for a particular publisher. But although the editor tried her very best to convince everybody to buy this book, it was finally turned down because of the topic."

Let's Be Friends Again is a sensitive story about an older brother's anger followed by forgiveness. "Very young children have the wonderful talent of changing from enemies to best friends from one moment to the next. Forgiving and forgetting comes naturally. But the older child finds it harder to deal with forgiveness, perhaps because our society endorses the concept of punishment. Being taught forgiveness on one hand and 'getting even' on the other may cause conflict and confusion. The growing child needs reinforcement for the idea that his natural, loving instinct is the better choice."[1]

"Recently I sold a book to my European publishers based on an old Balinese folk tale. The story has a very provocative ending and was rejected by all my American publishers because they feared an outcry by parents and librarians similar to that which was evoked by Maurice Sendak's *Night Kitchen*. My European publishers could not understand this concern at all and seem to be more daring. A number of my other books which have been successfully published in Japan and Europe have not yet been released here—partly because they are definitely not 'main-stream' books."

Wilhelm's most popular character is a tall, white, shaggy dog named Waldo, who works from the heart. "When Waldo came into my life I soon realized that he was a very unusual dog with great strength, humor, and charm. In the beginning, I was his 'master,' but now I'm not so sure anymore. . . .

"Waldo, this wonderful shaggy dog has become a great hit in many countries. Perhaps Waldo is appealing to the kids in America because of the fact that half of them grow up today with only one real parent. Many of them are also missing a fundamental relationship with their grandparents, who are not always living close by. For thousands of years, in all major cultures, children were usually brought up by their grandparents and not by their parents, who were always too busy fighting for survival. From their grandparents the children received their inner security. Furthermore the average American family moves once every seven years, and a child's 'best friends' are lost. So there are a lot of children growing up very lonely in America, and this may explain why Waldo has special appeal to many of them."

Humor is an element of Wilhelm's expression that is very important to him and to which he gives special attention. "I feel that humor can be one of the most difficult forms of art— particularly when it should look 'easy' and 'effortless.' Good humor is never vicious at anybody's expense. It is the art form which can 'heal,' as Norman Cousins reminds us.

"Getting older is a great adventure and a true blessing for an artist, in particular when he works in a humorous, joyful style. Young people usually cannot be truly humorous. They still have to change the world and are singleminded. Youth seldom has the lightness required for supreme art. Look at Haydn, who wrote his happy trumpet concerto towards the end of his life. And Verdi was eighty when he created Falstaff. Besides, I don't grow old—I only grow up!

"To me, spirituality is probably the most important element in life, as we are all spiritual beings. Re-aligning with my true self and with God-energy has become very important to me. I do this in meditation to find the stillness from which I gain the energy and strength for my work.

"When I look at young readers from the spiritual viewpoint, I do not see them as children but as fellow souls who are probably much older and wiser than I. This is always a very humbling realization for me, which I frequently need whenever I get carried away in my own 'self-importance.'"

FOOTNOTE SOURCES

[1] Elizabeth H. O'Neil, "Snoopy, Move Over. Waldo Is Here.," *Westport News* (Conn.), August 5, 1987.

We grew up together, but Elfie grew much faster than I did. (From *I'll Always Love You* by Hans Wilhelm. Illustrated by the author.)

FOR MORE INFORMATION SEE:

Telegram (Conn.), October 18, 1983.
Time, December 19, 1983.
Fairfield Citizen-News, January 27, 1984.
Junior Bookshelf, June, 1984.
Language Arts, January, 1986.
Trumbull Times (Conn.), July 24, 1986.
Mariner (Mass.), November 5, 1986.
Horn Book, September/October, 1988 (p. 658ff).
Westport News (Conn.) October 26, 1988.

WISLER, G(ary) Clifton   1950-

PERSONAL: Born May 15, 1950, in Oklahoma City, Okla.; son of Charles C. (a cotton executive) and Frances Joan (Higgins) Wisler. *Education:* Southern Methodist University, Dallas, Tex., B.F.A., 1972, M.A., 1974. *Home:* 1812 Savage Dr., Plano, Tex. 75023. *Agent:* Peekner Literary Agency, 3418 Shelton Ave., Bethlehem, Pa. 18017.

CAREER: Author. Denton High School, Denton, Tex., teacher, 1972-73; Ben C. Jackson Middle School, Garland, Tex., teacher, 1974-84; Bowman Middle School, Plano, Tex., teacher, 1986-87. *Member:* Western Writers of America, Society of Professional Journalists, Authors Guild. *Awards, honors:* American Book Award nomination, 1980, for *My Brother, the Wind;* Golden Spur Award for the Best Western Juvenile Book, 1984, for *Thunder on the Tennessee; The Raid* was exhibited at the Bologna International Children's Book Fair, 1985; *The Antrian Messenger* was selected one of Child Study Association of America's Children's Books of the Year, 1987.

WRITINGS:

My Brother, the Wind, Doubleday, 1979.
A Cry of Angry Thunder, Doubleday, 1980.
Winter of the Wolf, Elsevier/Nelson, 1981.
The Trident Brand, Doubleday, 1982.
Sunrise, Ace-Tempo, 1982.
Thunder on the Tennessee, Lodestar, 1983.
The Chicken Must Have Died Laughing, Perfection Form, 1983.
A Special Gift, Baker Books, 1983.
Buffalo Moon, Lodestar, 1984.
The Raid, Lodestar, 1985.
West of the Cimarron, Zebra, 1985.
Antelope Springs, Walker, 1986.

(Jacket illustration by Ed Martinez from *Thunder on the Tennessee* by G. Clifton Wisler.)

The Antrian Messenger, Lodestar, 1986.
Starr's Showdown, Fawcett, 1986.
Spirit Warrior, Zebra, 1986.
High Plains Rider, Zebra, 1986.
Texas Brazos, Zebra, 1987.
Purgatory, Fawcett, 1987.
The Wolf's Tooth, Lodestar, 1987
This New Land, Walker, 1987.
Abrego Canyon, Fawcett, 1987.
Texas Brazos: Fortune Bend, Zebra, 1987.
Comanche Summer, Zebra, 1987.
Illinois Prescott, Zebra, 1987.
Texas Brazos: Palo Pinto, Zebra, 1987.
Return of Caufield Blake, M. Evans, 1987.
Thompson's Mountain, Zebra, 1987.
Comanche Crossing, PaperJacks, 1987.
South Pass Ambush, Fawcett, 1988.
Texas Brazos: Caddo Creek, Zebra, 1988.
The Wayward Trail, Fawcett, 1988.
Avery's Law, PaperJacks, 1988.
Ross's Gap, Walker, 1988.
The Seer, Lodestar, 1989.
Sweetwater Flats, Fawcett, 1989.
Prescott's Trail, Zebra, 1989.
Esmeralda, Walker, 1989.
Lakota, M. Evans, 1989.

SIDELIGHTS: "I was born May 15, 1950, in Oklahoma City, Oklahoma, and grew up in Dallas, Texas. Like many a Dallas boy, I was smuggled across the Red River as a child from my native state and converted into a Texan. In my early days, roaming the Casa View neighborhood of East Dallas, I doubt

many of my friends or teachers would have figured me for a writer. I didn't take my studies very seriously and had a bad habit of daydreaming and showing up late. In third grade I had a 'crack the whip' teacher who worked the worst of these bad habits out of me, and a fourth-grade teacher who encouraged me to write stories for class and articles for our school paper. Sometimes I wonder where I might be had not these two ladies crossed my path—or if they'd come along in the wrong order.

"In 1961 two major changes came to my life. First we moved from Casa View to a brand new house and neighborhood, leaving behind what was a safe harbor and venturing into the unknown. That same spring I joined a Boy Scout troop and began a lifelong adventure. For a city boy, those first trips into the country were a revelation. I learned about plants and trees and stars, and I found a closeness for the earth my grandfather used to talk about. I also discovered I had a rare talent for taking old stories and making them into tales of high drama and adventure. By age thirteen I was the acknowledged troop storyteller, and for the first time I began entertaining others with my own tales.

"It took a good deal of work and considerable encouragement to get me from oral storyteller to writer, though. As many people raised in the southwest, I had a constant battle with English grammar. My friends and I simply didn't speak that language, and I struggled upstream against a mounting current of gerunds, tenses, and conjugations. Teachers kept after me, though, often offering me extra-credit writing assignments to make up for test scores. Then, while a senior at Hillcrest High School, I came under the influence of Mrs. Judy Jeffress. In her journalism classes I learned to juggle the parts of a sentence and breathe fresh life into verbs. Later, while writing sports stories and editorials for the Hillcrest *Hurricane,* I got my first by-lines and recognition as a writer. I'd found my calling!

"Having graduated high school in 1968, I set off for the wider horizon of university life. I entered Southern Methodist University and became one of only four freshmen to serve on the *Daily Campus* staff, writing sports. While at SMU, I had a chance to travel with the track squad, cover major sports events, and come into contact with major forces in the world of journalism. How often does a guy get to sit down at a table and talk to Harry Reasoner or Sam Donaldson? I interviewed Ken Kesey and Janis Joplin.

"In 1970 I felt myself headed for a career as a newspaperman. Then I had the misfortune of reinjuring a knee and undergoing surgery. Four months on and off crutches had a terrible effect, and I was anxious to escape come summer. I took a job as a youth counselor at Camp Grady Spruce, run by the Dallas YMCA, and found I had a rare talent working with young people. The next summer I worked as a leader for underprivileged kids at Boy Scout camps. Two things happened to me there. I dusted off my old campfire tales and became convinced I should get an education certificate and try teaching school.

"In 1972 following graduation I set off for Denton, Texas, where I became the journalism teacher and newspaper-yearbook sponsor. A great bunch of young people and supportive administrators and colleagues helped me through a marvelous first year. I left Denton to return to SMU and pursue my masters degree. Thereafter I accepted a position as an English teacher at Ben Jackson Middle School in Garland, where I worked from 1974-1984. It was while at Jackson, sharing some of my stories with students, that I was encouraged to try my hand at a novel. The result, *My Brother, the Wind,* was published in 1979 and went on to be nominated for the American Book Award.

"Some forty-two books later, I still look back fondly on those early days for the valuable lessons they taught *me,* and for the many fine friends I made.

"My stories come from a number of sources. There are those, like *Winter of the Wolf,* which grew out of old campfire stories I told. Others, like *Thunder on the Tennessee* and *The Wolf's Tooth,* spring forth from historical events and out of the pages of yellowing letters and diary entries. *The Antrian Messenger* and *The Seer,* like most sci-fi, I suppose, are born from imagination and wonderment. And in their pages live characters that have come to be good friends.

"Currently I am settling into my new house in Plano, Texas, preparing to work on a new book and recovering from a week in the wilds with the Boy Scouts."

WRIGHT-FRIERSON, Virginia 1949- (Wrightfrierson)

PERSONAL: Surname is prounced Fry-erson; born October 8, 1949, in Washington, D.C.; daughter of Marshall Sheldon (an engineer) and Helen (a naturalist; maiden name, Duckson) Wright; married Dargan Frierson, Jr. (a statistician and director of academic computing department), August 28, 1970; children: Dargan Michael, Amy Marguerite. *Education:* Attended Art Students League, 1969; University of North Car-

Virginia Wright-Frierson with daughter, Amy Marguerite.

olina, Greensboro, B.F.A., 1971; graduate work at University of Georgia, studied abroad in Cortona, Italy, 1971, and University of Arizona, Tucson, 1974-76.

CAREER: Painter, 1971—; Tucson Public Schools, Tucson, Ariz., assistant director of Title III, 1972-74, director of art resource center, 1974-76; University of North Carolina, Wilmington, instructor, 1978-80; Museum School, Wilmington, N.C., teacher, 1980-88; free-lance illustrator, 1980—. Artist-in-residence, Cortona, Italy, summer, 1989. Lecturer at schools and libraries. Board member of Arts Council of Lower Cape Fear, Wilmington, N.C., 1988—; board member of children's schools. *Exhibitions:* Tucson Museum of Art, Ariz., 1971, 1976; Cortona, Italy, 1971; Chuck Winter Art Gallery, Tucson, 1971-77; Brown Gallery, Scottsdale, Ariz., 1974-77; St. John's Museum of Art, Wilmington, N.C., 1977-88; Jill Flink Fine Art, Raleigh, N.C., 1978-88; New Elements Gallery, Wilmington, 1982-88; Weatherspoon Gallery, Greensboro, N.C., 1983; Tarboro Memorial Gallery, N.C., 1984; Wilson Art Gallery, N.C., 1984; Georgia Museum of Art, 1989. *Member:* National Museum for Women in the Arts, Raleigh Contemporary Gallery, St. John's Art Museum, North Carolina Art Museum. *Awards, honors: When the Tide Is Low* was named an Outstanding Science Trade Book for Children from the National Science Teachers Association and the Children's Book Council, 1985, and one of Child Study Association of America's Children's Books of the Year, 1986.

ILLUSTRATOR:

Betty Jo Stanovich, *Big Boy, Little Boy,* Lothrop, 1984.
Sheila Cole, *When the Tide Is Low,* Lothrop, 1985.
Loraine Aseltine, *First Grade Can Wait,* A. Whitman, 1988.

WORK IN PROGRESS: Flowers for All Seasons by Anita Holmes to be published by Bradbury Press; *The Rains Come to the Desert.*

SIDELIGHTS: "I have loved to draw and paint since I was two years old. Shortly thereafter, I decided that I wanted to write and illustrate children's books when I grew up! All through my years of schooling, I drove my teachers crazy by constantly writing little stories and drawing endless pictures to go with them (instead of listening to the math and geography lessons). I decided to attend the University of North Carolina at Greensboro rather than attending an art school after high school because I wanted a well-rounded education.

"The University of North Carolina at Greensboro offered a wonderful art department, so I studied there for four years and received a B.F.A. in painting in 1971, after a rigorous training in traditional drawing and painting methods—working from the figure and still life. I also enjoyed many courses in sculpture, ceramics, printmaking and film. In the summer of 1969, I worked at the Art Students League. I married Dargan Frierson in 1970, the summer before my senior year—and we both spent the entire summer of 1971 in Cortona, Italy. I painted as a graduate student as he accompanied me out in the fields. We sipped wine and expresso and travelled all over the country enjoying the architecture and museums.

"I decided not to pursue my illustration dreams until I had children of my own, but to become a professional painter. So I continued my studies, taught art and exhibited in many galleries and museums in Arizona and North Carolina. Our son was born in Wilmington, North Carolina in 1978. When he was three, after I had read a million children's books and

enjoyed the illustrations, I decided I was ready to try to enter this new career. I sent a story and photos of my paintings to William Morrow (publishers), and after a *long* year of correspondence, finally received a manuscript and contract for *Big Boy, Little Boy*—my first book. The star was my little boy and it also featured my mother. I finished my second book a week before my daughter, Amy, was born in 1984.

"I have continued to paint my own watercolors and oils and to exhibit them every several months in galleries and museums in the state. I have written several books, one of which is now under consideration with a publisher and I am preparing to work on a forty-eight page picture book.

"I have enjoyed my children immensely over these years and spend *much* time with them, reading, drawing, talking, playing, going to the library and the beach (we live about fifteen minutes from a wonderful beach), visiting our close and loving families, and having lots of company here.

"My working time this year has come when my children are at school (Amy went three mornings a week). I work like a maniac during these mornings, since the time is so limited and so precious. It is not easy! I have parented and painted for ten

She caught hold of the swing and pulled it back, back as high as could be. ■ (From *When the Tide Is Low* by Sheila Cole. Illustrated by Virginia Wright-Frierson.)

CHERYL ZACH

years and while I will forever treasure the years when my kids were small, I do welcome the opportunity to spend a little more time on my painting, reading, friendships, travel, study, teaching, and other interests. This fall, my youngest will attend preschool five mornings a week—a wealth of time for my work, comparatively, though I'll miss those mornings with her. There is not enough time or love or energy for everything in these years. My challenge has been to work at a balance and to do the best that I can at all my jobs. My kids are wonderful and my husband is very supportive.''

HOBBIES AND OTHER INTERESTS: Reading, travel, gardening, photography, racquetball.

ZACH, Cheryl (Byrd) 1947-
(Jennifer Cole)

PERSONAL: Born June 9, 1947, in Clarksville, Tenn.; daughter of Smith Henry (a military non-commissioned officer) and Nancy (a sales manager; maiden name, LeGate) Byrd; married Q. J. Wasden, June 2, 1967 (divorced September, 1979); married Charles O. Zach, Jr. (president of a die casting company), June 20, 1982; children: (first marriage) Quinton John, Michelle Nicole. *Education:* Austin Peay State University, B.A., 1968, M.A., 1977. *Politics:* Democrat. *Religion:* Episcopalian. *Home:* Bellflower, Calif. *Agent:* Richard Curtis, 164 East 64th St., New York, N.Y. 10021. *Office:* 9157 Belmont St., Bellflower, Calif. 90706.

CAREER: Harrison County High School, Miss., English teacher 1970-71; free-lance journalist, 1976-77; Dyersburg High School,

Dyersburg, Tenn., English teacher, 1978-82; writer, 1982—. *Member:* Romance Writers of America, Society of Children's Book Writers, Southern California Council on Literature for Children and Young People, PEN, Phi Kappa Phi. *Awards, honors:* Golden Medallion Award for Best Young Adult Novel from the Romance Writers of America, 1985, for *The Frog Princess,* and 1986, for *Waiting for Amanda.*

WRITINGS:

JUVENILE

Los Angeles (nonfiction), Dillon, 1989.

YOUNG ADULT ROMANCE NOVELS

The Frog Princess, SilhouEtte, 1984.
Waiting for Amanda, Silhouette, 1985.
Fortune's Child, Silhouette, 1985.
Looking Out for Lacey, Fawcett, 1989.

"SMYTH VS. SMITH" SERIES

Oh, Brother, Lynx Books, 1988.
Stealing the Scene, Lynx Books, 1988.
Tug of War, Lynx Books, 1988.
More Than Friends, Lynx Books, 1989.
Surprise, Surprise, Lynx Books, 1989.
Growing Pains, Lynx Books, 1989.

UNDER PSEUDONYM JENNIFER COLE; YOUNG ADULT ROMANCE NOVELS

Three's a Crowd, Fawcett, 1986.
Star Quality, Fawcett, 1987.

Too Many Cooks, Fawcett, 1987.
Mollie in Love, Fawcett, 1987.

ADULT ROMANCE NOVEL

Twice a Fool, Harlequin, 1984.

Zach's books have been published in French, German, Dutch, and Swiss. Contributor of articles, poems, and stories to magazines and newspapers, including *Writer, Romance Writers Report,* and *Fiction Writers Monthly.*

WORK IN PROGRESS: A humorous fiction book for younger readers, entitled *Benny and the Peanut Butter Contest;* an adult mystery novel.

SIDELIGHTS: "Because my father was a career army man, I led a gypsy's life as a child, changing schools ten times in twelve years. I was born in Tennessee and have lived in Georgia, Mississippi (the Gulf coast), Germany, and Scotland.

"I read early and well, and a deep love for books perhaps made it inevitable that my oldest and greatest ambition would be to create my own. I wrote poems, stories, and plays during childhood and won writing awards in college, but commercial success eluded me. I married, had children, taught school, and continued to write when I could.

"At my first writing conference, at Vanderbilt University in the late seventies, I discovered that writing was not just an art form but also a business. After the first shock, I decided that I wanted my writing to be read, so I began to pay attention to marketing as well as craftsmanship.

"After years of trying to write 'on the side,' while going to school, teaching, and raising my two kids, I remarried, moved to California, and took a year to pursue my lifelong ambition. Thirteen months later, I sold my first novel. My books have been published in six countries outside the United States.

"I came into writing for young people almost by accident, but I do have strong convictions about its importance. I believe young readers deserve the best, and writers for young people have even more responsibility as far as truth and excellence than writers in general.

"My books are sometimes triggered by incidents I have witnessed or situations of which I have been a part. My first young adult novel, *The Frog Princess,* was suggested by an incident I noted while I was still teaching high school. Although the story grew and changed as I wrote it, its origin was one moment of acute awareness in an ordinary classroom setting.

"My latest YA series, ''Smyth vs. Smith,'' draws on my experiences as a step-parent. With so many step or blended families in America today, I thought this was a situation to which many teens could relate, and about whose hilarious and poignant moments they would enjoy reading.''

Zach offered the following advice to aspiring authors of the young adult genre: "Writing a young adult novel with an authentic teen voice requires the author to see the world with double vision—both as the child he was and the adult he is. We have all lived through adolescence, endured its pains, joys, and frustrations. Delving into your own teen-age memories will enable you to relive those strong, sometimes overwhelming emotions and recreate them in your fiction, producing the immediacy and validity that the genre demands.

"Do you remember your first date? (Could you ever forget it?) The first time someone asked you out? The first time that special person kissed you? The sweating palms, the rumbling stomach, the anguished attempts at achieving poise that often failed you at the most crucial moments—these feelings are universal and timeless. Attributing such emotions to your characters will give them depth and reality, propel them off the page and into full dimension.

"Then, returning to your adult perspective, examine these characters. Reliving your own emotions will give your characters validity and elicit the essential reader sympathy. As the writer, you must add the exterior polish. Emotions do not change, nor do many of the 'first' experiences—first date, first kiss, first car, etc. But the outer trappings—clothes, fads, slang—do.

"To make your teen characters ring true to young adult readers, you must substitute observation for nostalgia. Watch today's teenagers in their natural settings—schools, restaurants, movies, malls, beaches, among others. Notice that they wear Reeboks or Nikes, not saddle shoes; acid-washed denim, not poodle skirts. Note the music coming from a teenager's Walkman, the activities that attract teens as participants or observers. And if you don't enjoy spending time with teens, beware: writing YA novels may not be for you. Immersing yourself in the lives of your teenage characters as you write your novel will be difficult unless you have a genuine liking for this age group.

"After creating strong, believable characters, you must grapple with the related question of conflict and plot. What is your character's problem, and how will he or she solve it? Looking at this from your perspective as a teenager will help you avoid a common pitfall among would-be YA authors: an adult-centered plot rather than one that is teen-centered. Again, think back to your own adolescence. What was your biggest problem and how did you handle it? Did your older sister steal your boyfriends? What did you do about it? Were you and your best friend in love with the same person? How did you work it out? Allowing your character to cope with his or her problem in a manner consistent with the charcter's age shapes your plot outline.

"Reverting to your adult viewpoint allows you to check your plot for possible flaws. Most of all, remember that the conflict must be solvable by your teen protagonist. Having an adult, friendly or not, step in to deal with your young hero's problem is a fatal mistake. When my shy, teenaged protagonist in *The Frog Princess* is elected class president because of a cruel joke, no adult can be allowed to solve her dilemma for her. Kelly has to solve her problem by herself, gaining self-confidence as well as the respect of her classmates in the process.

"Having looked at your conflict through your young protagonist's eyes should also protect you from another common pitfall—the condescension that creeps in when the writer's 'adult' side has not been effectively exorcised. The problems you faced at thirteen or fifteen or seventeen were real and vital and soul-shaking: they mattered. The fact that getting a date for the big dance or outshining your older brother seems a minor worry now does not lessen its original importance. Remembering this should deter you from talking down to your teen readers, or even worse, preaching to them. Problem solving and moments of revelation can come only through your teen protagonist, and cannot be superimposed by an intrusive author. At the end of *The Frog Princess,* Kelly receives a compliment from Tony, the good-looking classmate she has secretly admired, despite the dirty trick he played on her earlier. But by now she has realized that 'Tony would smile only for party-pretty girls in new dresses,' and decides this guy is not worth any heartache.

"Having believable characters, a strong but age-appropriate conflict and logical plotting, what next? Dialogue is just as crucial in teen fiction as in adult novels, with an added twist—the challenge of 'current' teen slang. Your child's eye will remind you of basic interests—friends, school, family problems—but dialogue is one element of your novel that may benefit most from your adult/detached writer's perspective.

"What about current slang—often a double-edged sword? Watch out for outdated expressions. An anachronistic slang word will alert readers—and editors—that the author isn't paying attention. Teen catchwords change quickly. The expression you hear today may be 'out' by the time your book gets into print. So use even the most up-to-date slang judiciously, to add flavor but not overpower the other essentials.

"What about setting? Unless your book takes place during a holiday period, school will probably be part of your background. In some ways, schools are unchanging, but in others they may have altered greatly since your own student days. Take a look at the schools in your neighborhood. What are the kids studying, what are they doing for extracurricular activities? Read student newspapers; they will inform you about student activities, opinions, and interests.

"Remember your first rule, however: Look at the school scene through a teen's eyes, not through those of a curious adult. To a fourteen-year-old, the essential part of the school day will most likely take place before, between, and after classes.

"And when you return to your adult viewpoint, consider other, more novel settings. Editors sometimes complain about overused lunchroom scenes. This doesn't necessitate moving your story to exotic locales. My YA novel, *Too Many Cooks,* in which the action centers on a small catering business, won critical praise for its 'vivid and unusual' setting.

"Last, point of view. Most YA novels are written either from first person—the 'I' viewpoint—or third person limited—looking inside one or two main characters. Both have advantages and pitfalls. First person can lend an impression of immediacy and help the writer focus strongly on the protagonist. It can also be limiting, presenting only what your main character witnesses.

"Using third person lets you present more than one viewpoint, widening the scope of your novel. But switching viewpoints must be done skillfully and not too often, or your book will sound choppy and confuse your reader. Accidental switches in points of view are one of the most obvious signs of a beginning writer and throw up a red flag to editors. While viewing the situation through your eyes as an adolescent will enable you to make the point of view authentic, you must go over your manuscript carefully from your perspective as an adult. . . .Your double vision will aid you in crafting a satisfying and special YA novel."[1]

FOOTNOTE SOURCES

[1]Cheryl Zach, "Double Vision: A Special Tool for Young Adult Writers," *The Writer,* November, 1988.

ZIMMERMANN, Arnold E(rnst Alfred) 1909-

PERSONAL: Born August 25, 1909, in Munich, Germany; son of Walther E. (a gallery director) and Maria (Seybold) Zimmermann; married Elizabeth Lloyd-Jones (a knitting writer and designer), July 27, 1937; children: Thomas S., Caroline L. Schwartz, Margaret G. Swansen. *Education:* Attended T.

ARNOLD E. ZIMMERMANN

H. Munich, Weihenstephan, 1932-34. *Home and office:* Babcock, Wis. *Agent:* c/o Schoolhouse Press, 6899 Cary Bluff, Pittsville, Wis. 54466.

CAREER: Rheingold Breweries, Brooklyn, N.Y. assistant master brewer, 1937-46; Peoples Brewery, Trenton, N.J., master brewer, 1946-49; Joseph Schlitz Brewing Co., Milwaukee, Wis., head maltster, 1949-53, assistant master brewer, 1953-58, master brewer at Milwaukee plant, 1958-61, director of brewing at all plants, 1961-63, vice-president of brewing, 1963-70; writer and illustrator, 1970—. *Member:* BMW Motorcycle Association.

WRITINGS:

JUVENILE; SELF-ILLUSTRATED

Fafnerl, the Ice Dragon, Crossing Press, 1973.
Troll Island, Crossing Press, 1977.
The Tale of Alain, Schoolhouse Press, 1983.

OTHER

Catalog: Gaffer's Book of Improbable Cats (self-illustrated), Schoolhouse Press, 1987.

ADAPTATIONS:

"The Tale of Alain" (videocassette), Schoolhouse Press, 1988.

WORK IN PROGRESS: The Lonesome Lake, a book about the seasons going past the lake, way up North, and how they affect land and animals, for all ages.

SIDELIGHTS: "My children's books are, I'm afraid, not the instructive books, which are preferred by schools and which often are very dry. And, again, they are not the 'blow'em up, shoot'em up' stories, which to my ancient view, warp children's imaginations. The books concern themselves mostly with nature; which, alas, humanity is trying hard to lose.

"I started to write stories—short stories—for my grandchildren after we bought an old schoolhouse with forty acres on both sides of a river. The kids loved the short stories and so the books gradually emerged. They were all read to them during their preschool years and they actually knew them by heart.

"As they grew older, I fitted a book to their age: *The Tale of Alain.* They loved it. Many children loved it. As I am very clumsy as a salesman, and as Schoolhouse Press concerns itself mainly with knitting literature, *Alain* was never very widely advertised. However, I am satisfied to see from letters from parents *and* children that I give some pleasure to children. . . .

"I am looking forward to the reception and the effect of the video version of *Alain.* The text is read by my English-born wife, Elizabeth, and the film shows my hand with paintbrush working in the pen and ink drawings with watercolour. This holds the children's attention and makes them follow and remember the story with an additional impetus.

"I have written a number of short stories both in English and German, some of them for my grandchildren which have never been published.

"Both my great-grandfather and my grandfather: Reinhard Sebastian and Ernst Reinhard Zimmermann are to be found in the International Artist Lexicon. My father, after having had his own art gallery, became Director General of the Glaspalant art exhibition, an annual affair of world renown until its unfortunate demise by fire in 1930.

"I have been a motorcyclist from my twentieth year and still ride a BMW with my wife, Elizabeth, as pillion rider. I wrote several articles on trips and also reminiscences which were publicized in the National BMWOA news as well as in the Madison BMW Club news.

"Since my retirement in 1970, we have lived in the country. My wife has two books on knitting published by Scribner's. We travel, going back to Europe frequently. We speak German and French fluently; I also speak Spanish. We enjoy riding through the enchanting Mississippi hills."

ZINDEL, Paul 1936-

PERSONAL: Born May 15, 1936, in Staten Island, N.Y.; son of Paul (a policeman) and Betty (a practical nurse; maiden name, Frank) Zindel; married Bonnie Hildebrand (a novelist), October 25, 1973; children: David Jack, Elizabeth Claire. *Education:* Wagner College, B.S., 1958, M.Sc., 1959. *Agent:* Curtis Brown, Ltd., 10 Astor Pl., New York, N.Y. 10003. *Office:* c/o Harper & Row, 10 East 53rd St., New York, N.Y. 10022.

CAREER: Allied Chemical, New York, N.Y., technical writer, 1958-59; Tottenville High School, Staten Island, N.Y., chemistry teacher, 1959-69; playwright and author of children's books, 1969—. Playwright-in-residence, Alley Theatre, Houston, Tex., 1967. *Member:* Playwrights Unit, Actors Studio.

PAUL ZINDEL

AWARDS, HONORS: Ford Foundation Grant, 1967, for drama; *The Pigman* was selected one of Child Study Association of America's Children's Books of the Year, 1968, and received the *Boston Globe-Horn Book* Award for Text, 1969; *My Darling, My Hamburger* was selected one of *New York Times* Outstanding Children's Book of the Year, 1969, *I Never Loved Your Mind,* 1970, *Pardon Me, You're Stepping on My Eyeball,* 1976, *The Undertaker's Gone Bananas,* 1978, and *The Pigman's Legacy,* 1980.

Obie Award for the Best American Play from the *Village Voice,* Vernon Rice Drama Desk Award for the Most Promising Playwright from the New York Drama Critics, and the New York Drama Critics Circle Award for Best American Play of the Year, all 1970, and Pulitzer Prize in Drama, and the New York Critics Award, both 1971, all for *The Effect of Gamma Rays on Man-in-the-Moon Marigolds;* Honorary Doctorate of Humanities from Wagner College, 1971; *The Effect of Gamma Rays on Man-in-the-Moon Marigolds* was chosen one of American Library Association's Best Young Adult Books, 1971, *Pigman,* 1975, *Pardon Me, You're Stepping on My Eyeball!,* 1976, *Confessions of a Teenage Baboon,* 1977, *The Pigman's Legacy,* 1980, and *To Take a Dare,* 1982; *Media & Methods* Maxi Award, 1973, for *The Pigman.*

Confessions of a Teenage Baboon was chosen one of New York Public Library's Books for the Teen Age, 1980, *The Effect of Gamma Rays on Man-in-the-Moon Marigolds,* 1980, 1981, and 1982, *A Star for the Latecomer,* 1981, and *The Pigman's Legacy,* 1981, and 1982.

WRITINGS:

YOUNG ADULT, EXCEPT AS NOTED

The Pigman (ALA Notable Book; *Horn Book* honor list), Harper, 1968.
My Darling, My Hamburger, Harper, 1969.
I Never Loved Your Mind, Harper, 1970.

I Love My Mother (juvenile; illustrated by John Melo), Harper, 1975.
Pardon Me, You're Stepping on My Eyeball!, Harper, 1976.
Confessions of a Teenage Baboon, Harper, 1977.
The Undertaker's Gone Bananas, Harper, 1978.
(With wife, Bonnie Zindel) *A Star for the Latecomer*, Harper, 1980.
The Pigman's Legacy, Harper, 1980.
The Girl Who Wanted a Boy, Harper, 1981.
(With Crescent Dragonwagon) *To Take a Dare*, Harper, 1982.
Harry and Hortense at Hormone High, Harper, 1984.
The Amazing and Death-Defying Diary of Eugene Dingman, Harper, 1987.
A Begonia for Miss Applebaum, Harper, 1989.

ADULT

When Darkness Falls, Bantam, 1984.

PLAYS

"Dimensions of Peacocks," first produced in New York, 1959.
"Euthanasia and the Endless Hearts," first produced in New York at Take 3, 1960.
"A Dream of Swallows," first produced Off-Broadway, April, 1962.
The Effect of Gamma Rays on Man-in-the-Moon Marigolds (first produced in Houston, Tex. at Alley Theatre, May, 1964; produced Off-Broadway at Mercer-O'Casey Theatre, April 7, 1970; ALA Notable Book; illustrated by Dong Kingman), Harper, 1971.
And Miss Reardon Drinks a Little (first produced in Los Angeles at Mark Taper Forum, 1967, produced on Broadway at Morosco Theatre, February 25, 1971), Dramatists Play Service, 1971.
The Secret Affairs of Mildred Wild (first produced in New York City at Ambassador Theatre, November 14, 1972), Dramatists Play Service, 1973.
Let Me Hear You Whisper [*and*] *The Ladies Should Be in Bed* ("Let Me Hear You Whisper" was televised on NET-TV, 1966; "The Ladies Should Be in Bed" was first produced in New York, 1978), Dramatists Play Service, 1973, *Let Me Hear You Whisper* (published separately; illustrated by Stephen Gammell), Harper, 1974.
Ladies at the Alamo (first produced at Actors Studio, May 29, 1975, produced on Broadway at Martin Beck Theatre, April 7, 1977, produced as "Ladies on the Midnight Planet," in Hollywood at Marilyn Monroe Theatre, 1982), Dramatists Play Service, 1977.
"A Destiny on Half Moon Street," first produced in Florida at Coconut Grove, winter, 1985.
"Amulets against the Dragon Forces," first produced in New York at Circle Repertory Company, March 23, 1989.

SCREEN AND TELEVISION PLAYS

"Up the Sandbox" (based on Anne Roiphe's novel), National, 1972.
"Mame" (based on Patrick Dennis' novel *Auntie Mame*), Warner Bros., 1974.
"Maria's Lovers," Cannon Films, 1984.
"Alice in Wonderland," CBS-TV, December 9, 1985.
(With Djordje Milicevic and Edward Bunker) "Runaway Train" (based on a screenplay by Akira Kurosawa), starring Jon Voight, Eric Roberts and Rebecca De Mornay, Cannon Films, 1985.
(With Leslie Briscusse) "Babes in Toyland," NBC-TV, 1986.

Contributor of articles to newspapers and periodicals.

ADAPTATIONS:

"The Effect of Gamma Rays on Man-in-the-Moon Marigolds" (television), National Educational Television (NET), October 3, 1966.
(Also author of screenplay) "The Pigman" (cassette; filmstrip with cassette), Miller-Brody/Random House, 1978.
"My Darling, My Hamburger" (cassette; filmstrip with cassette), Current Affairs and Mark Twain Media, 1978.

SIDELIGHTS: **May 15, 1936.** Born in Staten Island, New York. Coming from a broken home, Zindel never knew his father very well. "Mother was a girl in her twenties when my father left. She used to have to fight to get the allowance from him and tried to keep us together, moving from apartment to apartment. . . ."[1]

"My sister and I would see my father just about every other Christmas. Mother would take us to the Staten Island terminal and put us on the ferry, and when we got to the other side, my father would be waiting. Once or twice, he wasn't there. You could hardly blame him. It must be pretty traumatic when a man hasn't seen his kids in two years, so he takes a drink. . . .

"Once, I had a whole week together with my father, up at Star Lake. My mother would never give my father a divorce, you see, so he simply lived with a woman without benefit of clergy, and they had a marvelous life together. So this one time, my father took me up to where the woman's family lived at Star Lake. I was ten, and oh, God, what a jackass I was! On the train going up, we had lobster, and believe me, there was ample to eat for any normal boy. But my father liked to be flashy—he even took me to Toots Shor's one time—so he asked me if I wouldn't like another lobster, and in my childish ignorance I said yes, I would like another lobster. So there I sat in that dining car, eating twenty dollars worth of lobster.

"Then, when we got to Star Lake, I made the faux pas of all faux pas. It was Thanksgiving, and these very intelligent, very refined people had prepared a lovely dinner. . .a turkey, home-made this, home-grown that, and the woman's mother had baked a marvelous pumpkin pie. While everyone was savoring this culinary creation, I—being a perfect gentleman—said, 'Gee, this pie tastes good. It tastes just like the kind my mother makes with Flako pie crust mix.'"[2]

". . .I found out there was another world beyond that mother and sister of mine. A world where I learned there were fresh vegetables, and that you raised the seat up to urinate. Because, boy, was I pistol-whipped when I was a boy. So when my aunt says: 'You were *really* a good boy,' I know 'good' means I really was kept under control."[3]

It was a struggle for Zindel's mother to raise the children and make a living to support the family. "She worked at everything, nursing, real estate, a hot dog stand and inventions, but we usually lived in a shambles."[1]

". . .She and my father had had a lovely home in Oakwood on Staten Island and when their marriage broke up, she couldn't afford to keep it. But Mother just wasn't meant for apartment living. She couldn't stand anyone telling her what to do. One landlady told her how to hang her wash and plant her rosebushes, and the crowning touch that made us depart from that residence was when the landlady planted sunflowers beneath our window. They grew and they grew until they were right outside our window, and Mother felt she was being watched.

"We did manage to get a house once, in Travis. We lived there for four years—my crucial years, my adolescence. Mother

(From the Pulitzer Prize-winning stage production "The Effect of Gamma Rays on Man-in-the-Moon Marigolds." Starring Sada Thompson [center], it opened April 7, 1970 at the Mercer-O'Casey Theatre.)

(From the movie adaptation of Zindel's play "The Effect of Gamma Rays on Man-in-the-Moon Marigolds," starring Joanne Woodward [right]. Released by Twentieth Century-Fox in 1972.)

got the house for five dollars down, a phenomenal maneuver on her part. We lived next door to a black family—the only one in town—and we became friends. It was just our two families against that whole Polish town. But our house was a shambles. I had a teacher who suddenly needed an exhibit for a science fair and when she heard that I had made a terrarium, she said, 'We've got to have a look at it immediately.' She drove me home and we went out into the back yard to look at the terrarium, complete with black widow spider. The next day in school—and I'll never forget this—she said to the class, 'I have been teaching in this school for twenty years and I never realized until yesterday what poverty there is in this town.'

"Mother always had a load of animals. At one time, we had twenty-six collies. Breeding dogs was one sure way to make money, Mother decided. 'Lassie' was very popular then and she was convinced that collies would sell like hot cakes. But things got out of hand. Little collies kept falling out of big collies, and eventually everyone in town got a free collie. We built a kennel for them outside, but Mother couldn't bear to leave them out over night, so finally we gave them one whole room inside the house.

"Mother used to kill a lot of them. I'd come home from school and find that one of the dogs was missing. It would turn out that he had bitten somebody and Mother was afraid that they'd come and take the dog away, so, she'd have it 'put to sleep,' as she phrased it. Then she would cry for days."[2]

"Our home was a house of fear. Mother never trusted anybody, and ours wasn't the kind of house someone could get into by knocking on the front door. A knock at the door would send mother, sister and me running to a window to peak out."[1]

"She instilled in me the thought that the world was out to get me. . . ."[4]

". . .I felt worthless as a kid, and dared to speak and act my true feelings only in fantasy and secret. That's probably what made me a writer."[5]

"When I write, I hear the voices of my mother and sister. I'm writing from their voices in a metaphor I know about."[1]

Zindel was provided with few resources at home to challenge his young mind. "I came from a home that never read books. We had no books in the house. We had no desire to have books in the house, and I find that kids are very much a product of their homes. That old-fashioned saying is quite true, and so we had no politics. We had no books, no theatre. We had none of those things."[6]

Staten Island became his playground and entree into other cultures. ". . .South Beach was Sicily; Stapleton was Killarney; Silver Lake was Alexandria; Tottenville was The Congo. I have not the least doubt I would have emerged staggeringly polylingual if that Woman Scorned [his mother] had been a mixer.

"And each town offered a lush new backdrop: St. George—a buzzing city, hordes rushing on and off the five-cent ferry; Oakwood—a wooded backyard, pheasant families parading beneath hanging fat apples; Travis—a mad tiny airport, weekend pilots in Piper Cubs who circled above their lovers' homes and tossed bottles of Chanel No. 5 affixed to midget parachutes. And a mulberry tree. It was a time when Kilbasi, pepperoni and knockwurst were the relentless culinary dividers of this little island in New York Bay.

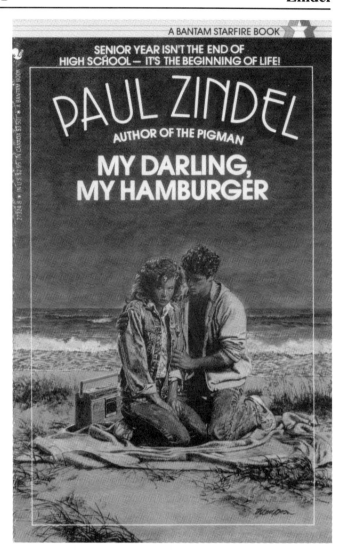

He could tell he had said the wrong thing. ■ (From *My Darling, My Hamburger* by Paul Zindel. Cover illustration by John Thompson.)

"By the time I was ten I had gone nowhere but had seen the world."[7]

With an active imagination, Zindel managed to keep himself entertained. ". . .I remember a love of marionettes—nautical, laughing, demoniacal. Some I fashioned myself. One—a grotesque sailor—was given to me for my second birthday. I recall cardboard boxes housing cycloramas, crepe-paper palm trees back-lighted by flashlight batteries with bulbs attached by twisted paper clips. The aquariums—two gallons, five gallons, twenty gallons. I sat for hours looking in at guppies hunting their young through forests of elodea. An insectarium, incredible centipedes, plump red ants—a sinister black spider unearthed in the backyard of the Travis home where I lived for my fifth Easter. I remember [that] terrarium, green silent stalks as magical to me as any bug, fish or puppet. Then there was the crippled boy who cried 'Shazaam' to become Captain Marvel—and Wonder Woman with her transparent lasso and magic girdle. And there was the terrifying world at the Empire Theater where Batman and friend were nearly murdered each Saturday morning.

"What a great love I had of microcosms, of peering at other worlds framed and separate from me."[7]

1947. Landed his first role in a play. "One day I tired of eavesdropping on the world and decided to enter it.

"At last, a part!

"I was eleven years old and selected to be one of the comic characters to make up the entourage for a 'Tom Thumb Wedding' to be held at the Dickinson Methodist Church. For those who have never heard of a 'Tom Thumb Wedding,' it is an esoteric celebration in which children who do not know what they are doing march down an aisle in a mock ceremony while their parents stand in pews and grin a lot. I believe only Sigmund Freud would know what the hell they are grinning at. Anyway, some woman with a heightened sense of character assassination designated me to portray B. O. Plenty and carry a Sparkle doll. This was my first clue that as a child I physically resembled a rather tall chicken with a thyroid condition. I was so hurt and angry at the casting I silently prayed during the wedding for the cute little boy and girl playing Tom and his bride to mature into dwarfs. I waited two years to be offered another part. Finally, it came. I was Santa Claus in the seventh-grade Christmas extravaganza at P.S. 26. Needless to say, I did not receive plaudits for my performance as a *bewhiskered* chicken with a thyroid condition.

"In the eighth grade I considered that perhaps I was trying in the wrong way to enter into the real world, so I launched my career as a vocalist. I sang 'Till the End of Time' and 'I'm Looking Over a Four Leaf Clover,' a capella for my eighth-grade shop class. I am afraid both the location and the selections were ill-chosen, and if the teacher had not been in the room, chisels and hacksaws would have gone flying through the air. And I suppose my final gesture toward being an active participant in this world was when I volunteered at the Ritz Theater to be swung around at 180 rpms by a roller-skating acrobat who supplemented the flick."[7]

Zindel wrote his first play in high school. "I decided that even if I could not succeed in the real world, perhaps my appointed role in life was to help other people succeed. I do not quite know how, but some of my classmates got the impression I had a strange sense of humor: *macabre,* I believe, was the summoned term. A group of the student officers asked me to help create a hilarious assembly sketch which would help sell G.O. cards. I gave them a version of 'The Monkey's Paw,' which has a final moment when a corpse, having been buried for six months, returns home. This is not especially the meat from which comedies are carved. My only other script contribution was an idea for a Senior Day sketch in which, as Dean Martin sang, 'When the Moon Hits Your Eye Like a Big Pizza Pie,' some mozzarella masochist got it in the face."[7]

1951. Contracted tuberculosis. ". . .I. . .was whisked off to a sanitorium at Lake Kushaqua, New York, where once again the world became something. I could look at only through a frame.

"Big deal, Paul Zindel—fifteen years old, tubercular, drab, loveless and desperate."[7]

Zindel's first original play was inspired by his time at the sanatorium. "A year and a half of feeding hummingbirds from vials of sugar water goes by and I return, cured and shy, to my high school and there write a play for a contest sponsored by the American Cancer Society. The plot: a pianist recovers from a dread disease and goes on to win tumultuous applause at Carnegie Hall for pounding out 'The Warsaw Concerto.' For this literary achievement I was awarded a Parker pen."[7]

By the time Zindel finished school, he had attended four different high schools. "I went to PS 8 and I went to PS 19 and

I went to PS 26 and I went to Port Richmond High School. See, even though we moved, we did a lot of lying to make believe we stayed in the district."[3]

Majored in chemistry at Wagner College in Staten Island. Zindel found a mentor when he took a creative writing course taught by Edward Albee. "He was one of my primary inspirations in writing plays. I felt very grateful because he took time."[3]

During his last year in college, Zindel wrote his second original play: "'Dimensions of Peacocks,' the title being my subtle way of expressing a fascination with the psychiatric term dementia praecox—which has nothing to do with the theme. It is the story of a misunderstood youth whose mother is a visiting nurse with a penchant for stealing monogrammed linen napkins from her patients by stuffing them down her bra."[7]

A few years later when Edward Albee's play "Who's Afraid of Virginia Woolf" was in previews, he and Zindel had a disagreement which ended their acquaintanceship permanently. "When you're young and someone famous comes your way, you want to hear him and be with him all of the time. But the parting of ways must come."[8]

"Now we smile politely when we pass each other in elevators on the way to a Dramatist Guild meeting."[8]

Zindel's father died in 1957. ". . .He had just retired and went up to a log cabin, a fishing shack, in Star Lake, N.Y., and he just keeled over. And he was with that woman he was with. . .many, many years."[3]

1958. Received B.S. in chemistry, and a year later his M.Sc.

Though he had already written two original plays, Zindel did not see a professionally produced play until he was twenty-three. "Lillian Hellman theatrically baptizes me with my first real play, 'Toys in the Attic,' in 1959. I behold for the first time Maureen Stapleton, unbelievably incandescent, a priestess of human laughter and pain. I remember thinking I had at last found what would be my religion, my cathedral.

"And at this point I cannot stop my typewriter from spilling out the experience which exploded my consciousness in a way that protects me from being a *dumb* playwright. It was early one summer evening about ten years ago. I was walking through Greenwich Village with a friend I had reason to believe possessed psychic powers. He has since gone mad. But on that evening he made me pause at an alley between two apartment houses. He told me he felt something strange was going to happen in that spot, although he did not know what or when. I did not pay much attention to his remark and we went on our way to see 'The American Dream' at the Cherry Lane Theater. It was two hours later that we were back out on the street when suddenly my friend began to run. He cried out:

"'Something's going on in the alley!'

"The alley was several blocks away but I ran with him anyway, thinking it was just a lot of nonsense. When we reached the alley, we saw twenty or more people hanging out their windows yelling, throwing money—coins and dollar bills—down to an old woman hovering over a row of garbage pails. She was stuffing the garbage into her mouth and ignoring the money as it fell around her. That incident haunted me. Shortly after I met Edward Albee and told him about it and how much it disturbed me. I could not understand why the woman had not picked up the money to buy food.

Jacket from Zindel's first juvenile book. ■ (From *I Love My Mother* by Paul Zindel. Illustrated by John Melo.)

" 'She was doing penance,' he told me quietly, simply." [7]

Ignited by his first theatrical experience, Zindel became an avid Tennessee Williams fan. ". . .I never missed an opening night of a Tennessee Williams play, except the revival of 'The Glass Menagerie,' which I've *never* seen. Of course, I've read the play many times. I used to run into Williams at least once a year. One time it would be in a Greenwich Village bar, another time at the theater. At the premiere of 'Night of the Iguana,' I cornered him in the lobby during intermission, only to have him whisked away by two men. Every time I would see him, I would say, 'Mr. Williams, I admire your plays so very much.' " [2]

1959-1969. Taught chemistry and physics at Tottenville High School on Staten Island. During his ten years of teaching, Zindel continued to write plays. His first real success came in 1964 when *The Effect of Gamma Rays on Man-in-the-Moon Marigolds* had its premiere at Houston's Alley Theatre. *Marigolds* is the story of a young girl, Tillie, who lives with her epileptic sister and her abusive mother, Beatrice. When Tillie receives recognition at school for her science project, it is clear that she will be able to break free from her mad family and find fulfillment. "*Marigolds* was written when I was twenty-

five-years-old. One morning I awoke and discovered the manuscript next to my typewriter. I suspect it is autobiographical, because whenever I see a production of it I laugh and cry harder than anyone else in the audience. I laugh because the play always reminds me of still another charmingly frantic scheme of my mother's to get rich quick—a profusion of schemes all of which couldn't possibly appear in the play. . . .I remember an endless series of preposterous undertakings— hatcheck girl, PT boat riveter, and unlicensed real estate broker." [9]

"*Marigolds* is the kind of story that just sort of pops right out of you, because you've *lived* it. My mother *was*. . .Beatrice. I've exaggerated, of course. It's true that Mother did a lot of the mean things that Beatrice does, but she was also capable of enormous compassion. She had been a practical nurse, and people were always calling her when they got sick, and she'd be on the phone half the night dispensing medical advice. Mother was never as isolated as Beatrice; she would occasionally get out and mix with people. She even had a great capacity for laughter. But she was always glad to get home, to shut the door on everything. She was afraid people were commenting on her appearance, making fun of her clothes. To tell you the truth, Mother was a beautiful example of paranoia. Only, in her case, it was *right* to be paranoiac.

(From the musical "Mame," starring Lucille Ball. Screenplay by Paul Zindel, it was produced by Warner Brothers/ABC in 1974.)

"I'm very bad on dates, but I think it was in 1963 that my agent sent *Marigolds* to Nina Vance at the Alley Theater in Houston. She told me later that she probably would never have read it, except that it had a gold cover and it looked so nice that she took it home with her. It was first produced at the Alley Theater in May, 1964. . . ."[2]

1966. Television version of *Marigolds* produced by National Educational Television. Charlotte Zolotow, editor for Harper & Row saw the production. ". . .Charlotte Zolotow. . .tracked me down and got me to write my first novel, *The Pigman*. She brought me into an area that I never explored before, my own confused, funny, aching teenage days."[5]

"I was flattered that someone would call me up and tell me they thought I had talent and offer me an advance."[10]

The Pigman was instrumental in establishing the realistic teenage novel as a distinct genre. In this story, two high school sophomores, John and Lorraine, befriend an elderly man they call "The Pigman" because his name is Pignati and he collects china pigs. Mr. Pignati, who is senile, becomes a substitute parent neither has ever known. He brings joy into their lonely lives until, inadvertently, John and Lorraine cause the Pig-

man's death. Only upon his death, do they realize their responsibility to others. Diane Farrell, in her *Horn Book* review stated: "Few books that have been written for young people are as cruelly truthful about the human condition. Fewer still accord the elderly such serious consideration or perceive that what we term senility may be a symbolic return to youthful honesty and idealism."[11]

A London *Times* reviewer added: ". . .an unpleasant book in some ways, but the issues are starkly real."[12]

1967. Zindel took a leave of absence from teaching and went to Houston on a Ford Foundation Grant as playwright-in-residence for the Alley Theater.

1968. Before seeing the semi-autobiographical *Marigolds* on stage, Zindel's mother passed away. ". . .I returned to my mother's house knowing she had only a few months to live; she was unaware of the fact that she was dying. We had long before made that peace between parent and son which Nature insists not happen until the teen years have passed. During that privileged time just before she died, we enjoyed each other as friends. If she felt strong on a particular day she'd ask to go for a car ride. She loved burnt-almond ice cream, shrimp in lobster sauce, and flowers in bloom. On one of our trips we discovered a grove with a family of pheasants, a floor of lilies of the valley, and a ceiling of wisteria. Always we talked of the past—of her father, of his vegetable wagon in old Stapleton, of a man who rented a room in her father's house in which to store thousands of Christmas toys. There was always the unusual, the hilarity, the sadness. In her own way she told me of her secret dreams and fears—so many of which somehow I had sensed, and discovered written into that manuscript next to my typewriter. . . ."[9]

". . .Mother, *did* see *Marigolds* on television and she *loved* it. She always said that it was going to be a great big hit one day."[2]

1969. Feeling that he could be of more assistance to teenagers by writing for them, Zindel quit teaching high school for good. ". . .I took an informal survey to find out what books young people were reading, and I discovered that there weren't many writers who were getting through to them. There was *Catcher in the Rye,* from which so much teen-age literature stems, but I discovered that many teen-agers didn't really understand what it was about.

"And when I started reading some teen-age books myself, what I saw in most of them had no connection to the teen-agers I knew. I thought I knew what kids would want in a book, and so I made a list and followed it."[10]

"I write for the people who don't like to read, as a rule. I found that the academic students, the ones from better homes and gardens, so to speak, were able to enjoy a whole range of material. Some were even able to enjoy Shakespeare! But as a rule, that left out an enormous body of students. I found even the subject of chemistry becoming too sophisticated and leaving behind a whole lot of kids, and even those from better homes and gardens weren't able to catch on to the new chemistry. And they had no need for it. They had need for other, more immediate bodies of information."[6]

Zindel's second young adult novel was published by Harper & Row. *My Darling, My Hamburger* is the story of a young girl with abusive parents who gets pregnant in high school and turns to an illegal abortionist.

Marilyn R. Singer, in a *School Library Journal* review, had mixed reactions to this second story: "[*My Darling, My Hamburger* is a] skillfully written story of four high school seniors. . .that has tremendous appeal on the entertainment level, but that totally cops out on the issues raised: sex, contraception, abortion. . . .The teenagers here are the most realistic of any in high-school novels to date: they have appropriate feelings and relationships; smoke, drink, swear; have refreshingly normal sexual thoughts and conflicts. The dialogue and description are so natural and entertaining (and often very funny) that the author disarms his audience (anyone who writes so convincingly must be a friend) while planting mines of moralism: *pot and sex are destructive.*"[13]

John Rowe Townsend, in his *New York Times* review of the book considered *My Darling, My Hamburger* ". . .to be a better novel than *The Pigman.* . . ." Although, "as a work of literary art this is more a promise than an achievement, but it's quite a big promise and it's not a negligible achievement."[14]

Ever since the appearance of his first two books, Zindel's novels have been the objects of a good deal of controversy and evaluation. On the one hand, they have been described as humorous and honest, but, on the other, they have been condemned as "hack work" and slick "con jobs." Lavinia Russ,

for instance, praised Zindel in a *Publisher's Weekly* review as being ". . .one of the brightest stars in the children's book sky. When Paul Zindel's first book *The Pigman* appeared, it was so astonishingly good it made your reviewer feel like some watcher of the skies when a new planet swims into his ken. When his second book arrived and topped his first, even Keats could offer no poetry to express the joy it brought, the assurance that Mr. Zindel was no one-book writer."[15]

Whereas, Josh Greenfeld in a *New York Times* book review criticized Zindel for a lack of honesty: "How do you reach the young, the teen-agers? In books, as in life, I do not know. But neither, I think, does Mr. Zindel. For I do know that fiction must offer truth in the guise of illusion, not illusion instead of the truth. And the one thing our Now children can sense most assuredly, as they peer across that well-known gap at their generators, is the scent of adult con.'"[16]

Because Zindel's young adult novels have recurring themes of abusive adults and desperate teenagers, he has met with criticism. He believes that he is confronting the reality of teenage life. "Teenagers *have* to rebel. It's part of the growing process. In effect, I try to show them they aren't alone in condemning parents and teachers as enemies or ciphers. I believe I must convince my readers that I am on their side; I know it's a continuing battle to get through the years between twelve and twenty—an abrasive time. And so I write always from their own point of view."[17]

"The way I see my world is reflected in what I write. I find the way I see the world constantly undergoes transition. This is part of a maturation process, part of the experiences that go on. But again very seriously I feel there's a type of biological clock that allows certain insights into the world and into life, and those change. The fearlessness that teenagers have about

What I'm going to confess here is so mind-boggling that it may haunt you the rest of your life. ■ (From *Confessions of a Teenage Baboon* by Paul Zindel. Jacket illustrated by Fred Marcellino.)

(From Zindel's Off-Broadway production of ''Amulets Against the Dragon Forces,'' starring
Matt McGrath and John Spencer. Premiered at Circle Repertory Company, April, 1989.)

death is no longer a fearlessness that I have. When I look at most of my work I see the words 'bathos' and hyperbole ringing out, which was once diagnosed as my style of seeing things—things exaggerated. In that exaggeration I am able to see the world exaggerated as a place of home which, in a sense, can be the dream of the nonexistence of death. Through bathos and hyperbole I can see the world as one of the most hilarious and comic places that there can be to live. Then, by the use of these qualities again, I can look at another element and see the world as quite ghastly, see it through very morbid eyes and find everything threatening and dangerous. So there's a great complexity of these feelings.

"These themes have been repeated in my work. So in a sense, what I'm telling you is self-analysis which really is not as valuable as a person with a more objective viewpoint, the critic, the reader who follows my works, who can look at them and see the themes which are repeated over and over again and that in a sense tell what the author's true vision of the world is. So what I think of the world really is reflected through my books. It's in transition and like the motion of being keys on a piano: I just play different ones at different times, but what I do learn now, and what I'm concerned about now, is how to maintain the most sensible level of happiness and fulfillment for myself, while at the same time trying to satisfy the demands of society which are to bring innovation to civilization, to institutions, to make contributions which make the world a better place to live. So that really I try to satisfy both. I see the world as a problem solving situation, and the solution of those problems through fiction seems to be the adventure that I've chosen for myself."[6]

Zindel's mother's prediction came to pass when on **April 7, 1970,** *Marigolds* opened Off-Broadway at the Mercer-O'Casey Theatre to rave reviews. He received the Drama Critics Circle Award, the Obie for the best American play, and the Drama Desk Award for the most promising play. *Marigolds* was then moved to Broadway to the New Theatre. Zindel became the second Off-Broadway playwright to win the Pulitzer Prize for Drama. "I was watching 'King Kong' on TV when the news came about the Pulitzer Prize. All I knew was that whatever this prize was, it was going to make me have more friends and maybe bring love into my life because I was a very unhappy person. I was immediately whisked off to Hollywood. It was all very preposterous and exciting and corrupt and fun and damning and useful. The prize brings with it many curses and many blessings."[5]

The play's success brought financial rewards. "The first thing you do when you are handed a lot of money, you have the power to be whoever you were inside all along. Everybody says, 'Oh, he's so ugly now that he's become famous.' They're always complaining about people who suddenly become mean. You're mean all along; it's just when you have the money you have a chance to test that meanness. You also find out all the things you thought were a god, or all the things that limited you are no longer a proper excuse. The first thing you should do is crack up. It's like all the stops are pulled out. It's very easy, like I used to do, to go off on tremendous benders to Mexico and team up with lots of young kids, and try to keep up with their water glasses of stingers as they down them and rush down the coast and go swimming with pearl divers. You're on a path to really crack up."[18]

February 25, 1971. Zindel's next play *And Miss Reardon Drinks a Little* opened on Broadway at New York's Morosco Theatre. The story involves the three Reardon sisters who have been permanently scarred by a neurotic, tyrannical mother, now deceased. "I now know how much of the family is in the play. I have felt faint and even had to leave the theater because

seeing the scenes played was such an overwhelming experience. I'm just beginning to understand the role of the emotions in our lives."[19]

With the emotional exhaustion of reworking the play (originally written in 1966), and the disappointment of mixed reviews, Zindel entered psychoanalysis. "The pattern is set when you're born. Children come into the world in good shape, usually. But they don't own the world. They are ruled. And parents are cruel in ways they don't recognize, really hard on kids. Even good, caring, loving parents. That situation makes for masochism in the child, any child, because nobody can measure up to expectations. Then the kids go to school where they learn the formal way of pretending to behave according to acceptable values. But they're still warped children, suppressing deep feelings that have to come out some way. That's when the masochism becomes hostility. . . .Most grow up to release hostility in humor, but usually it's hurtful humor. All the pain felt and inflicted comes from feeling inferior inside.

"To linger in that state and really sink to the depths of self-pity is worthless. It can lead to suicide, at worst, or lasting misery. The thing, then, is to pull yourself out of masochism, hostility, and up to the next stage: setting goals. But this can cause more trouble, the exaggeration of creative plans, getting into unreality, larger-than-life dreams of glory."[20]

". . .I began having heart attacks. They weren't real. I was down in Mexico, and starting in August I had violent heart spasms, which they said was angina. From there it went to brain tumors. From there it went to potassium deficiency.

"I had a checkup, two weeks in the hospital, and started to go to a psychoanalyst. Oh, well, yes—I'd had fifty sessions of therapy when I was fifteen and out of a TB sanitorium, with a man that never said *one word* to me.

"So now I'm driving, I'm on the road to Virginia, and I have a seizure: palpitations, malaise. I had a six o'clock appointment I wanted to keep, and I'm lying there in the motel in the position good for heart patients, saying: 'Jesus, they told me this was imaginary.' And then I remembered Freud, and remembered having passed some sign on the road.

"I couldn't remember exactly, but I did remember Freud writing about a certain gate and graveyard in Vienna that whenever he looked up at it, something written on it, he passed out. I knew if I could think of that sign I passed just before the attack. . . .

"I had to think about it for about half an hour. I was even going to drive back and look at it. Now this is what the sign said: MARYLAND.   This   is   my   mother. . .buried in. . .WOODLAND. The moment I realized that, the whole illness just fell right off me and I was stark raving healthy."[3]

October 25, 1973. Married Bonnie Hildebrand. ". . .She was publicity director at the Cleveland Playhouse when they were doing *Marigolds*. She's a girl from New York who had a Gypsy Rose Lee type of mother who trained Bonnie to tap-dance on toe. She died when Bonnie was sixteen, leaving her with the major talent of tap-dancing on toe, which was going out of fashion.

"When I met Bonnie she was married to a psychologist who was running suicide clinics. She divorced him about a year later and we started living together. At that time I was going to a psychoanalyst six days a week, and this psychoanalyst made me pay $360 a week whether I was in town or not.

"I decided not to let him get away with that, so if I was out of New York I would call him and take the hour on the phone, which he resented. Eventually I got smart and decided to let Bonnie take over a few of those hours when I was away. . . ."[20]

1974. Son, David, born; two years later daughter, Elizabeth Claire. "Fatherhood? I really wanted it. You see, I really think I had one enormous teenage from thirteen to around thirty-seven. . . ."[20]

Struggling to overcome many old fears, Zindel made an effort to break down personal barriers, but was unable to entirely avoid a mid-life crisis. "I was afraid of flying for fifteen years, but last May [1975], I booked eleven flights in a row, including Leningrad and Moscow. Luckily we took the baby along, a great icebreaker. People would come running up and we'd have these baby parties in front of the Museum of Religion and Atheism.

"But in Paris, after two months of traveling, I got ill, had a breakdown of the mental processes. Because you can only take so many images without your brain going kaput. I heard Candy Bergen on the tube say the same thing happened to her in China. But what it was, I was turning forty."[20]

1977. Zindel's play, *Ladies at the Alamo,* opened on Broadway. In it Zindel continued his exploration of women with five strong females who are involved in a power struggle for control of an important theater complex in Texas. "This play was a complete departure for me. Until now, I've written mainly very personal psychological dramas like *Marigolds*. With *Ladies* I've relied more on my imagination and technique and less on my memories."[21]

Zindel and his family moved to California. "I think I was headed very much to becoming a first class hack in this town. I think it was because I had bought the whole California dream.

"I married a wife who had many aspirations as a princess. We have children who go to the best schools. We're wedged in between Walter Matthau and Angie Dickinson with Roger Moore across the road. I felt suddenly I was maybe ten steps ahead on some kind of game where I didn't belong.

"I also found it was a major corruption to my writing and I also kind of knew what I was doing 'cause I did pull a novel out of it."[10]

By **1981,** he was ready to return to New York and to Broadway. "I'm excited to be coming back, I'm going to do my best to get to the top of the heap. I'm not cynical about Broadway, it's terrific. It's the platform for our best writers, and the marketplace of our dreams."[22]

"No human being particularly loves the microcosm to which he is born. His life is a wandering from one sphere to another, each equally filled with imperfection. But it is a part of the human spirit for man to stalk a perfect world, a world he can control. In that is the primordial thrust which demands that Theater exist. The uniqueness of the Theater is that it is the ultimate companion of reality. If one can cause a moment to happen on the stage, it is quite possible that one can make it happen in reality. The Theater is the least illusionary phenomenon in the world. Other mediums can cut, fade, lip-sync, overlap, dissolve, but a moment must be truer, more real on the stage.

"Because Theater demands greater honesty, people now wonder if it is dying. It just happens that little honesty can emerge at this particular time of chaos in our world because nobody knows what the hell is going on. No wonder no one's writing anything terribly honest. Frauds succeed right and left in television and the movies because there are more guiles, more hiding places for their dishonesty. Unhappily, at this moment even our theaters are laced with transient fakers—special effects personnel who are determined to lure the public by being cruder, lewder and nuder. . . ."[7]

"I think the theater is becoming a director's world. Technique, special effects, a lot of theatrical tools. I love the tools, I love the nudity, the pigments opening up, but as far as *content*—there is no content.

"I feel that the playwrights are failing. They seize on the most obvious problems and present them in a scientific, journalistic manner, gleaning from the surface. They are titillated by the obvious and they fail to articulate the atomic age. Arthur Kopit failed to accomplish anything for the poor Indians or for anyone else in 'Indians.' Sam Shepard merely mentions obvious problems in 'Operation Sidewinder,' without adding any understanding, any new insight."[2]

"Sometimes the audience overtakes certain aspects of its Theater. At the moment, the lives of the audiences are often far more theatrical and dramatic than what is available to them on the stage. The public has stolen the greasepaint and raped the wardrobe mistress. Histrionics have taken to the streets—braying, battling and bludgeoning. Our country has taken on the accoutrements of theater. But no one can kill Theater. It can become dormant for a period of time, but Theater is so inextricably a voice, a device for survival, that man will rediscover it within himself time and time again. Thank God, the theatrical drought cannot ever last for too long a time. Man eventually tires of dishonesty and crawls off alone, perhaps in a dark place, to commune with his instinct once more. His dream is of a brilliant world, a universe too colossal and golden for him alone to create in totality, and so he marks out a space in the sand. Into it he places actors, and to those actors he gives words. Move for me. Dance for me, he whispers. Here in this place I will glimpse what paradise can be."[7]

FOOTNOTE SOURCES

[1]"Zindel Having Problems and Lots of Fun Too," *Morning Telegraph,* July 30, 1970.
[2]Guy Flatley, "And Gamma Rays Did It!," *New York Times,* April 19, 1970.
[3]Jerry Tallmer, "Hearts and Marigolds," *New York Post,* May 8, 1971.
[4]Stephen M. Silverman, "How *Moon's* Zindel Stays Happy in His Work," *New York Post,* March 6, 1978.
[5]Sidney Fields, "Author Has Chemistry for Kids," *Daily News,* March 9, 1978.
[6]Paul Janeczko, "In Their Own Words: An Interview with Paul Zindel," *English Journal,* October, 1977. Amended by P. Zindel.
[7]Paul Zindel, "The Theatre Is Born within Us," *New York Times,* July 26, 1970.
[8]Laurie Winer, "A Talk with Paul Zindel," *Other Stages,* May 20, 1982.
[9]P. Zindel, *The Effect of Gamma Rays on Man-in-the-Moon Marigolds,* Bantam, 1971.
[10]Sean Mitchell, "Grown-up Author's Insight into Adolescent Struggles," *Dallas Times Herald,* June 27, 1979.
[11]Diane Farrell, *"The Pigman,"* Horn Book, February, 1969.
[12]Peter Fanning, "Nasties in the Woodshed," *Times Educational Supplement* (London), November 21, 1980.
[13]Marilyn R. Singer, *"My Darling, My Hamburger,"* School Library Journal, November, 1969.

[14]John R. Townsend, "It Takes More than Pot and the Pill," *New York Times Book Review,* November 9, 1969.

[15]Lavina Russ, *Publishers Weekly,* September 22, 1969.

[16]Josh Greenfeld, *New York Times Book Review,* May 24, 1970.

[17]Jean Mercier, "Paul Zindel," *Publishers Weekly,* December 5, 1977.

[18]T. H. McCulloh, "The Effect of Planets on Paul Zindel," *Drama Logue,* July 22, 1982.

[19]*Sunday News* (New York), March 14, 1970.

[20]J. Tallmer, "Paul Zindel," *New York Post,* November 20, 1976.

[21]Patricia Bosworth, "The Effect of Five Actresses on a Play-in-Progress," *New York Times,* April 3, 1977.

[22]Rebecca Moorehouse, "Stardust and Marigolds," *Playbill,* September, 1981.

FOR MORE INFORMATION SEE:

New York Times, June 27, 1965, October 4, 1966, April 8, 1970, April 19, 1970, July 26, 1970, February 26, 1971, March 8, 1971, April 3, 1977 (section 2, p. 1), April 8, 1977, October 23, 1981 (p. C2), May 19, 1981.

Horn Book, February, 1969 (p. 61), April, 1970 (p. 171), June, 1971 (p. 308), October, 1976.

Times Literary Supplement, April 3, 1969 (p. 355), April 2, 1971 (p. 385), December 10, 1976 (p. 1549), April 7, 1978 (p. 383).

School Library Journal, November, 1969 (p. 137), April, 1980 (p. 129), October, 1980 (p. 160).

Village Voice, April 16, 1970.

Time, April 20, 1970, May 17, 1971.

Harold Clurman, "Theatre," *Nation,* April 20, 1970.

Scholastic Voice, April 27, 1970.

Library Journal, June 15, 1970 (p. 2317).

Tom Prideaux, "Man with a Bag of Marigold Dust," *Life,* July 4, 1970.

New Yorker, December 5, 1970, March 6, 1971, November 25, 1972.

Washington Post, January 27, 1971.

New York Sunday News, March 14, 1971.

Newsday, May 4, 1971, May 8, 1971.

Martha E. Ward and Dorothy A. Marquardt, *Authors of Books for Young People,* Scarecrow, 1971.

Variety, June 17, 1972, July 28, 1982 (p. 18), August 20, 1982, April 20, 1983 (p. 188), December 18, 1985 (p. 66).

English Journal, November, 1972 (p. 1163).

Elementary English, October, 1974 (p. 941).

James T. Henke, "Six Characters in Search of the Family: The Novels of Paul Zindel," *Children's Literature,* 1976.

Contemporary Literary Criticism, Volume 6, Gale, 1976, Volume 26, 1983.

Patricia O'Haire, "Five for the 'Alamo,'" *Daily News* (New York), February 15, 1977 (p. 22).

Bulletin of the Center for Children's Books, May, 1978, October, 1978, December, 1984.

Stanley Hoffman, "Winning, Losing, but above All Taking Risks: A Look at the Novels of Paul Zindel," *Lion and the Unicorn,* fall, 1978.

Children's Literature Review, Volume 3, Gale, 1978.

D. L. Kirkpatrick, editor, *Twentieth-Century Children's Writers,* St. Martin's, 1978, 2nd edition, 1983.

(From the movie "Runaway Train," starring Jon Voight. Zindel co-authored the screenplay for the 1985 Golan-Globus production.)

David Rees, "Viewed from a Squashed Eyeball," in *The Marble in the Water: Essays on Contemporary Writers of Fiction for Children and Young Adults,* Horn Book, 1980.

Times Educational Supplement, November 21, 1980 (p. 32).

Voice of Youth Advocates, October, 1981 (p. 40).

"A Theatregoer's Notebook," *Playbill,* October, 1981.

Sally Holmes Holtze, *Fifth Book of Junior Authors and Illustrators,* H. W. Wilson, 1983.

Dictionary of Literary Biography, Volume 7, Gale, 1983, Volume 52, 1986.

Publishers Weekly, January 6, 1984, July 26, 1985.

"Peoplescape," *Los Angeles,* March, 1984.

Wilson Library Bulletin, December, 1984, January, 1985.

Journal of Youth Services in Libraries, fall, 1988 (p.71ff).

A Notice about the Index

In response to suggestions from librarians, *SATA* indexes will no longer appear in each volume but will be included in each alternate (odd-numbered) volume of the series, beginning with Volume 58.

SATA will continue to include two indexes that will cumulate with each volume: the **Illustrations Index,** arranged by the name of the illustrator, gives the number of the volume and page where the illustrator's work appears in the current volume as well as all preceding volumes in the series; the **Author Index** gives the number of the volume in which a person's Biographical Sketch, Brief Entry, or Obituary appears in the current volume as well as all preceding volumes in the series.